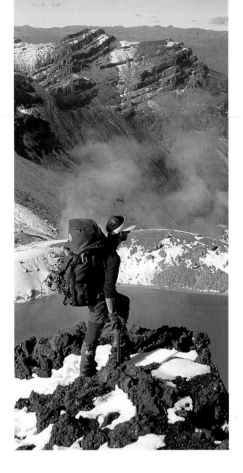

TOP TREKS
OF THE WORLD

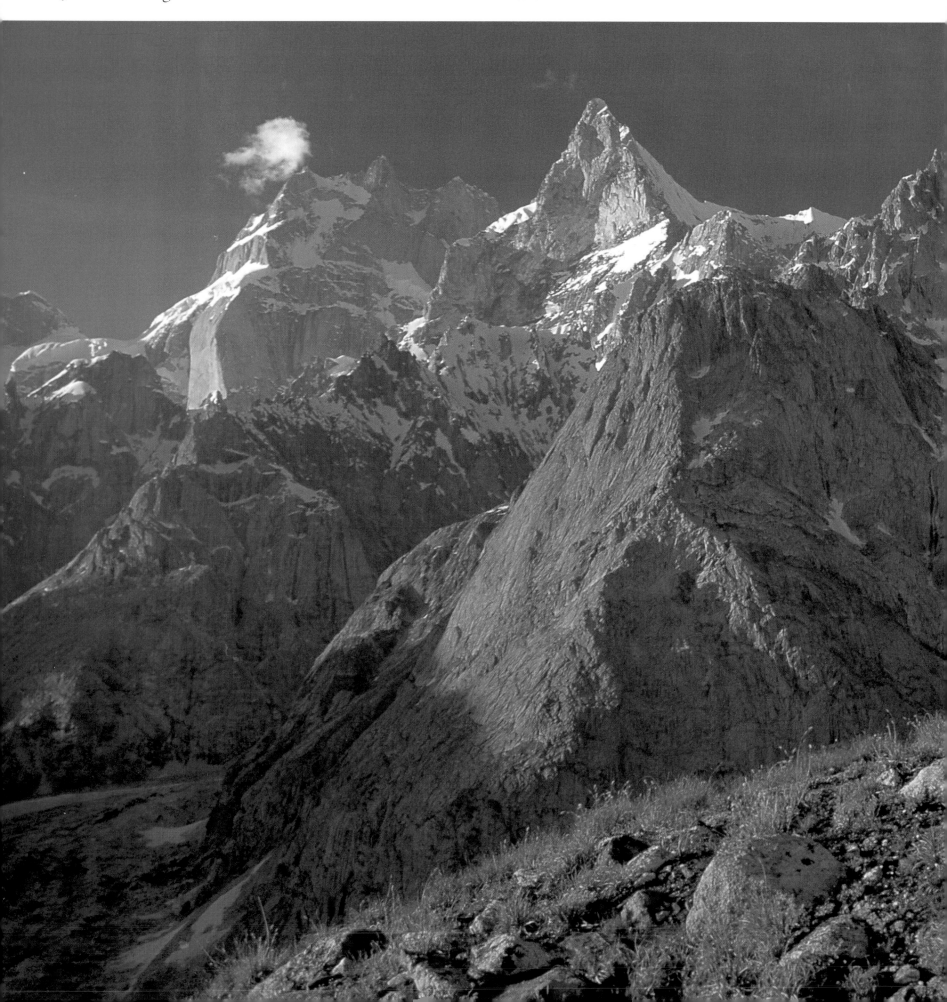

Ulysses Press   *general editor* – STEVE RAZZETTI

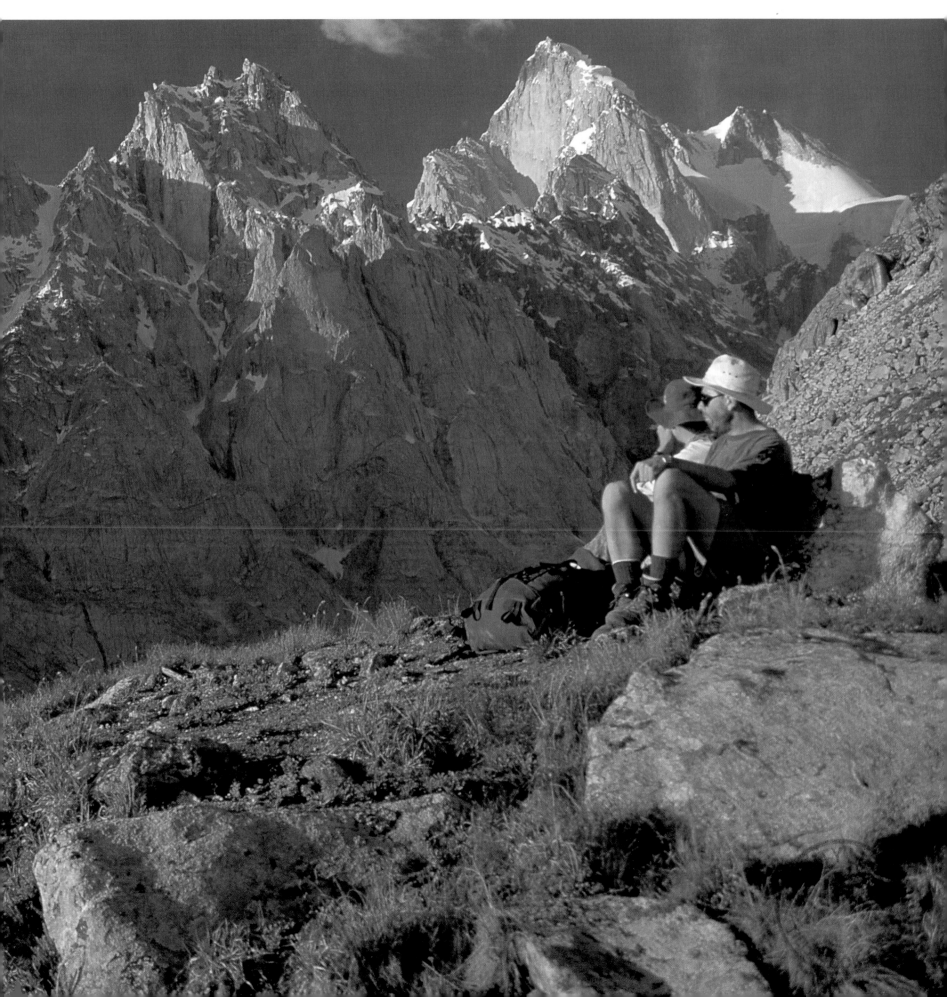

Published in the United States by
Ulysses Press
P.O. Box 3440
Berkeley, CA 94703
www.ulyssespress.com

ISBN 1-56975-302-4
Library of Congress Control Number: 2001092291

Distributed in the United States
by Publishers Group West

First published in Great Britain in 2001 by
New Holland Publishers
London • Cape Town • Sydney • Auckland

MANAGING EDITORS Claudia dos Santos,
Mari Roberts
MANAGING ART EDITOR Peter Bosman
COMMISSIONING EDITOR Simon Pooley
EDITOR Ingrid Schneider
CARTOGRAPHY John Loubser, John Hall
PICTURE RESEARCH Sonya Meyer, Zuné Roberts
ILLUSTRATOR Steven Felmore
PRODUCTION Myrna Collins
INDEXER AND PROOFREADER Sean Fraser

REPRODUCTION BY
Hirt & Carter (Pty) Ltd, Cape Town

PRINTED AND BOUND IN SINGAPORE BY
Tien Wah Press (Pte) Ltd

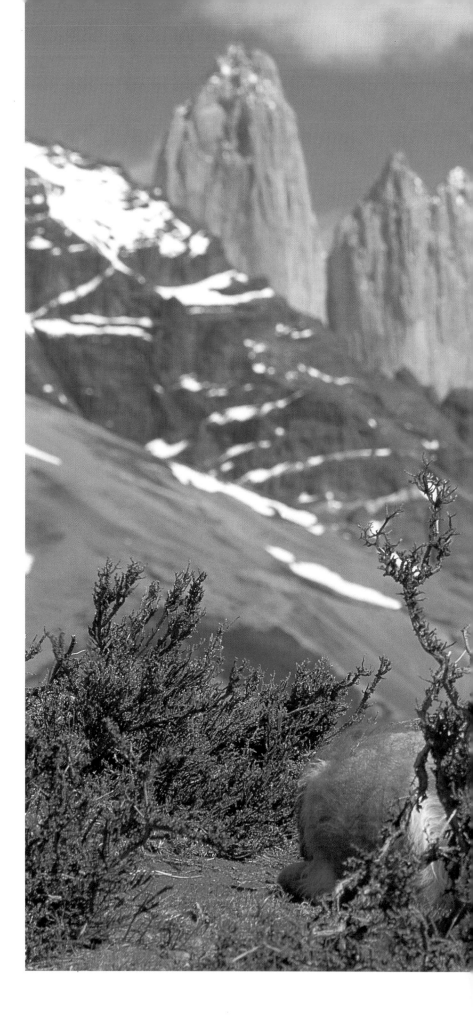

HALF TITLE *Looking down on Emerald Lake, Tongariro National Park. The high mineral content of the water in these old volcanic craters brings about their unique colour.*

TITLE *From a flower-strewn meadow high above the Biafo Glacier in Pakistan's central Karakoram, The Ogre and Latok peaks are sensationally revealed.*

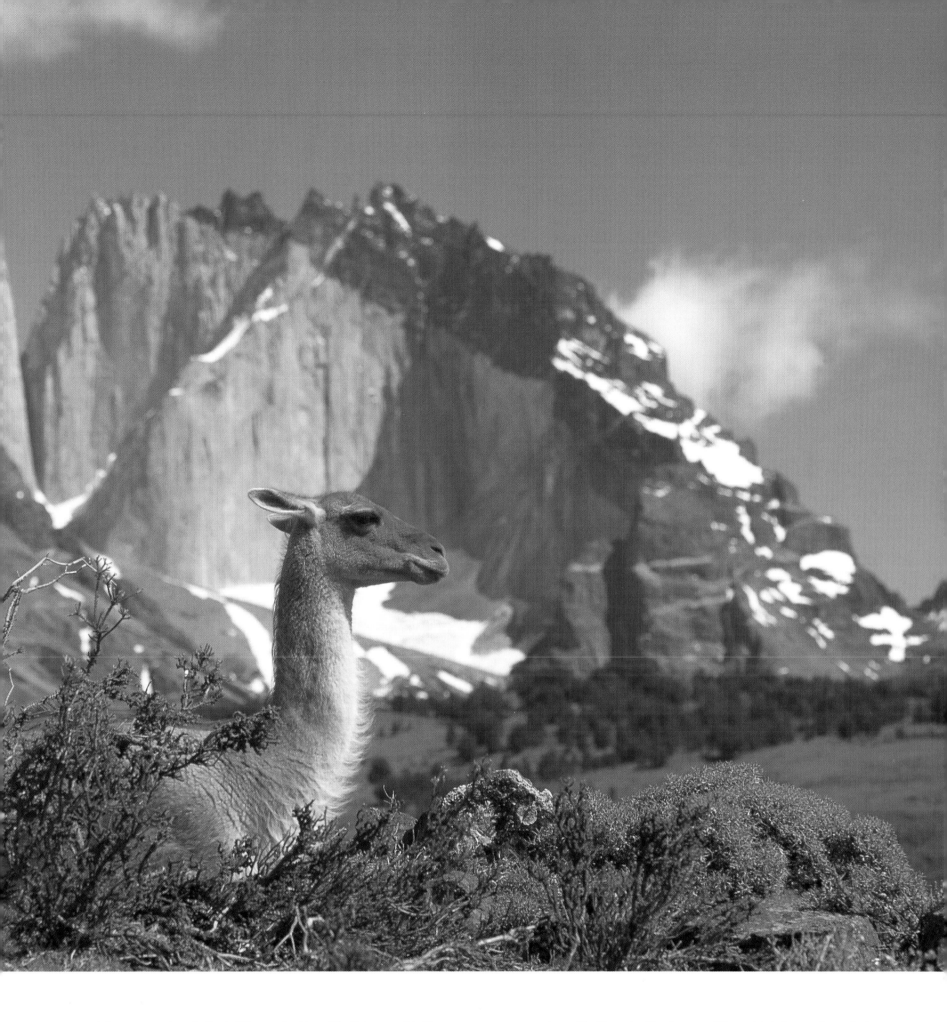

ABOVE *A lone guanaco poses in front of the granite spires of the Paine massif in Torres del Paine National Park. On the right, the intriguingly named Nido Negro de Condores.*

FOLLOWING PAGES *The Tongariro Crossing, one of the most popular one-day walks in New Zealand, forms part of the Round the Mountains trek in Tongariro National Park.*

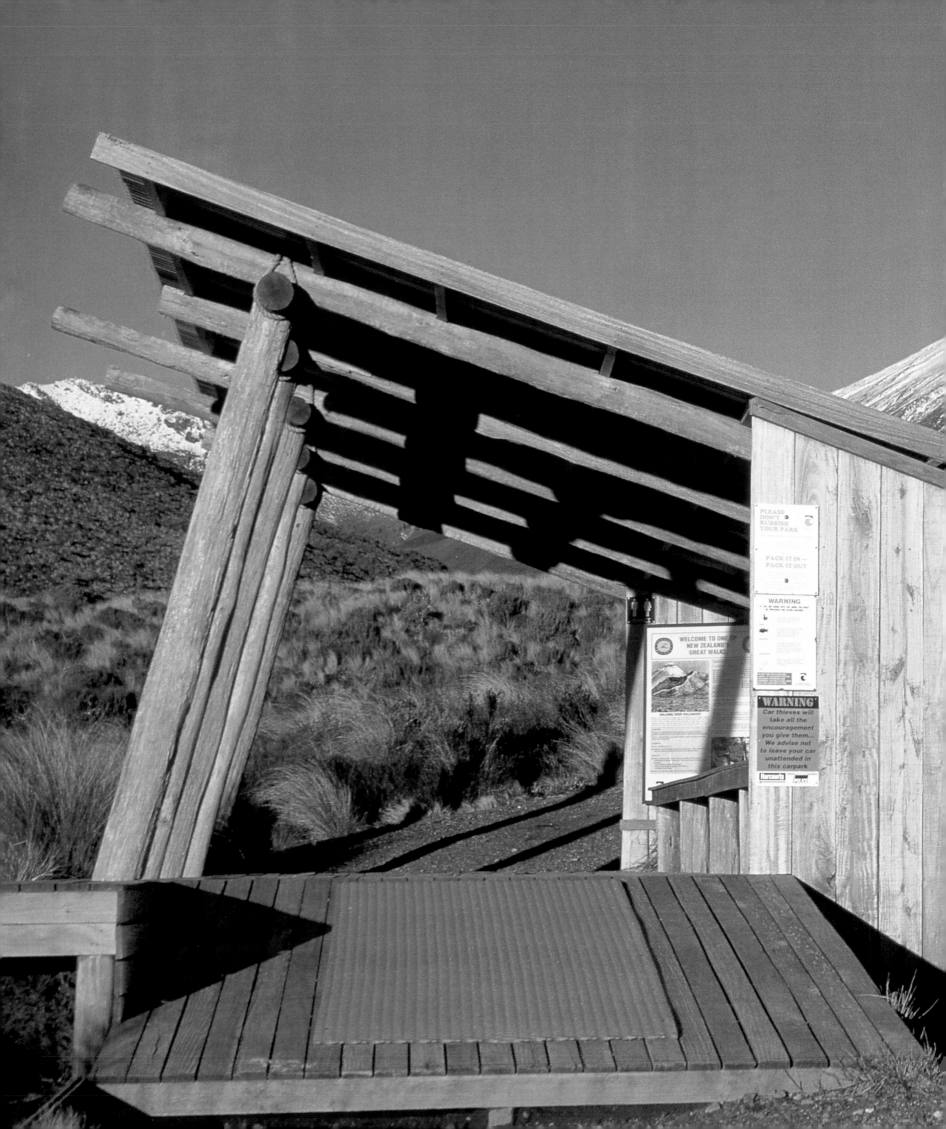

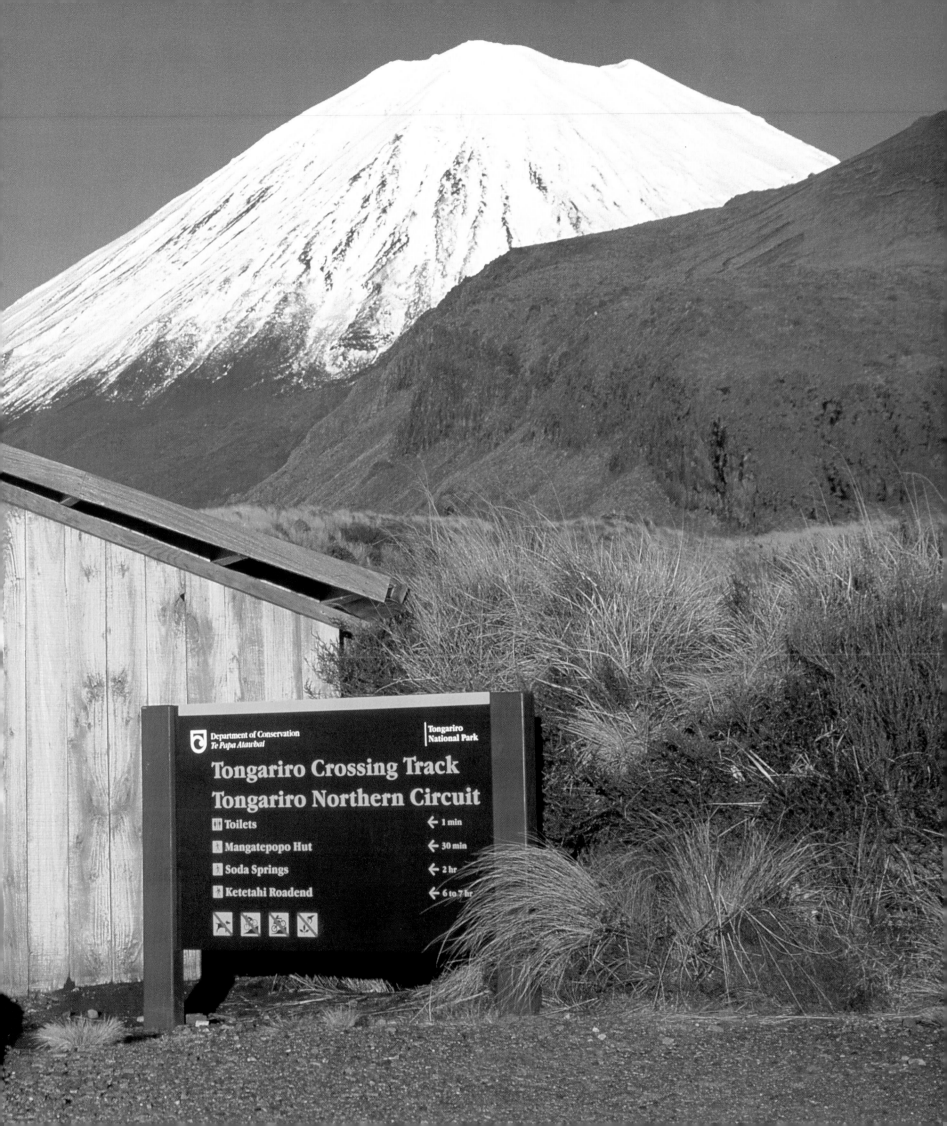

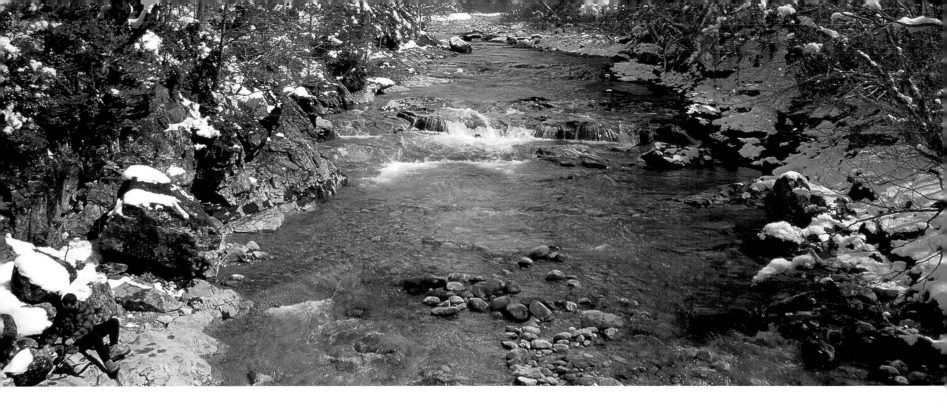

CONTENTS

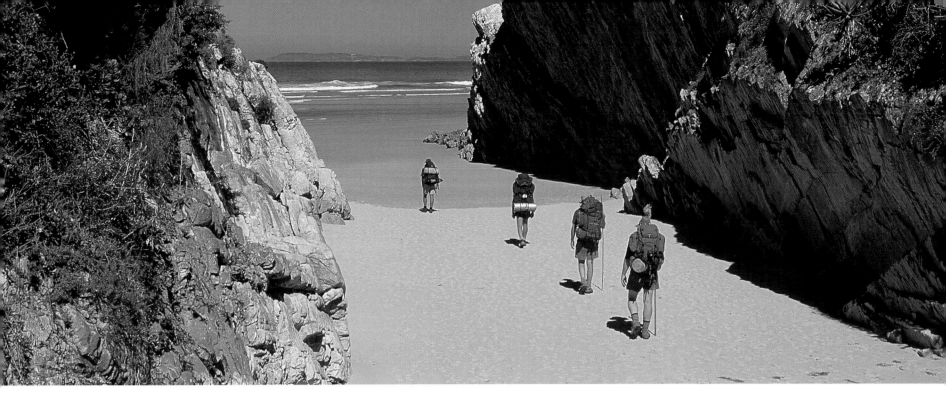

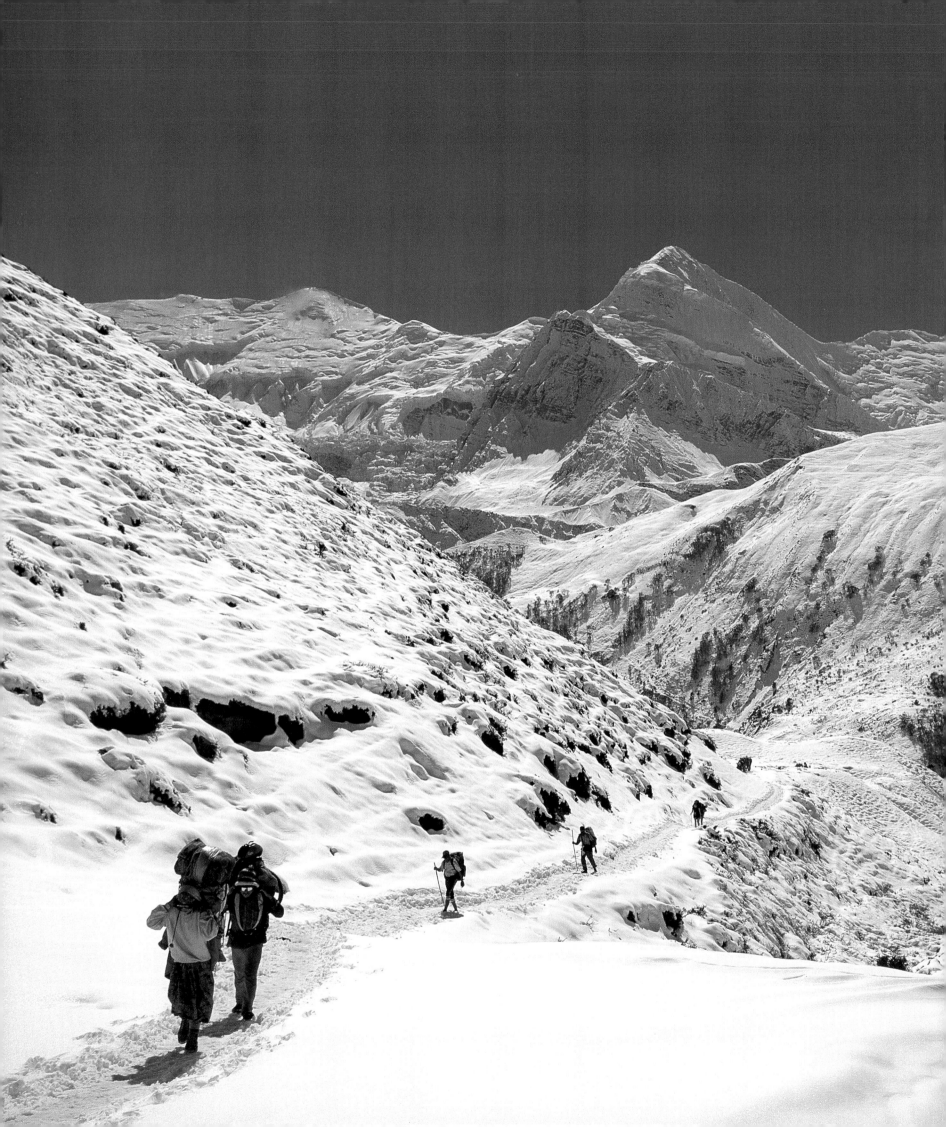

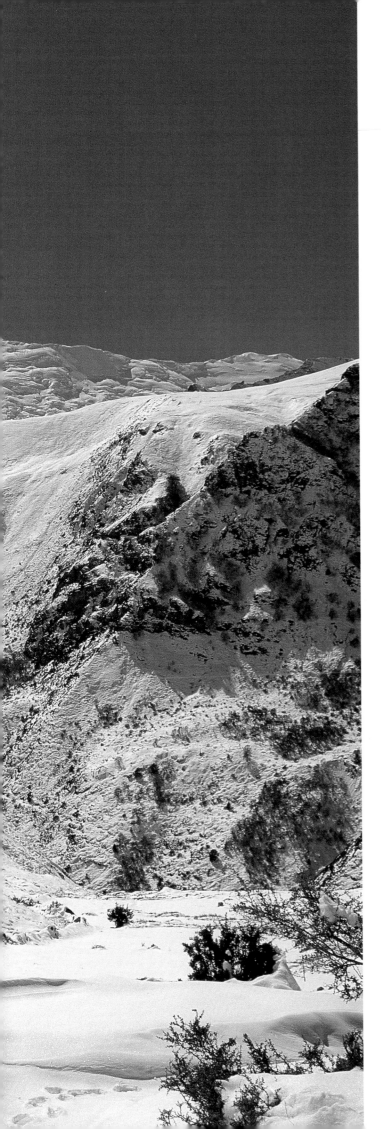

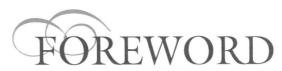

FOREWORD

'The body roams the mountains and the spirit is set free...'

Thus wrote the 17th-century Chinese poet Hsu Hsia-k'o. It has long been a favourite of mine although I'm tempted to substitute for mountains the all-embracing term *wild places*. Despite having spent a lifetime climbing and travelling among mountains, I have also found spiritual refreshment, if not the same heady adrenaline, in the desert, on the empty savanna and on the ocean.

So much of our time is dominated by the effort of surviving the hassles of modern existence that it is all too easy to feel like an insignificant ant on the global anthill. Having lost sight of what being is all about, we can regain our perspective amid the wild places.

I know an English hill that rises like the bows of a great ship above a wide green vale. Its summit, encircled by the prodigious mound-and-ditch ramparts of a prehistoric hill fort, rises but 190m (630ft) above the sea. But when the wind bends the yellow grass and the clouds scud close overhead this is as stimulating a place as many a mountaintop. I go there often to reassure myself that there is more to life than cameras and computers, e-mails and invoices.

It is not easy to define a wild place. Beauty is in the eye of the beholder. All is relative.

Not often do we find the opportunity to enjoy the really wild places – today they are few and far between. Perhaps primeval imperatives are their defining qualities. The finding of food, drink and rest for instance, the quest for somewhere to sleep, the search for the onward route. Sometimes even the business of staying alive. The escape from civilization is not from but to reality.

This book will lead you to such wild places. These are special journeys carefully selected by experienced travellers. They are practical objectives for the keen walker yet challenging enough to be memorable adventures. Above all, they will refresh the spirit.

That great Scottish mountain explorer Norman Collie once wrote:

'... the land of the great woods, lakes, mountains and rushing rivers is still mysterious enough to please anyone who has eyes to see, and can understand.'

Go then and enjoy.

JOHN CLEARE, WILTSHIRE, ENGLAND

PREVIOUS PAGES, LEFT TO RIGHT *A hiker absorbs the wonders of spring on the banks of the Ordesa River in the Pyrenees; the end is in sight! Trekkers on the Otter Trail approach Nature's Valley.*
LEFT *The trail from Manang to Thorung Phedi, Nepal. The first snows of winter transform the Marsyangdi Valley above Manang into a glistening wonderland.*
OVERLEAF *Camp in the ablation valley on the north side of the Hispar Glacier at Haghura Shanga Lichang, Pakistan. A welcome, verdant oasis amid such a dramatic and apparently lifeless landscape.*

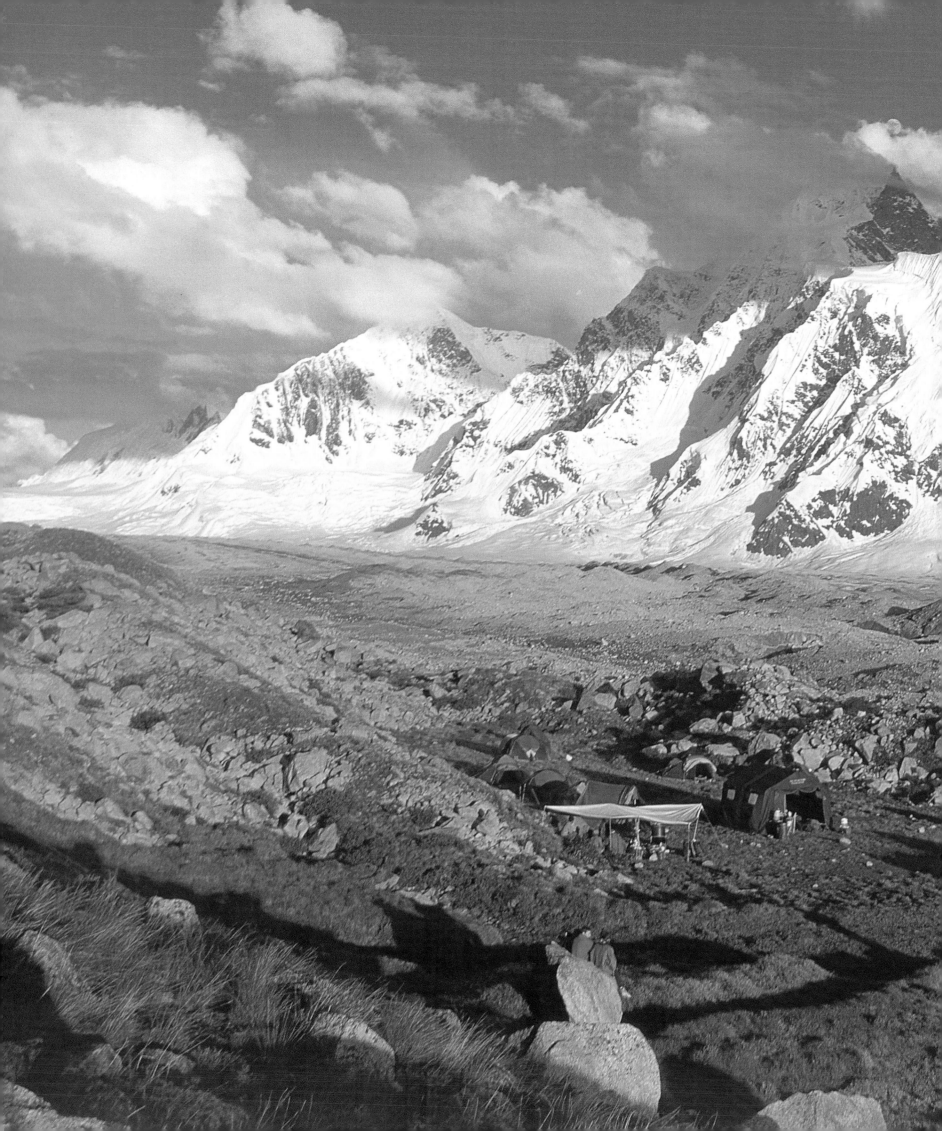

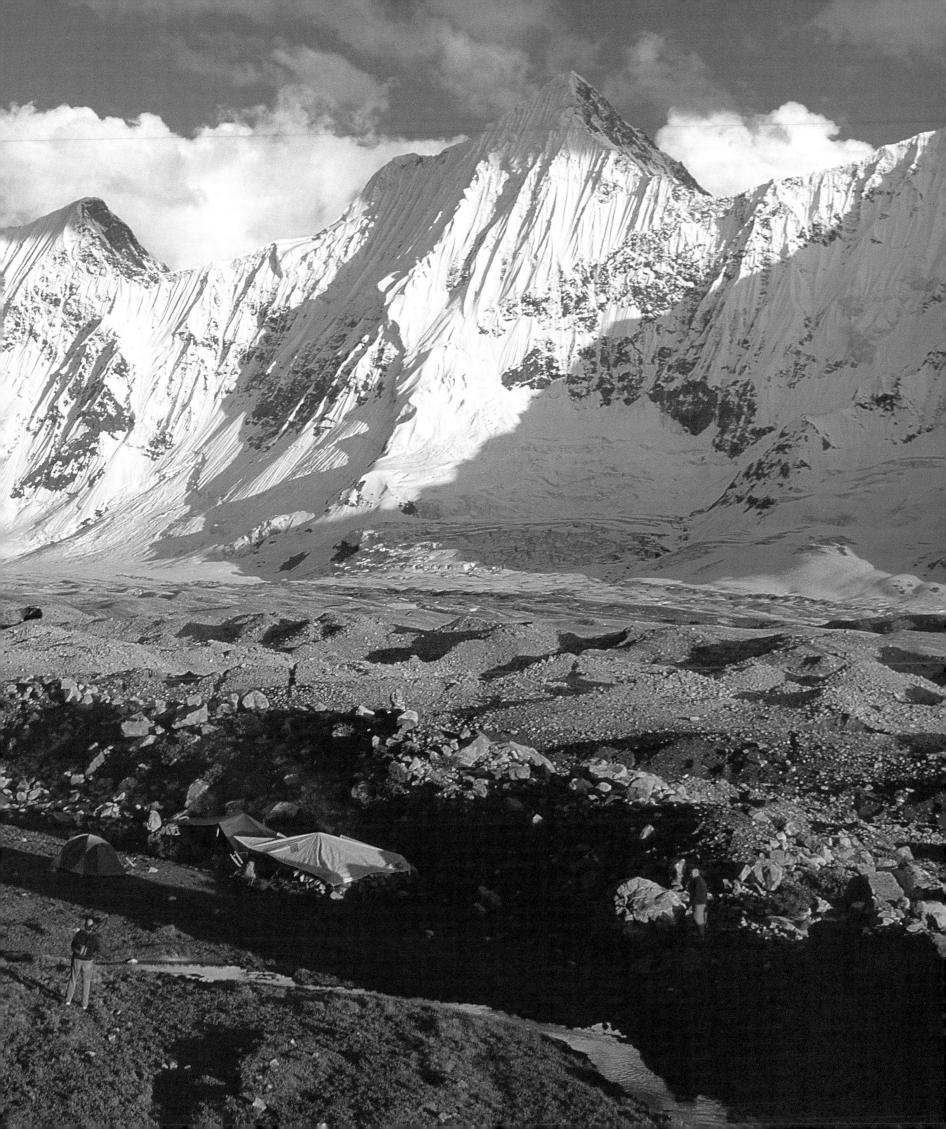

INTRODUCTION

by Steve Razzetti

Humanity has always exhibited a strong itinerant tendency. Prehistoric man pursued the animals he hunted out of Africa across Europe and Asia, arriving in Australia some 50,000 years ago. In a similar fashion, he crossed from Siberia into Alaska and the Americas approximately 14,000 years ago. The earliest recorded exploits of mankind the explorer are found in Egyptian hieroglyphics dating from 4000BC, and until AD1500 the most accomplished explorers and cartographers came from the Chinese and Arab worlds.

In the 14th century, somewhat late in the race to explore the planet, several colourful characters sailed from the ports of Europe motivated initially by the two perennial pillars of human endeavour – commercial development and religious proselytism. With the 15th century came the Renaissance, the rise of assertive sovereign states – England, Spain, Portugal and France – and the beginning of the

that travelling on foot in remote areas has become any less strenuous than it was in the past. In order to complete your journey as safely and enjoyably as possible a considerable amount of forward thinking and preparation is called for.

Many of the destinations featured in this book are in extremely remote and inaccessible corners of the world, in countries where the luxuries of efficient and dependable internal transport, clean food and drinking water are still but dreams. Planning and successfully completing a trip in such places requires both a degree of patience and a willingness to be flexible. Things break down. Weather is fickle. Communications are unreliable. Be prepared to think on your feet, remain positive, and adapt your plans according to the conditions you encounter once you arrive. Define the success of a trip not by the goals achieved but by your level of enjoyment!

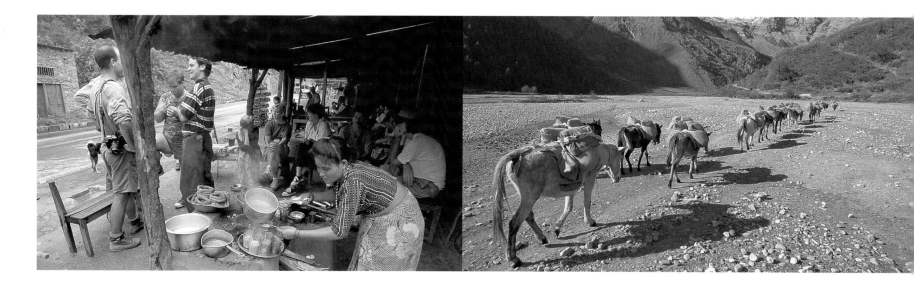

colonial era. At the same time, the growth of a wealthy merchant class throughout Europe led to a flowering of artistic activity and scientific endeavour. By the 17th century, these Renaissance ideals began to find expression in the motivations of travellers, and from this period to the present day there extends a rich literary tradition encompassing the accounts and illustrations of those who travelled for the sheer pleasure of travel itself, as well as those who sought scientific, anthropological and geographical knowledge.

Distant and exotic corners of the world are becoming increasingly accessible, but the ease with which an air ticket or holiday booking is obtained does not mean

Choosing an appropriate mode of wilderness travel or a 'trekking style' is your first step, and an enlightened decision early on will greatly enhance your chances of a thoroughly rewarding journey. Essentially there are four options: backpacking (carrying everything yourself), relying on locally available accommodation and food (known as 'tea-house' trekking in Nepal), expedition mode (hiring local porters or pack animals yourself) and booking with a commercial operator (who will arrange everything for you). Your choice may be limited by where you wish to travel and the length of time you have at your disposal, but briefly, the advantages of each are explained in the following pages.

ABOVE *Local cuisine is sampled at a tea-house rest stop in Nepal. Food and lodging require little effort or planning with this mode of travel.*

ABOVE *Pack animals – mules, horses, yaks, llamas – even sheep! – are often used to carry travellers' luggage in wilderness areas. Careful packing and strong duffles are essential.*

BACKPACKING: This gives you absolute freedom and flexibility on the one hand, but commits you to lugging heavy packs and relying on lightweight, freeze-dried foods on the other. You may well cover less ground, and making sure you have energy left at the end of a gruelling day to set up camp, collect fuel, fetch water, cook and clear up is paramount. Your time spent in the wilderness will be limited by how much food and fuel you can carry.

TEA-HOUSE: Depending on where you travel, this approach can vary from absolute luxury to real hardcore. On popular trails in Nepal, local hostelries have evolved into sophisticated affairs offering private rooms, under-table heating, hot showers, sun terraces and a range of cuisine and beers almost equal to that found at resorts in the Alps. Here you may reasonably contemplate a three-week outing carrying only your clothes and sleeping bag. Adopting such a mode in the

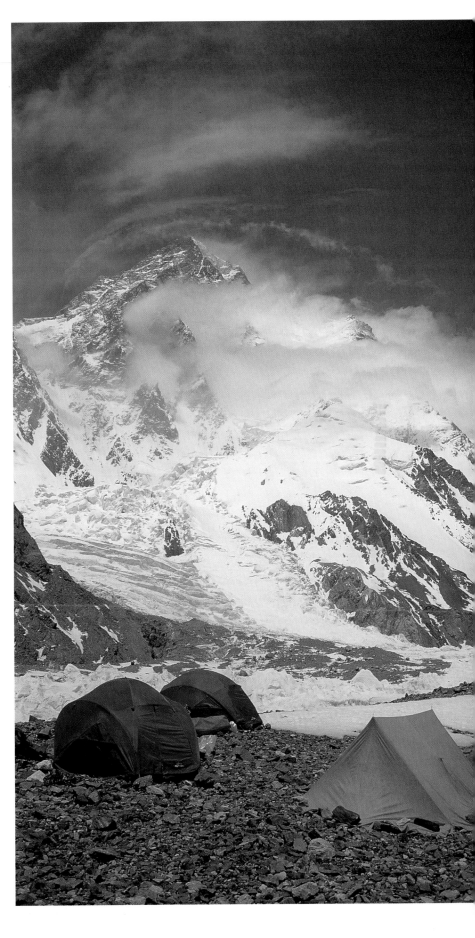

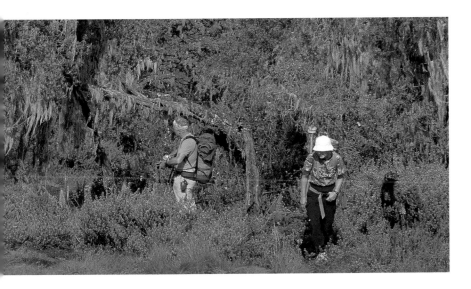

Karakoram, however, would demand knowledge of several local languages and commit you to sleeping in hovels and eating bread and goat meat daily. The extent of your wanderings will be limited by the availability of food and shelter.

EXPEDITION: For a group of friends with a shared objective, this has to be the best and most economical way to go. By hiring local porters or pack animals you can effectively become a self-contained unit for a month or more and adapt your plans to meet conditions as the journey unfolds. In the Himalaya and Andes, this is particularly appropriate, and by travelling with a team of locals you benefit from their knowledge of the terrain and learn some of their language and customs.

ABOVE *Trekkers near Mackinder's Camp, Mount Kenya. Carrying your own pack and gear may limit your time outdoors but you are sure to enjoy it alone.*

ABOVE *Base camp for K2, on the Godwin-Austen Glacier. Tents for expedition-style trekking in regions such as this should be able to cope with heavy snow and gale-force winds.*

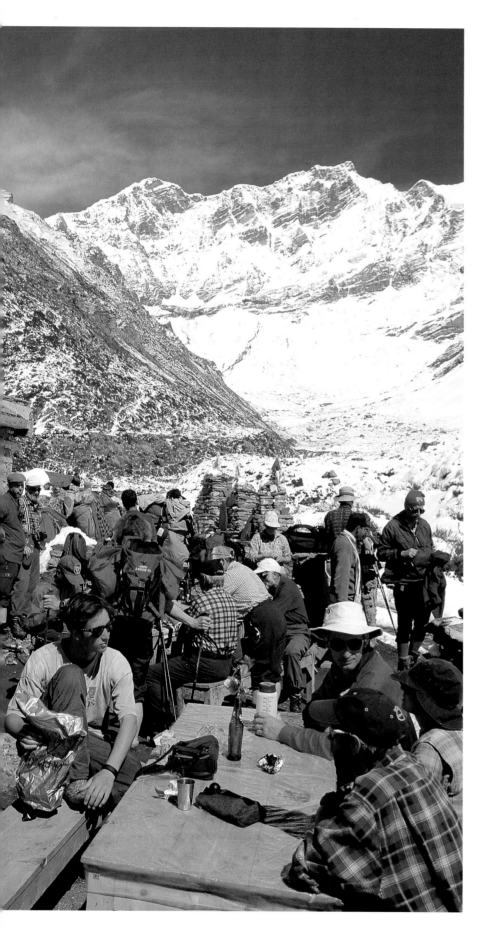

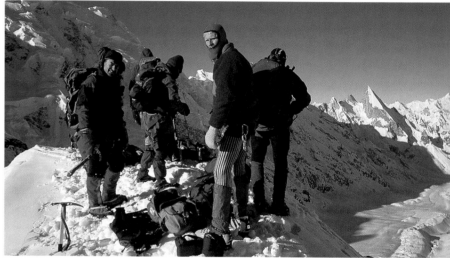

COMMERCIAL OPERATOR: 'Adventure travel', arranged through one of the burgeoning number of agencies specializing in wilderness areas, may be a contradiction in itself; nevertheless, this mode of travel is more popular today than ever before. By signing up for a set tour on given dates you spare yourself the time and effort involved in organizing the logistics of the trip, but you also commit yourself to travelling on a prearranged itinerary in the company of a group of strangers. For many people who lead busy professional lives at home this is the only feasible option, but it does require an astute choice of operator and a particular level of social skills.

Given that most of us today lead fairly sedentary lives, careful consideration should be given to the level of fitness required for a long walk in the wilderness. Certainly, you will achieve a degree of fitness during a trek, but the fitter you are

at the start, the better your body's chance of coping with the rigours of prolonged, vigorous exercise. Similarly, remaining healthy in a wilderness environment requires a few precautions and skills. Common sense indicates a thorough medical and dental check-up before departure and, for certain countries, a programme of inoculations may be prudent. A comprehensive medical first-aid kit is essential.

Most of the treks described in this book reach altitudes at which, without proper acclimatization, the symptoms of Acute Mountain Sickness (AMS) may manifest in some or all of a group. Make a point of understanding the basic physiology of this potentially serious condition. AMS can kill. Be aware that its

ABOVE *While the festive social 'scene' of tea-house trekking may appeal to some, those seeking tranquility may prefer to travel in a self-sufficient private group.*

ABOVE *The ascent of a technically straightforward peak, such as the Gondokoro Peak in Pakistan, serves as perfect acclimatization for the more challenging Gondokoro La crossing.*

onset has absolutely nothing to do with age, gender, level of fitness or experience, and be prepared to adjust your itinerary to allow for different speeds of acclimatization among your group. The simple rule of thumb is that you should never continue your ascent with symptoms of AMS and that if your symptoms worsen while remaining at the same altitude you must descend.

Similarly, most of the treks in this book are in regions where strong sun and dry air combine to make dehydration a very real danger. The symptoms of dehydration are often very similar – and the condition almost as serious – to those of AMS. Consuming ample, safe drinking water is of paramount importance. Bringing water to a rolling boil – at any altitude – is now accepted to be enough to sterilize it, but in many field situations this is not feasible. Tincture of iodine is similarly reliable and careful consideration of the size and quality of water bottles is important.

Other points to consider before dashing off into the hills include insurance and how to organize a rescue in case of an accident. Standard travel insurance is unlikely to be sufficient, and you should carefully choose a policy from one of the many specialist brokers selling expedition cover. Read the small print and think ahead to how you will communicate with your insurers should a rescue or evacuation be urgently required. Consider also how you will carry your money and convert it into local currency – Quechua Indians in Peru are unlikely to recognize travellers' cheques or accept credit cards.

As a matter of polite sensitivity and ecological awareness, give due consideration to both the cultural and environmental impact of travelling in remote areas. By definition, many such places are home to both fragile ecosystems and unique communities of people with traditions far removed from our own. Make your trip

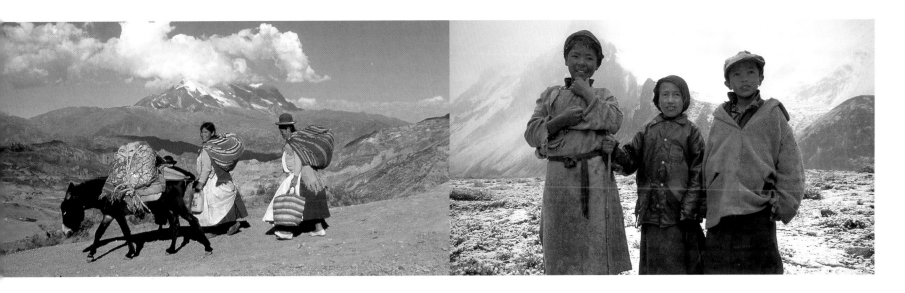

Outdoor equipment has benefited hugely from recent innovations and technology, and the fabrics used in modern mountain clothing have revolutionized the levels of comfort they provide. Before buying expensive items, acquaint yourself with the climatic extremes and temperature variations you are likely to encounter. Hi-tech fabrics and state-of-the-art design may make life in cold, wet and windy environments bearable, but before you part with large amounts of money for designer desert wear and end up looking like a cross between Indiana Jones and James Bond, consider going ethnic. Traditional dress in many of the world's hotter locations is by far the most practical, comfortable and cheapest attire.

as eco-friendly as possible by adopting and sticking to suitable strategies for waste disposal, toilets, cooking fuels, etc. Be aware of local dress codes, domestic etiquette and appropriate behaviour, and if you are a keen photographer be prepared to sacrifice your desire for a picture if a local person is unhappy about being photographed. Always ask permission first.

Finally, get out there and explore. Discover new heights, take in your surroundings, appreciate local cultures and take time to reflect on the wonderful experiences that you are bound to encounter.

But most importantly, have fun.

ABOVE *Local folk, such as these Aymara Indians in Bolivia, lead simple, contented lives and respond with enthusiasm to those with an interest in their culture and language.*

ABOVE *The Westerner's urge to hand out sweets has turned children along the popular trails in Nepal into persistent beggars and should be stoutly resisted. Frienship is enough.*

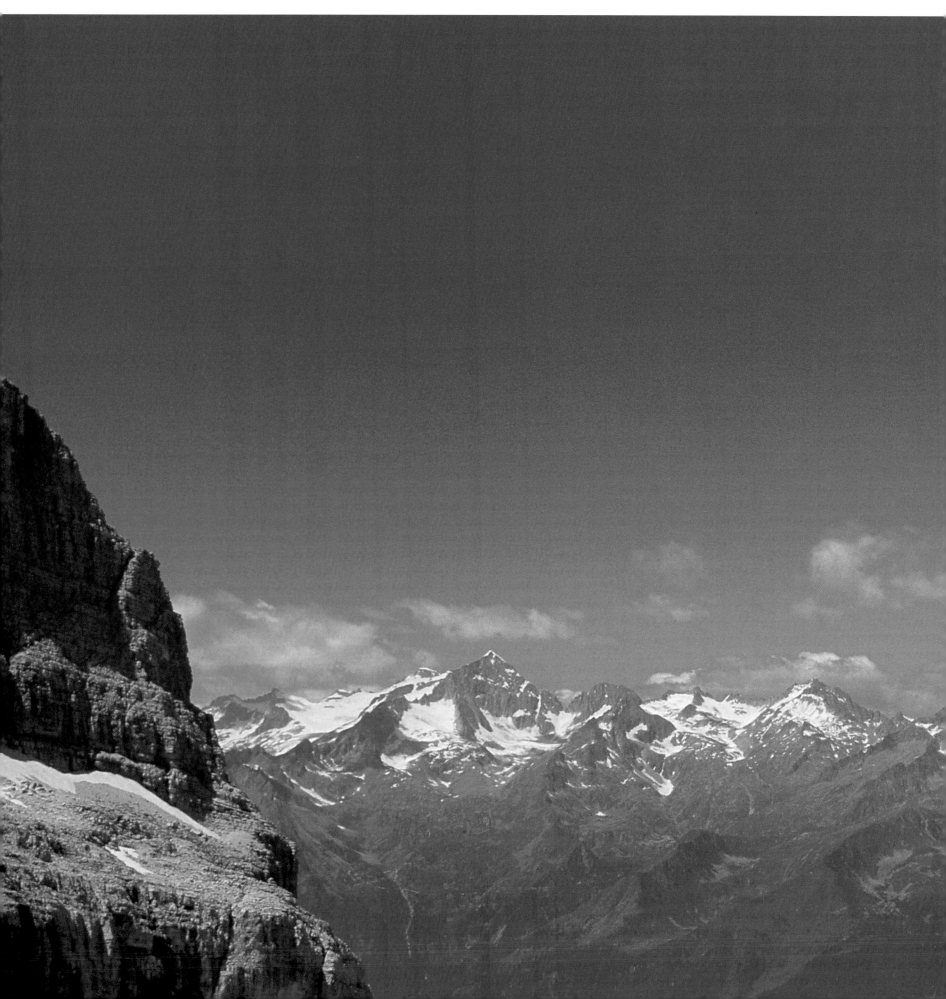

EUROPE

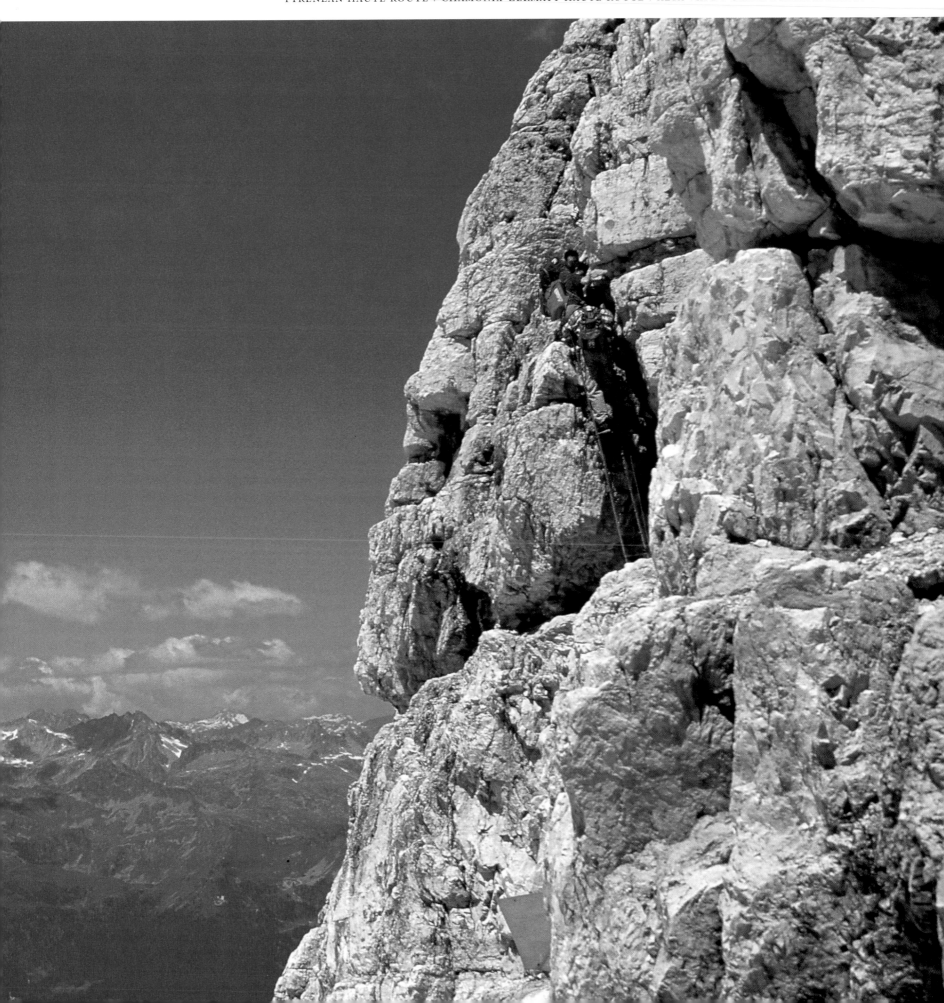

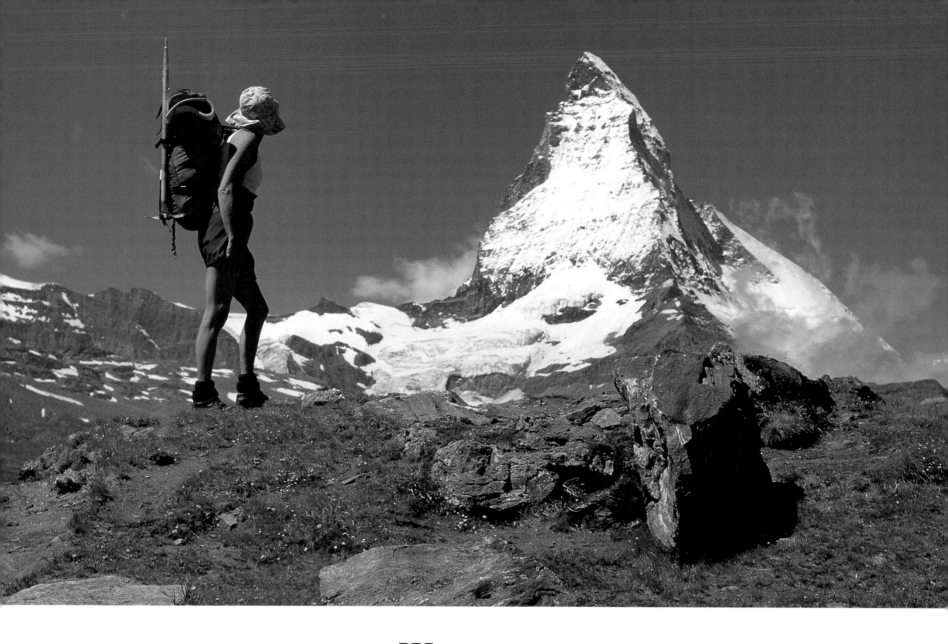

EUROPE

Our nature lies in movement;
complete calm is death.

PASCAL

ABOVE *The imposing and characteristic pyramid form of the Matterhorn is so completely arresting it will mesmerize trekkers for hours at a time.*

OPPOSITE *A trekker makes his way along the grassy trails of the Dolomites, the Sella Towers forming a typical backdrop.*

PREVIOUS PAGES *The* vie ferrate *(iron ways) in Italy are not for the faint-hearted! Often completely exposed to the elements, they offer memorable routes up precipitous rockface.*

While it is patently true that many of the world's continents spawned magnificent, diverse and sophisticated civilizations long before the advent of the Christian Era and the rise of European power, it is an undeniable fact that the world we live in today – for better or for worse – is largely the product of European endeavour.

European cultural and economic values were vigorously and often forcefully exported to the farthest-flung corners of the globe during the colonial era, and had profound influences on everything from population patterns to architectural styles. Language is perhaps the simplest and most telling barometer of this outflowing tide of ideas. To travel in South America one must speak Spanish; in North America, the entire Indian subcontinent, Australia and New Zealand, English will suffice; and on the vast continent of Africa, French, German, Portuguese, English and Dutch all have their places.

Against a background of post-war reconstruction, economic depression and the sudden realization that world domination was a thing of the past, many Europeans looked to their own countries for avenues of escape and adventure again, and found that they were sitting on a gold mine. Alpinism may have started in the Victorian era and initially been the preserve of the middle and upper classes, but after World War II things rapidly changed. Guide books and magazines proliferated, climbing, walking and cycling clubs sprung up in every city, long-distance footpaths were conceived, built and waymarked, newspapers avidly reported the daring exploits of all sorts of adventurers and the era of *the great outdoors* began.

Included here are the quintessential adventurous long-distance treks in Europe's most spectacular and celebrated mountain wilderness areas. All are challenging, both physically and logistically, all are popular

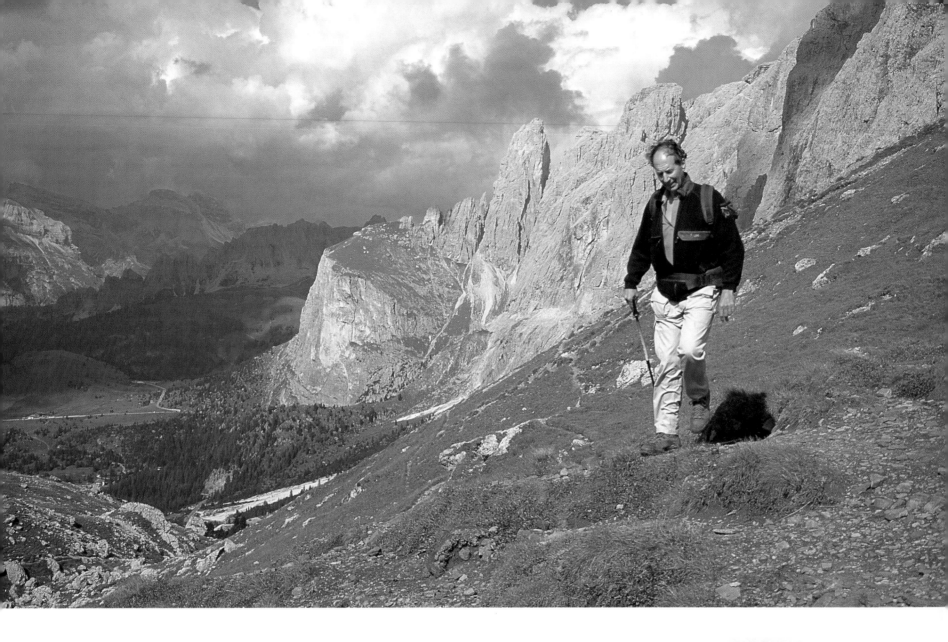

and all will leave you wondering why Europeans ever ventured abroad in search of adventure when such wonders are to be found on their doorsteps.

In the Alps, the classic Haute Route between Chamonix and Zermatt – from Mont Blanc to the Matterhorn – covers a distance of 65km (40 miles), across 11 passes among the mightiest alpine 4000m (13,000ft) peaks. The Alta Via 2 from Bressanone to Feltre through the Dolomites in Italy's South Tyrol is a fairyland feast of perpendicular pink limestone towers, *vie ferrate* and idyllic forested valleys.

Second only to the Alps in terms of mountain grandeur in Europe, the Pyrenees contain over 120 summits in excess of 3000m (9800ft) and form a formidable natural frontier between France and Spain. Overlooked by mountaineers and hikers for decades while the Alps stole the limelight, the lonely valleys and vast tracts of pristine upland wilderness that constitute the bulk of the range have only been discovered by outdoor enthusiasts relatively recently. In the pages that follow, you will find a tantalizing description of part of the Haute Route Pyrénéene (HRP) – the 45-day odyssey along the crest of the range from Atlantic to Mediterranean.

Corsica may appear as an island in your atlas, but in reality it is simply a range of mountains in the Mediterranean. Though administered by the French for 200 years, it belongs – geographically, historically and linguistically – to Italy, and has had a colourful and often violent past. The interior consists of impenetrable, labyrinthine valleys and stark, arid peaks of grey and pink granite, many of which rise to over 2000m (6500ft). Along the crests of these mountains from Calenzana to Conca, the 180km (120 miles) Grande Randonnée (GR20) is a serious but popular undertaking.

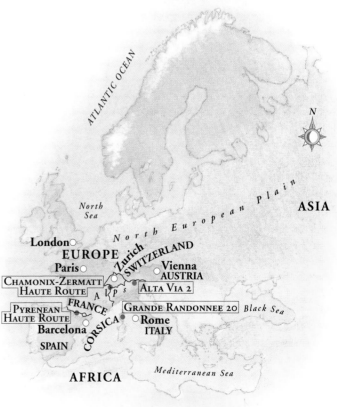

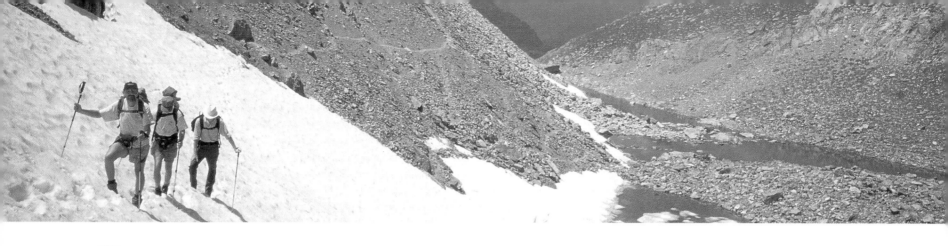

PYRENEAN HAUTE ROUTE

by Hilary Sharp

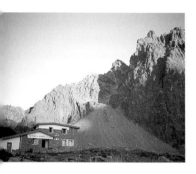

The Pyrenees run between the Atlantic Ocean and the Mediterranean, forming the frontier between France and Spain. Legend has it that in ancient times Hercules could not resist seducing Pyrène, the beautiful daughter of the King of Cerdagne, before setting off on a mission. In despair at her lover's departure, the princess took off in pursuit, only to be slaughtered by wild animals. On his return, devastated by grief, Hercules built a tomb around his beloved, piling up huge rocks that became the Pyrenees.

The peaks here are smaller than in the Alps but no less impressive and there is a marked contrast between the ridged sierras of the Spanish side and the steep forested valleys of the French side of the massifs. The Pyrenees contain three national parks, two of which feature on the Pyrenean Haute Route: the French Parc National des Pyrénées and the Spanish Parque Nacional de Ordesa y Monte Perdido.

The first real explorer of this wild country was French geologist and botanist, Louis-François Ramond de Carbonnières who, from 1787, climbed many peaks and passes. In 1802 he was a driving force behind the first ascent (by two French guides, Laurens and Rondau, and a Spanish shepherd) of Monte Perdido, at 3355m (11,008ft) the third highest peak in the range. One of the indigenous flowers of the Pyrenees is named Ramondie des Pyrénées, in his honour.

The Haute Route Pyrénéene (HRP) begins at the Lac de Bious d'Artigues, a deep blue lake dominated by the Pic du Midi d'Ossau (2884m; 9462ft), prominent and easily recognizable by its double summit. The trail leads under the south face of the mountain and circles east around it, passing through meadows which in summer are blue with wild irises. Higher up, yellow-spotted gentians replace the irises, until the

rocky boulder field above the Lac de Peygeret. The arduousness of the final section of the climb is mitigated by the fine views and on arrival at the Col de Peygeret (2300m; 7500ft) you are rewarded with the impressive south face of the Pic du Midi d'Ossau just above. Ahead are the summits Palas (2974m; 9758ft) and Balaitous (3144m; 10,315ft), which indicate the direction of the next day's walk, and just below, next to its glittering lake, is the Refuge de Pombie.

In the early morning the sun catches the top of the Pic du Midi d'Ossau, turning the face orange as you descend meadows strewn with foxgloves and the blue thistle-like Pyrenean eryngo. If you're lucky you'll see herds of isards, the Pyrenean chamois, running on the high slopes. Lower down, horses and donkeys graze peacefully, while shepherds tend sheep. The Arrious Valley provides the main ascent on this day, with a pleasant steady climb out of the woods and into open country littered with boulders, to the Col d'Arrious (2259m; 7412ft).

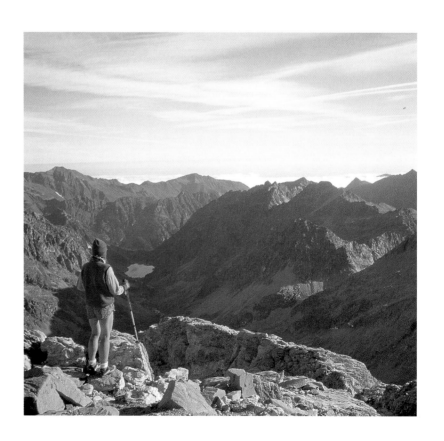

TOP *The final slopes below the Col de la Fache (2664m; 8741ft) can remain surprisingly snowy. A slip here would result in an icy dip in the Lac de la Fache.*

INSET *An early start from Refuge de Pombie allows you to enjoy the sunrise at the Pic du Midi d'Ossau (2884m; 9462ft).*

RIGHT *The Petit Vignemale is a fine diversion, with excellent views in all directions. Here, looking north across the Pyrenees National Park and the Lac de Gaube.*

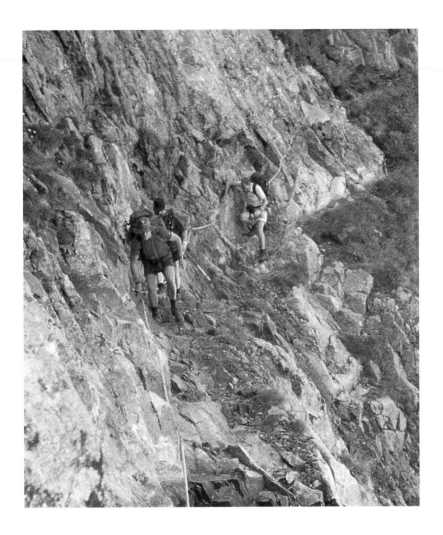

ABOVE *The Passage d'Orteig provides a spectacular finish to the day, traversing high above the Lac d'Artouste to reach the Arremoulit Refuge.*

The Arremoulit Refuge can be reached by two possible routes. If it is wet or stormy you must take the path that descends to the Lac d'Artouste, and then follow a clear and easy path back up to the refuge. In dry conditions, however, it is much more interesting and less arduous to take the Passage d'Orteig, which winds its way round the hillside high above the lake and along a short section of exposed cable handline. The excitement is fairly short-lived and you soon reach the safety of relatively flat ground and the hut, situated among several azure blue lakes – tempting, but glacially cold.

The Col d'Arremoulit (2448m; 8032ft), reached by following a cairned path through boulders, brings you to the Spanish border and a superb panorama – the distant summit of Lurien (2753m; 9033ft) behind and ahead, the high peak of Balaitous with its reflection in the lake below. The path leads around the Arriel lakes and then takes a traverse eastwards, contouring the hillside, high above the Rio Aguas Limpias, to the dammed Respumoso Lake. Flowers are abundant – houseleeks, gentians, rhaetian poppies, leopard's bane, thrift, wild chives and, of course, irises – and there is an endless vista of distant mountains. Above the lake is a new refuge, handy for cold drinks on a hot day before tackling the hard, hot climb back to France. The path passes a beautiful lake where a refreshing swim will make the next bit seem less difficult.

The return to France at the Col de la Fache (2664m; 8741ft) provides stunning views of Vignemale, at 3298m (10,821ft) the highest of the French Pyrenean peaks. A long, steep descent will test tired legs. The Refuge Wallon is visible long before you reach it, but suddenly, just when you've had enough, the rocks give way to grassy pasture and the hut in a fine open setting.

From Wallon the route crosses the river and makes its way into the Gave d'Arratille Valley. A pleasant wending path rises near the river past stunted pine trees to the Lac d'Arramatille, colonized by abundant white flowers. The climb onwards to the Col d'Arratille (2528m; 8294ft) is quite arduous and once again you pass into Spain, this

LOCATION The Pyrenees massif, which sits astride the French–Spanish border.

WHEN TO GO July, August and the first half of September.

START The Lac de Bious d'Artigues, accessible by bus and taxi from nearby towns, including Lourdes.

FINISH Gavarnie. Twice daily bus service runs to Lourdes.

DURATION 10 days. This is just a section of the long Haute Route Pyrénéene, which takes about 45 days.

MAX ALTITUDE Monte Perdido (3355m; 11,008ft).

TECHNICAL CONSIDERATIONS This a non-glaciated trek but some sections of trail are very exposed and care and judgement must be used in bad weather. Monte Perdido can be climbed without crampons and ice-axe only when it is clear of snow late in the season. Le Taillon is a relatively easy ascent but is quite long and still requires care in route finding. Petit Vignemale has an obvious route to the top, but in exposed places a fall would have dire consequences. There is some avalanche danger. Ask at the local tourist office if unsure about conditions.

EQUIPMENT Standard trekking gear. Huts provide blankets and food.

TREKKING STYLE Backpacking, although it is possible to overnight in huts instead of tents. All food must be bought before start. Only place on trek to buy food is Gavarnie.

PERMITS/RESTRICTIONS None.

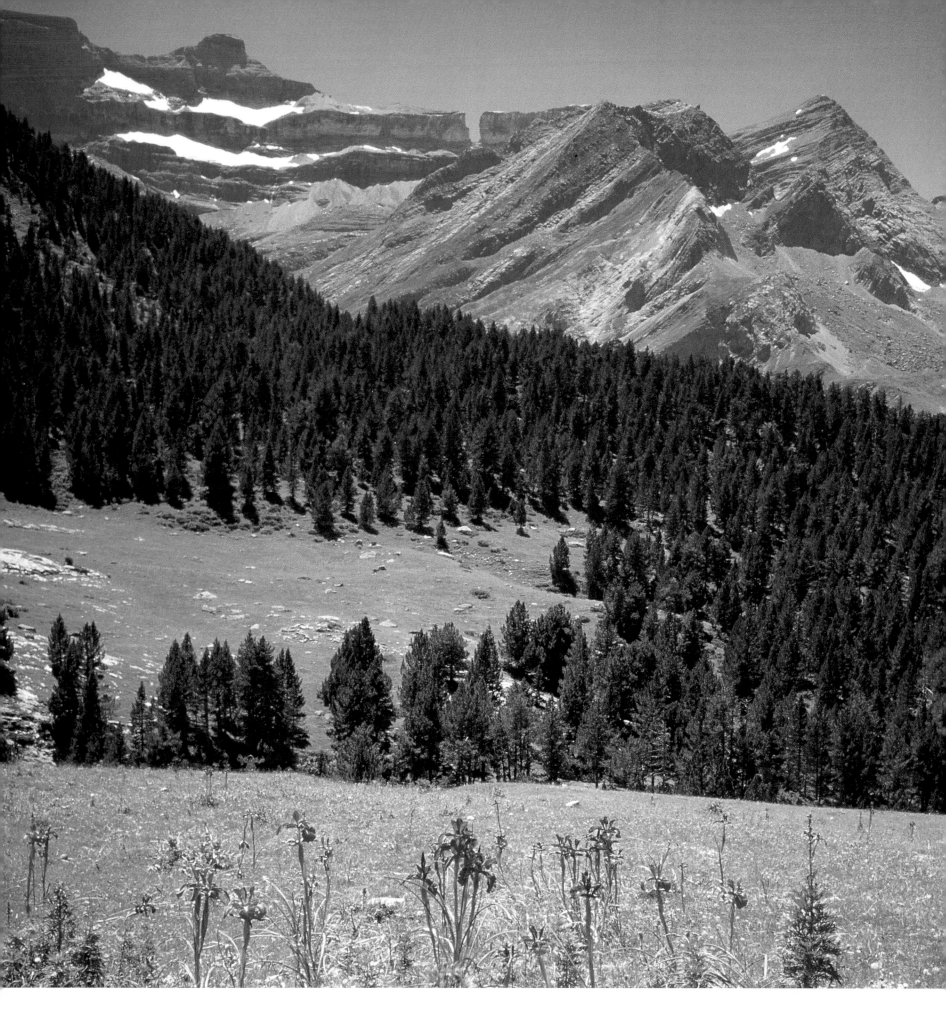

ABOVE *Blue irises provide a colourful foreground for this distant view of the Brèche de Roland, seen here from the slopes below the Refuge des Espuguettes.*

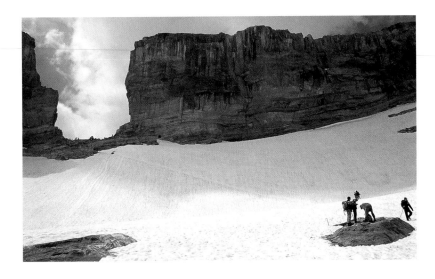

time just for an hour or so, before hurrying back over the Col des Mulets (2591m; 8501ft) to discover Vignemale's impressive north face and glacier. The first ascent of this mountain was made by Henri Cazaux and Bernard Guillembet in 1837. However, it was the Irish–French Count Henry Russell who, having fallen in love with the summit, made the Vignemale truly famous when in 1899 he purchased a 99-year lease of the peak for the sum of one franc a year. He excavated a number of small caves from the rock around the summit to allow him to spend time up there with his friends. These now tend to be inhabited in the summer by penniless climbers.

The Refuge des Ourlettes de Gaube is a rather basic refuge, redeemed by its fine position under the towering face of Vignemale and by the smiling welcome of the hut guardians. A graded zigzagging path leads easily from the hut to the Hourquette d'Ossoue (2734m; 8971ft) but progress will be slow as your gaze is constantly drawn to the orange glow of the rising sun kissing the summit of Vignemale. From the Hourquette Pass, the Refuge de Baysellance is just a short walk away, but first the summit of the Petit Vignemale (3032m; 9948ft) to the south calls, giving a quick ascent and excellent views of the Ossoue Glacier leading to the summit of Vignemale itself.

From the refuge, the path descends relentlessly and in the high season there will doubtless be many people toiling upwards. Be sure to peer into Henry Russell's caves on the way down. After a couple of exposed sections, you reach the flat boulder-strewn area before the Ossoue Dam, which provides a perfect lunch spot and the opportunity for bathing sore feet in the icy waters of the river. The dam is at the roadhead, but Gavarnie is several kilometres away. Unless you're a fan of road walking, it is best to take the path that winds up above the road, through meadows of irises, gentians, houseleeks and orchids. This route is long, but the views are very satisfying: looking back, Vignemale and Petit Vignemale dominate the horizon, while ahead lies the striking pyramid of the summit of Pimené, situated just above Gavarnie. A final 20 minutes on tarmac leads into town, where the return to civilization is a little rude – the streets here are usually teeming with people, and horse droppings, this being the preferred transport for reaching the famous and impressive Cirque de Gavarnie.

ABOVE *The northern slopes beneath the striking Brèche de Roland often remain snowy throughout summer. The trail is clearly seen here in the snow.*

The trek could finish here but it would be a shame not to continue and discover Spain's Ordesa region, just across the Franco–Spanish border. Home to some of the most spectacular scenery in the Pyrenees, one of the highlights is the Ordesa Canyon, a deep and impressive gorge sculpted long ago by glaciers.

Spain is reached via the Refuge des Espuguettes, Cirque d'Estaubé and the Brèche de Tuqueroye (2669m; 8757ft) and Monte Perdido is seen in all its glory. The 'lost mountain', so-called because from France it is blocked from view by the frontier peaks, provides a popular ascent both by its glacier and a non-glaciated route, later in the season. Head south past the Lago de Marboré into the Cirque de Puneta to the Refugio Ronatiza Pineta, keeping a lookout for the famed lammergeier (vulture) overhead.

The Faja de Pelay trail takes the southern side of the Ordesa Canyon, its huge red walls towering all around, while below the fast-flowing Rio Arazas carves out the gorge. At the base of the gorge, there are two options for reaching the nearest accommodation in picturesque Torla: a long road walk or the GR11 through the trees. This section has to be reversed the next day, making for a steep climb up the canyon slopes along a *via ferrata* to reach the Faja de las Flores trail, which traverses in a superb position across the exciting north face of the canyon. This section is unforgettable, due both to its exposure and to the incredible sculpted walls of the canyon below. Head up past the Casteret Cave, a major cave system that holds ice year round, to the amazing rocky notch of the Brèche de Roland (2807m; 9210ft), and back into France. Stop and savour this final highpoint of the trek, gazing out to the distant mountains and hazy plains of Spain.

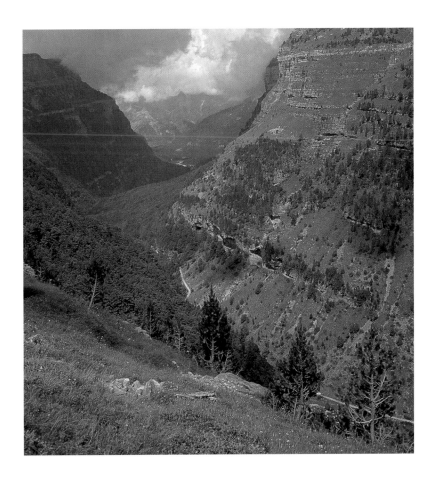

ABOVE *The impressive steep cliffs of the Ordesa Canyon are seen to great advantage from the Faja de Pelay path, which cuts high above the canyon.*

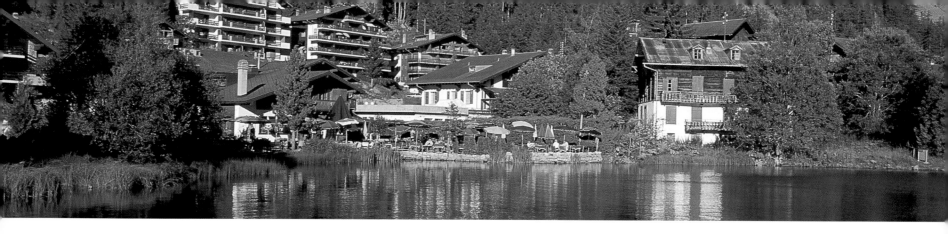

CHAMONIX–ZERMATT HAUTE ROUTE

by Hilary Sharp

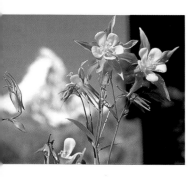

The Haute Route glacier walk from Chamonix to Zermatt passes through many of the high Pennine peaks and is one of the most beautiful walks in the Alps. Established in 1861 by members of the British Alpine Club, together with local guides, the route was originally known as the High Level Road. Today, it is very often done on skis in the spring, but is still a highly popular walk in the summer.

In 1741, British adventurers, William Windham and Richard Pococke, arrived in Chamonix with the purpose of exploring the glaciers they had seen glinting in the distance from the Geneva plains. Their journey was widely regarded as reckless and foolish as not only was access to the Chamonix Valley long and difficult, it was generally believed that the glaciers were inhabited by evil spirits and to venture into their midst would invite misfortune.

The men and their entourage were not daunted, however, and their glowing reports of the glaciers enticed many visitors to the Alps over the next few decades. In 1786, Jacques Balmat and Gabriel Paccard, both natives of Chamonix, made the first ascent of Mont Blanc, marking the beginning of modern alpinism. Many summits were climbed soon after, but the steep-sided Matterhorn remained virgin well into the 19th century. Englishman Edward Whymper, one of the most prolific alpinists of all times, had his heart set on this ascent. In 1865, competing against Jean Antoine Carrell from Italy, Whymper and his party reached the top of the Matterhorn, only to endure a terrible accident during the descent when four of his party fell to their deaths.

There are several variations to the Haute Route today, but the Chamonix to Zermatt option seems to be the most popular way, both in terms of route and direction. Chamonix is a major French alpine town situated in the shadow of Mont Blanc, at 4807m (15,772ft) the highest peak in Western Europe. Zermatt is the Swiss version, its mountain backdrop the unforgettable Matterhorn, unique for its soaring pyramid shape. There is no real reason why you shouldn't go from Zermatt to Chamonix, but tradition and force of habit mean that this is rarely done.

The trek actually starts at the head of the Chamonix Valley at the village of Le Tour. The path to the Albert Première Refuge takes a rising traverse around the

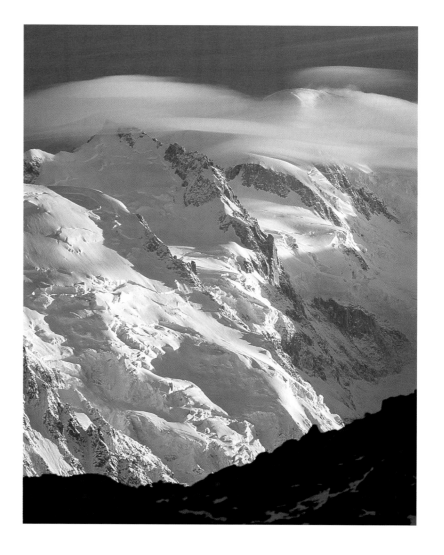

TOP *The charming alpine resort of Champex enjoys fabulous views of the Grand Combin across its perfectly kept lake. This is certainly a place to linger.*

INSET *Wildflowers are one of the joys of summer trekking. Pictured here, an alpine columbine growing near Zermatt, with the Matterhorn beyond.*

ABOVE *Mont Blanc dominates Chamonix, it's immense glaciers descending in a chaotic tumble to the narrow valley below.*

OPPOSITE *Here on the Trient Plateau with the Chardonnet beyond, trekkers take a mid-morning break from glacier travel.*

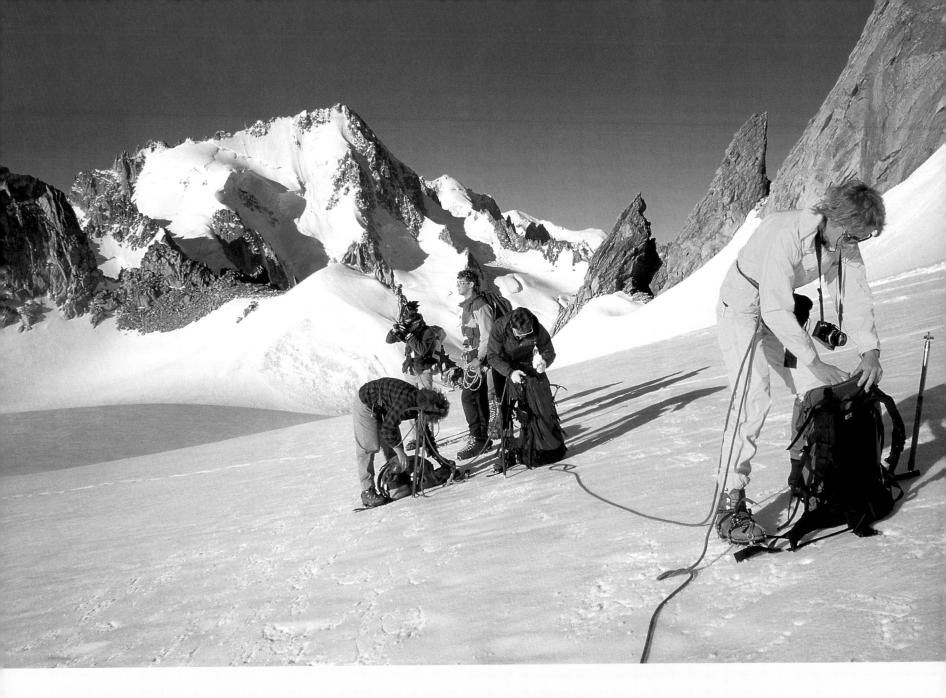

LOCATION The Pennine Alps, situated in the Western Alps bordering France, Switzerland and Italy.

WHEN TO GO July, August or early September. Earlier in the year there is likely to be fresh snow, which makes for difficult walking and can be dangerous. After September the weather is less likely to be stable and huts are closed.

START Le Tour at the head of the Chamonix Valley. Accessible by bus from Chamonix.

FINISH Zermatt. Train services run from Zermatt down to the main Rhône Valley.

DURATION 8 days. Allow extra days for bad weather.

MAX ALTITUDE The Pigne d'Arolla (3796m; 12,455ft)

TECHNICAL CONSIDERATIONS Trek takes place almost entirely on glaciers, so an awareness of weather and snow conditions is necessary. Must be experienced in glacier travel. It is essential to consult a detailed guide book for this route as well as the map.

EQUIPMENT Basic glacier travel kit: Crampons, ice axe (55–60cm for an average-sized person), harness, crevasse rescue equipment (minimum requirement: 2 prussik loops, a long sling, 5 karabiners and an ice screw), rope (30m long and at least 8mm thick).

TREKKING STYLE Backpacking or hut-to-hut. Huts along the route provide food and bedding. Reservations are recommended in the holiday season.

PERMITS/RESTRICTIONS None.

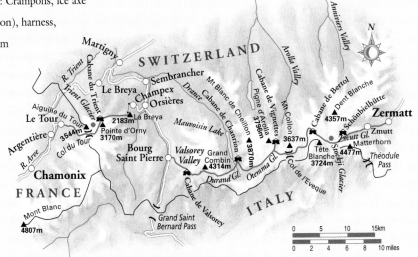

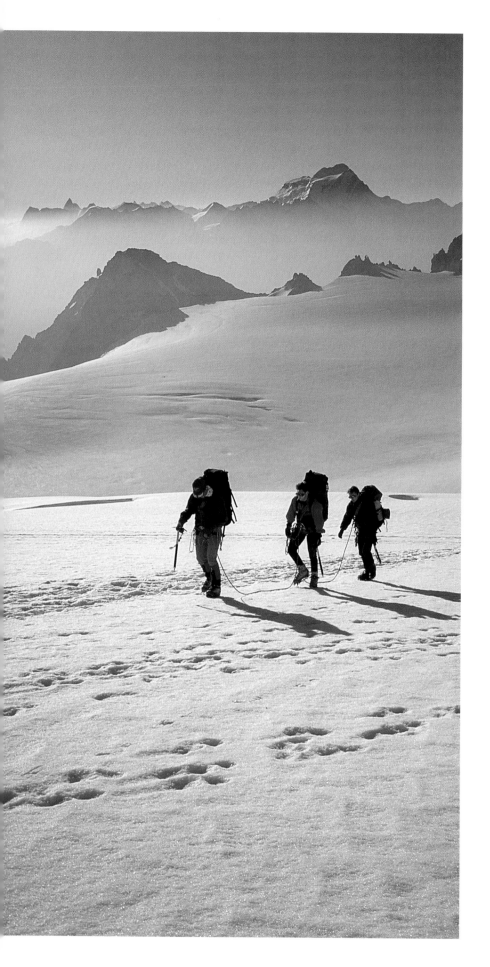

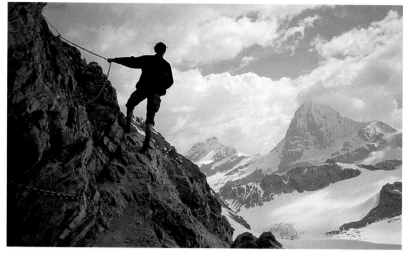

ABOVE *A trekker takes full advantage of the solid chains of this* via ferrata *to admire the spectacular Dent Blanche from a view point near the Bertol Hut.*

hillside, onto the glacial moraine leading to the hut. Perched just above the Glacier du Tour, this hut enjoys spectacular glacier and summit views. However, it is one of the most popular in the Alps and always busy. If you plan to ascend the Aiguille du Tour (3544m; 11628ft), a good beginner's peak, then it would be wise to overnight at the hut, otherwise press on.

Just beyond the hut you'll set foot on the first glacier. Your objective, the Col du Tour (3281m; 10,765ft), is up at the head of the glacier, and this gives access to the Trient Glacier, which forms a huge plateau where it would be quite easy to get lost in bad weather. The Cabane du Trient is to be found under the Pointe d'Orny at 3170m (10,400ft) and enjoys superlative views of the northern side of the Aiguille du Tour and the Aiguilles Dorées – for your first night in the mountains you won't be disappointed.

During the next day's descent down the left bank of the Orny Glacier, you can admire the spectacular profile of the rock spire of the Clochers du Portalet, before continuing down the pleasant, well-worn path eventually leading to the chairlift of La Breya, which delivers you to the outskirts of Champex. Champex is a fine place to enjoy a break, before taking the bus or taxi to Bourg Saint Pierre.

A good path leads out of Bourg Saint Pierre, starting off relatively gently up the Valsorey Valley, then steepening with a section of chains and cables. The Valsorey Hut is perched at 3030m (9940ft), under the southwestern slopes of the huge bulk of the Grand Combin (4314m; 14,154ft). The next stage is serious and should not be attempted in bad weather. Climb up northeast behind the hut and make an eastward traverse to the Plateau du Couloir (3664m; 12,022ft). This can vary dramatically from easy snow early in the season to ice and scree later. From the plateau, which is immediately under the Grand Combin, you head down onto the Glacier du Sonadon, which is quite flat at this point. The Col du Sonadon (3504m; 11,497ft) is directly ahead to the east and is easily crossed en route to the Durand Glacier.

Descending the glacier to the valley above Mauvoisin Lake, you come out at the bridge at 2182m (7159ft). Climbing and glacier walking all done for the day, you can relax and enjoy the wonderful views of the Grand Combin, La Ruinette and,

ABOVE *Trekkers heading off across the Glacier du Tour. Setting off in the early morning ensures you will travel on snow when it's hard and avoid the heat of the day.*

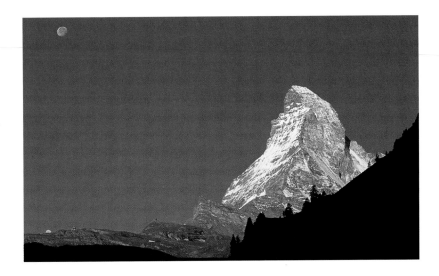

ABOVE *The distinctive profile of the Matterhorn dominates the final part of the Chamonix–Zermatt trek and contrasts starkly with the glaciated slopes of Mont Blanc.*

down the valley, the Mauvoisin Lake itself, formed by what is allegedly the biggest dam of its kind in the world. The Cabane de Chanrion is just 280m (920ft) above.

Two choices present themselves for the next day, and the decision of which route to take depends largely on the weather. The first possibility, taking the Otemma Glacier, involves no technical difficulties and stays relatively low, making it a good choice in less than perfect weather. The second, up the Brenay Glacier, involves a section of steeper ground to pass a serac barrier and also allows for the ascent of the Pigne d'Arolla (3796m; 12,455ft). This is a fine peak to include on the way if you can, with no technical difficulties. The splendid views are definitely one of the highlights of the trek, with Mont Blanc de Cheillon (3870m; 12,700ft) to the west and Mont Collon (3637m; 11,933ft) to the east.

Whichever route you choose, you end up at the Cabane des Vignettes, situated on a rocky promontory. Perched high above the Arolla Valley, with the rocky summits of the Aiguille de la Tsa, the Dents de Bertol and the Bouquetins right opposite, a night spent here will be unforgettable.

From the hut you need to reverse the Otemma route as far as the Col de la Chermotane (3053m; 10,017ft), then continue up the glacier below the western flank of Mont Collon to the Col de l'Eveque (3392m; 11,129ft), whence descend the Haute Glacier d'Arolla until it picks up the path to the Plans de Bertol. Enjoy a welcome rest before tackling the steep but well-marked trail, and then the snow of the Bertol Glacier to the Col de Bertol at 3279m (10,758ft). The hut is just above to the north of the pass, high on the rocks, accessed by chains and ladders and surrounded by a sea of glaciers.

As you pass from French- to German-speaking Switzerland, you'll be getting closer to Zermatt and you will definitely want the camera at the ready for your first view of the Matterhorn in all its magnificence. In good weather, the traverse of the flat upper section of the Glacier du Mont Miné will pose no problems, taken in a generally southeast direction to obtain the fantastic viewpoint of the Tête Blanche (3724m; 12,218ft). Here is the view you've dreamed of: the Matterhorn and the Dent Blanche close up, with the Zermatt peaks in the distance.

It will be difficult to drag yourself away and continue down onto the Stockji Glacier, which is heavily crevassed – tear your gaze away from the visual delights of the peaks and watch out for holes. From the rocky lump of the Stockji, a steep zigzag path descends to gain moraines leading to the Schönbiel Glacier. Cross the glacier and pick up the path, snaking up through steep ground to reach the hut.

Staying at the Schönbielhütte is an experience you don't want to miss. A fit party could certainly continue on to Zermatt, and if it is nightlife and shops you're after then go for it. This hut occupies such a marvellous position, however, with the north face of the Matterhorn right opposite the front door, that it is hard to imagine how anyone could want to pass it up. The Matterhorn (Monte Cervino in Italian, meaning the Stag Mountain) is such a unique summit that it is totally absorbing to study the different faces and ridges. Its neighbour, the Dent d'Herens (4171m; 13,685ft) is equally spectacular and this visual treat is simply unforgettable.

The next day there will be plenty of time for a leisurely stroll down to the 'real world'. A good trail cuts above the left bank of the Zmutt Glacier, eventually passing through the charming hamlet of Zmutt, one of the oldest hamlets in the area. Its importance dates back to Roman times when it was the last staging post before the long climb up to the Théodule Pass, the route used to travel over to Italy. It is worth stopping for refreshments here and exploring the traditional houses.

Stroll down into Zermatt past numerous ancient chalets and meadows bursting with brightly coloured gentians, orchids, geraniums, hawksbeards and rampions – a welcome contrast after days of snow and ice – then celebrate!

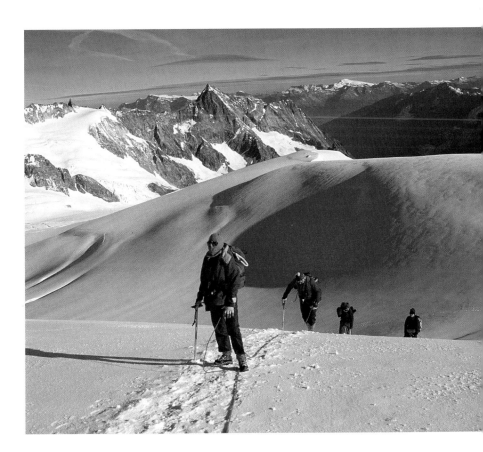

ABOVE *Trekkers stop to rest, ascending the Glacier du Mont Miné. Walking on glaciers in the sun is an exhausting experience but the view more than compensates for the effort.*

29

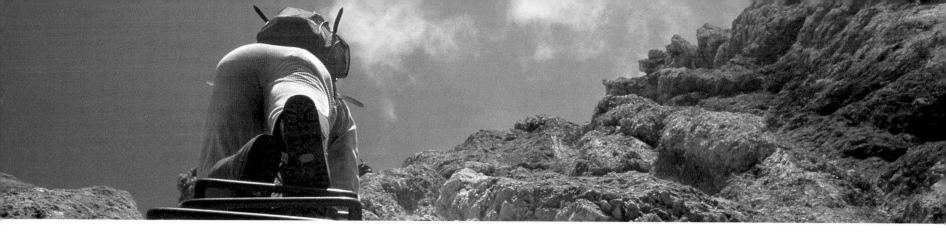

ALTA VIA 2

by Hilary Sharp

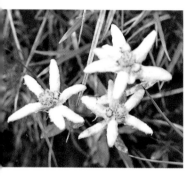

Situated at the eastern end of the Alpine chain, the Dolomites form part of the region of South Tyrol. The Tyrol overlaps Austria and Italy and, until World War I, South Tyrol was part of the Austro-Hungarian Empire. In 1918, the Treaty of Versailles gave South Tyrol to Italy but its population remained German speaking. It seems that in this region of Italy, people still feel more Austrian than Italian and if there's one essential thing you must know before going to the Dolomites, it is that every place has two names – an Italian and an Austrian one – which are usually not even remotely similar to each other. The town of Bressanone, for example, is also known as Brixen, the Rifugio Genova is the Schluterhütte – get used to this peculiarity and you are on your way to understanding the Dolomites.

The name 'Dolomites' is thought to come from that of the Marquis de Dolomieu, a French geologist who analyzed the unusual rock of the region in the 18th century. However, the area's original appellation, Monti Pallidi (Pale Mountains), gives a more graphic description of the limestone spires for which this area is known. The presence of magnesium in the rock gives it a rosy tinge and spectacular sunrises and sunsets are just one good reason to trek here.

World War I saw many fierce and drawn-out battles between Austria and Italy in this mountain range, and the troops often overcame the rocky obstacles by means of cables, metal rungs and other ironware hammered into the rocks. These *vie ferrate* (iron ways) have become a Dolomites tradition and today many of these equipped scrambles have been set up to allow the rocks to be climbed for pleasure. Nevertheless, despite much barren rugged scenery, the Dolomite trekker will also walk through flower-strewn meadows and pastoral green valleys. The area is hiker-friendly, with vast networks of footpaths, beautifully maintained and well marked, and several *alta via* (high routes) traversing the region. One of the best is the Alta Via 2, a section of which is described here.

The Alta Via 2 begins in the northwestern corner of the Dolomites, leading downward across the region to finish at its southern extremity. It crosses many of the mas-

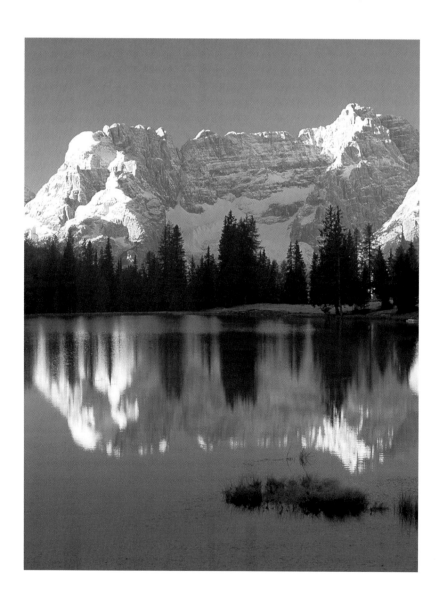

TOP *Ascending a typical* via ferrata. *Although extremely daunting in appearance, these iron ways can be climbed easily and provide fabulously exposed trekking.*

INSET *At first glance rather nondescript in appearance, closer inspection of the Edelweiss – white star – flower reveals tiny yellow flowers, hidden among large, woolly silver bracts.*

RIGHT *Fresh snow coats the Marmolada, the highest summit in the Dolomites. Seen to great advantage from a number of viewpoints, the most popular is the Vial del Pan.*

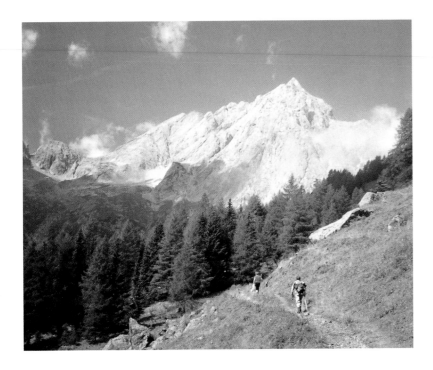

sifs en route. A week's trek doing part of the Alta Via can take in the Odle, Puez, Sella and Marmolada massifs (or groups, as they are called in the Dolomites).

The trek begins in Bressanone (Brixen), an elegant and charming town whose history dates back more than a thousand years. Bressanone has interesting cobbled streets with narrow alleys and arches and very much the flavour of the Austrian Tyrol, with leather breeches and apple strudel in abundance. The first day out of town involves quite a long grind up to the Rifugio Plose. Accessible by ski lift and also by car, the footpath is good, but most people choose not to spend the night here, preferring to take the lift up and head for the Rifugio Genova (Schluterhütte).

The views are immediately spectacular towards the Odle group where the summit of Sass de Putia is visible among the spiky peaks. A gentle stroll along a path bordered by juniper and blueberry bushes, provides a good warm-up as far as the Passo Rodella, after which a steep climb offers the first taste of real trekking in the Dolomites. The well-made path winds up initially through pine forests and then emerges to rocks and scree. Although beautifully maintained, the path is just the wrong angle and surprisingly tiring. Walkers are generally glad to reach the Forcella della Putia at 2361m (7746ft) for a well-earned rest.

Given adequate time and energy, it is highly recommended that you continue up the excellent trail to the Sass de Putia. At 2875m (9433ft), this is a fine peak, with a short *via ferrata* to attain the final summit. All of the *vie ferrate* mentioned here can be done without equipment, but that doesn't mean there are no dangers. Caution should be exercised at all times. In bad weather, the rock quickly becomes very slippery, and on this peak a fall in the wrong direction would take you over the steep west face.

ABOVE *Walking in the Dolomites is not all about rocky, barren scenery. The trail up to the Rifugio Falier takes you through beautiful forests and meadows.*

RIGHT *Equipped with metal aids varying from cables to ladders to iron rungs, via ferratas provide routes across terrain that would otherwise be out of bounds to hikers.*

The second day begins gently, with superb views – ahead to the Piz Duleda (2909m; 9544ft) and, behind, the Sass Putia. The next objective, the Forcella della Roa (2616m; 8583ft), is altogether too obvious – a deep notch up ahead – but for now enjoy the pastoral surroundings and look out for early morning chamois. The Forcella is reached by a steep, but mercifully short scree ascent, and views of the distant valley and the Piz Duleda just east of the pass are fabulous. From this point there are at least two possibilities to cross the ridge to reach the Puez Alps, the most direct of which includes a few cables on the steep parts and arrives on the ridge under the Piz Duleda, which can provide a pleasant diversion. A stroll through slopes studded with tiny alpine flowers such as toadflax, glacier crowsfoot and rock jasmine, above an impressive drop to the Vallunga, with views of the Sella group and the summit of the Sassolungo (3181m; 10,437ft), takes you quickly to the Rifugio Puez. This easily accessible hut attracts an impressive lunchtime trade, but most of these visitors will descend later in the day.

From Puez, the trail south is a delight in the early morning, with the welcome rays of the sun and distant views of the glistening snowy summits of the Ötztal Alps. Ahead is the Sella group, reached by descending from the Passo del Cir (2466m; 8091ft) through a forest of unusual red and orange limestone spires. The Passo Gardena provides civilization of sorts – prepare for chaos in the summer – and basic provisions can be bought here.

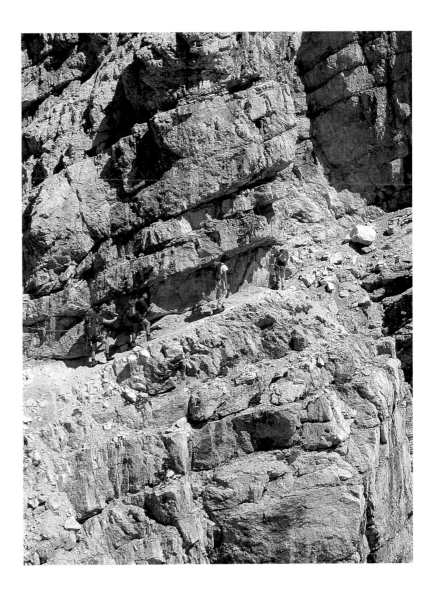

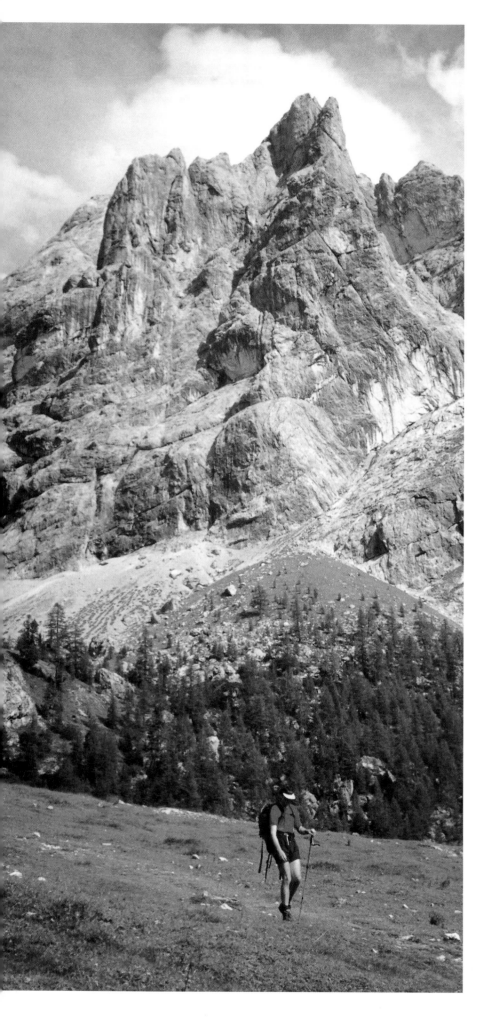

A well-marked path tempts many walkers up the Val Setus. Rather dauntingly numbered 666, the trail zigzags relentlessly up scree to a *via ferrata* that exits on a rocky plateau by the Rifugio Pisciadu and its lake. Staying here would give you time to ascend the Cima Pisciadu (2985m; 9794ft), just above. Continuing on up steep scree gives access to a barren plateau and a lunar landscape. From here, the quick, steep ascent of Piz Boé (3152m; 10,342ft), which includes a short *via ferrata*, is a must. The summit is unlike any other, with its hut and strange square aerial, rather like a drive-in movie screen – not a place to linger.

Either return to the hut or traverse the peak, the next objective being the bleak Forcella Pordoi (2829m; 9282ft). The way down from here takes a narrow couloir of scree, very steep and quite intimidating – like looking down a snow slope just before launching off on skis. An adventurous soul took to skiing scree slopes in the Dolomites in the early '80s and it is almost possible to see why.

Leading on from the Passo Pordoi is the famous path the Vial del Pan, the Grain Route used for smuggling in the 17th century. The path gets very busy – partly due to its views of the Marmolada, at 3343m (10,968ft) the highest summit in the Dolomites, but also because it is flat. The views of the Marmolada Glacier and the imposing rocky summit of the neighbouring Gran Vernal, along with the numerous alpine flowers found here (including gentians, anemones, edelweiss and vanilla orchids), make for a memorable walk. Spend the night at one of the hotels on the shores of the Lago de Fedaia, under the glaciated slopes of the north face of the Marmolada. The Marmolada formed the Austro-Italian frontier before 1919 and consequently saw a lot of fighting. As the Marmolada Glacier recedes, tunnels carved in rock and the remains of wooden shelters are emerging at 3000m (10,000ft) and above, testament to the immense effort put in by the troops who fought here.

Two options exist to cross the Marmolada. The glacier itself can be crossed via the Forcella della Marmolada (2910m; 9550ft), after which a steep descent and short *via ferrata* lead to the Rifugio Contrin. The alternative is a long but incredibly scenic route circumnavigating the mountain via Malga Ciapela then up past the Rifugio Falier, under the orange and gray walls of the Marmolada's south face, an important rock-climbing site. The Passo di Ombretta (2702m; 8865ft), with its bright red bivouac hut, is reached after a long ascent, and meadows filled with edelweiss, field gentians and houseleeks lead down to the Rifugio Contrin, a large, interesting building owned by the Italian Army in a fine setting below the Cima Ombretta (2931m; 9617ft).

From the Rifugio Contrin, a pleasant path climbs up into rockier terrain, past remnants of barbed wire and tin cans, poignant reminders of the war, to the Passo Cirelle (2683m; 8803ft) and an endless vista of misty mountains. The descent to the Rifugio Fochiade allows a last jaunt down a steep trail before lunch at Fochiade, after which the end of your trek at the Passo di San Pellegrino (1919m; 6296ft) is just a stroll away.

LEFT *Having attained the Passo di Ombretta and admired the Marmolada up close, the trail to the Rifugio Contrin leaves the rocky profile of the Cima Ombretta behind.*
OPPOSITE *The inspiring view from the Passo del Cir extends across the Passo Gardena to the Sella range beyond, a mass of limestone towers.*

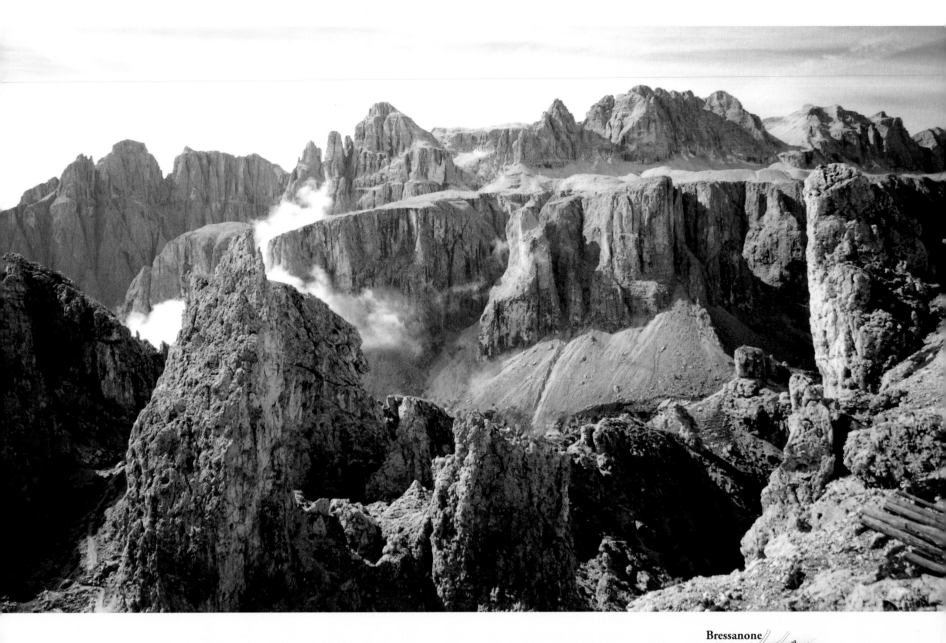

LOCATION Eastern end of the Alps, just south of the Austro-Italian border.

WHEN TO GO July to early September. Any earlier and there is likely to be considerable snow remaining on the high passes; any later and refuges may be closed and fresh snow may fall at low altitudes.

START Bressanone (Brixen). Reached by road from Italy or Austria. Regular train services from Innsbruck.

FINISH: Passo di San Pellegrino. Daily bus service to Bolzano and on to Bressanone in July and August only. If visiting out of season, arrange a taxi before starting the trek.

DURATION 6 to 8 days; approx. 75km (45 miles).

MAX ALTITUDE Forcella della Marmolada (2910m; 9547ft).

TECHNICAL CONSIDERATIONS Care should be taken on the *vie ferrate* – this is not a walk for those who don't like exposure. Crossing of the Marmolada (optional) usually requires ice axe, crampons and a rope, and knowledge of glacier travel. Scrambling is moderate in difficulty. Several long and steep ascents and descents for which trekking poles will come in handy.

EQUIPMENT Huts provide beds, blankets and pillows. Sheet sleeping bag a requirement. Food is excellent and self-catering is usually not an option in the huts on this trek.

TREKKING STYLE Backpacking, or hut-to-hut. Basic picnic supplies available at huts and at road passes.

PERMITS/RESTRICTIONS None.

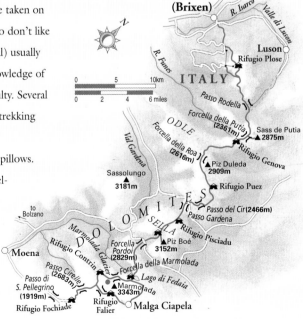

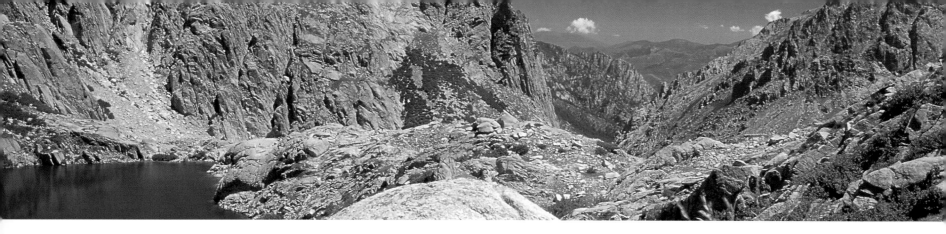

GRANDE RANDONNEE 20 (GR20)

by Hilary Sharp

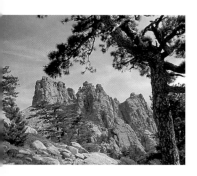

Corsica, *ile de beauté* in French, and known by the Greeks as *kalliste* – the 'most beautiful' – is situated just 160km (100 miles) south of the French Mediterranean coast and 80km (50 miles) west of the Italian coast. A French region or *département*, Corsica (*la Corse* in French) is really a rocky massif in the sea. Although its highest peaks only reach 2700m (8800ft) they hold snow for a substantial part of the year and, despite the Mediterranean location and the beautiful sandy beaches, the Corsican mountains are renowned for sudden and violent changes of weather.

Walking Corsica's mountains, you will feel you have stepped back in time. Most people live on the coast, and there are less than 10 people per square kilometre living in the mountains where life is hard and the farmers scrape a living from their sheep, goats and cows. The once infamous Corsican bandits and their vendettas are history, albeit quite recent, and there is a trend of emigration from villages in the hills to the big coastal towns and even the mainland.

At around 180km (110 miles) in length and involving some 9700m (31,800ft) of ascent, the Corsican high-level long-distance walk is regarded as one of the toughest of the European *grande randonnées* (big walks). It is also considered to be one of the finest of its kind. Officially named the Grande Randonnée 20 (GR20), this route begins in the northwest and makes its way along the most mountainous spine of the island, staying high almost all the time, to finally emerge near the attractive beaches on the southeast coast. The Parc Naturel Régional de la Corse (PNR) was created in 1972 to protect the whole of the mountain chain, and all the refuges found along this trail are owned by the PNR.

TOP *The Lac de Capitello at the head of the Restonica Valley looks tempting from above, but closer inspection reveals how icy the waters really are!*

INSET *The granite needles and Corsica pines of Bavella form one of the most classical attractions on the island.*

ABOVE RIGHT *The Refuge de Carozzu is left via a splendid new suspension bridge, which provides some early-morning excitement.*

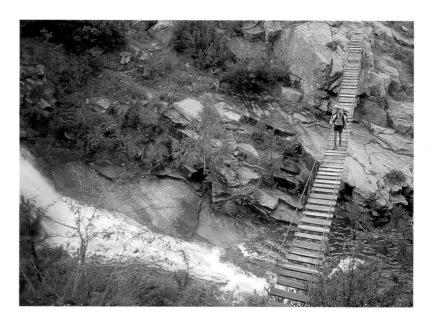

The trek begins in the small village of Calenzana, just north of Calvi, erroneously claimed to be the birthplace of Christopher Columbus. From the relatively low altitude of 275m (900ft) in Calenzana, the first day's walk takes you to the dizzying heights of 1570m (5150ft). You'll soon escape the oppressive summer heat as you climb up into the hills and the wonderful views back to the north coast provide welcome excuses to rest, while ahead lie the tempting rocky peaks, rugged and mysterious. When you've finally toiled your way over two cols, you will arrive at the Crête de Fuca where the terrain eases up and a pleasant stroll leads around to the Ortu di u Piobbu Refuge.

Although this route is liberally supplied with huts, which are wardened to make sure you pay your dues, there is no reliable provision of food. Gas stoves and pots are provided, but in the height of the season you may have to queue to use these. Hut places are allocated on a first-come, first-served basis, so there is always the possibility that you will arrive and find the hut full. It is essential that you carry minimum camping equipment, at least a bivvy bag and stove, if not a tent. Sleeping bags are necessary even in the huts, as are sleeping mats, although the hut sleeping platforms do have mattresses.

The next day's walking is more gentle, although equally spectacular and varied; at times rocky, at times among juniper and scented alder bushes, with views dominated by the summit of Monte Cintu, at 2706m (8878ft) Corsica's highest summit.

The Refuge de Carozzu (also known as the Refuge de Spasimatu) is surrounded by soaring cliffs, most of which feature rock-climbing routes. This hut usually offers basic provisions, including rough red wine and dark Corsican beer made from chestnuts. From the Carozzu hut, a rather wobbly suspension bridge takes you to some innocuous-looking granite slabs. Climbing up these in dry conditions you will not be aware of the challenge that can ensue in the rain when the slabs become a potential death trap. Surmounting the crest under the Muvrella summit, you'll be rewarded with a wonderful panorama, with Monte Cintu in the foreground much closer now.

The descent is steep and a little tortuous, taking you to the tiny hamlet of Haut Asco, at the end of a road, where there are at least two refuges and a hotel. An extra day spent here would allow an ascent of Cintu, which has a marked and cairned path to its summit. At Haut Asco you are poised to tackle the crux of this route, the Cirque de la Solitude. This imposing granite combe is surrounded by rocky spires, and the surrounding crest was first traversed by the bold Austrian adventurer, Felix von Cube, at the beginning of the 20th century. It took him several attempts to find the key to this section, but today the presence of chains and cables makes the passage relatively straightforward if somewhat daunting.

Beyond the Bocca Minuta on the other side of the cirque is the Tighiettu Refuge, an alternative base for an ascent of Monte Cintu. Just below the hut is one of the delights of walking Corsica's high mountains – a *bergerie* (shepherd's dwelling) where local food can be bought. Regional specialities tend to revolve around goat or sheep – the cheese sandwiches are fabulous, as are omelettes filled with brocciu cheese. These shepherds live by the age-old practice of transhumance – they bring the animals up into the high pastures during the summer months, descending as the year goes on to spend winter down in the valleys.

The next refuge, Mori, is nestled under two interesting summits, both of which beg to be climbed if you can spare a day. The Paglia Orba is ascended by an intricate gully-and-ledge system, while the Capu Tafunatu is climbed via its very characteristic hole – *tafunatu* in Corsican dialect – carved out of a flawed patch of granite by wind and rain.

The lovely pastoral Golo Valley, with its fabulous swimming pools, leads to forests of distinctive Corsican pines, past the spartan hotel at Castell di Vergio and on towards Lac de Nino. Here wild horses graze beside the still waters of the lake, which harbours bushes of fragile aquatic plants. The Manganu Refuge is just beyond the Bergerie de Vaccaghia and attracts a lot of visitors, partly due to its relatively easy access from nearby roads, but also as it is ideally situated for one of the gems of the GR20 – the Restonica Valley. The route traverses the head of the valley via the stunning Brèche de Capitello, at 2200m (7300ft) the highest point on the trek. Arrive here early and you'll ascend in the shade, emerging into golden sunlight through the narrow rocky col. Views from the ridge are immense; to the east, the Lac de Melo and the Lac de Capitello, their inky depths glistening temptingly below; to the west, the distant villages of Soccia and Orto, misty in the morning light. The intricate trail finally leads to the Col de la Haute Route (2206m; 7238ft) where a whole new vista opens up, looking southeast across to the Monte d'Oro.

RIGHT *The northern section of the GR20 follows a spectacular trail through quite steep and rocky terrain.*

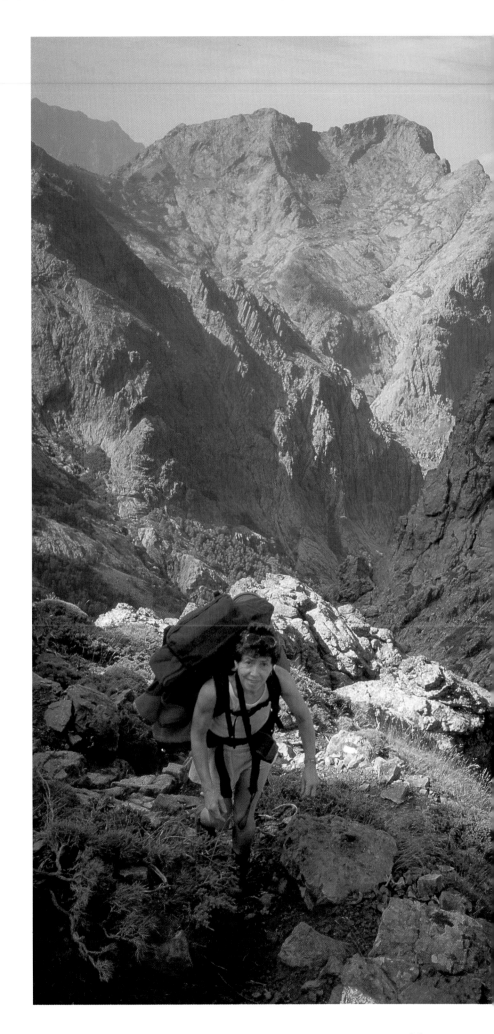

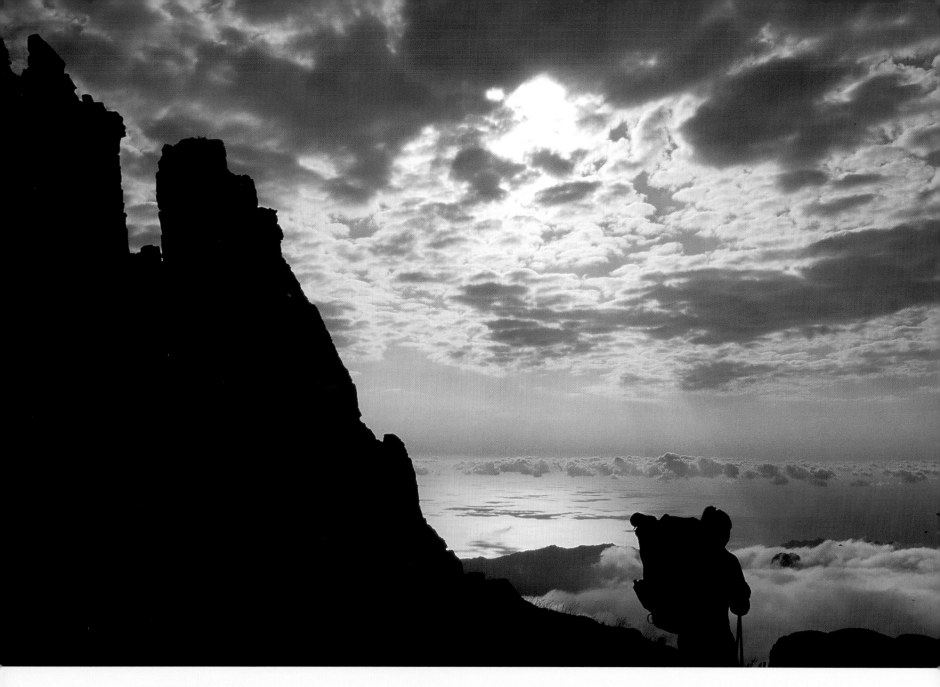

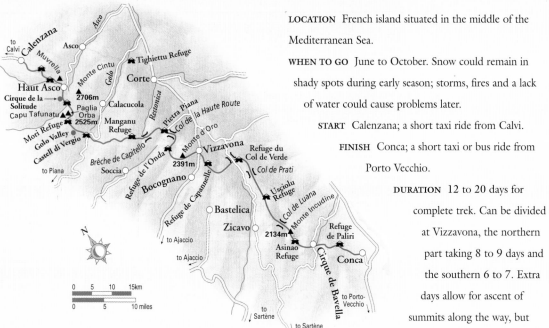

LOCATION French island situated in the middle of the Mediterranean Sea.

WHEN TO GO June to October. Snow could remain in shady spots during early season; storms, fires and a lack of water could cause problems later.

START Calenzana; a short taxi ride from Calvi.

FINISH Conca; a short taxi or bus ride from Porto Vecchio.

DURATION 12 to 20 days for complete trek. Can be divided at Vizzavona, the northern part taking 8 to 9 days and the southern 6 to 7. Extra days allow for ascent of summits along the way, but time is easily lost due to bad weather or the need to leave the route to buy additional food.

MAX ALTITUDE Brèche de Capitello (2200m; 7300ft).

TECHNICAL CONSIDERATIONS Terrain requires a good head for heights. Some easy scrambling.

EQUIPMENT Sleeping bag, mat, bivvy bag, stove and food are minimal requirements. Tent is advisable.

TREKKING STYLE Backpacking. Huts along the trail do not guarantee food supplies, but have toilet facilities and cold showers. Water source at huts can run low late in the season. Very basic food supplies can be bought at *bergeries*, and at several places en route, notably Haut Asco, Castell di Vergio, Vizzavona, Capanelle and Col de Verde.

PERMITS/RESTRICTIONS Camping along the trail is only permitted in the vicinity of huts.

From the Pietra Piana hut there are two choices – either a valley walk past the Bergerie de Tolla, or a shorter version along the ridge heading south. The Refuge de l'Onda is the last stopover before the valley where civilization will be rediscovered. Vizzavona marks the dividing point between the north and south sections of the trek, although distance-wise it's a little over halfway. The southern part of the GR20 is markedly different in scenery, with rolling grassy hills and wonderful views of the coast.

Steep forest leads out of Vizzavona, over the Bocca Palmente and past the rather old Refuge de Capanelle. A continuing traverse through beech trees brings you out at the Col de Verde, where there is also a refuge. The next climb is most rewarding. After a long toil, the Col de Prati is reached at 1840m (6040ft) and the views are breathtaking – this is the first time you'll see the southeast coast, and you will begin to realize just how far you have come. A fantastic ridge provides a scenic walk to the Usciolu Hut, with panoramic views of the coastline. Surrounded by beech forest again, the trail opens out onto a plateau where streams wind their way through lush green grass dotted with deep blue monkshood. From the Col de Luana the way is more than obvious – up – to the only true summit actually on the GR20 route, Monte Incudine (2134m; 7031ft).

A quick descent leads to the Asinao Refuge, from where it's only a short way to one of the most famous spots on the island, the Cirque de Bavella. The path weaves in and out of the weird and wonderful sculpted rock formations, the granite spires sometimes swirled in bands of early morning mist rising from the valley. Bavella has accommodation and bus services but it's worth staying at the next hut, Refuge de Paliri, if only for the views of the Italian coastline, Monte Christo and the neighbouring island of Sardinia. The last day is as good as all the others, with many impressive granite spires, orange in the morning rays. After reaching the narrow gap of the Bocca Usciolu, it's downhill all the way, the southeast coastline beckoning you, until suddenly you emerge from the footpath onto the road next to the welcome fountain of Conca.

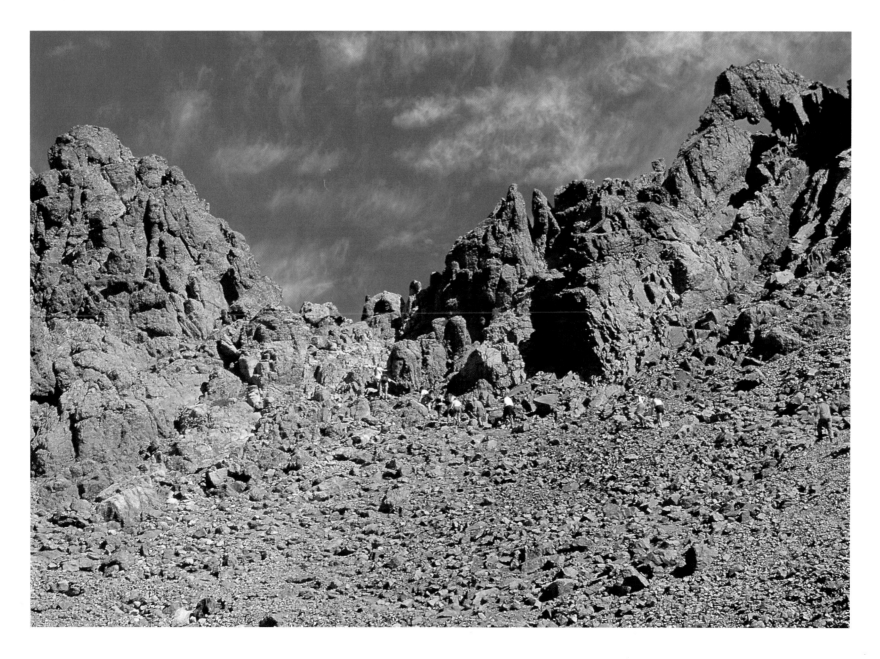

OPPOSITE *Early morning at the Cirque de Bavella. A trekker enjoys a few minutes of solitude before descending to reality at the Col de Bavella.*

ABOVE *The impressive eroded hole of the Capu Tafunatu, viewed here from the neighbouring Paglia Orba, provides a good objective for a day's walk.*

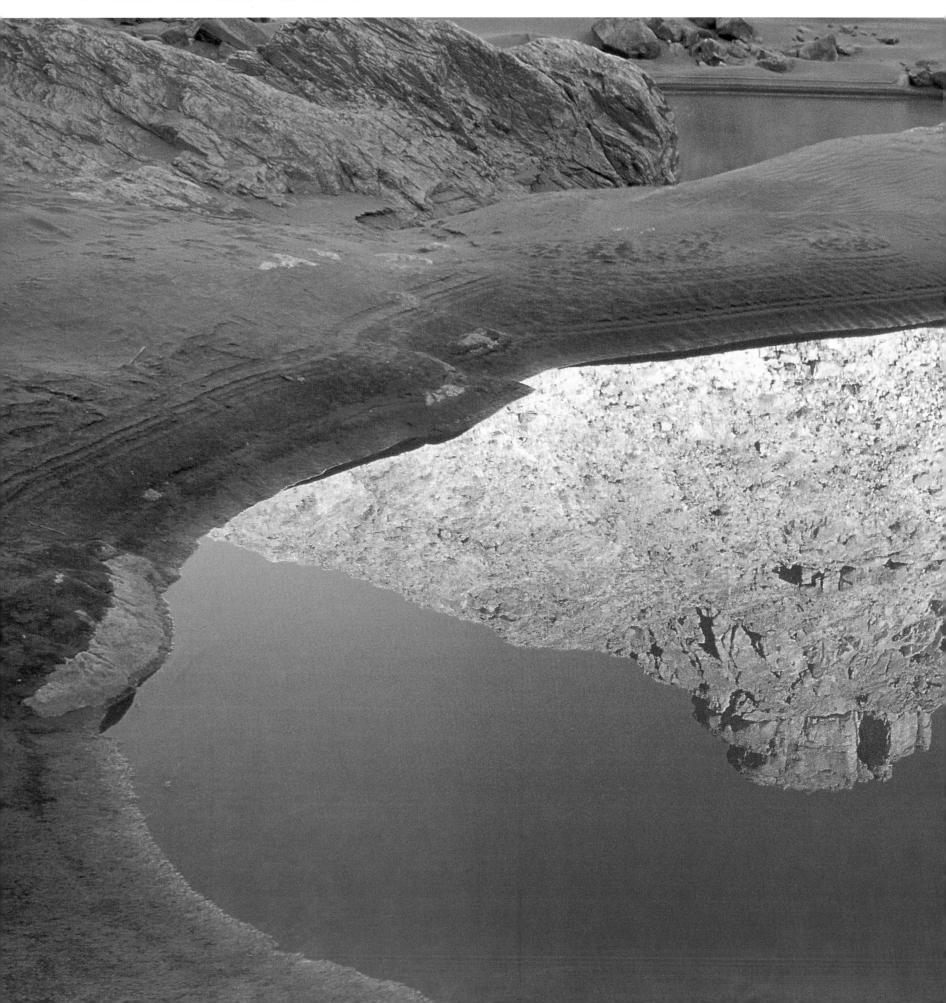

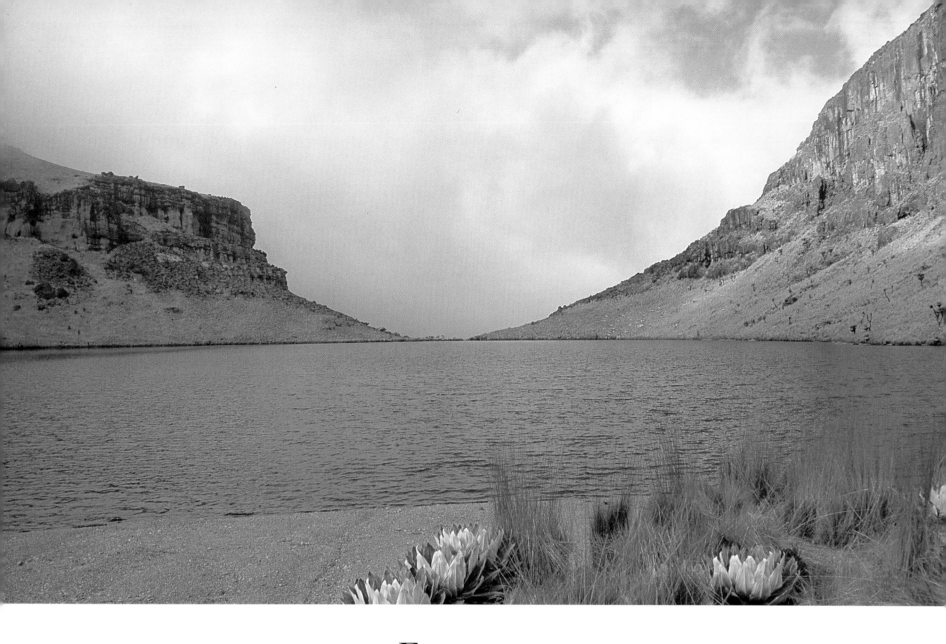

AFRICA

He who does not travel does not know the value of men.

MOORISH PROVERB

ABOVE *Lake Michaelson, the pearl of the Gorges Valley, is a welcome overnight stop on the Chogoria Route to Mount Kenya.*

OPPOSITE *River-mouth crossings are a feature of South Africa's famous Otter Trail – this one at Elandsbos.*

PREVIOUS PAGES *A mirror to the dawn of time. The world's most ancient canyon is gouged by the Fish River in Namibia.*

Few places on earth elicit such intense and diverse emotions in travellers as Africa. Human history is now accepted to have begun here, with the archaeological and anthropological work of the Leakeys in Kenya and Tanzania confirming that the Rift Valley was indeed the 'cradle of humanity'.

Modern travellers may gaze in awe at the unbelievable diversity and sheer scale of the landscape, marvel at the wildlife and relish the exuberance of the African people, but in reality these are some of the poorest countries in the world. The hardships and deprivations of daily life for many here are almost inconceivable, yet in the face of such adversity somehow the human spirit flourishes and life is colourful, rich and full.

In the wake of centuries of colonization and exploitation, it is not surprising that the liberation of Africa has left much of the continent in a state of poverty. Communications, electricity, safe drinking water, transport – services taken for granted in other parts of the world – have yet to reach enormous tracts of Africa.

Sensitively managed tourism is one of the best hopes Africa has for emerging from the post-colonial mire and more enlightened governments on the continent have realized this and gazetted parks and reserves to preserve their natural heritage. Adventure travel – away from insular resorts and luxury hotels and out in the country at large – helps to break down cultural barriers and counter the ignorance upon which prejudice thrives. There is no finer way to see the real Africa, to physically experience the scenery and sense the unique colours and textures of the African bush, and these treks reveal the glory of the continent's landscape.

The Mediterranean coast of Morocco may be but an hour away from Spain by boat, but life in the arid, roadless interior of the high Atlas Mountains continues at a pace unchanged by the centuries. Among these forbidding peaks on the northern fringe of the Sahara live the Berbers, Morocco's original inhabitants, in

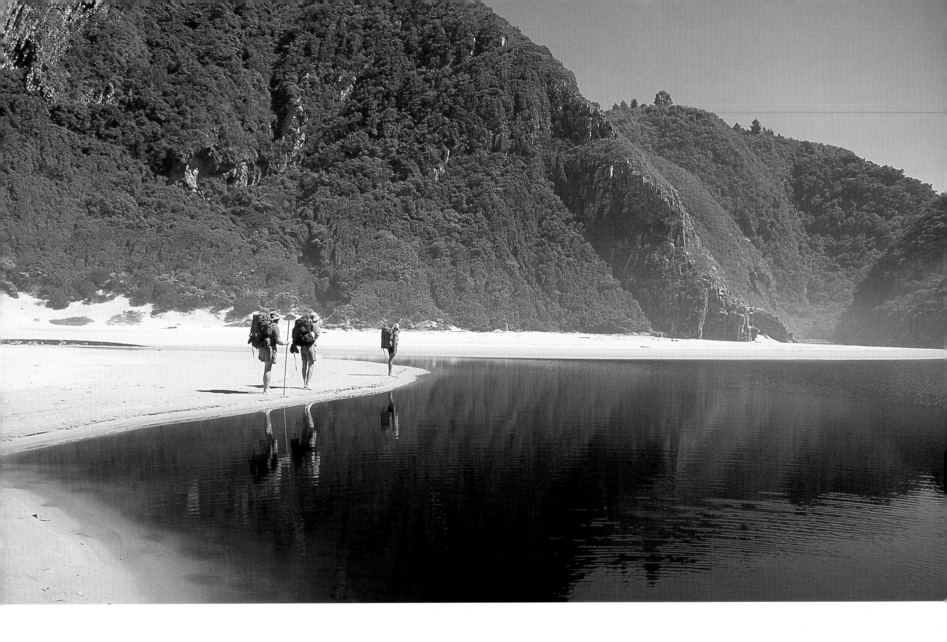

picturesque villages of clay and stone. The Atlas is the highest mountain range in North Africa, and though most visitors set their sights on the Jbel Toubkal massif, a traverse of the entire range reveals a broader and more stimulating canvas.

Some 6400km (4000 miles) south of the Atlas in Namibia, between the Namib and Kalahari deserts, the Fish River Canyon lies in a tract of land perhaps even more inhospitable than the Sahara. The road journey to the canyon from the town of Keetmanshoop is often described as the most desolate but magnificent in Namibia, and though the 86km (53 miles) hiking trail through the canyon itself is certainly not for the faint-hearted, it is surely one of southern Africa's most stunningly beautiful walks.

In complete contrast to the provocative emptiness of Namibia, the Indian Ocean coast of South Africa's southern Cape region is an Eden of cool leafy glades and secluded beaches, behind which rise the idyllic mountains of the Tsitsikamma range. By combining two of the well laid-out trails in the region, a circuit including all the highlights of this pristine enclave may be completed in 10 days.

No selection of treks in Africa, however short, could omit the fantastic highlands of Kenya's Rift Valley, and though Kilimanjaro in neighbouring Tanzania steals the glory as the highest summit on the continent, the hiking around Mount Kenya is unquestionably superior. Rising above a band of almost impenetrable forest, the mountain itself is surrounded by a rolling tract of magnificent high-altitude heathland and chaparral that affords fine views and gives a sense of space and perspective that is never attained on Kili. By combining the two most scenic approaches to the mountain with a circuit of the three principal summits, you will maximize your enjoyment of this, the pearl of East Africa.

EUROPE

AFRICA

MOROCCO
Marrakech
TICHKA TO TOUBKAL

Mediterranean Sea

SAHARA DESERT

Red Sea

Ethiopian Highlands

KENYA
Congo Basin
CHOGORIA & SUMMIT CIRCUIT ROUTES
Nairobi

Great Rift Valley

ATLANTIC OCEAN

NAMIBIA *Kalahari Basin*
Windhoek
FISH RIVER CANYON
SOUTH AFRICA
INDIAN OCEAN
Cape Town
OTTER & TSITSIKAMMA TRAILS

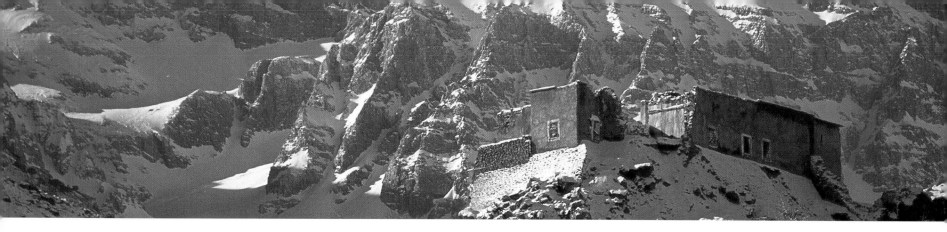

TICHKA TO TOUBKAL

by Hamish Brown

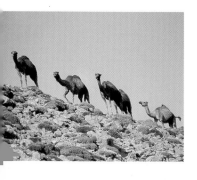

The South Pole was reached a dozen years before the highest summit of Morocco, Jbel Toubkal (4167m; 13,672ft), was first climbed by Europeans. The antagonism of Berber tribes kept the Atlas as *terra incognita* until France grabbed the country in 1912, making it the last country in Africa to be colonized. Toubkal was first climbed in 1923 by a French party. A Polish expedition explored the Western Atlas a decade later and a mere handful of surveyors would have seen the Tichka Plateau before World War II stopped mountain explorations. After the war, the struggle for independence kept Europeans away until 1956, and as a result it is only over the last 40 years that this mountain world, hardly changed in centuries, has become more widely known. The first complete Tichka to Toubkal trek was only undertaken in 1992, by myself – and was nicknamed 'The Wonder Walk'.

The Atlas Mountains sweep across southern Morocco, dividing plains and cities from the deserts fringing the Sahara. Marrakech is the gateway to the Atlas and from its rooftops the horizon is seasonably rimmed with improbable snowy mountains. Berber clans have occupied the Atlas for millennia, a tough, agricultural society, friendly and hospitable. On trek, their mules ensure unburdened freedom of movement, with enhanced camping and cooking facilities.

On this route trekkers will experience spectacular, varied scenery leading on, day by day, from the remote Tichka Plateau, down the forests and gorges and villages of the Oued Nfis (river), through a switchback of *tizis* (passes) to Imlil, and culminating on Toubkal, the highest peak in all North Africa. The trek normally takes two weeks, plus a couple of days at the start and finish for additional travel.

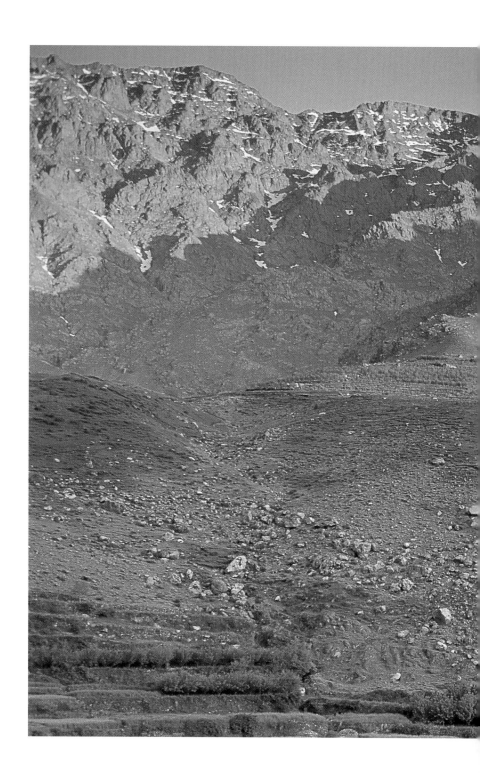

TOP *Every valley, clan or tribe once had its own* kasbah, *the defensive post for storing grain and treasured belongings. This ruin above Imlil has now been restored.*

INSET *Camels can be seen everywhere in Morocco, and are still widely used for off-road transport and pulling ploughs in tiny terraced fields.*

RIGHT *One of the attractions of trekking in the Atlas is the generally reliable weather. Sunsets are often colourful as in this view of the Aksoual and the Toubkal range.*

Trekkers fly in to Marrakech, changing at Casablanca. Several hotels offer a minibus service and will transport trekkers over the Atlas along the dramatic Tizi n' Test road to Taroudant, briefly meeting the trek route by the Oued Nfis. From Taroudant, a *camionette* (pick-up) takes the party from the city through unique argan forest, date palms, orange groves and walnut fields to the high, irrigated pastures of the Medlawa Valley, lodged in the heart of the mountains. The night is spent in the highest village, Awsaghmelt, in a friendly Berber house with traditional food and mint tea.

Early the next morning, trekkers are off, leaving the muleteers to strike communal tents, load the mules and follow after, soon overtaking and speeding on to the next site to have welcome tea ready for the arrivals. Tents pitched, there is usually time to relax or explore the flora and fauna, meet the local people and write notes, before dusk welcomes supper in the big tent and then it's time to sleep.

From Awsaghmelt the Medlawa path climbs upwards, twisting and turning for hours, to reach the Tizi n' Targa, a nick on the Tichka Plateau rim. At 3000m (10,000ft) some of the party may be puffing. The Tichka Plateau is a wedge-shaped hollow, the source of the Oued Nfis, rimmed with peaks, the outer sides falling precipitously for thousands of feet. Camp is a grass strip by the stream, dotted with mini daffodils early in season.

There is a real 'lost world' feel to the plateau, enhanced the next day when ascending the highest rim peak, Imaradene (3351m; 10,995ft). The exposed crest calls for some scrambling, and while the peak is being traversed the muleteers shift camp to the lower end of the plateau. The Oued Nfis gives a satisfying succession of oak forest, villages and pine forest before running parallel with the looping Tizi n' Test road, passing the historic sites of Tinmal and the Kasbah Goundafi to reach Ijoukak where the route forsakes the Nfis. Leaving the plateau, the Tiziatin forest (evergreen

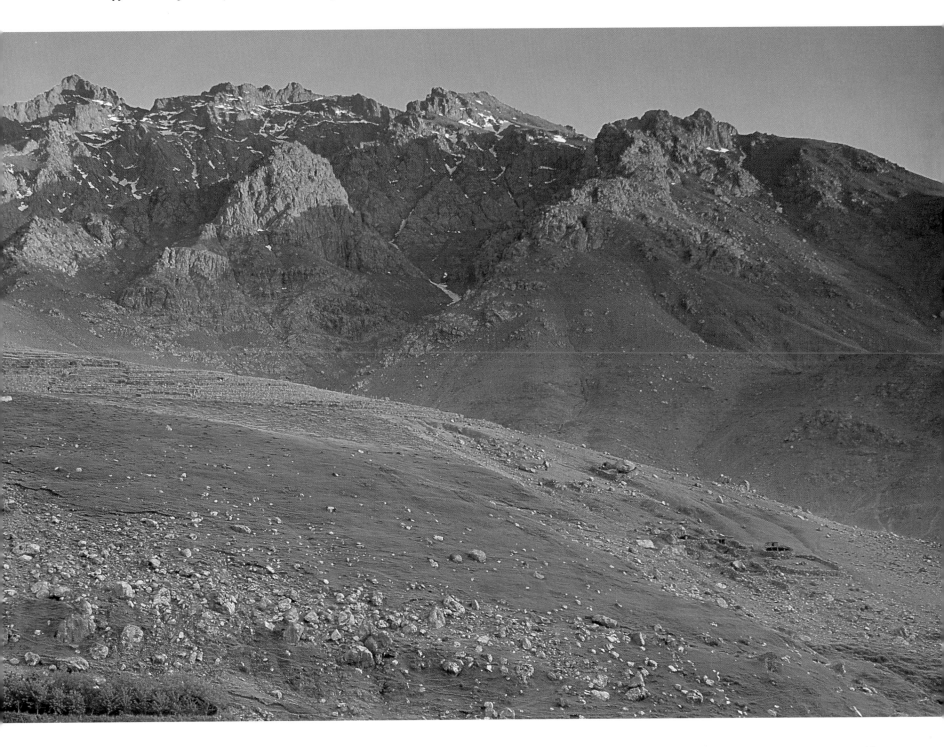

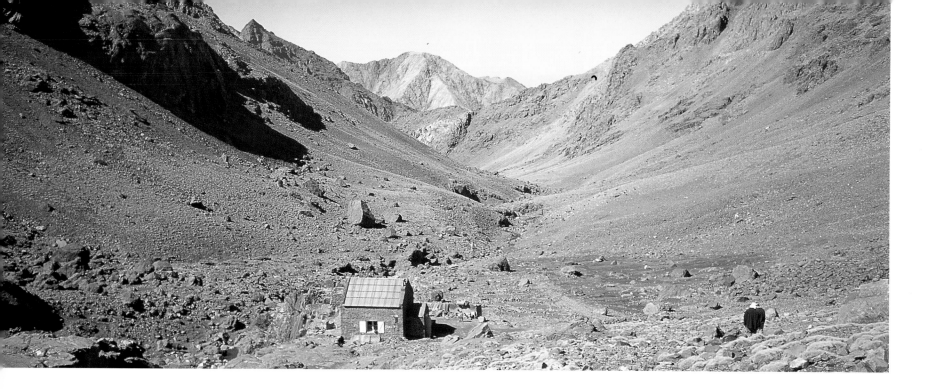

oak) is overlooked by rocky peaks and the river cuts deep through a granite gorge for one stretch. The peaks become ever wilder; Oumzra's triple summits to the north are glimpsed up a side valley as the first village, Agadir, is reached. Villages perch along the north side every few miles, linked by mule tracks, and accommodation in houses is an option. The architecture in the area relies entirely on local stone and timber, with water channels, terraced fields, almond and walnut trees adding a touch of luxury.

A few villages after Souk Sebt, the path enters forests of cool pine. Sleeping under the stars or swimming in river pools, each camp seems better than the last. The red soils of Africa end the rugged reaches of the valley and the river is followed on the north bank while the tarred road on the south side is rarely even noticed. Tinmal, a fortified mosque restored in the 1990s, is a starkly beautiful spot. From here, in the 12th century, the Almohads exploded to conquer Marrakech and create an empire reaching along North Africa and up through half of Spain.

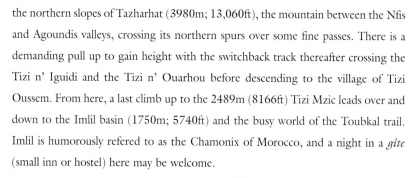

The riverside Kasbah Goundafi is the derelict palace of one of the tribal chiefs, also known as 'Lords of the Atlas', who controlled the Nfis and the Tizi n' Test – proving a thorn in the side of British explorers Cunninghame Graham and Joseph Thomson. It was the driving of tarred roads over the Atlas that really brought about the end of tribal power.

Much of the road traffic takes a break at Ijoukak so it is full of foodstalls and cafés, and gives another temptation for a roof overnight and a tasty *tagine* (casserole) supper. Plenty of uphill walking lies ahead – and there are two options. One heads up the Agoundis side valley and over the Tizi n' Ouagane (3750m; 12,300ft) to the hut for Toubkal – but this is only possible late in the season when clear of snow. The other, standard route, climbs high to traverse the northern slopes of Tazharhat (3980m; 13,060ft), the mountain between the Nfis and Agoundis valleys, crossing its northern spurs over some fine passes. There is a demanding pull up to gain height with the switchback track thereafter crossing the Tizi n' Iguidi and the Tizi n' Ouarhou before descending to the village of Tizi Oussem. From here, a last climb up to the 2489m (8166ft) Tizi Mzic leads over and down to the Imlil basin (1750m; 5740ft) and the busy world of the Toubkal trail. Imlil is humorously refered to as the Chamonix of Morocco, and a night in a *gîte* (small inn or hostel) here may be welcome.

An hour above Imlil lies Around, the last village on the trail towards Toubkal. The mountains close in and the path zigzags along to the sacred shrine of Sidi Chamharouch. The pass up to the east, the Tizi n' Tagharat (3442m; 11,293ft), was the ultimate height and distance reached by Hooker and Ball of the first real Atlas expedition in 1871. The Toubkal trail goes up like a coiled rope before a long rising traverse to the haven of the Club Alpin Française (CAF) refuge at 3207m (10,522ft).

From this mountain hut the summit of Toubkal (4167m; 13,672ft) takes three to four hours. The trail cuts up a steep slope into the hanging valley of Ikhibi Sud, then follows a crest up to the summit wedge of mountain. Few treks can have such a grand ending – all but one of the country's 4000m (13,000ft) summits cluster round, the massif rearing from the Haouz Plain to the north and the tawny desert to the south.

Toubkal is not the end of course. The toilsome boulders have to be descended – but how easy the path seems down to verdant Imlil. Even the drive out to Marrakech is fascinating and a couple of nights in this magical city will feel much more the *grande finale*.

TOP *The Toubkal (Neltner) Hut was built to facilitate the year-round popular ascent of Jbel Toubkal (4167m; 13,672ft), the highest peak in North Africa.*
CENTRE *Berber shepherds are often semi-nomadic, taking flocks to high pastures in summer, staying in basic* azibs *(stone shelters) or the black nomadic tents.*
OPPOSITE *Berber village houses always huddle together; in the past for defence and today in an attempt not to waste precious agricultural land.*

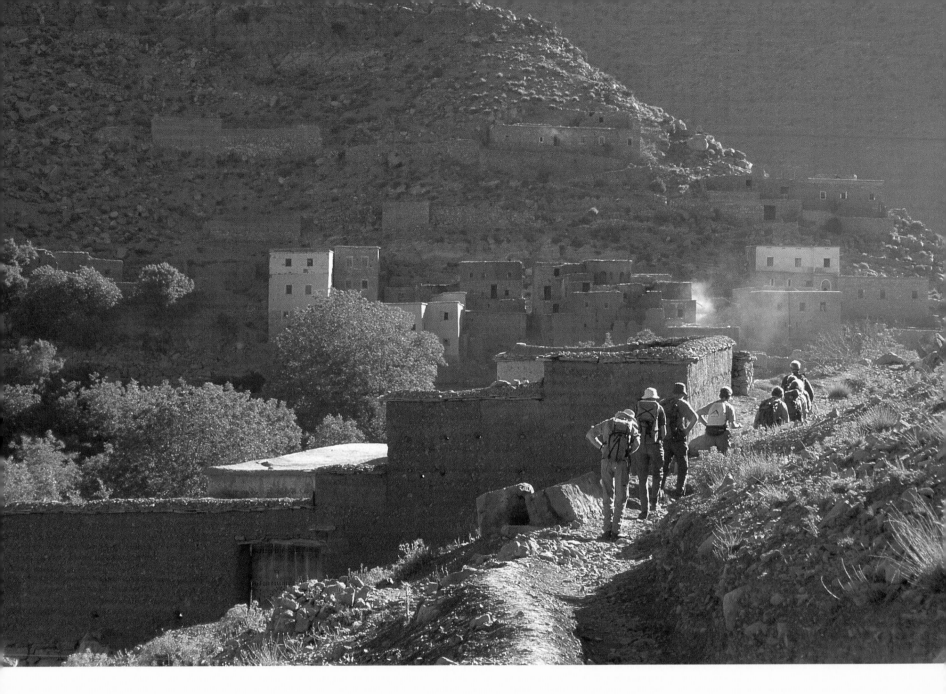

LOCATION High Atlas Mountains of Morocco, North Africa.

WHEN TO GO May to October.

START/FINISH Tichka Plateau, North of Taroudant; descending to Marrakech from Jbel Toubkal. Flights to/from Marrakech and hotel minibus for start/finish.

DURATION 14 to 18 days; 140km (80 miles). Add days at start/finish for access. The major peaks of Imaradene (start) and Toubkal (end) can be omitted if required, though they are not technical ascents.

MAXIMUM ALTITUDE Jbel Toubkal (4167m; 13,672ft).

TECHNICAL CONSIDERATIONS This is essentially a summer trek, the earlier dates being dependent on mule access to the Tichka Plateau, while Jbel Toubkal can bear summit snow into June. Take local advice. The trekking is mostly on good paths/tracks suitable for any fit person but there are some long ascents to *tizis*. Nights can feel cool, days can be hot and, while generally sunny, storms can occur during any season.

EQUIPMENT Clothing to cater for all seasons, tent, sleeping bag and mat. No short trousers. A large water bottle, sunblock and sunglasses are essential.

TREKKING STYLE Backpacking or expedition.

PERMITS/RESTRICTIONS Restrictions, fees, etc., are mercifully absent and trekking costs modest.

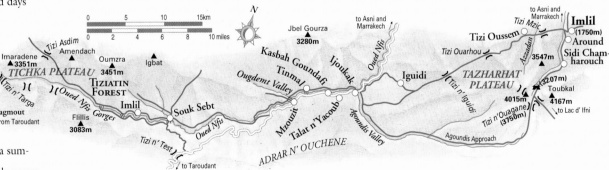

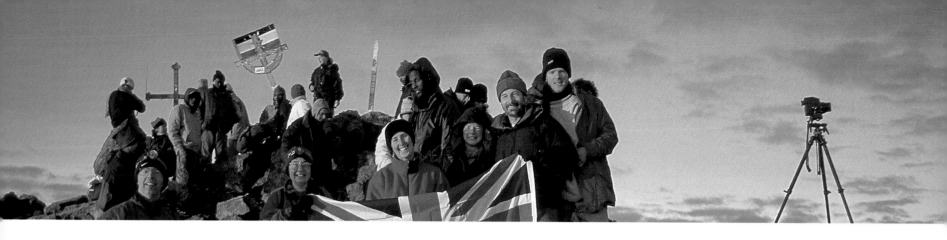

CHOGORIA & SUMMIT CIRCUIT ROUTES
by Steve Razzetti

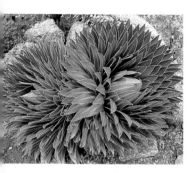

Stretching in an enormous arc from Syria to Mozambique, the Great Rift Valley is undoubtedly one of the most spectacular manifestations of plate tectonics on earth. Spanning over 4800km (3000 miles) and formed by the parting and sinking of the earth's crust along an ancient tectonic fault line, elevations on the valley floor range from 400m (1300ft) below sea level at the Dead Sea to over 1800m (5900ft) in Kenya. The vast majority of all the earth's volcanic and seismic activity occurs in the vicinity of such fault lines, and while there has been no volcanic eruption or major earthquake in Kenya for centuries, earth tremors may still occasionally be felt in the country's highlands.

In eastern Africa, the Great Rift Valley divides into the Western Rift and the Eastern Rift, with the latter bisecting the Kenyan Highlands between the Aberdare Range and the Mau Escarpment. Scattered along the Great Rift Valley are numerous extinct rift volcanoes, the highest in Kenya being Mount Kenya (5199m; 17,058ft) and Mount Elgon (4321m; 14,177ft). Mount Kenya is the second highest peak in Africa, after Kilimanjaro (5895m; 19,341ft) in neighbouring Tanzania, and today consists of the eroded magma core of a volcano that once exceeded 6500m (21,300ft) in height.

Kenya takes its name from this mountain, and the word is a corruption of the Kikuyu *Kere Nyaga* (meaning Mountain of Brightness). The Kikuyu believe the mountain to be the abode of their god Ngai, whom they refer to as *Mwene Nyaga* (Professor of Brightness). Located some 150km (90 miles) north of Nairobi and presenting an unforgettable spectacle as its rugged form soars above the fertile plains, Mount Kenya has blessed East Africa with a good deal more than its mere luminescence. In the immediate vicinity rise many rivers, fed by the melting snows above. These include the longest in the country, the Tana, which provides much of Kenya's supply of electricity.

Snow on the Equator? Ludwig Krapf, travelling inland from Mombassa in 1849 apparently doubted his own eyes as he described how he 'could see the "Kegnia" more

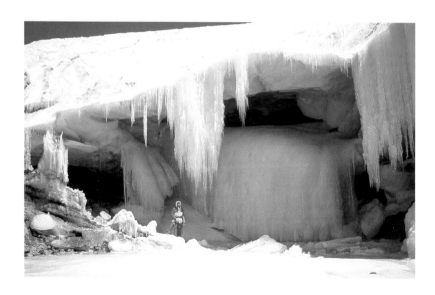

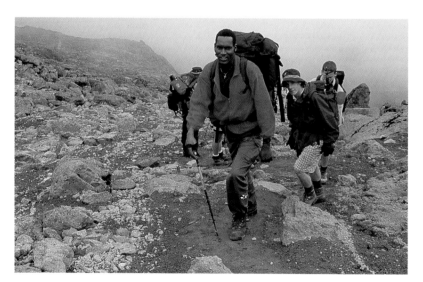

TOP *Trekkers celebrate the climax of their visit to Mount Kenya at sunrise on the rocky summit of Point Lenana.*
INSET Lobella keniensis, *one of three types of giant rosette plants found in East Africa. The others are* Carduus *and* Senecio.

ABOVE LEFT *Ice Cave beneath the Lewis Glacier near Curling Pond, a short walk from Austrian Hut. If the dramatic glacial retreat continues, such sights will soon disappear.*
ABOVE RIGHT *Ascending the trackless, rocky slopes above Lake Michaelson, on the toughest day of the approach to Austrian Hut.*

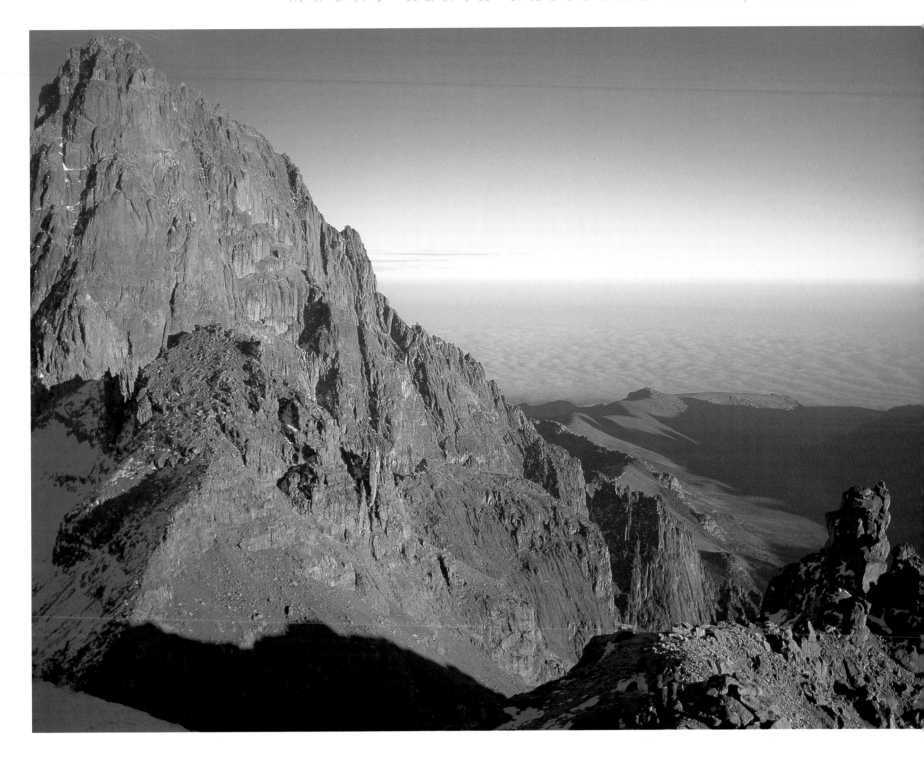

distinctly, and observed two large horns or pillars, rising over an enormous mountain to the northwest of Kilimanjaro, covered with a white substance.' His suggestions that there were perhaps snow-capped peaks in Equatorial Africa were ridiculed by geographical establishments back in Europe until, 33 years later, the affable Scot Joseph Thomson got closer. It certainly looked very much like snow.

The first European to make it through the surrounding jungle onto the mountain itself was an Austrian by the name of Count Samuel Teleki. He actually reached the snow line in 1887 and touched the stuff. Next came British geologist JW Gregory in 1893, who studied the physical structure of the mountain and gave European names to many of its prominent features, including the Teleki Valley on the Naro Moru side.

Sir Halford Mackinder made the first ascent of the highest peak of Mount Kenya in 1899 accompanied by alpine guides Ollier and Brocherel. In those days, the railway

ABOVE *Morning sun warms the colours of the precipitous crags of Nelion, seen here from the summit ridge of Point Lenana.*

had reached Nairobi but there were no roads. In the bush roamed elephant, lion, buffalo and rhinoceros, as well as local Kikuyu tribes displeased with Europeans trespassing on their sacred ground. To appease the locals, Mackinder named the highest summit (5199m; 17,058ft) after a Maasai *laibon* (witch doctor) named Mbatiang. The second highest (5198; 17,055ft) he named after Mbatiang's brother, Neilieng, and the third (4985m; 16,356ft) and fourth (4704m; 15,434ft) after his sons, Olonana and Sendeyo. The first three have commonly been anglicized to Batian, Nelion, and Lenana.

Thirty years later, on 6 January 1929, Englishmen Eric Shipton and Percy Wyn Harris established what is today known as the Normal Route up Nelion. Shipton

47

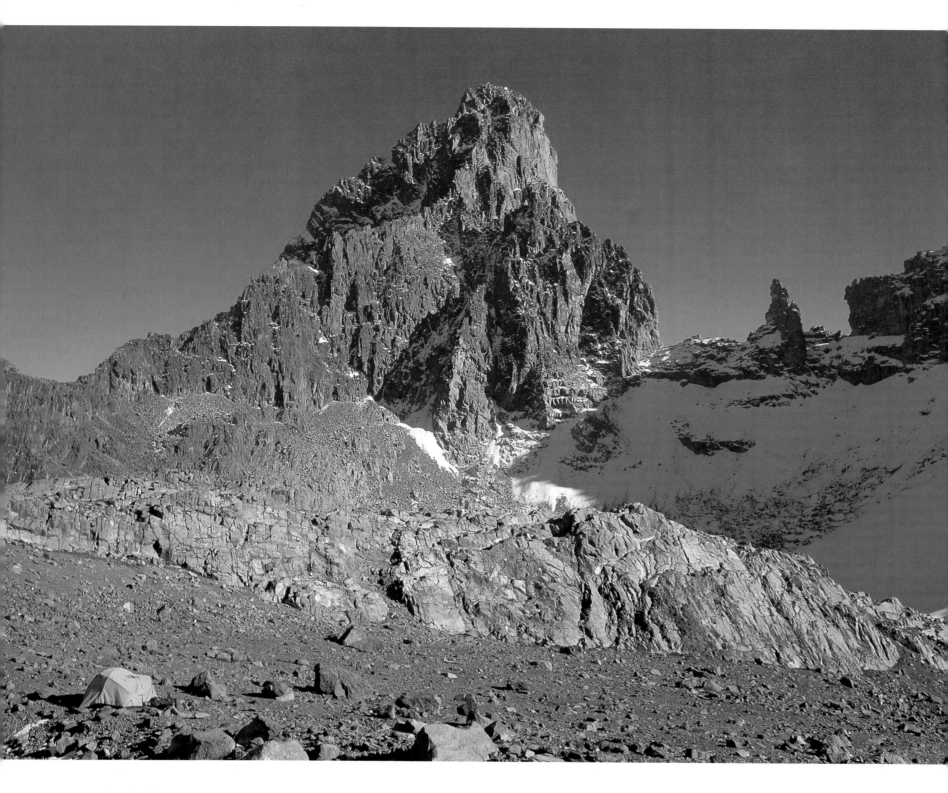

ABOVE *From this isolated, airy spot on a ridge just above Austrian Hut, the extent of the Lewis Glacier's retreat is clearly apparent.*

returned with Bill Tilman in August 1930 and completed both the first traverse of the mountain and the first circuit of the summits. After World War II, interest rapidly increased. In 1949, the ground above 3400m (11,100ft) was gazetted as a national park and the area mapped by the Colonial Surveys. That same year, the Mountain Club of Kenya was formed and soon huts were erected at various strategic locations.

Standing alone above the plains of the Rift Valley, Mount Kenya does not offer the opportunities for altitude acclimatization during the walk-in as do peaks of similar stature in the great ranges of the Himalaya and the Andes. Many trekkers underestimate both this fact and the seriousness of the terrain, and for them memories of aching limbs and pounding headaches will obscure those of the

ABOVE *From this isolated, airy spot on a ridge just above Austrian Hut, the extent of the Lewis Glacier's retreat is clearly apparent.*

magnificent views encountered. The Chogoria Route, pioneered in the 1920s by Earnest Carr, is the most beautiful approach and, at three days, by far the most gentle. Consider this especially if no prior acclimatization has been gained.

As with popular mountain journeys everywhere, there is much to recommend deviating from the main trails, and Mount Kenya is no exception. Instead of heading straight for Minto's Hut (4300m; 14,000ft) along the well-marked path from the Chogoria Park Gate and Mount Kenya Lodge, take your time and head off on the smaller track through rolling moorland to Lake Ellis for your first night's camp. Spend the second by the idyllic shores of Lake Michaelson and make for the Top Hut (4790m; 15,715ft) via Square Tarn and Tooth Col from there. The pristine splendour of these lakes and the country surrounding them is far removed from the overcrowded squalor of a night at Minto's.

Point Lenana commands breathtaking views of the adjacent higher summits, and is reached after only 45 minutes of easy scrambling from Top Hut. Most people do this by the light of their head torches before dawn and stand at the top, in the bitter chill, waiting to watch the glorious spectacle of the African sun soaring into the sky. There then ensues a mad rush back to the hut where hearty breakfasts are wolfed down and beelines made for the Teleki Valley and Met Station on the Naro Moru route far below. This is a shame, for an extra day or two spent completing the Summit Circuit Route really crowns what is undeniably the best high mountain walk in East Africa.

In either direction, the Summit Circuit Route can be completed by fit and acclimatized walkers in less than eight hours. In order to properly savour all its aspects, however, an extra night at Two Tarn Hut (4990m; 16,370ft) or Kami Huts (4425m; 14,518ft) is highly recommended. The former commands stunning views of the Tyndall Glacier and the west face of Batian, while the latter looks out over the summits of Sendeyo and Terere. The trails are thin and traverse loose ground. Navigation may be problematic as mists envelop the peaks daily, obscuring landmarks, but the Summit Circuit Route certainly is a challenging and spectacular climax to a traverse of Mount Kenya. Whichever option you choose, do not hurry out down the Naro Moru – the views back to the main summits from Mackinder's Camp are the best on the trip, and the vegetation on the final steep descent to the Met Station through the Vertical Bog absolutely surreal. Those craving a spot of unbridled luxury after all this exertion will not be disappointed at the Naro Moru River Lodge.

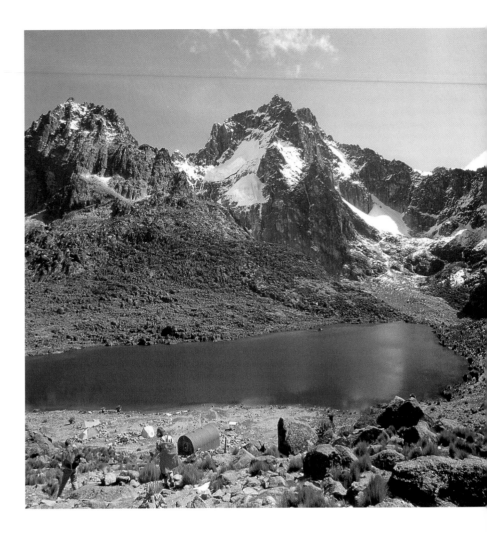

ABOVE *Batian and Nelion, separated by the Gate of the Mists, present a sensational view across Hut Tarn from Two Tarn Hut (4990m; 16,370ft).*

LOCATION East of the Rift Valley, Kenyan Highlands.

WHEN TO GO January to February, August to September.

START Mount Kenya Lodge (3000m; 10,000ft). International flights to Nairobi, then by road (3hrs) to the old Scottish mission station at Chogoria. There is a transit hotel here, and porters may be arranged. The *bandas* (huts) of Mount Kenya Lodge are 3.5hrs further by 4x4 if the road is dry.

FINISH Naro Moru Meteorological Station. The Naro Moru River Lodge operates a basic lodge and campsite here. The River Lodge is 1hr away by jeep, and from Naro Moru the journey to Nairobi takes 3hrs.

DURATION Minimum 6 days.

MAX ALTITUDE Point Lenana (4985m; 16,356ft).

TECHNICAL CONSIDERATIONS Acclimatization is a must.

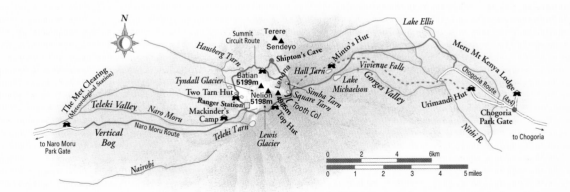

EQUIPMENT Self-sufficient camping recommended, especially if the Lakes Ellis/Michaelson diversion is planned, either through an agency in Nairobi or organized on the spot at Chogoria. There are huts at most of the other preferred campsites, but they are often noisy and crowded.

The exception is Austrian Hut, which will sleep at least 30.

TREKKING STYLE Backpacking or expedition.

PERMITS/RESTRICTIONS None, but park and hut/camping fees must be paid on entry (in US Dollars).

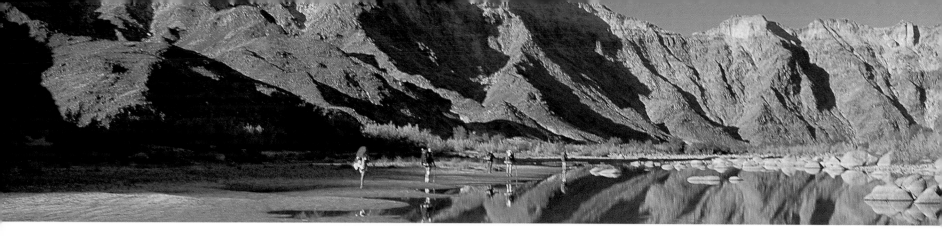

FISH RIVER CANYON

by Mike Lundy

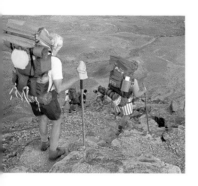

The Fish River Canyon is one of the biggest river-gouged canyons in the world, second only to the Grand Canyon in Arizona, USA. In the same class as Victoria Falls and Kilimanjaro, it ranks as one of Africa's great natural wonders. The deafening silence, the unadulterated solitude and the billion stars every evening combine to provide a profoundly inspiring experience, and cleanse the soul.

The ancient sediments and lava forming the bottom of the canyon were originally deposited between 1800 and 1000 million years ago. Between 500 and 300 million years ago, during the Gondwana Ice Age, a series of north–south fractures were deepened by southward-moving glaciers. Incision by the Fish River, in warmer times during the last 50 million years, has given the canyon its present shape.

Proclaimed a natural monument in 1962, six years later the Fish River Canyon was declared a game reserve by the South African government, which at that time was administering the mandated territory of South West Africa. The canyon is situated in the southwest corner of what became in March 1990 Namibia, a country bigger than France and the United Kingdom combined, but with a population of only 1.5 million. It is over 600m (2000ft) deep in places and stretches for more than 160km (100 miles). The trek itself covers more than half that distance, and takes five days to complete. Parts are so narrow that you feel you can almost reach out and touch both encroaching cliffs. As you progress downstream, the canyon widens until at its broadest it is a gaping 27km (17 miles) across.

Before you begin your descent, pause to look down on this awesome sight from the Northernmost Viewpoint. Hell's Corner glowers back at you, but further downstream the vista is breathtaking, particularly in the early morning when the steep cliffs are awash with colour. The steep descent to the canyon floor is a journey through

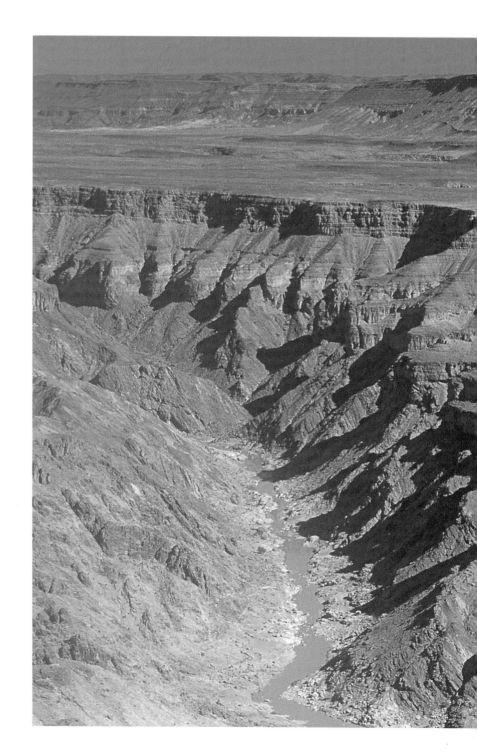

TOP *Nearing the halfway point of the trek, the canyon walls continue to tower over hikers, imparting mixed feelings of awe and total insignificance.*

INSET *Descent into the abyss of the Fish River Canyon, with the help of chains. Walking sticks are a useful aid in boulder hopping and river crossings.*

hundreds of millions of years of the earth's geological history. The river's shining ribbon gets closer and closer, until at last, an hour or so after beginning your descent with the aid of chains, you are able to plunge gratefully into the enormous pool waiting at the bottom, deep in the belly of the world's oldest canyon.

The first 16km (10 miles) to Palm Springs are notoriously rugged and slow, as the terrain is predominantly made up of large boulders interspersed with soft sand – not to mention the odd river crossing. For all the effort required, however, this is still the most rewarding and beautiful part of the canyon. There is no marked trail but there is also no way you can get lost between the two enormous walls which dictate your route. There are also no set overnight stops. Simply call a halt for the day on any suitable terrain an hour before sunset. (After which it rapidly becomes dark and the temperature plummets.)

Not long after starting down the canyon you will be surprised to come across the remains of two motor scooters. They are the result of a harebrained expedition against all the advice of the authorities by the Cape Town Vespa Club in 1968.

A little while before you see the palm trees at Palm Springs, your nose will tell you that you are close. The 57°C (135°F) spring water is rich in fluorides, chlorides and sulphides, the latter being responsible for the rotten egg smell. This, despite the odour, is a great spot for a rest or even overnight, where weary limbs can be rejuvenated in the comfortably hot waters. The palm trees, while splendid specimens, are somewhat incongruous here. They are not indigenous

BELOW *The Fish River Canyon, showing just a hint of its full majesty. The trek is a roller-coaster ride down the world's oldest and second largest canyon.*

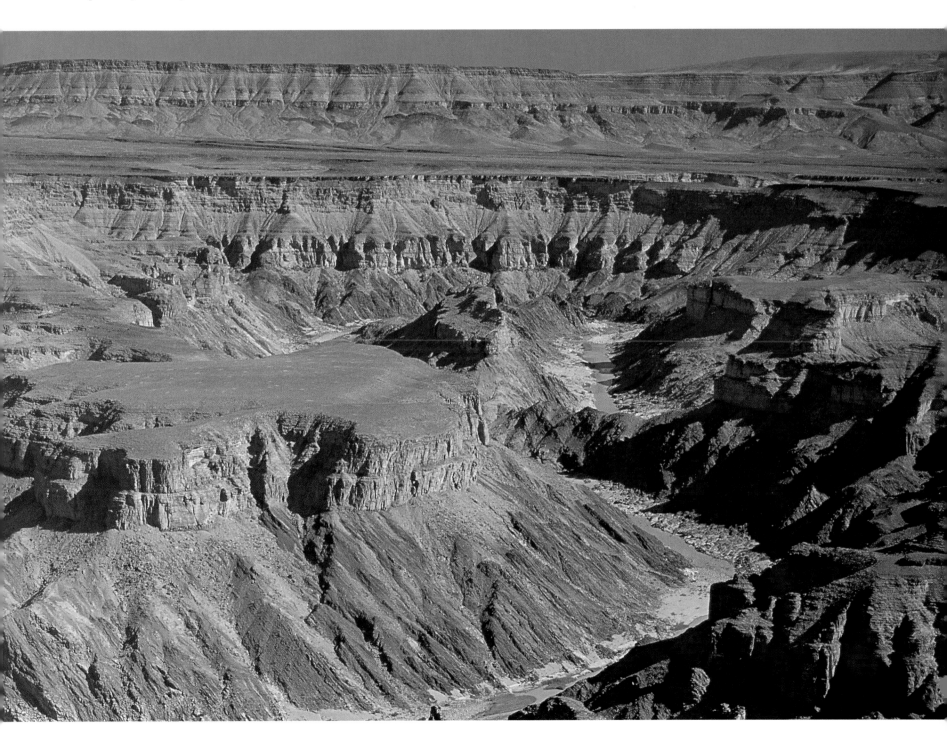

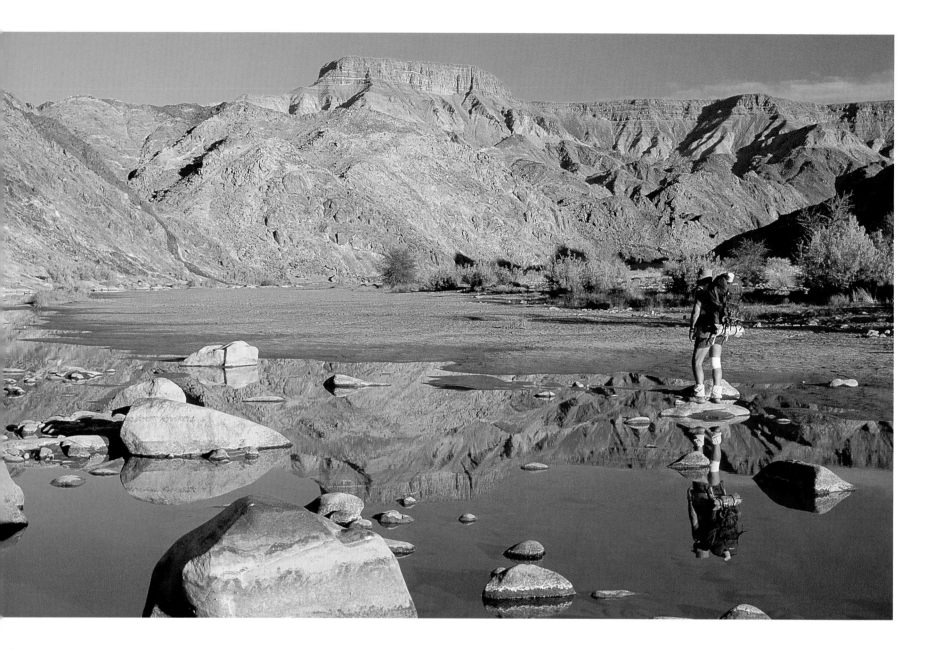

to southern Africa and their presence has given rise to several stories. The most popular and likely of these is that they grew from date stones discarded by two German prisoners of war, who had escaped from the POW Camp at a nearby place called Aus during World War I.

After Palm Springs, the going becomes easier and Table Mountain, a large flat-topped mountain (not to be confused with the larger Table Mountain, internationally recognized symbol of Cape Town, some 900km [560 miles] to the south), comes into view, offering help for orientation during the next few serpentine turns in the river.

The third day brings a series of interesting rock formations and pinnacles in such intriguing creations as the Three Sisters and Four Finger Rock. Once you leave the latter behind, the canyon begins to widen, the claustrophobic cliffs moving slowly further apart. It is in the region of these rock formations that you might find the uneasy relationship between leopards and baboons can sometimes be too close for comfort. It is not uncommon for an evening's silence to be shattered by the bloodcurdling screams of baboons under attack, as nature takes its course uncomfortably nearby.

Following a couple of shortcuts over ridges in the loop of hairpin bends, the canyon begins to widen, and you might see horse-like spoor, or dung. Unfortunately, this is

ABOVE *Reflections in time and space. June and July are ideal months to avoid either too much or too little water.*

probably all you will see of the shy Hartmann's mountain zebra, as they quench their thirst only under cover of darkness. There are two other species of zebra in southern Africa, but Hartmann's is endemic only to isolated mountainous areas of Namibia and southern Angola. More frequent sightings of the majestic kudu, a large antelope with twisted horns, are likely.

On the fourth day, you might stumble across a German grave, its occupant enjoying for all eternity the rare solitude of this desert wilderness. Germany occupied Namibia as a colonial power for some 30 years before World War I, and fierce fighting with Nama tribesmen took place in this area. Lieutenant von Trotha was shot in the back during a skirmish in 1905 and buried where he fell.

On the final day, the canyon opens out into a wide open space and the trail continues mostly on soft sand. By now you have surely heard the call of Africa – the plaintive and haunting sound of the fish eagle, arguably the most regal and awe inspiring of all the raptors – and glimpsed some of its stars: the klipspringer

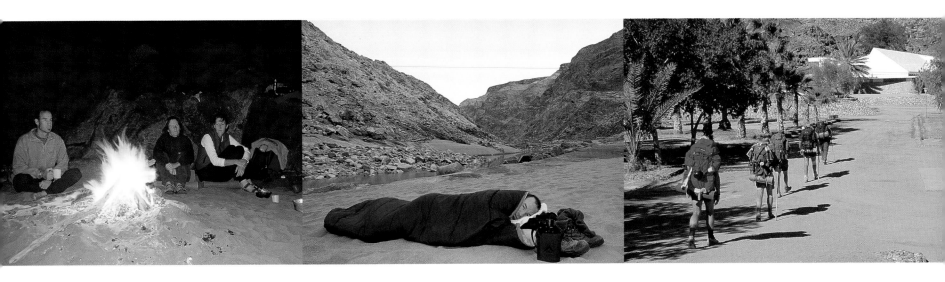

('rock jumper' buck) poised gracefully on the tips of its hooves like an agile ballet dancer. You would also have seen among the sparse vegetation the tree most associated with Namibia, the quiver tree, so named because the native Khoi people used the hollowed trunk of this aloe-like euphorbia as a quiver in which to carry their arrows. Confined mainly to the riverbanks, the camel thorn offers welcome shade and the ebony, with its drooping branches, gives the impression of wilting in the heat. Far from it. You have to be a survivor in this harsh wilderness.

The Fish River Canyon trek ends at Ai-Ais (pronounced 'Eye-Ice'), paradoxically the Nama word for 'burning water', and the healing hot springs at this luxury oasis will soothe your aching joints. The resort, established in 1971, was almost entirely washed down the river one year later, during the biggest flood in recorded history.

Namibia is a country that draws visitors back. It is hard to pinpoint why. There are miles of seemingly nothing, but there is an allure, a mystique about that nothing. The densely wooded lush green hills of the north, the arid desert plains of the south and the aptly named Skeleton Coast, constantly at war with the cold south Atlantic Ocean, show her in some of her moods. The title of a recent book on Namibia, however, puts it all into perspective: *Namibia – The land God made in anger*. Trek through the Fish River Canyon and you will see what God makes when He is really angry.

ABOVE, LEFT TO RIGHT *After a stiflingly hot day of 40°C (104°F), a campfire keeps trekkers warm during the near-freezing desert night – extremes are part and parcel of the Fish River Canyon; the reliable weather conditions in the canyon mean that trekkers need not carry tents and can appreciate the magnificent night sky by sleeping under the stars; the end is in sight – Ai-Ais beckons weary hikers with hot springs, ice-cold beer and comfortable beds. And this oasis is not just another mirage!*

LOCATION Namibia; near the border with South Africa.

WHEN TO GO Mid-April to mid-September. June and July are the best months. Due to extreme weather conditions, the canyon is closed during the remainder of the year.

START Hobas, 10km (6 miles) from the canyon, 650km (404 miles) from Windhoek, 900km (560 miles) from Cape Town or 1200km (750 miles) from Johannesburg.

FINISH Ai-Ais; hot-spring oasis in the semi-desert. Range of accommodation from luxury apartments to basic huts and permanently erected tents with camp beds. Spa complex has a restaurant, filling station and swimming pool.

DURATION 5 days. 100km (60 miles) along the entire river course, or around 86kms (53 miles) using short cuts.

MAX ALTITUDE 820m (2700ft).

TECHNICAL CONSIDERATIONS None.

EQUIPMENT Lightweight boots, clothing to cater for all seasons, high SPF lotion and a hat are absolutely essential. A tent is not necessary, as you can sleep in the open, but a survival bag is recommended. Wood is scarce, so take a stove. Large water bottle advisable.

TREKKING STYLE Backpacking.

PERMITS/RESTRICTIONS Groups can consist of 3 (min) to 40 (max) people. A medical certificate of physical fitness, issued within 40 days of the trek, must be submitted to the ranger at Hobas before starting. For permits apply to the central reservations office of Namibia Wildlife Resorts Ltd in Windhoek.

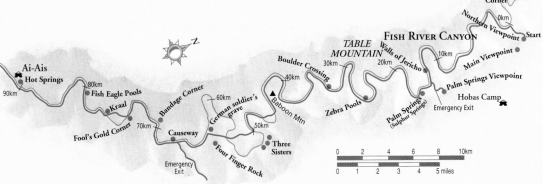

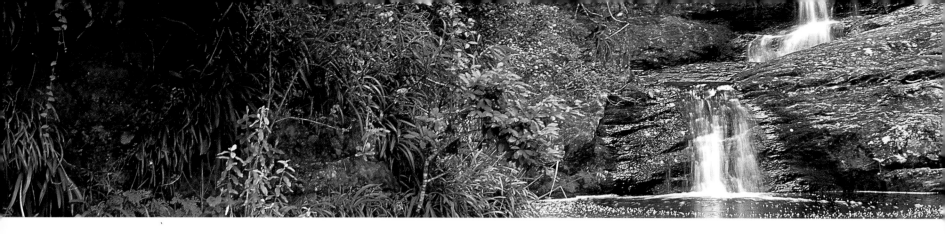

OTTER & TSITSIKAMMA TRAILS

by Mike Lundy

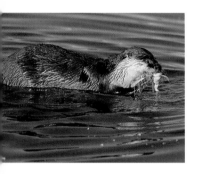

The original inhabitants of this southern tip of Africa were the Khoisan or Bushman people. Light-skinned and small in stature, they more than made up for their lack of size with superb hunting and survival skills. They called this place *Tsitsikamma* – where the clear waters begin – for these verdant mountains are the birthplace of many a river that gurgles its way down to the sea and adulthood.

Situated about two-thirds of the way between the coastal cities of Cape Town and Port Elizabeth, the Tsitsikamma Otter Trail Circuit is a combination of two popular South African trails – the inland mountainous Tsitsikamma Trail and the spectacular coastal Otter Trail. This 10-day adventure takes you from a ragged coastline of untamed beauty, to the tall mountains of the Tsitsikamma, with its dark primeval forests of tree ferns and *fynbos*.

Unique to this small corner of Africa, *fynbos* is a group of flowering shrubs that make up a botanical treasure, unrivalled anywhere else on the planet. The plant world is divided into six distinctly separate regions, called Floral Kingdoms. The smallest of the six areas by far is the Cape Floral Kingdom – but it is also the richest, with nearly 9000 different species of flowering plants confined in an amazing concentration to a tiny corner of the southwestern tip of Africa. The richness and abundance of the flora is well illustrated by heather of the genus *Erica*. The well-known heath flora of Europe has 21 species of *Erica*. Here can be found no less than 657 *Erica* species.

The Tsitsikamma National Park was established in 1964 and the trail system a short while later in 1968. The park encompasses 80km (50 miles) of pristine coastline and mountain retreat and extends three nautical miles out to sea – for there is even an underwater trail; the only one in Africa.

The Tsitsikamma and Otter trails were the first ones in a planned interconnecting network of hiking trails throughout South Africa. The National Hiking Way System, as it was to be called, never in fact interconnected, but has spawned a large number of treks throughout the country. At the last count, there were 375 listed walks and trails in South Africa alone, with a further 78 in neighbouring countries.

The 10-day trek starts at the spectacularly situated Storms River Mouth rest camp. From here trekkers set out westward along the wild coastline, moving through dense indigenous forest and emerging every so often at a secluded beach or a breathtaking viewpoint. Huge jagged rocks stick straight out of the sea, guarding the coast like sentries. This is not a place you would choose to be shipwrecked. The path winds up and down steep wooded hillsides occasionally interrupted by a river. The coastal section of the trek takes five days, and being only 43km (27 miles) one might be tempted to think it is a walk in the park. It isn't. In fact, the second half of the trek, the Tsitsikamma Trail, is a lot longer at 72km (45 miles), but easier. Take your time on the coastal section.

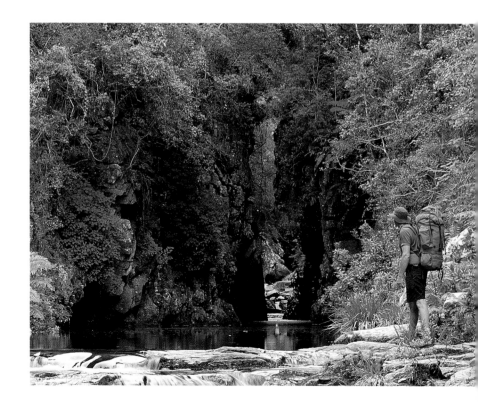

TOP *Day two brings together a blend of splashing silver and verdant green in peaceful harmony. One of many waterfalls – this one between Ngubu Huts and Kleinbos.*
INSET *Due to its acute senses of smell and hearing, the Cape clawless otter is very seldom seen. Despite this fact, the elusive animal lends its name to the trail.*
RIGHT *A trekker stops to admire the surroundings – a Garden of Eden complete with swimming pool – at Kleinbos on day two.*

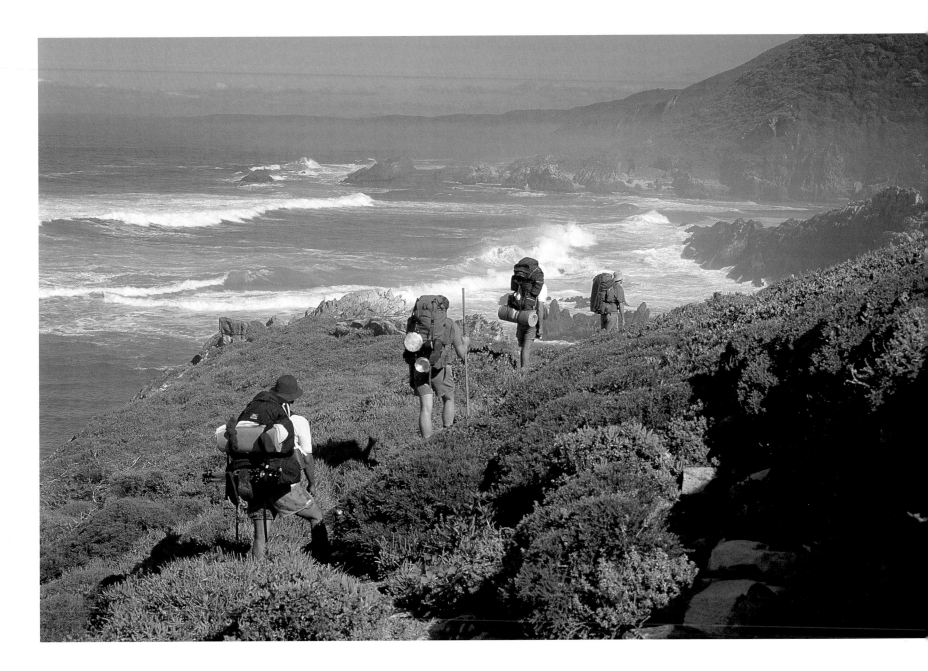

The first part of the trek involves a fair bit of rock scrambling and boulder hopping, just on and above the high-water mark. This short section to the first overnight hut (4.8km; 3 miles) is something of a baptism of fire. At least it is for inexperienced trekkers, who can't quite seem to make the jump to the next rock, without climbing all the way down, and laboriously up again. Soon, however, all frustrations are washed away at a beautiful waterfall cascading into a deep, dark swimming pool.

A mere three hours after starting will bring you to the first overnight huts – Ngubu Huts – named after the park ranger who helped to develop the trail and subsequently died in a fire. There are two spartan log cabins at each coastal overnight stop. They each sleep six people in bunks with foam mattresses, and have a table and two benches. Water and firewood are usually provided, but not guaranteed.

The second day of the trek is a spectacular combination of steep ascents and descents, with Skilderkrans (painted cliffs) being a highlight. From here you can see much of the Otter Trail in both directions. A detour from the trail to Blue Bay is a must. It is only 10 minutes down to a superb sandy beach – one of the few on this rugged coast. Make the most of it before facing the slog back uphill again to the main trail.

ABOVE *The Otter Trail winds its way along the coast, often emerging out of the bush onto cliffs that offer spectacular vistas of the crashing Indian Ocean.*

The following day, after more ups and downs, you might get the feeling you are being watched. You are – by cheeky little vervet moneys or brightly plumaged Knysna loeries. This day ends with a crossing of the mouth of the Lottering River to reach the Oakhurst Huts on the opposite bank. They could not be closer to the crashing waves where bottlenose dolphins frolic in the tumbling translucent breakers.

The fourth day brings with it the most feared obstacle on the trek – the Bloukrans (blue cliffs) River crossing. Its perceived dangers are almost without fail blown out of all proportion, and hikers often sleep fitfully the night before in fearful anticipation. Strong currents and deep water at high tide are factors that warrant some consideration, but provided the crossing is undertaken at low tide, there is little to worry about.

The last day on the coast starts with a climb to a high plateau, before plummeting down to the seemingly endless beach at the aptly named Nature's Valley, the trek's mid point. The squabbling gulls; the rare African black oystercatchers trying to lure you

55

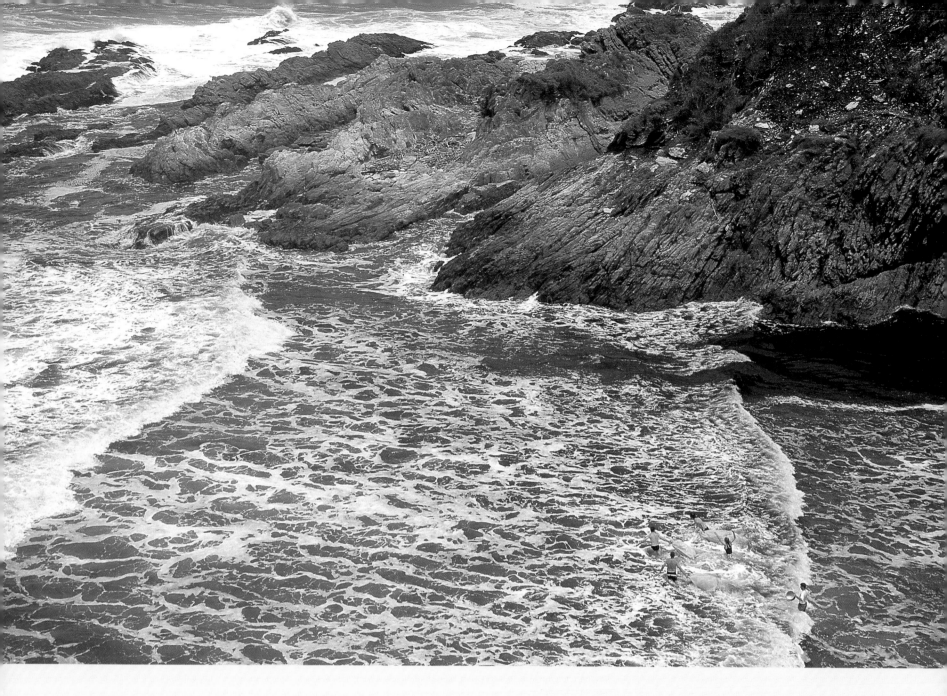

WHEN TO GO Although this is a year-round rainfall area, avoid August to November when it is above average. Warmest months are December to March with an average temperature of around 20°C (68°F).

START/FINISH Storms River Mouth; 500km (310 miles) east of Cape Town; 250km (150 miles) west of Port Elizabeth.

DURATION 10 days. Otter Trail is 43km (26 miles), Tsitsikamma Trail 72km (48 miles).

MAX ALTITUDE 740m (2400ft).

TECHNICAL CONSIDERATIONS None.

EQUIPMENT Standard hiking gear, plus sleeping bag. Must be self-sufficient in food.

TREKKING STYLE Backpacking, although both trails have huts for overnight stays. Otter Trail huts have 6 bunks each (2 huts at each stop); Tsitsikamma Trail huts have 30 beds each.

PERMITS/RESTRICTIONS Permits are required for both the Otter and Tsitsikamma trails and can be obtained from the SA National Parks for the Otter Trail and from the SA Forestry Co Ltd (SAFCOL) for the Tsitsikamma Trail. It is difficult to get permits for the Otter Trail due to popularity.

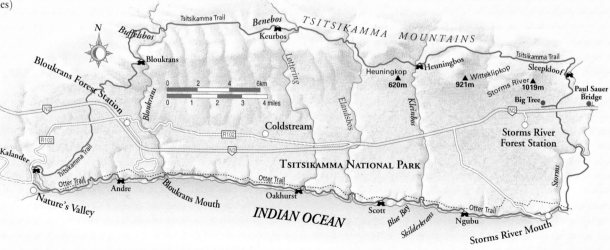

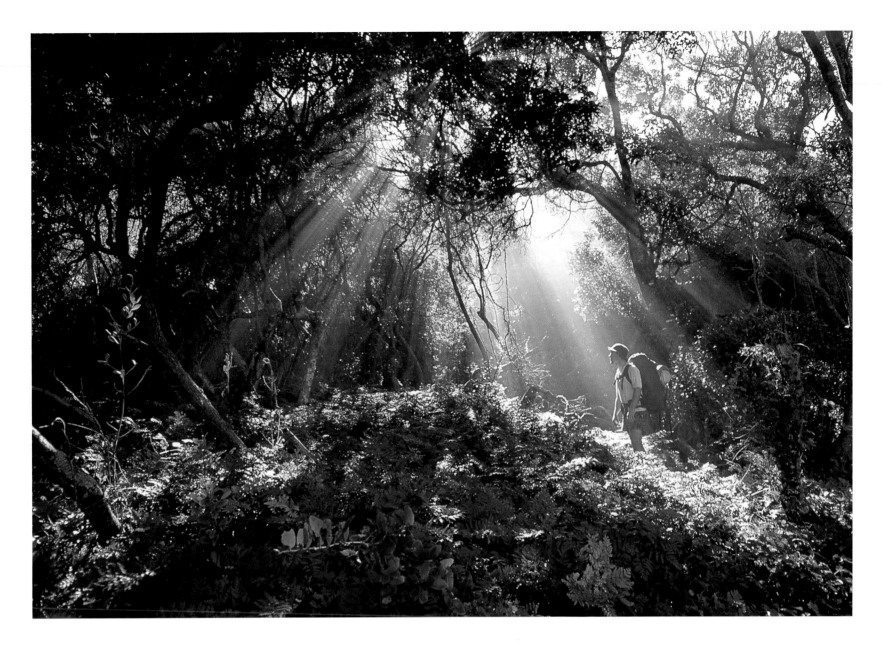

OPPOSITE *The incoming tide is not a good time to cross the Bloukrans River mouth; but these hikers know it is a great deal safer than the outgoing tide!*

ABOVE *Filtered sunbeams add peace and tranquility to the inland Tsitsikamma Trail, contrasting markedly with the frenetically noisy seashore of the Otter Trail.*

away from their defenceless chick; the solitary cormorant drying himself out in the crucifix position – these coastal birds will not be following you into the mountains.

Re-stock provisions at the local shop, and head on into the Tsitsikamma Mountains, jealously hiding their primeval forests, *fynbos*, and sparkling swimming holes. Unlike the coastal log cabins, the mountain huts accommodate 30 people, so be prepared to share with interesting strangers. Perched precariously on a cliff edge, your first night in the mountains at the Bloukrans Hut is a fitting end to the day – the view is for ever.

Like the coastal trail, the second day in the mountains is a day of ups and downs, with Buffelsbos (buffalo forest) and Benebos (bone forest) adding a touch of nostalgia. Elephant and buffalo once roamed these forests in great numbers; alas, it took European colonists less than 100 years to wipe them out. Surviving are a large number of tree ferns, making a forest glade look like a scene from 300 million years ago. The rocks are decorated with nature's paintbrush – lichens in every shade of yellow, red, orange, black, white and grey.

The following day takes you past Formosa Peak: at 1675m (5496ft) the highest peak in the Tsitsikamma range. Three river crossings and a walk along an old wagon track will bring you to your penultimate overnight stop at Heuningbos (honey forest). The track was built in 1834 in order to exploit the indigenous forests. Regrettably, a number of these have now been replanted with alien pines of European origin.

The ninth day of the trek reaches the highest point of the trail (740m; 2400ft), making it probably the most strenuous day's hike. There is a superb view over the rolling forests to the Storms River Gorge and your last overnight hut, perched on the edge of a headland way below, at Sleepkloof. There you will most certainly sleep, but the name actually means 'dragging ravine', and refers to the logs that were taken out through it.

The final lap is mostly downhill, and rather sadly crosses a national road, bringing you back to the real world with a jolt. The icing on the cake, however, is to cross the Storms River Mouth on a pedestrian suspension bridge, all the while wondering if it is really safe. It is. And you have conquered 10 days of Africa's finest.

ASIA

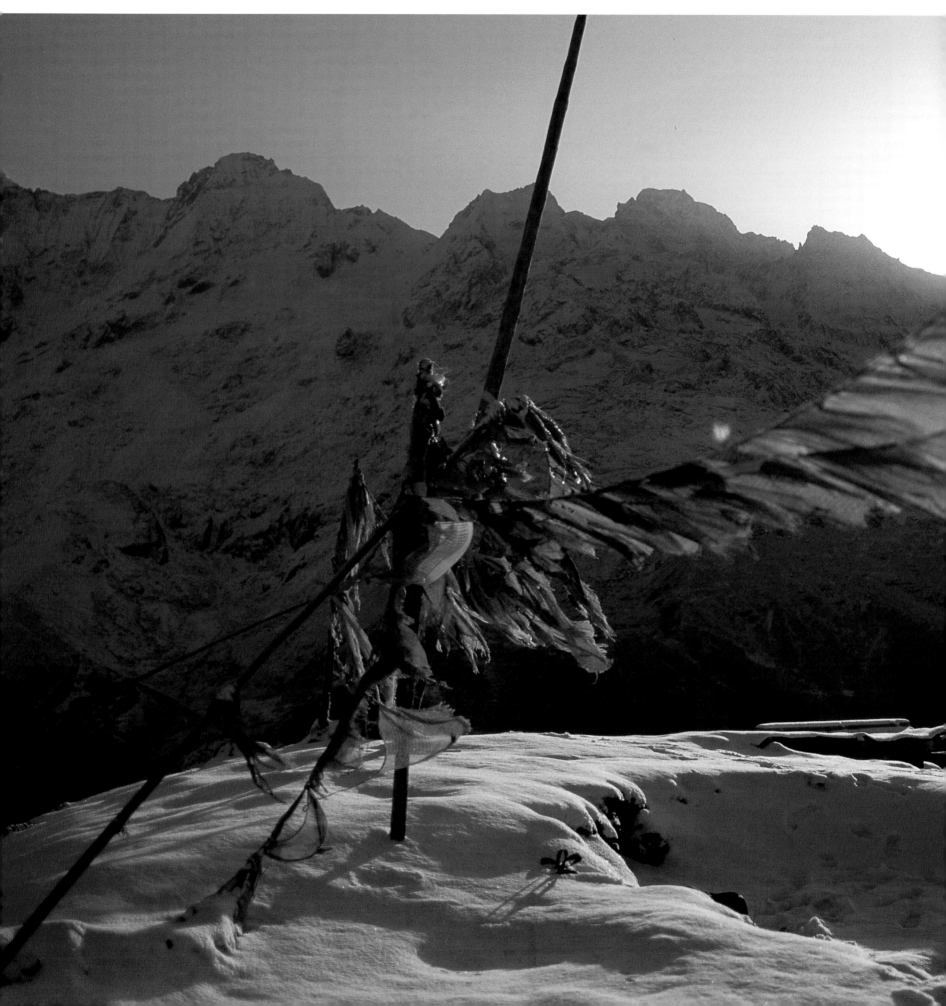

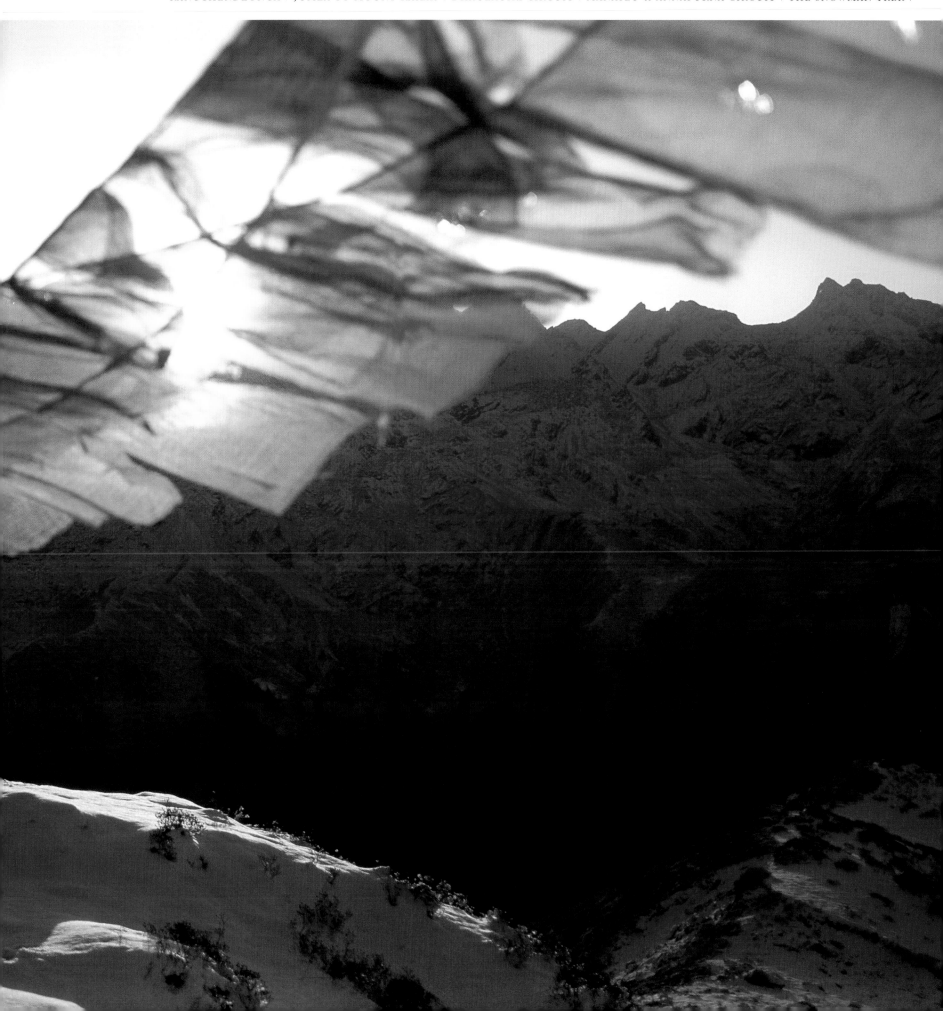

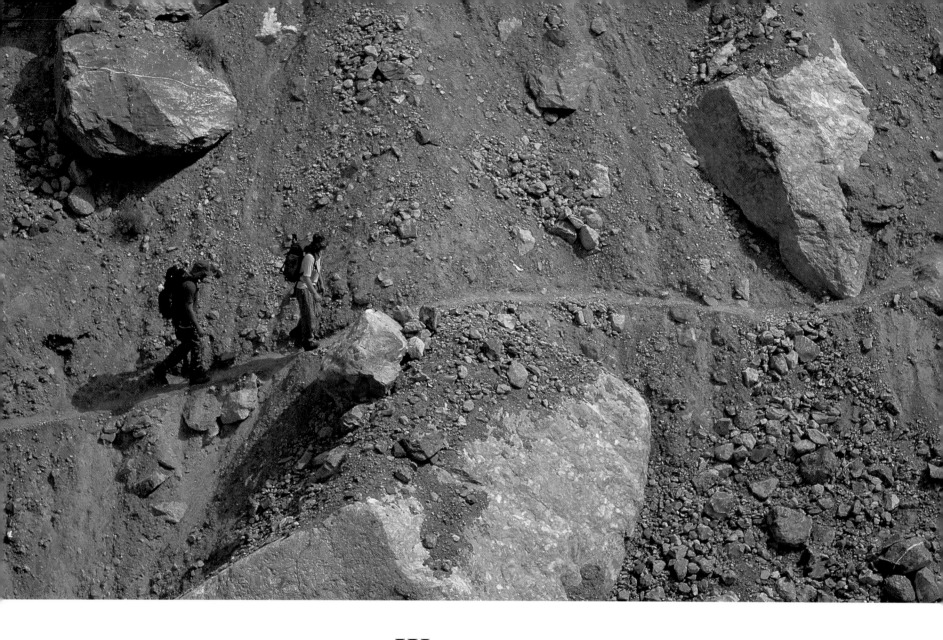

ASIA

I am a wayfarer, and ever I wander through the world seeing the marvels thereof.

SHIHABUDDIN SUHRAWARDI, 1153–91

ABOVE *The mountain deserts of Pakistan present trekking conditions entirely different from those in Nepal – less of the huge ascents and descents, but much rougher underfoot.*

OPPOSITE *Trekkers crossing a bridge over the upper Dudh Khola just below Bimthang in Nepal. Beyond is the mighty Himlung Himal, just one of a broad vista of stunning peaks revealed during a crossing of the Larkya La.*

PREVIOUS PAGES *At Dzong Ri, the colourful flags of Tantric Buddhism flutter in the wind, carrying prayers to the gods.*

With coastlines on the Arctic, Pacific and Indian oceans and the Mediterranean and Red seas, Asia is the largest of the continents. Its boundaries encompass the enormous peninsulas of Arabia, India and Indo-China, and upon its soil ancient civilizations sprung up in Mesopotamia (Iraq) and the Indus valley 4000 years before the birth of Christ.

The ebb and flow of empires and invasion have left the lands of the continent with a fantastically diverse cultural heritage, and the hand of nature has conspired to enrich this even further by throwing up the highest, most formidable natural frontier on earth – the Himalaya – against which the tides of commerce, Islam, Hinduism and Buddhism have surged over the centuries. Nowhere else on earth can mountaineers and trekkers combine the joys of pursuing their vocations with the release of travelling amid hills and valleys so thoroughly imbued with spirituality and sanctity.

Mention Pakistan or the Karakoram in the company of those who have travelled there and they will recall the sincere hospitality and camaraderie shown to visitors by the hardy Moslem inhabitants of the northern areas. Tourist infrastructure may be primitive, but the rewards reaped by those who venture into these lands of intense, dazzling sunlight, sweltering heat and range upon range of unbelievably rugged mountains are profound. The treks included here – to K2 via the Gondokoro La and the traverse of the Biafo–Hispar – are arguably the toughest and most committing in the book, but also the most dramatic.

Kashmir, the Himalayan Eden over which Pakistan and India have squabbled for so long is, sadly, off-limits for trekkers today, but beyond lies an arid tract of Indian mountain country every bit as alluring. Ladakh and Zanskar may not have the 8000m peaks and enormous glaciers of the Karakoram, but they

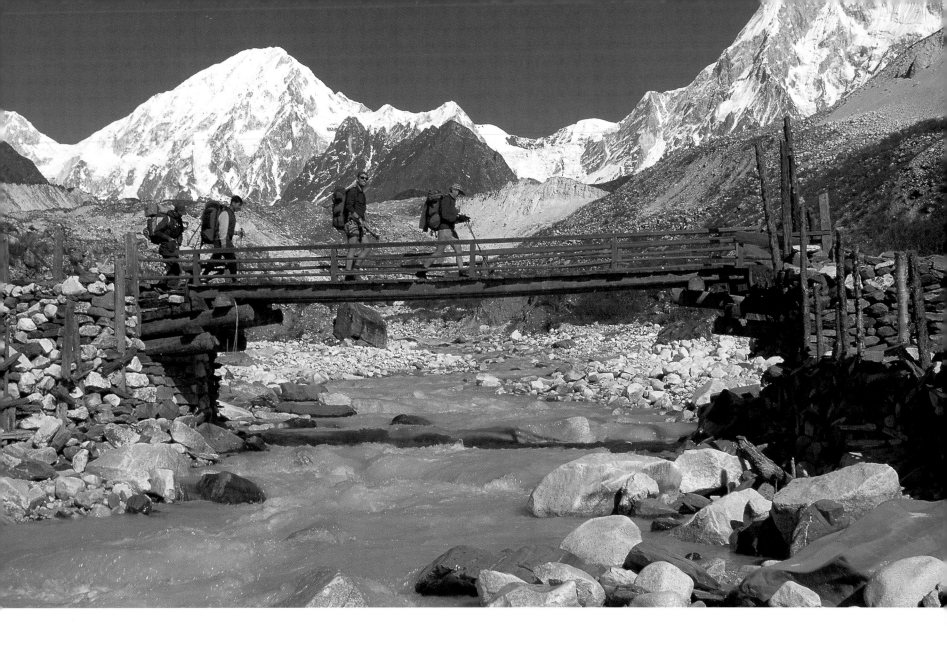

are populated by a gentle people of Tibetan Buddhist faith who have kept their traditions alive. Of the many excellent trekking routes possible in the region, none is more scintillating and challenging than the long passage south from Lamayuru in Ladakh through the heart of Zanskar to Manali.

Nepal needs no introduction as a destination for trekkers. It was here, in the 1960s, that the first commercial trekking companies sprung up, and it remains a Mecca for mountain lovers everywhere. In Kathmandu, the bustling capital of this tiny mountain kingdom, medieval temples nestle next to cyber cafés and trekkers will find that the friendly Nepalis have learned to cater for their every need. Though many of the more famous trails are very busy these days, it is still very easy to escape the crowds.

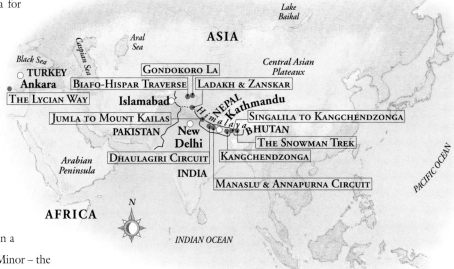

East of Nepal, closer to the life-giving monsoon that sweeps in from the Bay of Bengal, the Himalayan chain is at its most verdant and secretive. In Sikkim it has recently become possible to approach the mighty Kangchendzonga along the Singalila ridge, while in Bhutan the Snowman Trek is perhaps the most spectacular and least known trail in the entire Himalaya.

Finally, with one foot in Europe and the other in Asia, Turkey has long been a pivotal force shaping the history of both. On the Mediterranean coast of Asia Minor – the peninsula known today as Anatolia – the ancient region of Lycia was coveted by Persians, Rhodians and Romans alike. The newly opened trail along the rugged coastline is sure to become a classic.

61

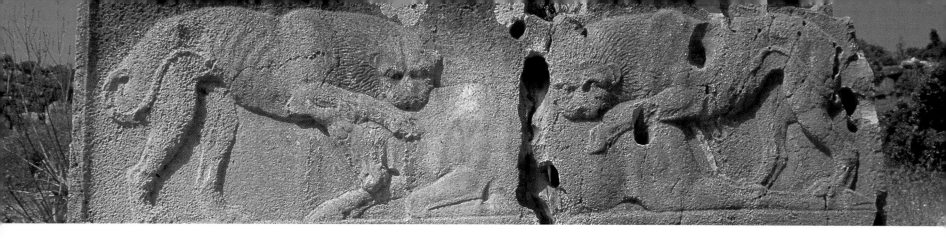

THE LYCIAN WAY

by Kate Clow

Lycia is the mountainous bump on the south coast of Turkey, where the Taurus range plunges into the glittering Mediterranean. The Lycian Way follows Greek and Roman roads and aqueducts, traditional nomad trails and forest tracks around the coast, rising over ranges and diverting around deltas. Existing tracks have been linked up to form a continuous walking route that stretches over 530km (330 miles), soars along cliffs, winds through forests, pauses at deserted beaches and takes several detours inland. Old fishing villages, now tourist honeypots, such as Kemer, Kaş and Kalkan, offer supplies, accommodation and a break from the solitude of the trail.

Most Turks still work the land, some as shepherds, trekking up and down the mountains with their flocks on seasonal migrations. More recently, however, second-generation city-dwellers have rediscovered their ancestral lands; the Lycian Way marks a new recreational fashion, in imitation of European ways. It is sponsored (and signposted) by a major bank and waymarked in red-and-white flashes similar to the French *Grande Randonnées*. Trekkers are still rare on this new route; it is possible to walk for a week without meeting a soul. The most popular section is the diversion to Mount Olympos – the physical and spiritual highpoint of the walk.

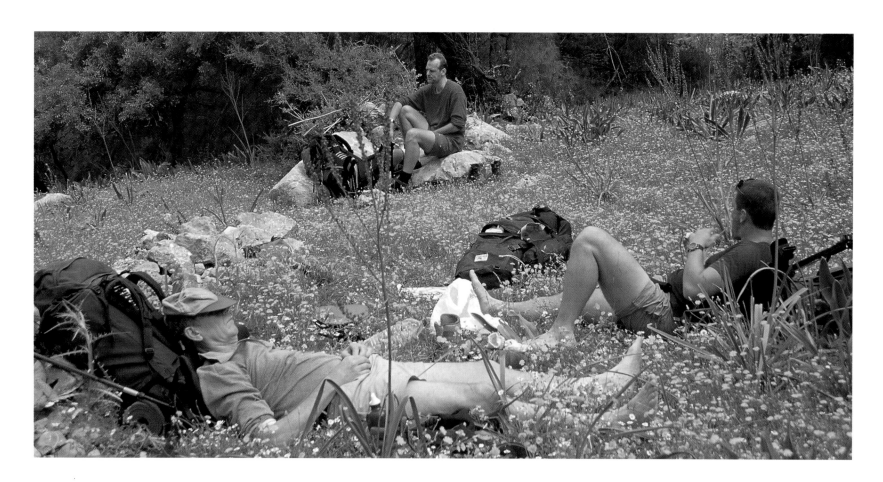

TOP *A relief on the tomb of the royal dynasty at Xanthos, from the 4th–5th centuries* BC, *showing lions attacking a deer.*

ABOVE *A group of trekkers resting on a* yayla *(summer pasture) after the rigorous hike up the slopes of the Musa Dağı.*

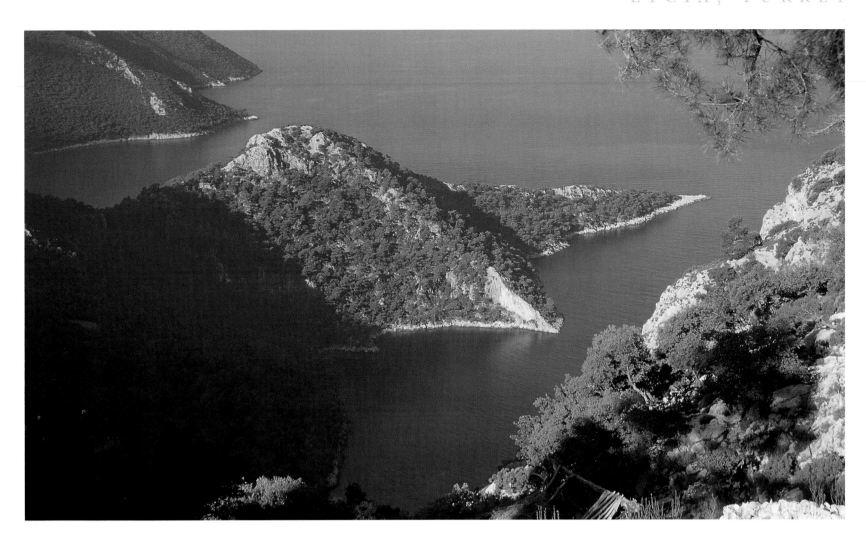

Lycia was originally a client state of the Hittite Empire, established in central Anatolia about 1800BC. Pushed southwards by new invaders, they intermixed with Greek settlers and established an artistic, wealthy culture, supplementing farming and fishing with mercenary warfare – Lycian contingents fought at Troy and Salamis. After Alexander's death (323BC), the Seleucids and then the Romans ruled Anatolia, but allowed the Lycians, now Greek speaking, freedom to form a unique democratic league. After centuries of prosperity, by the 6th century most of the population had succumbed to plague and Arab pirates. The Lycian peninsula lay almost deserted until the arrival of the Turks in the 15th century.

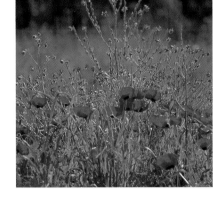

The first, and greatest hero to travel the Lycian Way was the Macedonian king, Alexander the Great. With a mission to free the Greek cities of Asia Minor from Persian rule, he entered Lycia at present-day Fethiye, with his army of 10,000 foot soldiers. He traversed the mountain of Baba Dağı en route to the superbly fortified stronghold of Xanthos, where he accepted the surrender of the capital of Lycia. One by one, the other cities submitted, the representatives of Phaselis bringing him a gold crown. Alexander overwintered at Phaselis and, seated in the open-air theatre, must have contemplated Mount Olympos and the gorges to the north, which blocked his route. After winning local skirmishes he sent engineers to cut steps for the passage of his army. Alexander himself, with his closest companions, marched along the beaches, wading around rocky coastal spurs to rendezvous with his army on the plain at Antalya.

The Lycian Way trek starts at the crescent of golden sand called Ölü Deniz where a rash of hotels and pensions would more than accommodate Alexander's army. The route climbs abruptly up mule trails on the slopes of Baba Dağı, where paragliders soar in the westerly breezes and waves pound the rocks far below. The first day's trek descends past a restored mill house to Faralya, where a friendly village pension offering excellent local cooking is perched on cliffs above Butterfly Valley. After this comfortable night, you're mostly on your own, winding through farmland and forest, with glimpses of the wide sea and occasional passing boats. The switchback climb between strawberry trees and pines that rises from Kabak Valley is probably the most beautiful track in Turkey.

The first Lycian city en route is Sidyma, where ancient stones have been adapted to the daily needs of a beekeeping and farming community, a temple doorway supports tumbling cottages, a few inscriptions are incorporated into the mosque walls and a stone sarcophagus is used as a toolshed.

TOP *A view over Yedi Burun (seven capes), a series of spectacular headlands facing into the prevailing westerly wind and sheltering deserted beaches.*

ABOVE CENTRE *The Lycian Way is ablaze with wild flowers in spring – anytime between January and May, depending on altitude.*

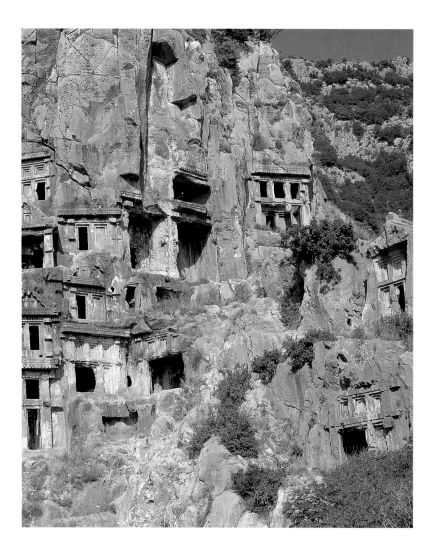

ABOVE *Early explorer Charles Fellows reported that these Lycian rock-cut tombs overlooking the Roman theatre at Myra were once painted in rainbow hues.*

dot remote paths. The hilltop site of Phellos, where a huge sculpted relief of a bull shows the skill of ancient artists, commands views to the Greek islands and is the starting point for a sheer descent to the resort town of Kaş.

From here, the route hugs the coast, winding through thyme-scented maquis to the ruins of Aperlae, where ancient stone tombs guard a shallow bay. Past here is the flower-filled fishing village of Üçağız, and then Myra, legendary home of St Nicholas. Above Myra, in May, the trekker can observe migration first hand – goats rush eagerly to their upper pastures, spewing spring flowers from chomping jaws. The route climbs past the ruins of a Byzantine church and a hermit's cell to İncegeriş Hill at 1811m (5942ft). The coast, from the islands of Üçağız to the limestone ridge of Cape Gelidonia, is spread like a carpet below. A steady descent by Roman road leads to Finike, an orange-growing town, and across a delta to the southernmost point of Lycia. The Cape is marked by a remote lighthouse, where it is possible to stay the night. Climb the tower to watch the rising sun paint the world in rose and gold.

Turning north, the going gets tough. After a few energetic days switchbacking over forested ridges, the route turns inland to the saddle of Mount Olympos, where huge cedars guard the pass at about 1800m (5900ft). For the brave and experienced, there is a chance to reach the summit at 2366m (7763ft) – to be greeted by misty views of rolling ridges silhouetted in deep indigo against the shining sea. The less adventurous can bypass the peak, visit the theatre at Phaselis, and relax where Alexander once sat. Beyond Mount Olympos, a series of tiny summer villages offer a chance to stay with the locals. The route finishes with a descent of a deep, silent valley to the sea, and a final two-day climb to 1500m (5000ft). It emerges on a narrow ridge with a breathtaking drop into a canyon below, and views beyond to the bay and your destination city – Antalya. A couple of hours along the ridge is the nearest village of Hısarçandır, a long walk or a short car ride away from civilization.

A steep downhill coastal track between Sidyma and an ancient fort at Pydnai is a real test for a trekker with a full pack – the track is slippery with loose rocks and the ancient kerbstones have long collapsed. The route drops into orchid-filled forest and crosses wheatfields to the village of Gavurağılı (meaning Christians' enclosure), where descendants of the ancient Greeks sheltered their flocks until their return to Greece in the chaos after World War I. Only a few old people remain in the decaying balconied houses set among olive trees and vegetable gardens.

Round the point, past the battlemented fort of Pydnai, is a 12km-long (7.5-mile) beach leading to Patara, once the chief harbour of the Lycian homeland. Windblown sand and silt have extended the delta of the Xanthos River out to sea, burying the site of Patara and creating fertile soil for tomato cultivation. The Lycian Way circles the delta, first through mimosa planting, then following the courses of the aqueducts that supplied Xanthos and Patara from the hills above. The Patara aqueduct is borne over dry valleys on an impressive syphonic pipeline made of 1000 stone blocks, each weighing 600kg (1300lbs), a 2000-year-old engineering marvel.

Following still-used nomad trails to the high pastures of Bezirgan, the trail enters a stark world where the season is two months behind the sunny coast below. Wind-sculpted rock formations tower over gushing springs and brilliant scarlet anemones

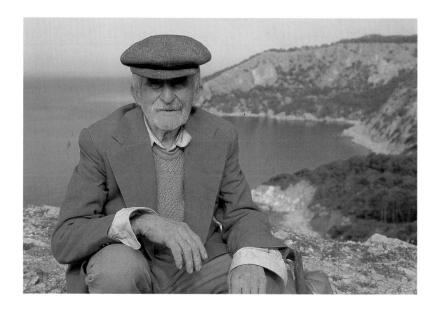

ABOVE *Suleyman, one of four remaining residents in Gavurağılı, walks part of the Lycian Way every Friday on his way to the mosque.*
OPPOSITE *Cape Gelidonia lighthouse. In earlier days, the cape and the adjoining five islands were a shipping hazard on the route from Egypt and Syria to Greece and Rome.*

LOCATION Turkey's Mediterranean coast; trail runs between Fethiye and Antalya.

WHEN TO GO Mid-September to November is sunny and colourful. February to May, spring flowers are wonderful.

START Ölü Deniz, 20mins by public minibus from Fethiye. Nearest airport is Dalaman, 2hrs drive from Ölü Deniz.

FINISH Hısarçandır, 30mins by minibus or taxi from Antalya. Nearest airport is Antalya.

DURATION 30 days; 530km (330 miles).

MAXIMUM ALTITUDE Mount Olympos (2366m; 7763ft).

TECHNICAL CONSIDERATIONS Trek starts moderately and becomes tough; the more remote sections should not be attempted alone. Allow time to acclimatize and take plenty of water. No large-scale local maps available. For latest information on the trail, check out www.lycianway.com

EQUIPMENT Lightweight tent, sleeping bag, cooking equipment, thick-soled boots, lightweight clothing according to season, sunglasses and sunscreen, swimming gear. Supplies available at villages along the way.

TREKKING STYLE Backpacking.

PERMITS/RESTRICTIONS Camping is forbidden in Culture Ministry historic sites, but possible in many places along the trail. Huge Anatolian sheepdogs can be a menace; a dog-scaring whistle is recommended.

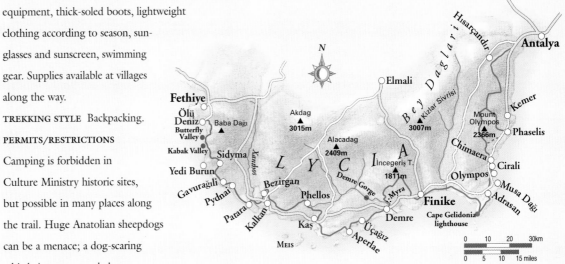

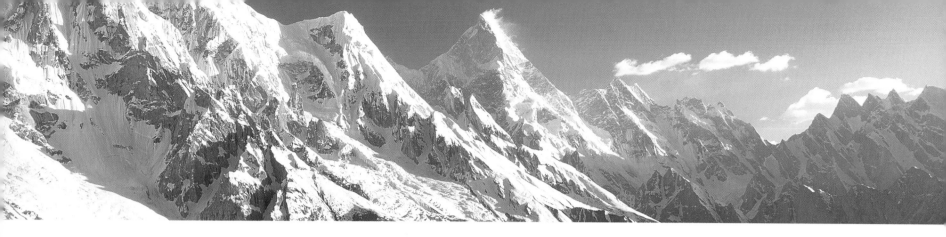

GONDOKORO LA – HUSHE TO CONCORDIA

by Steve Razzetti

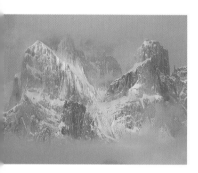

Named after an ancient pass across the watershed between the Indian Ocean and Central Asia, the Karakoram is unquestionably the most savagely beautiful range of mountains on earth. Extending for some 320km (200 miles) from the Hindu Kush in the west to the Ladakh range and the Greater Himalaya in the east, the peaks of the Karakoram are situated along some of the most mobile fault lines on earth, and while tectonic forces push the summits skywards, enormous glaciers and tumultuous rivers tear them down again. To travel in the Karakoram is to witness perhaps the greatest exhibition of active geology the world has to offer.

Everything about the Karakoram is extreme. Four of the world's fourteen 8000m peaks – K2, Broad Peak, Gasherbrum I and Gasherbrum II – tower over one glacial system, the Baltoro. No fewer than 36 summits exceed 7300m (24,000ft), while literally hundreds exceed 6000m (19,600ft). These are some of the most heavily glaciated mountains outside of the polar regions, and the seven largest glaciers (Biafo, Hispar, Baltoro, Gasherbrum, Chogo Lungma, Siachen and Batura) all cover areas of over 350 square kilometres (217 square miles). In summer, valley temperatures frequently exceed 40°C (104°F) and the unbelievably fierce heat of the sun melts the high glaciers and snowfields at an incredible rate, turning the rivers below into thundering torrents which carry the highest volume of sediment of any rivers on earth. Such is the power of these mighty streams that boulders the size of office blocks flip and boom along their beds like autumn leaves blown across a pavement by a light breeze.

Though Englishman Godfrey Thomas Vigne was the first European to really penetrate far into the Karakoram, it was Thomas Montgomerie of the Survey of India who first realized their true stature. In 1856, from a distant survey station atop the peak of Haramukh in Kashmir, he triangulated a series of 32 peaks to which he gave the prefix 'K' for Karakoram. When his observations were finally computed in 1858, K2 was found to be the second highest mountain in the world, and the currently accepted figure for its height is 8611m (28,268ft).

Fellow countryman Henry Haversham Godwin-Austen got the first close look at K2 in 1861. At the end of a truly epic expedition, during which he discovered the Hispar Glacier and crossed the Hispar Pass (*see page 70*) before descending the

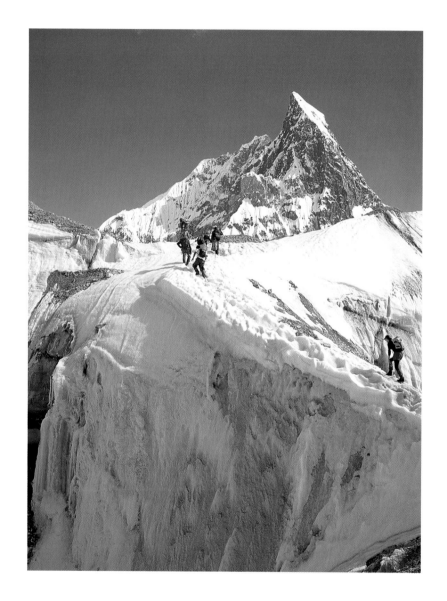

TOP *The awesome north face of Masherbrum (7821m; 25,661ft) and peaks lining the southern flanks of the upper Baltoro Glacier after spring snowfall.*
INSET *The soaring granite needles of the Trango Towers are undoubtedly the climax of the mountain architecture that lines the northern flank of the Baltoro.*
ABOVE *Returning to Concordia from K2 base camp through a heavily crevassed section of the Baltoro, with Mitre Peak towering overhead.*

Biafo Glacier to the village of Askole, he made a brief sortie onto the Baltoro Glacier. Determined to actually see K2, he gave up following the Baltoro and ascended a spur above the camp now known as Urdokas to a point where he was able to sketch just the summit of the monstrous pyramid that towered over the intervening ridges.

The seminal visual record of these peaks made by the celebrated Italian photographer Vittorio Sella during the Duke of Abruzzi's expedition in 1909 really brought this area to the attention of the mountaineering world. Using a large camera capable of exposing 30x40cm glass plates, Sella recorded over 800 superlative images during the expedition, and prints were subsequently acquired by such august bodies as the Royal Geographical Society and the Alpine Club in London and the National Geographic Society in Washington. Italian interest in K2 never waned, and in 1954 Ardito Desio led the expedition that succeeded in making the first ascent.

Trekking to Concordia, the confluence of the Baltoro and Godwin-Austen glaciers that lies at the very heart of the Karakoram, is a difficult undertaking. Though Skardu, the sleepy capital of the Pakistani province of Baltistan in which the highest of the Karakoram peaks are situated, is served by daily scheduled air services from Islamabad, mountain weather is notoriously fickle and flights are

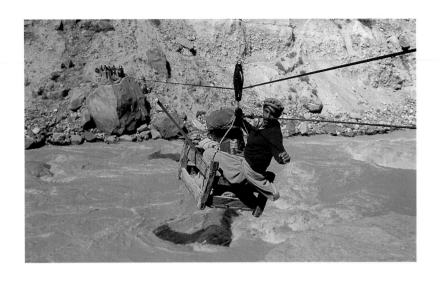

ABOVE *Crossing the raging waters of the Braldu River by* jhola *at Chongo. Depending on the condition of the road, this may or may not be necessary.*
BELOW *Ascending rocky ground above the upper Gondokoro Glacier with Layla Peak beyond. Use of helmets on this crossing is advised as stonefall is guaranteed.*

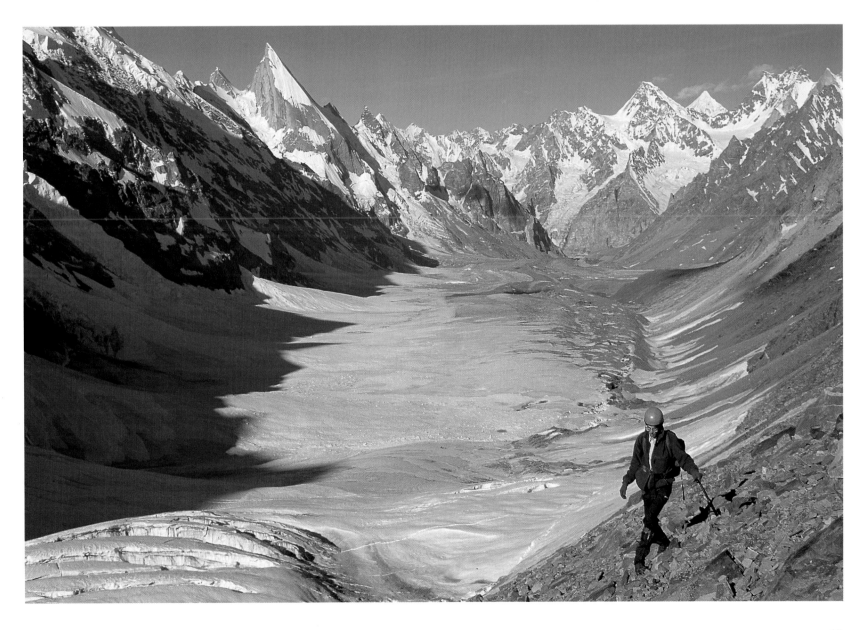

LOCATION Karakoram Range, Baltistan province, northern area, Pakistan.

WHEN TO GO Early June to early September.

START Hushe village; international flights to Karachi or Islamabad (recommended), then by air (1hr) or road (Karakoram Highway, 18–30hrs) to Skardu. Overnight there, then to Hushe by jeep (10hrs).

FINISH Askole village; jeep to Skardu (6–10hrs depending on road conditions), then by air or road to Islamabad/Rawalpindi.

DURATION 22 days; 130km (80 miles).

MAXIMUM ALTITUDE Gondokoro La (5585m; 18,324ft).

TECHNICAL CONSIDERATIONS Party must consist of proficient glacier travellers and be equipped for both roped glacier travel and crevasse rescue. Some fixed ropes may be required on the upper sections of the Gondokoro La. Some stone fall danger here also – helmets recommended.

EQUIPMENT Plastic boots, crampons, harness and glacier travel/rescue equipment.

TREKKING STYLE Expedition. Must be completely self-sufficient.

PERMITS/RESTRICTIONS Trekking permit and a liaison officer now required for this route (it's close to the disputed border with India). Permit only available through trekking agent in Pakistan. *Note:* Licensed Pakistani mountain guides may double as liaison officers.

often cancelled. Until 1986, those seeking to approach K2 and its mighty neighbours faced a gruelling expedition justly considered among the toughest treks in the world. From Skardu, reached as now by air or an epic two-day drive up a spur of the frequently cut Karakoram Highway, jeeps would ply the arid Shigar Valley to Dassu, the portal of the Braldu Gorge. In three days the precarious trail, swept sometimes by the tumultuous river, sometimes by dangerous stonefall, led to the oasis of Askole. The route continued via the sweltering heat, freezing nights, hair-raising river crossings and the torturous Baltoro moraines to Concordia, the Gasherbrums, Broad Peak and K2. Expeditions returned by the same route. Then came a man called Ali Mohammed from the village of Hushe.

His home lies at the head of a previously obscure valley to the south of Masherbrum, visited only briefly by the infamous American travelling couple Fanny Bullock Workman and her husband William Hunter Workman in 1911 and by sporadic expeditions to the south face of Masherbrum until the 1980s. The hardy men of Hushe regularly work as high-altitude porters on the Baltoro and, in 1985, Ali Mohammed was employed by an expedition attempting Chogolisa, a 7654m (25,112ft) peak on the upper Baltoro. Looking south across a nearby col from a camp high on the peak, he was amazed to see the unmistakable form of Layla Peak, an elegant spire on the Gondokoro Glacier, just above his village. He decided to attempt to get home via this tantalizing shortcut, succeeded, and thus discovered the Gondokoro La (5585m; 18,324ft).

Hushe was already fast gaining a reputation among trekkers and mountaineers in the mid-1980s, and Ali Mohammed's discovery suddenly opened up the possibility of a circuit trek taking in the most picturesque of the four glaciers above Hushe village, a high pass offering breathtaking views of K2, Broad Peak and the entire Gasherbrum group, and a visit to Concordia concluded with a walk out down the Baltoro to Askole. Among aficionados of the wild and adventurous, this route has become something of a cult classic.

The village of Hushe can be reached by jeep in approximately 10 hours from Skardu, and the men there have organized themselves to cater for trekkers and mountaineers

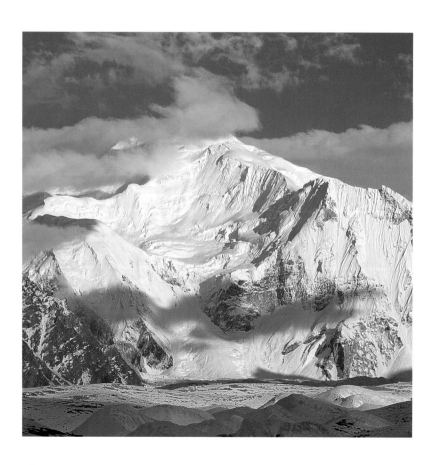

LEFT *Baltoro Kangri (7312m; 23,989ft), often referred to as 'The Golden Throne' above Concordia, which in turn is known as 'The Throne Room of the Mountain Gods'.*

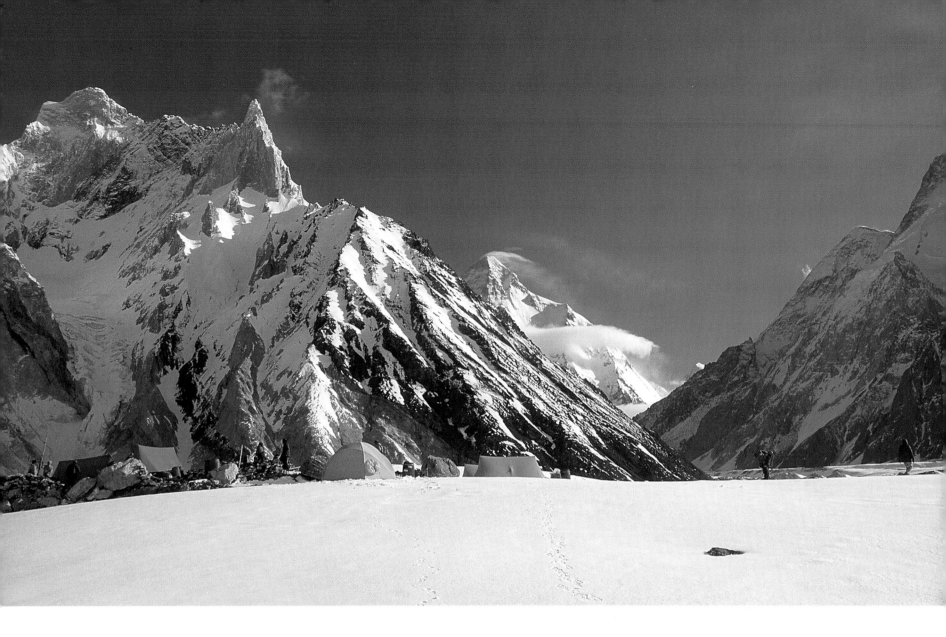

wishing to travel by this route. Calling themselves the Hushe Mountain Rescue Team, at the beginning of each season, in late May, they fix ropes on the difficult sections, place bamboo bridges across crevasses and establish permanent camps at the base of the pass on either side. For a fee they will even guide people across.

This route is certainly not for those without a head for heights, and a level of competence in navigating and traversing glacial terrain is essential. It qualifies as a serious expedition, and for those wishing to experience the joys of mountaineering without actually venturing onto a major peak it is unbeatable. Many people acclimatize for the crossing by ascending the technically straightforward Gondokoro Peak (5656m; 18,557ft) above the Gondokoro Glacier and, having crossed to Concordia, spend a few days visiting the base camps of the Gasherbrums, Broad Peak and K2 before heading off down the Baltoro. As a result, one is treated to a jaw-dropping parade of mountains right until the end, with the Mustagh Tower, the north face of Masherbrum, the Trango Towers, Uli Biaho, the Cathedral Spires and Piaju Peak saved as treats for the final few days.

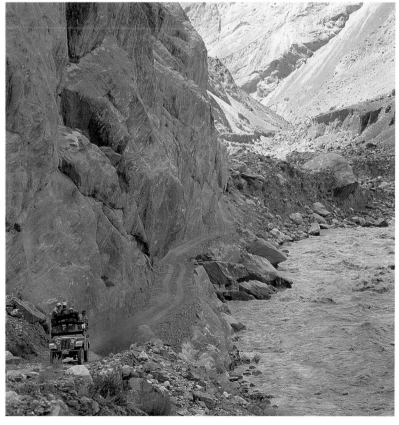

ABOVE *Camp on the Baltoro at Concordia, with Crystal Peak and Marble Peak on the left, and the monstrous pyramid of K2 distant up the Godwin-Austen Glacier.*
RIGHT *A jeep makes its way along the newly dynamited but often impassable road through the Braldu Gorge between Dassu and Chongo.*

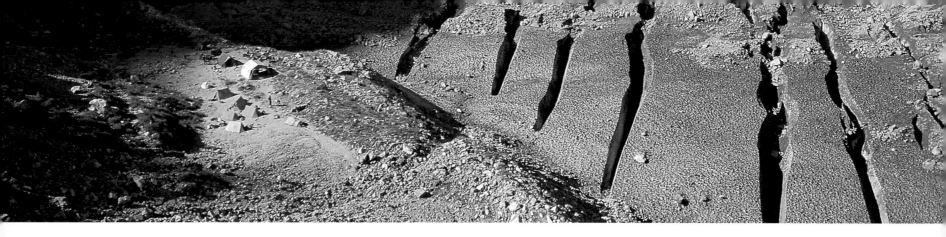

BIAFO–HISPAR TRAVERSE

by Steve Razzetti

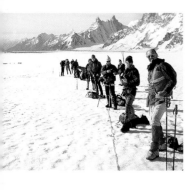

K2 and the host of other mighty peaks surrounding the upper Baltoro Glacier have long attracted the attention of the world's leading explorers and mountaineers, but one other enigma of the Central Karakoram had geographers guessing as to its true identity well into the 20th century. Lukpe Lawo, or 'Snow Lake', the vast névé basin from which the Biafo and Hispar glaciers radiate, embodies perhaps more than any of the region's magnificent mountains all that is unique about the Karakoram.

Cutting an enormous swathe through the heart of the Central Karakoram, the Biafo–Hispar forms one of the longest continuous expanses of glacial ice outside of the polar regions – a total of almost 130km (80 miles). Snow Lake was for years believed to be a genuine ice-cap, and many fantastic legends grew around it before its true nature was established. The first explorer to set eyes on the Biafo Glacier was a British sportsman by the name of H Falconer in 1838, while Henry Haversham Godwin-Austen discovered the Hispar when he reached the crest of the Nushik La from the south in 1861. However, the real extent of this glacial superhighway was not realized until Englishman Sir Martin Conway's expedition 31 years later.

Conway made the first crossing of the Hispar Pass (5151m; 16,900ft) on 18 July 1892. Though he also traversed the Biafo Glacier to Askole, he did not attempt to survey Snow Lake. This omission, and his tantalizing descriptions of the place, enticed an American couple whose names will forever be associated with the early exploration of the area. Fanny Bullock Workman and her husband William Hunter Workman devot-

ed themselves to the Karakoram. Between 1898 and 1908 they made no less than seven major expeditions to the region, and published many lavishly illustrated books and articles about their travels. In 1908, they followed Conway over the Hispar Pass, from which Fanny made her famous ascent of Workman Peak and estimated the area of Snow Lake to be in excess of 700 square kilometres (435 square miles).

Only in 1939, on the brink of the outbreak of World War II, was this enormous glacial wilderness accurately surveyed, during a phenomenal expedition that represented the climax of the career of Britain's most celebrated and accomplished mountain explorer. During the second of his epic trips to the Karakoram, Eric Shipton and his colleagues conducted a survey that was to produce a map of extraordinary accuracy. This work was to be the opening phase of a mammoth 16-month mountain odyssey, but even in the most remote Karakoram, momentous events cannot be ignored by men of the world. The party had split into several units for the purpose of conducting their work, and, approaching a prearranged rendezvous on Snow Lake, Shipton recounted: 'When at last we were within earshot, Russell shouted out the

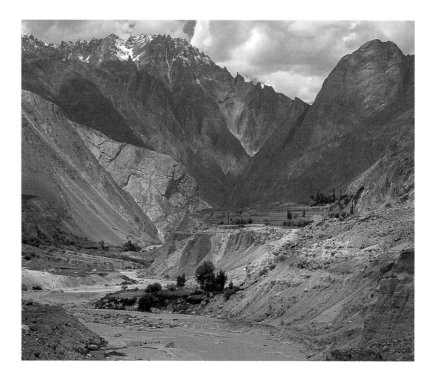

TOP *A bird's-eye view of Namla, the first camp on the ascent of the Biafo from Askole. As the summer progresses, the crevasses widen into yawning chasms.*

INSET *Trekking group roped together on the upper Biafo Glacier, where the sheer scale of the landscape is almost overwhelming.*

RIGHT *The irrigated fields of Askole village stand out in verdant contrast against the barren splendour of Braldu Valley, with the entrance to Braldu Gorge in the distance.*

OPPOSITE *Travelling unroped above the snowline should not be contemplated. However, when travelling with just one companion and unsupported, it may be the safest option.*

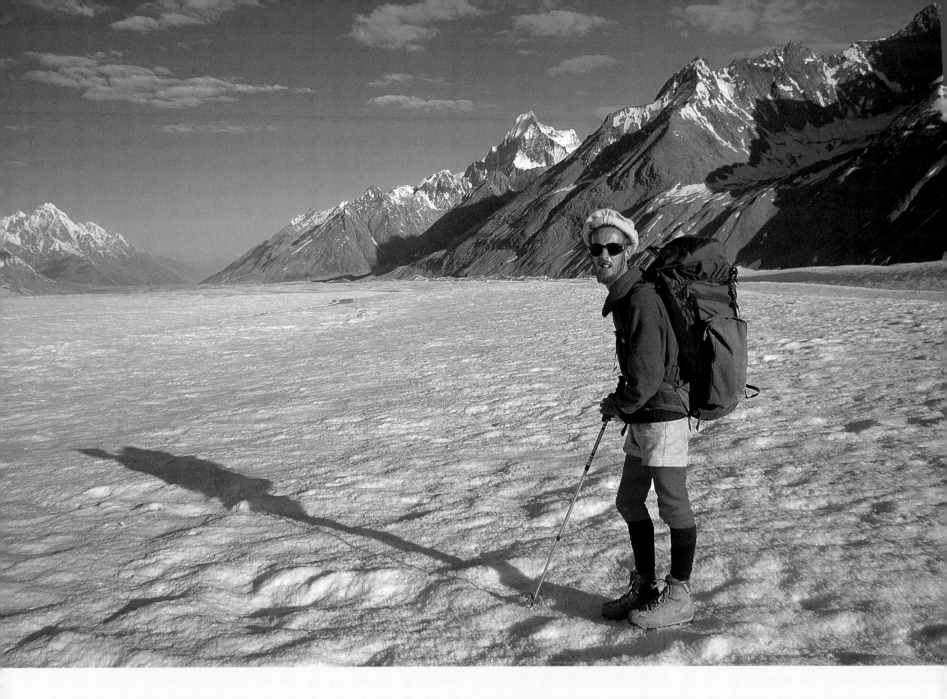

LOCATION Central Karakoram, Pakistan.

WHEN TO GO June to September.

START Askole village. International flights to Karachi or Islamabad, then by air (1hr) or road (KKH, 18–30 hrs) to Skardu. Overnight there, then to Askole by jeep (6–10hrs).

FINISH Nagar village. Jeep to Karimabad (on the KKH in the Hunza Valley), then by bus or jeep to Gilgit (3–4hrs). Gilgit–Islamabad by bus (14–18hrs) or air (45mins).

DURATION 14–20 days, depending on side trips, pace and weather.

MAXIMUM ALTITUDE Hispar Pass (5151m; 16,900ft).

TECHNICAL CONSIDERATIONS Party must consist of proficient glacier travellers and be equipped for both roped glacier travel and crevasse rescue.

EQUIPMENT Harness and glacier travel/rescue equipment.

TREKKING STYLE Expedition. Self-sufficient all the way.

PERMITS/RESTRICTIONS Open zone, no permits required.

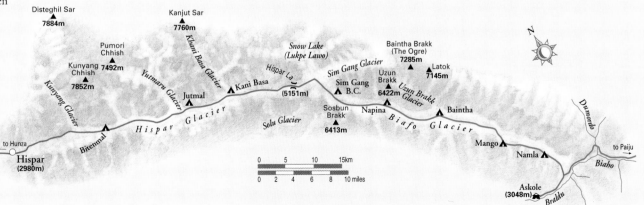

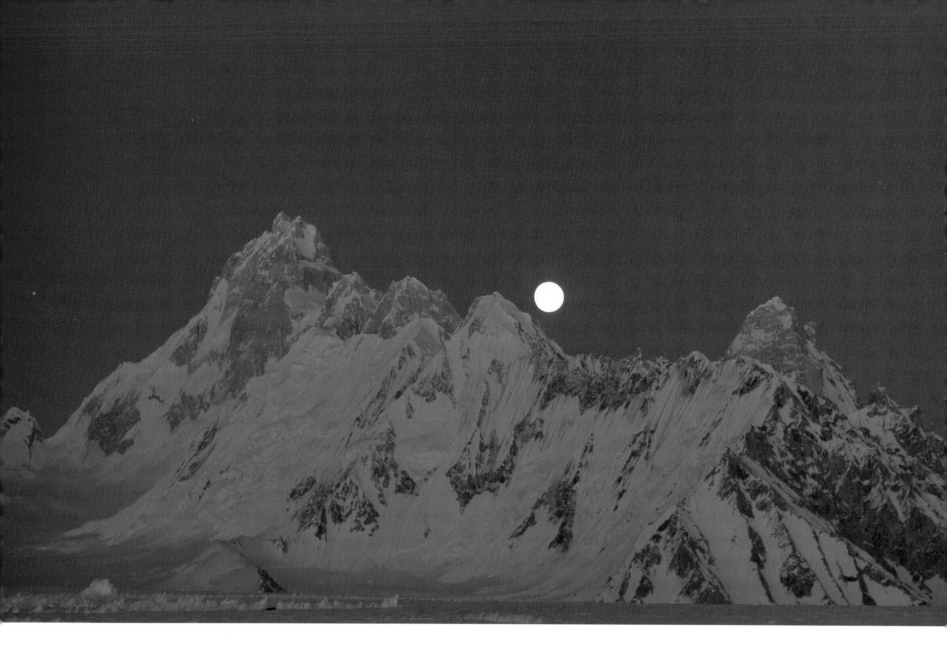

ABOVE *The full moon rising behind The Ogre's fearsome north face, as seen from a camp on the crest of the Hispar Pass. On the right is Uzun Brakk, or 'Conway's Ogre'.*
BELOW *View down towards the Braldu Valley, Mango and Namla across the ablation zone at Baintha on the Biafo Glacier.*

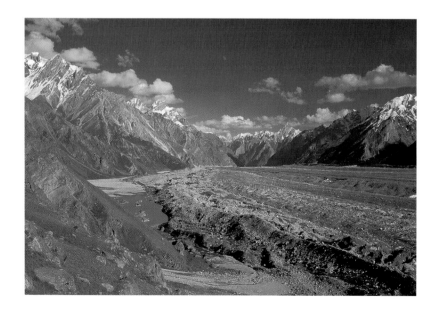

shattering news that England was at war with Germany. He had heard it on the tiny wireless receiving set we had brought to get time signals for our astronomical work. It was hard to realize the meaning of the disaster. Perhaps the London where we had planned this very venture was a chaos of destruction and terror. How fantastic, how supremely ridiculous it seemed in our remote and lovely world of snow and ice. As if to point the contrast, the mists cleared and for a moment the glacier was bathed in a sunset glow reflected from the high peaks. The great granite spires of the Biafo stood black against a deep blue sky. At least this mountain world, to which I owed so much of life and happiness, would stand above the ruin of human hopes, the heritage of a saner generation of men.'

For half a century the lonesome bears and snow-leopards of the Biafo–Hispar then had the place almost completely to themselves, watching the occasional mountaineering expedition that came to scale the pinnacles and spires lining these glaciers from solitary vantage points amid a vast mountain landscape. Facts and figures attest to glacial magnitude but utterly fail to convey the impact of the place in human terms. Shipton's survey revealed the area of Snow Lake to be but a tenth of that posited by the Workmans, but nevertheless where the Biafo flows south out of Snow Lake it is nearly 5km (3 miles) wide, a 1000m (3300ft) deep and moves over 100m (330ft) a year. Its cavernous crevasses could swallow entire apartment blocks.

Even today, with air services to Gilgit and Skardu and rough jeep tracks snaking their tentative way into the range's wild and desolate valleys, the Karakoram are a difficult proposition for those seeking to travel or climb there. However, the route from Askole to Nagar has been widely acknowledged as the quintessential Karakoram traverse.

Departing from the approach to K2 just beyond Askole, this challenging trek does not pass another human settlement until the penultimate day, when it reaches the village of Hispar. Leaving the comparatively busy mountaineers' trail up the Braldu Valley, it turns northwest onto the boulder-strewn lower reaches of the Biafo and instantly enters another world. The tip of this glacier, like all the major ice flows of the Karakoram, is hidden beneath the enormous mass of debris transported from above, and protrudes into the Braldu Valley to such an extent that it almost blocks it. In only a few places is the blackened, pock-marked and rapidly melting ice visible beneath the gravel and rocks, and walking on the surface is a tortuous and energy-consuming business at first. Only on the third day, as the route crosses to the northern flank, does a streak of white, clean ice appear in the centre and the going becomes easier.

Ahead, from very early on in the ascent of the Biafo, a spectacular array of enormous snow-capped peaks appears on the horizon, luring the traveller onward. These are the Latoks and Baintha Brakk, given the ominous sobriquet 'The Ogre' by Sir Martin Conway. From the third-stage camp at Baintha, an easy climb can be made to the summit of Baintha Peak (5100m; 16,700ft) for panoramic views of the magnificent mountain architecture that lines the upper Biafo and its tributary, the Uzun Brakk. From the gently angled slopes above this camp, where a rest day is almost mandatory

so that your porters can bake bread and feed themselves up for the rigours ahead, the full extent of The Ogre's formidable defences is revealed. The epic first ascent of this desperately difficult mountain was made in 1977 by British mountaineers Doug Scott, Chris Bonington and Mo Antoine, and it has never been repeated.

However dramatic the perspective on the south face of The Ogre may be from above Baintha, it is surpassed by that on the north face from the Hispar Pass itself where, given good weather, a camp should be made. A more sensational location could not be imagined, as the angle of the seemingly interminable snow slopes that lead up to the pass gradually eases and imperceptibly the ground begins to descend again to the west. To the east, the vast whiteness of the Sim Gang Basin and Snow Lake are surrounded by a host of perpendicular peaks, over which the shadowy north face of The Ogre broods like a menacing spectre.

Both sunrise and sunset from this bird's-eye viewpoint can only be described as mind-blowing, yet unbelievably, the biggest mountains are still to come. The Hispar is a more difficult glacier than the Biafo, and its enormous northern tributaries descend from an unbroken mountain chain that includes the summits of Kanjut Sar, Disteghil Sar, Pumori Chhish and Kunyang Chhish, all well over 7000m (23,000ft). By the time you join the tourists relaxing in the comfortable hotels of Karimabad in Hunza you will surely have earned your Karakoram stripes.

BELOW *Crossing the Kani Basa Glacier, the first of four major tributaries of the Hispar that have to be negotiated on this route.*

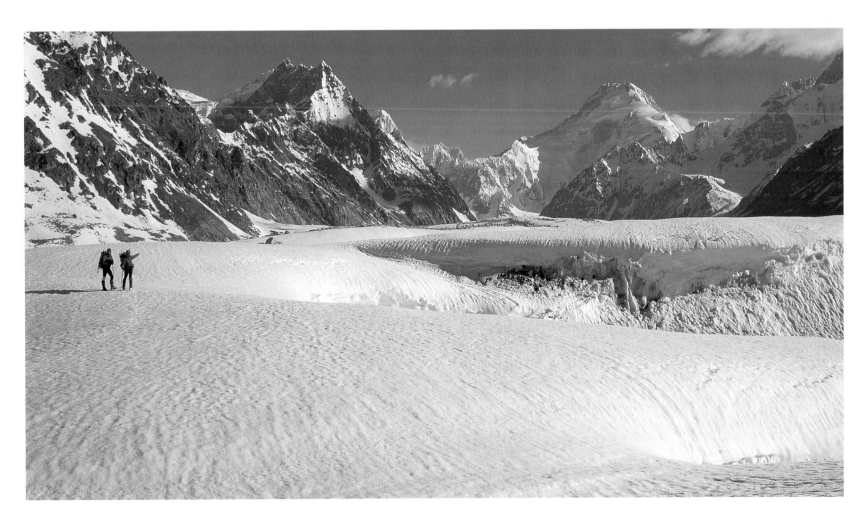

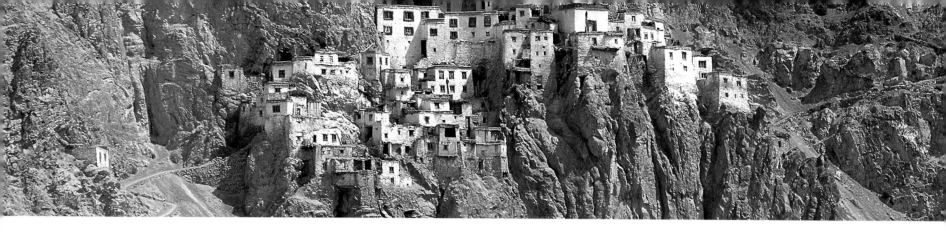

LADAKH & ZANSKAR

by Steve Razzetti

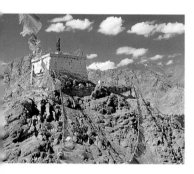

Zanskar and Ladakh are the most remote of all India's Himalayan domains. Secreted among rugged, torrent-filled defiles and stark, barren mountains, the precious patchworks of irrigated fields that surround scattered villages throughout the region appear like vibrant emerald jewels set in a desolate crown of thorns. Perched atop unlikely spurs and cliffs, often commanding breathtaking views of the surrounding countryside, numerous Buddhist monasteries or *gompahs* add splashes of brilliant white to the soaring browns and greys of the scene. With a landscape that frequently elicits comparisons with the moon, the high mountain deserts of Ladakh are not everyone's idea of bliss, but the area certainly has a powerful and undeniable magic.

Bounded in the north and east by the Karakoram and Kailas ranges and in the south by the Great Himalaya, the Ladakh and Zanskar ranges do not attain the great heights of their neighbours. They are, however, just as complex and contain sufficient summits in excess of 6000m (19,600ft) to catch heavy winter snowfall. Being north of the Himalayan rain shadow, Ladakh and Zanskar are not afflicted by

the monsoon, but under the fierce summer sun the high snowfields and glaciers melt rapidly, turning the rivers below into raging torrents. Many of the valleys become impassable for this reason, and the major trails often surmount huge ridges in order to avoid dangerous gorges. The name Ladakh means 'land of the passes', and summer trekking here often involves hair-raising river crossings, especially on the less frequented routes.

The history of Ladakh is one of conquest and acquisition, with rulers constantly having to fend off Tibetan and Kashmiri designs on their territory. Due to its rich and vigorous Buddhist cultural heritage, Ladakh is often referred to as Little Tibet, but in truth it has never been ruled by the Dalai Lama in Lhasa. The forcible conversion of neighbouring Kashmir to Islam in the 13th century effectively brought the separate kingdoms of Ladakh and Zanskar closer together, and the zenith of Ladakh's power came in the 17th century, at the beginning of which the king, Senge Namgyal, built the Potala-like palace at Leh. Zanskar has effectively been a dependency since that time.

The first European to reach Ladakh was a Portuguese layman by the name of Diogo d'Almiera, who spent two years in the vicinity around the year 1600. He was followed, briefly, by the Jesuit priests Francesco de Azavedo and Giovanni de Oliviero in 1631, and by Ipolito Desideri in 1715 during his mammoth journey from Srinagar to Lhasa. Another century passed before the influence of the British East India Company reached Leh, in the persons of William Moorcroft and George Trebeck. They found the Ladakhi authorities most suspicious of their motives, and in his narrative of events Moorcroft relates how the *Khalun* (king) of Ladakh had heard that 'it was the practice of the English to appear at first in the guise of merchants, merely to gain a footing in the country, and

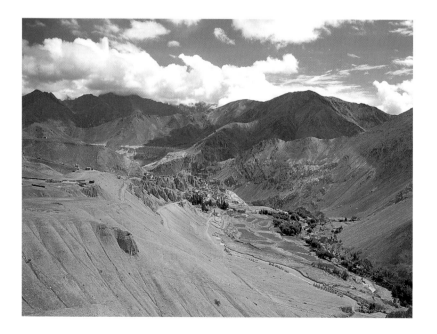

TOP *The maze of monks' quarters and temples that makes up Phuktal Gompah, clinging to the sheer cliffs above the Biri Chhu.*

INSET *Prayer flags at a gompah in the Indus valley near Leh.*

BOTTOM LEFT *There has been a monastery at Lamayuru since the 10th century. Once a major staging post on the Srinagar–Leh caravan route and home to over 200 monks, it now houses only 30 and is the starting point for the trek south across Zanskar.*

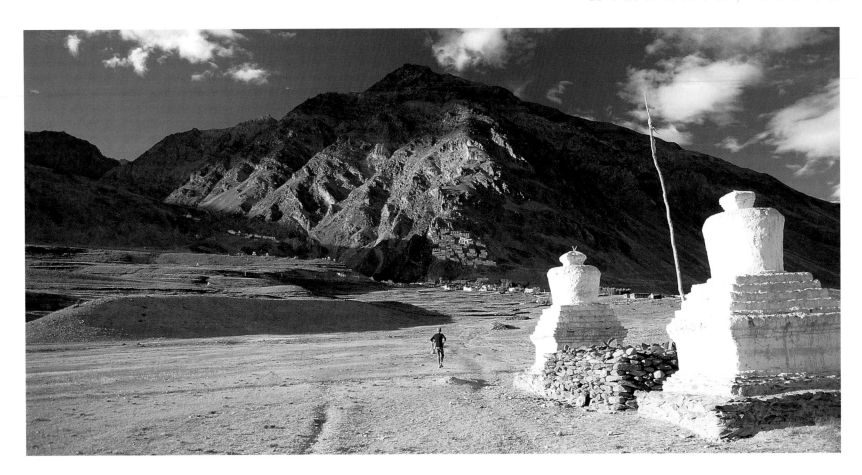

that, having effected this, they speedily brought it under their authority.' Barely two decades elapsed before the *Khalun's* apprehensions were borne out.

Western interest in the history of Zanskar began with a chance meeting between an Englishman and a Hungarian on the caravan route between Srinagar and Leh, in 1822. William Moorcroft was travelling under the auspices of the East India Company, while Alexander De Körös was returning from Leh having failed to get further towards Yarkand in his quest to discover the origins of the Hungarians. Moorcroft aroused De Körös' interest in things Tibetan, and in June 1823 the latter arrived in Zanskar where he spent 16 months compiling a Tibetan grammar for the British Government.

Ladakh may be remote, but Zanskar is both remote and almost inaccessible. Translated from the Tibetan *Zangs-dkar* (white copper), after the precious mineral found in this area, the territory consists essentially of lands drained by the two major tributaries of the Zanskar River, and covers 4800 square kilometres (3000 sqaure miles) of extremely mountainous terrain at an average elevation of 4000m (13,000ft).

Before the coming of the rough road into Zanskar from Kargil on the Srinagar–Leh 'Beacon Highway', Padum, the tiny capital, was effectively cut off from the outside world for most of the year. Zanskar's isolation and obscurity have served to preserve it as a rare enclave of untrammelled Tibetan culture, carrying its rich

ABOVE *The whitewashed walls of Karsha Gompah cling to the rocks above the Zanskar River opposite Padum. The largest monastery in Zanskar, it is home to 150* gelug-pa *or yellow-hat monks and is overseen by the Dalai Lama's younger brother.*

BELOW, LEFT TO RIGHT *A group of Ladakhi ladies at the Hemis festival, Ladakh; the magnificent new Maitreya or Future Buddha statue at Thikse Gompah; a masked participant in the ritual dances of the Hemis festival.*

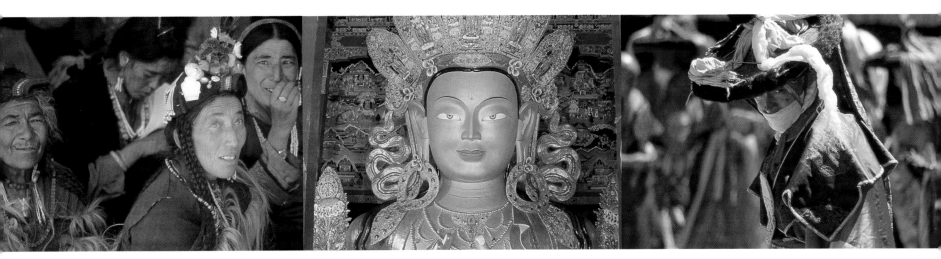

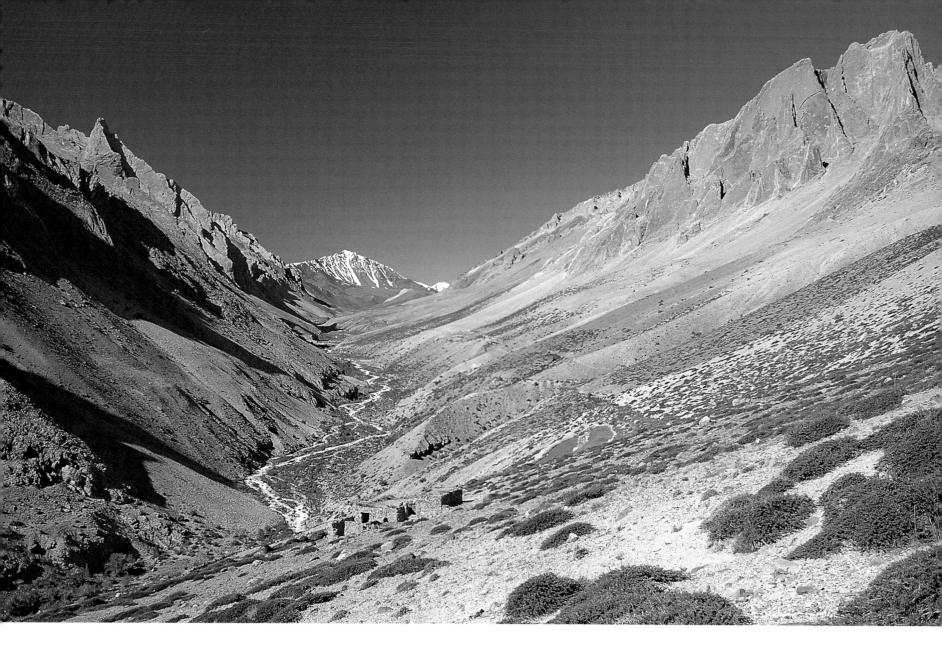

heritage of Tantric Buddhism into the 21st century largely intact. The monasteries tucked away among the arid mountainfolds of the country are living examples of an ancient tradition that has been violently obliterated in its Tibetan homeland.

The mountains and valleys of Ladakh and Zanskar are bisected by a complex network of trails and passes, making the area a paradise for trekkers prepared to ad-lib with their itineraries. Tourists may wander the open areas without permits or other bureaucratic hindrance, but the sparse population and barren land make self-sufficient travel essential. Many fine itineraries can be undertaken, tailored according to a party's level of fitness and interest in Buddhist culture, but if there is one outing that combines the best of both mountain scenery and monastic splendour it is surely the traverse of Zanskar from Lamayuru to Darcha. Very few treks offer the combined attractions of sustained cultural interest and scenic diversity over such a long and challenging walk.

The walk begins beneath the fantastic spectacle of Lamayuru, where the monastery's superbly preserved medieval buildings sit perched astride a spur, amid a bizarre and alien landscape of wind-eroded hillsides and sculpted cliffs. Today, the trail bypasses both the village and the monastery, but one can still follow the ancient caravan route a way up on foot past crumbling *mane* walls towards the Fatu La from the monastery. The trail to Zanskar leaves Lamayuru down-valley, before sneaking off south up a

ABOVE *Ruins of a settlement in the Spantang Valley, en route to the Sirsir La from Hanupatta, are evidence of more prosperous times in the area's past.*

dry, stony defile towards the Prinkiti La, the first of eight passes between Lamayuru and Padum. Allow at least 10 days to complete this section and be prepared for plenty of tough climbs and knee-crunching descents. Local guides are strongly recommended as trails and bridges are frequently washed out. Available mapping is highly inaccurate and up-to-date route information is essential. Highlights of this walk into Zanskar are undoubtedly the fabulous monastery at Lingshot and the view from the Sini La at 5060m (16,600ft). Immediately to the east of the col is a dramatic rocky peak, but it is the vistas back north to the previous pass, the Sirsir La, and ahead towards Lingshot that really take the breath away.

Finally, from the Purfi La, the Zanskar Valley is revealed, and from a point just below the crest on the descent there is an awesome view into the formidable gorges through which the Zanskar River escapes north towards the Indus and Ladakh. During the long winter months, when the passes are closed, it is along the frozen surface of this huge river that the Zanskaris tentatively lead their yaks on trading trips to Leh.

The pace of life in Padum has picked up considerably with the coming of the road, but it is still a sleepy, dusty backwater. There are several very important monasteries

LOCATION Ladakh Himalaya, Jammu and Kashmir and Himachal Pradesh, India.

WHEN TO GO June to November. Like the Karakoram in Pakistan, the Ladakh and Zanskar ranges are mountain deserts that lie in the 'rain shadow' of the main Himalayan Range, and are barely affected by the summer monsoon.

START Lamayuru Gompah; international flights to New Delhi, then by air (1hr) or road (3 days) to Leh. Local transport (jeep or bus) to Lamayuru takes half a day.

FINISH Darcha; local bus to Manali (10hrs). Then either by road to Delhi (18hrs) or to Kulu by road (3hrs) and by air to Delhi (1hr). Alternatively, travel to Chandigar by road (8hrs) and on to Delhi by air (35mins). Note: the road conditions from Chandigar to Delhi are extremely dangerous.

DURATION 23 days minimum.

MAXIMUM ALTITUDE Shin-Kun La (5096m; 16,720ft) or Phirtse La (5250m; 17,225ft).

TECHNICAL CONSIDERATIONS None.

EQUIPMENT Self-sufficiency in accommodation, food and fuel strongly advised. Pack in strong duffles. Pack ponies are used on this route.

TREKKING STYLE Backpacking or expedition. Local accommodation is also possible, but unsophisticated and unsanitary.

PERMITS/RESTRICTIONS No permits required.

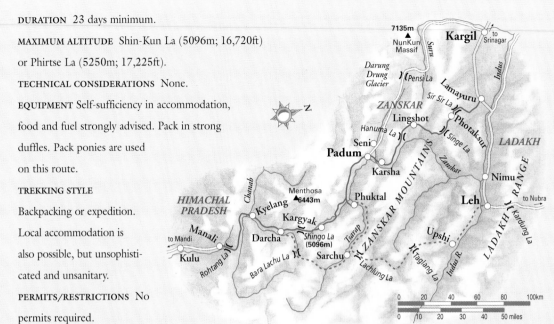

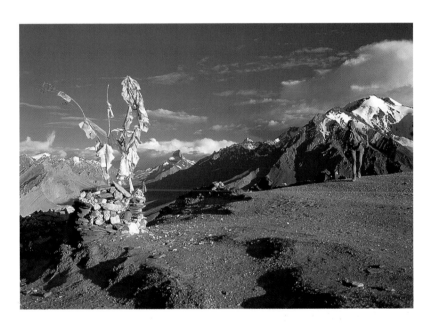

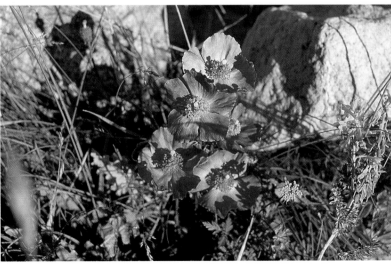

in the vicinity, however, making a couple of days' rest here more than worthwhile. Opposite the town on an incredibly steep hillside sits Karsha, the largest *gompah* in Zanskar and home to 150 monks. The lower *labrang* (assembly hall) is dark and unused today, but a torch reveals the crumbling walls, covered with exquisite frescoes and murals that are almost 1000 years old.

Padum is situated at the confluence of the two major tributaries of the Zanskar River, the Doda and Tsarap Chhu's, and the trail south to Darcha and Lahaul via the Shingo La initially follows the latter. Allow a minimum of seven days to reach Darcha. Compared to the intricate ridges and deep gorges traversed on the first half of the route, this section passes through enormous, sweeping landscapes of windswept plains and isolated farmsteads. Though it involves a short diversion into the valley of the Biri Chhu, on no account should a visit to Phuktal Gompah should not be missed. A more dramatic setting for a monastery could not be found. The whitewashed buildings appear to cascade out of an enormous cave high above the roaring waters of the river.

The last village in Zanskar is Kargyak, and south of this hamlet of 20-odd houses the trail passes beneath the Gumbarajon, a magnificent monolith of rock over 1000m (3300ft) high that would not look out of place in Yosemite. Beyond lies the Shingo La (5096m; 16,720ft), the only pass to be crossed between Padum and Darcha. This col may be snow-covered at any time of year, and the steep five-hour descent to the tiny campsite at Ramjak will make you thankful you chose to complete the route in this direction.

TOP LEFT *Late afternoon light casts the surrounding hills into gorgeous relief from the crest of the Sirsir La.*

LEFT *Several species of the Himalayan blue poppy grow in Ladakh and Zanskar, bringing a vivid splash of colour to the mountain deserts in late summer.*

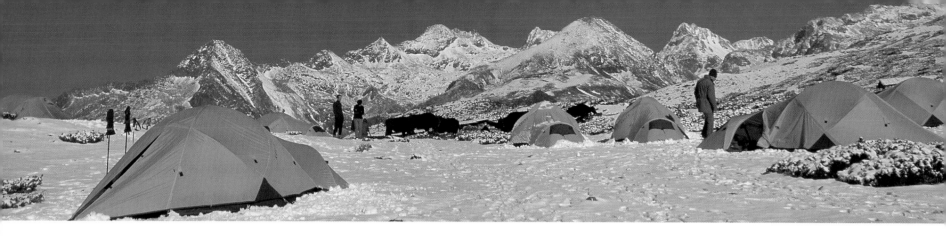

SINGALILA TO KANGCHENDZONGA

by Steve Razzetti

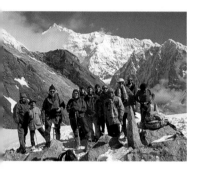

While the Nepal Himalaya and Tibet were off-limits to European explorers throughout the 19th century and for much of the 20th, the reverse was true of the Sikkim Himalaya. The delineation of the present boundaries of this tiny principality was determined by a treaty with the British in 1861, bringing to an end almost 200 years of invasions and uncertainty during which the country was overrun by both the Bhutanese and the Nepalese.

In 1888 an attempted invasion by the Tibetans, rebuffed with the assistance of a force dispatched by the government of India, finally precipitated the establishment of Sikkim as a protected Native State. It has been a part of India ever since. In geographical terms, the country may accurately be described as the catchment area for the Teesta River, bounded in the west by Kangchendzonga and the Singalila Ridge, and in the east by Pauhunri and the Donkya Ridge.

The first European to really explore the mountains of Sikkim was Major LA Waddell. Between 1888 and 1896, he made various journeys and actually crossed the Singalila Ridge via the Kang La to visit the Yalung Glacier. However, the development of Sikkim as a playground for the sportsmen of the Victorian Raj was largely due to one man. Claude White was appointed as the first Political Officer of Sikkim after accompanying the force sent to repel the Tibetans in 1888. It was White who first crossed the Goecha La from Dzong Ri to the Talung Glacier in 1890, explored the gorges between Pandim and Simvu and completed his journey with a trek out down the Talung River.

By the 1930s, Sikkim was firmly established as a favourite haunt for British mountaineers and naturalists. Government officials from Calcutta flocked to the hill stations of Darjeeling and Kalimpong to escape the oppressive heat and humidity of the Indian

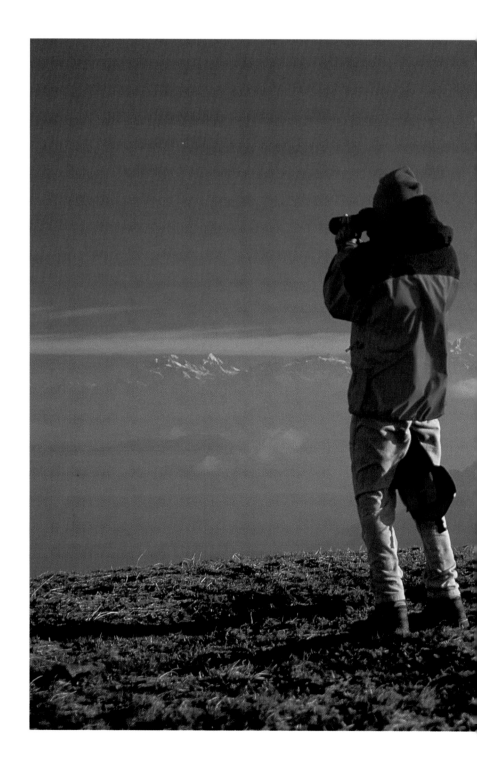

TOP *The peaks of the upper Singalila Ridge – Kokthang, Rathong and Kabru – seen from the camp at Dzong Ri in Sikkim.*

INSET *The climax of this trip – a trekking group on the Goecha La beneath the east face of Kangchendzonga.*

RIGHT *Looking towards Kangchendzonga and Jannu early in the morning from above Phalut on the Singalila Ridge.*

monsoon, and touring the mountain districts of Sikkim was definitely *en vogue*. The journals of the Alpine and Himalayan Clubs were crammed with accounts of exploits as Sikkim rapidly became one of the best known of all the Himalayan districts.

The Indian government today no longer grants foreigners quite as much freedom to roam these hills. Few places in the Himalaya require as much bureaucratic procedure to obtain the necessary permits, but trekkers should not be discouraged. The route affords magnificent perspectives on the peaks of the Singalila Ridge, Pandim and the east face of Kangchendzonga and reaches the heart of the Sikkim Himalaya.

Until 1999, the five-day hike to the Goecha La (4800m; 15,700ft) from the village of Yoksum was usually preceded by a gentle three- to four-day stroll along the Sandakphu section of the Singalila Ridge between Mani Banjang and Phalut, and an overnight stay at the town of Pemayangtse. Thus two short but very enjoy-able treks were interspersed with a couple of days' road travel and a night in a hotel. The second half of the trek commenced with a slither along leech-infested forest trails in the deep gorge of the Rathong Chhu, followed by the ascent of a steep and seemingly interminable ridge dividing the valleys of the Churong Chhu and Prek Chhu rivers. Emerging from the trees at Dzong Ri, trekkers were confronted with a mountain vista as breathtaking as any in the entire Himalaya. Ahead, the pyramid form of the Kangchendzonga towers over an intervening ridge. To the west are Kokthang, Rathong and Kabru, the magnificent peaks forming the northern part of the Singalila Ridge, rising towards their master in a series of spectacular snowy steps.

Miraculously, in the spring of 2000, the Indian authorities announced the opening of the previously off-limits section of the Singalila Ridge between Phalut and Dzong Ri. The frustration of being forced to divert from the spectacular

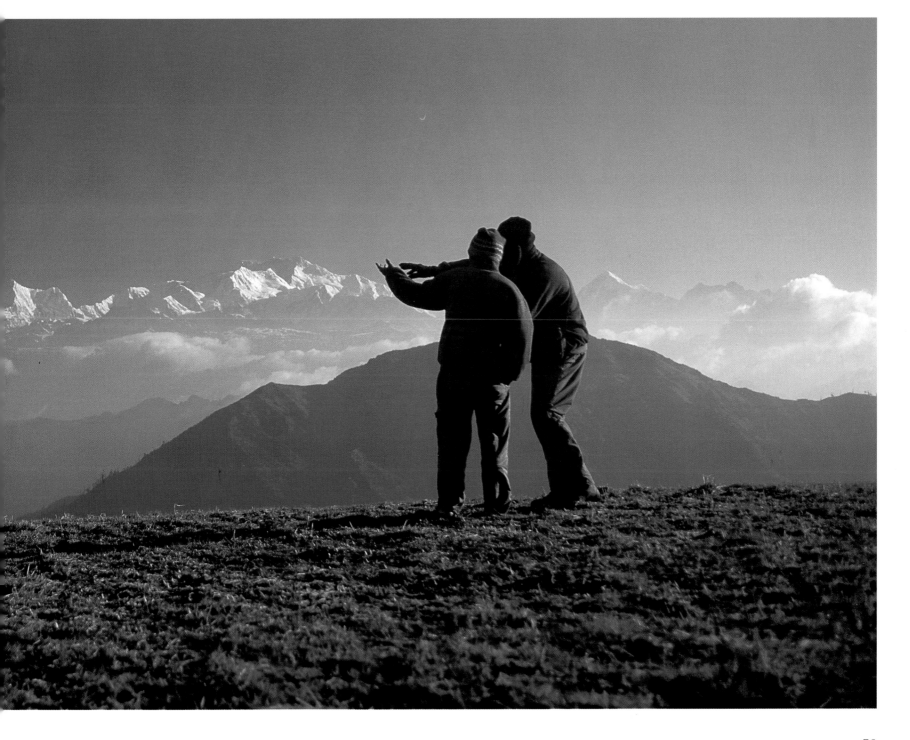

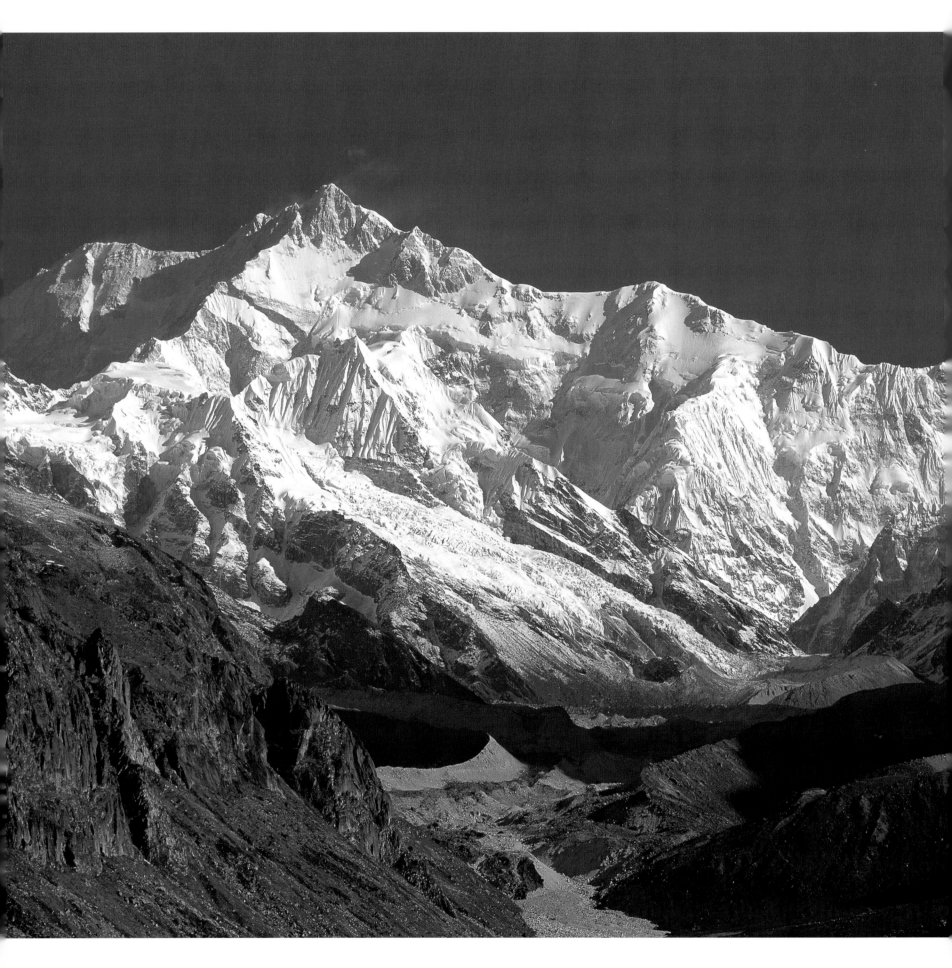

ABOVE *Under a blanket of snow, the awe-inspiring pyramids of the east face of Kangchendzonga beckon from Thanshing, Sikkim.*

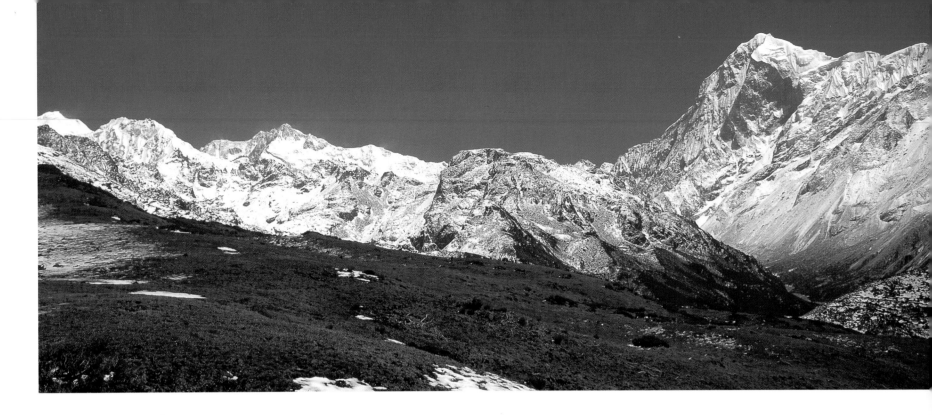

ridge-walk at Phalut no longer has to be endured. The entire walk from Mani Banjang to the Goecha La via Dzong Ri can now be completed in a sensational 15-day hike, before backtracking for a couple of days and finishing with the descent to Yuksom.

In spring, the Singalila Ridge yields only occasional tantalizing glimpses of the glistening white giants ahead, as the trail along its crest heads north through swirling mists and dense cloud forest and crosses entire mountainsides cloaked with enormous azaleas and rhododendrons in full bloom. Exotic orchids flower in dripping grottoes while luxuriant ferns cloak the ground beneath the trees in a dense tapestry of green. Eventually, however, the ridge has to be abandoned as the trail to Dzong Ri and Kangchendzonga plunges down to cross the Churong Chhu.

From the camp at Dzong Ri, under the brooding east face of Kangchendzonga, one can gaze into the tantalizing forbidden valley that leads immediately west to the Kang La and Nepal. To the north, the Prek Chhu cuts a spectacular cleft hard beneath the jagged ramparts of Pandim (6691m; 21,953ft) and thence to the Goecha La. Standing on this snowy col three days later, most visitors will lament the modern political constraints that preclude a more complete tour of the sensational Sikkim Himalaya.

ABOVE *From Dzong Ri, the approach to Kangchendzonga descends into the valley of the Prek Chhu and passes beneath the west face of Pandim.*

LOCATION Sikkim Himalaya, India.

WHEN TO GO March to May or September to December.

START Mani Banjang; international flight to Delhi, Bombay or Calcutta, then by train, bus or plane to Bagdogra (West Bengal) and up to Darjeeling by toy train, bus or jeep. Overnight in Darjeeling, then by road (4hrs) to Mani Banjang.

FINISH Yuksom; jeep or bus to Kalimpong or Darjeeling, then on to Bagdogra for rail, road and air links to Delhi, Bombay or Calcutta. Note: Land crossing into Western Nepal is also possible from Darjeeling.

DURATION 18 days.

MAXIMUM ALTITUDE Goecha La (4800m; 15,700ft).

TECHNICAL CONSIDERATIONS After snowfall, the Goecha La may not be reachable without an ice axe at least.

EQUIPMENT Need to be self-sufficient throughout.

TREKKING STYLE Backpacking or expedition. Some lodges available on the Singalila Ridge between Mani Banjang and Phalut, although no food.

PERMITS/RESTRICTIONS Trip may not be done independently; must hire local guide or agent. Permit for Phalut Dzong Ri section only available at tourist office in Gangtok. No fee for permits, but fees for yaks, porters, cameras and tents on a per day basis for trekking.

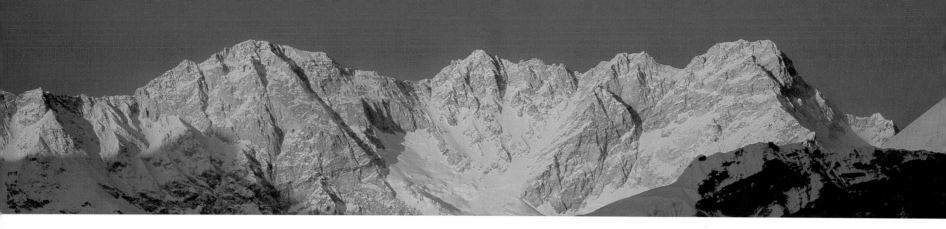

KANGCHENDZONGA

by Steve Razzetti

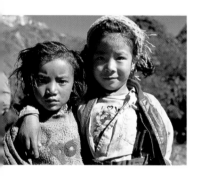

Hope Leezum Namgyal, crown princess of Sikkim, was adamant. Seeing my notes pertaining to our travels to Kanchenjunga she exclaimed, 'You cannot write the name like that! It means nothing! The mountain's true appellation is the Tibetan "Kang-Chen-Dzong-Nga", which translates as "Peak of the Five Great Treasuries of the Snows". As a matter of politeness we do not anglicize the names of mountains in Wales or Scotland, so why should you those of Sikkim and Tibet?' Kangchendzonga it is then!

Separated from the great peaks of the Khosi section of the Nepal Himalaya by the mightiest of all the country's trans-Himalayan rivers, the Arun, Kangchendzonga is often referred to as part of the Sikkim Himalaya. Unlike the other major summits of the Great Himalaya, Kangchendzonga does not merely lie on the crest of a ridge-system running east–west, but forms the centre of a giant cross, whose formidable lines radiate east, west, north and south from its 8598m (28,210ft) apex. Just 13m (43ft) short of K2, it is the third highest mountain in the world.

The western arm of this monumental intersection terminates at the summit of Jannu, itself one of the most spectacular peaks in the entire Himalaya, while the eastern arm descends to the Zemu Gap in Sikkim. To the south, the Singalila Ridge extends for a further 80km (50 miles), forming the border between Nepal and Sikkim. To the north, a complex and inaccessible chain of summits terminates at Jongsang Peak and the border with Tibet. Rising directly from the plains of India, the Kangchendzonga massif lies east of the protective barrier of the Siwalik Hills, which serves to trap the incoming monsoon clouds before they can unleash their deluge on the rest of the Nepal Himalaya. Consequently, these mountains receive

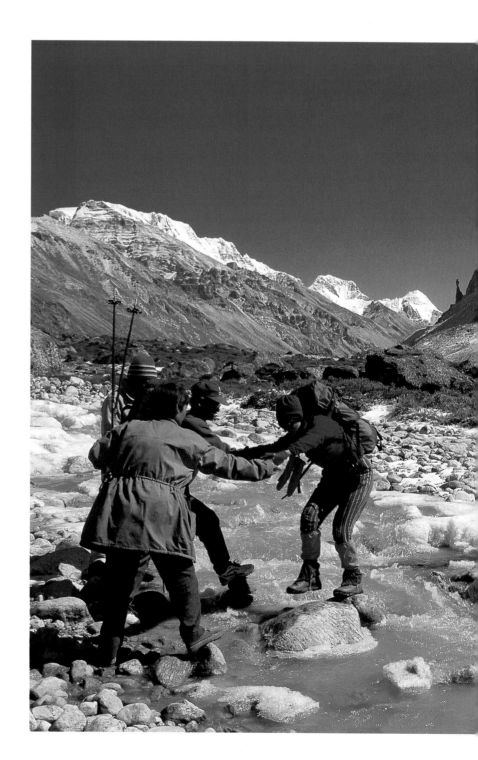

TOP *Sunset light on the south face of Kangchendzonga viewed from the lonely shrine at Oktang on the Yalung Glacier.*

INSET *Young bhotia girls at Phole village in the valley of the Ghunsa Khola. The Tibetan upper reaches of this valley were once part of neighbouring Sikkim.*

RIGHT *Stepping across a stream in the ablation valley on the northern flank of the Kangchendzonga Glacier at Ramtang. The rocks are completely encrusted with ice.*

the highest precipitation in Nepal, their summits adorned with phenomenal snow formations, while the valleys below are cloaked in unbelievably dense and lush jungle.

Clearly visible from the popular hill station of Darjeeling in West Bengal, Kangchendzonga attracted the attention of explorers long before the rest of Nepal. To this town, the sportsmen, loungers and ladies of the Raj fled to escape the oppressive heat and humidity of Calcutta. Nepal and Tibet were both forbidden to foreigners during the 19th century, and the first travellers to penetrate their borders did so clandestinely and at considerable risk to themselves and their local guides.

The first explorer to visit the Nepal side of Kangchendzonga was British botanist, Sir Joseph Hooker. His reports, published under the title *Himalayan Journals*, caught the attention of the Royal Geographical Society and the Survey of India, and the latter dispatched the *pundits* Sarat Chandra Das and Rinzin Namgyal to find out

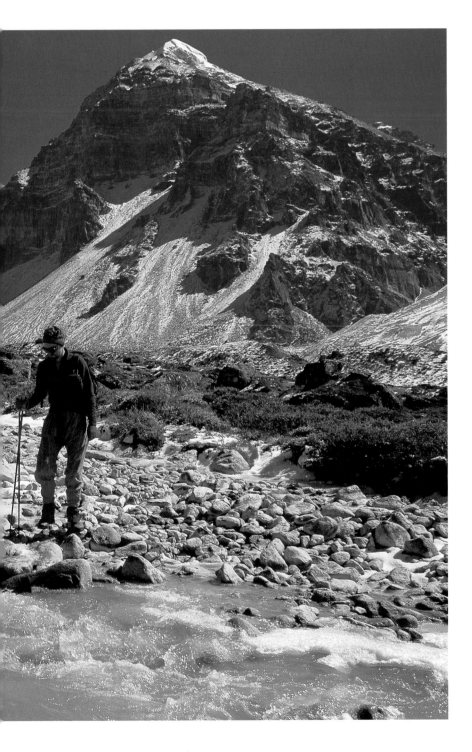

more. Chandra Das made two journeys into Nepal, one in 1879 and another in 1881, entering on each occasion across Singalila Ridge via the Kang La but crossing into Tibet via the Jongsang La in 1879 and the Nago La in 1881. In 1883, Rinzin Namgyal also entered Nepal across the Kang La from Sikkim and explored the upper reaches of the Yalung Glacier before retracing his predecessor's footsteps over the Jongsang La.

In 1899, it was Rinzin Namgyal whom the Englishman Douglas Freshfield chose to accompany his multinational party on what was undeniably the most important expedition in the history of Kangchendzonga. Setting off from Darjeeling, their aim was to circumambulate the entire massif. Accompanied by celebrated mountain photographer Vittoria Sella, his brother Erminio, mountain guide Angelo Maquignaz, Professor Edmund Garwood and Mr Dover, the Road Inspector of Independent Sikkim, the party initially followed Rinzin's journey of 1883 in reverse, entering Nepal across the Jongsang La. From here they proceeded down to the remote settlement of Ghunsa where, to their surprise, the inhabitants were not the slightest bit taken aback to find a party of 'palefaces' in their midst.

Continuing eastwards from the village into the valley of the Yamatari Chhu, Freshfield and his party crossed to the Yalung Glacier and the south side of Kangchendzonga via the lower of the two possible routes, the Chunjerma La. With their supplies running low and Rinzin ever more fearful of being apprehended by Nepalese frontier guards, they did not linger on the Yalung side of the pass. Gaining only fleeting glimpses of the Yalung Glacier and the peaks surrounding it through the gathering mists, they descended to Tseram, crossed the Simbua Khola and camped in the valley beneath the Kang La. Two days later they were sipping coffee and reading mail from home at Dzong Ri in Sikkim.

Trekkers wishing to visit the Nepal side of Kangchendzonga today will find the authorities in Kathmandu far more obliging, provided the necessary permits are applied for and conditions regarding self-sufficiency in food, fuel and accommodation met. Due to the extreme remoteness of the region, a thorough tour will occupy the best part of five weeks (30 days' walking). Those with less time at their disposal may want to consider the daily air services to the tiny landing strip at Suketar above the administrative centre of the district, Taplejung. By flying in and out, it is perfectly feasible to visit the Yalung Glacier and the south face of Kangchendzonga, cross either of the routes to Ghunsa and trek up to Pang Pema beneath the awesome north face before retreating back to Taplejung in a little over three weeks (23 days' walking).

The ideal starting point is Tumlingtar in the Arun Valley. From here, the trek leads into Taplejung across the Milke Danda ridge, from the crest of which the entire Kangchendzonga group presents itself in all its glory some 64km (40 miles) away. Ramze, the base camp on the Yalung Glacier for the South Face of Kangchendzonga, is an eight-day hike from Taplejung. Totally devoid of tea-houses and lodges, this walk offers a refreshing alternative to the crowded commercialism of the more popular regions of the country. Cutting through the grain of the land, however, it is not an easy undertaking. The first half of the trail winds through intensively farmed country, with quaint thatched farmhouses surrounded by lovingly tended gardens and shaded by some of the biggest poinsettia trees you will ever see. Testament to the hard work of the mountain folk of Nepal, the vast expanses of terraced rice paddies hereabouts are without equal. Beyond Yamphudin, the most remote hamlet

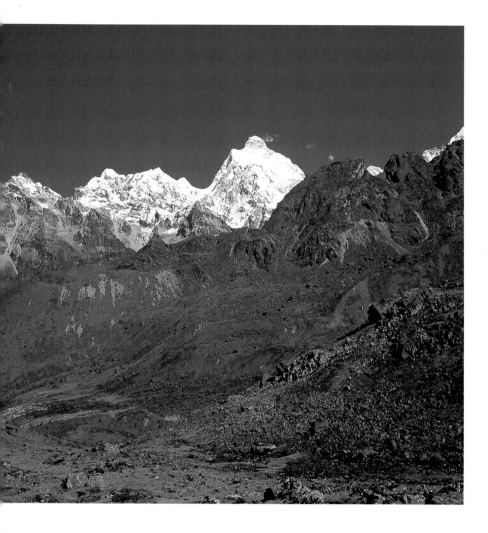

ABOVE *Though the Lapsang La may be higher, the stunning views of Jannu from the Mirgin La make this lower route an appealing alternative.*

passed on this route, the trail enters a region of pure mountain wilderness as it climbs steeply into forests of birch, conifer and rhododendron and crosses yet more ridges before finally approaching the south side of Kangchendzonga up the picturesque valley of the Simbua Khola. The stunning array of peaks that tower over the Yalung Glacier at Ramze is merely a taster of the splendours to come.

There are two possible routes across the watershed between the Yalung Glacier and the Ghunsa Khola Valley to the north. The Lapsang La (5100m; 16,700ft) is higher and involves traversing steep screes and boulder fields on both sides, but its mountain views are unquestionably inferior. The Chunjerma Route, known locally as the Selele Way after a summer grazing pasture on the Ghunsa side, only reaches 4500m (14,700ft) but the trail is far better and stays at a higher altitude for much longer. The Chunjerma route actually crosses two passes, the Sinion La (4440m; 14,570ft) and the higher Mirgin La (4570m; 14,900ft). The steep ascent above Tseram on the Yalung side offers superlative panoramas of the entire south side of Kangchendzonga, while from the prayer flags at the crest of the Mirgin La the views west across the Arun and north to the awesome ramparts of Jannu are simply magnificent.

Having walked in to Ramze, spent a day or two there and crossed north to Ghunsa, you will be sufficiently acclimatized to get the most out of the undisputed climax of this trek – the three-day hike up the Kangchendzonga Glacier from Ghunsa. On this stretch, a new, even more breathtaking vista is revealed at every turn until finally, as the tiny trail above the Kangchendzonga Glacier reaches the base camp at Pang Pema, the awesome North Face of Kangchendzonga appears. No mountain prospect on earth is more utterly overpowering as it soars to the heavens in perpetual shadow – foreboding, intimidating and absolutely amazing. For a bird's-eye view, ascend Drohmo Ri, the 6200m (20,300ft) 'hill' immediately above camp. Retreat to Taplejung takes a further seven days.

LOCATION Kangchendzonga Himal, eastern Nepal.

WHEN TO GO April to June or October to December.

START/FINISH International flights to Kathmandu, then by air (45mins) or road (night bus – 14hrs) to Biratnagar. Overnight there and then early morning STOL flight to Taplejung (30mins). Return by the same route.

DURATION Minimum 23 days.

MAX ALTITUDE Pang Pema (5100m; 16,700ft).

TECHNICAL CONSIDERATIONS If there is snow, parties opting to cross the Lapsang La (high route from Tseram to Ghunsa) should take an ice axe for cutting steps, especially for porters.

EQUIPMENT Need to be fully self-sufficient in accommodation, food and fuel throughout. People organizing treks themselves should ensure that porters have sufficient high-altitude clothing and adequate footwear. If providing this gear yourself, hand it out on the day it is required.

TREKKING STYLE Backpacking or expedition.

PERMITS/RESTRICTIONS Trekking permit required. Must be obtained through accredited agency.

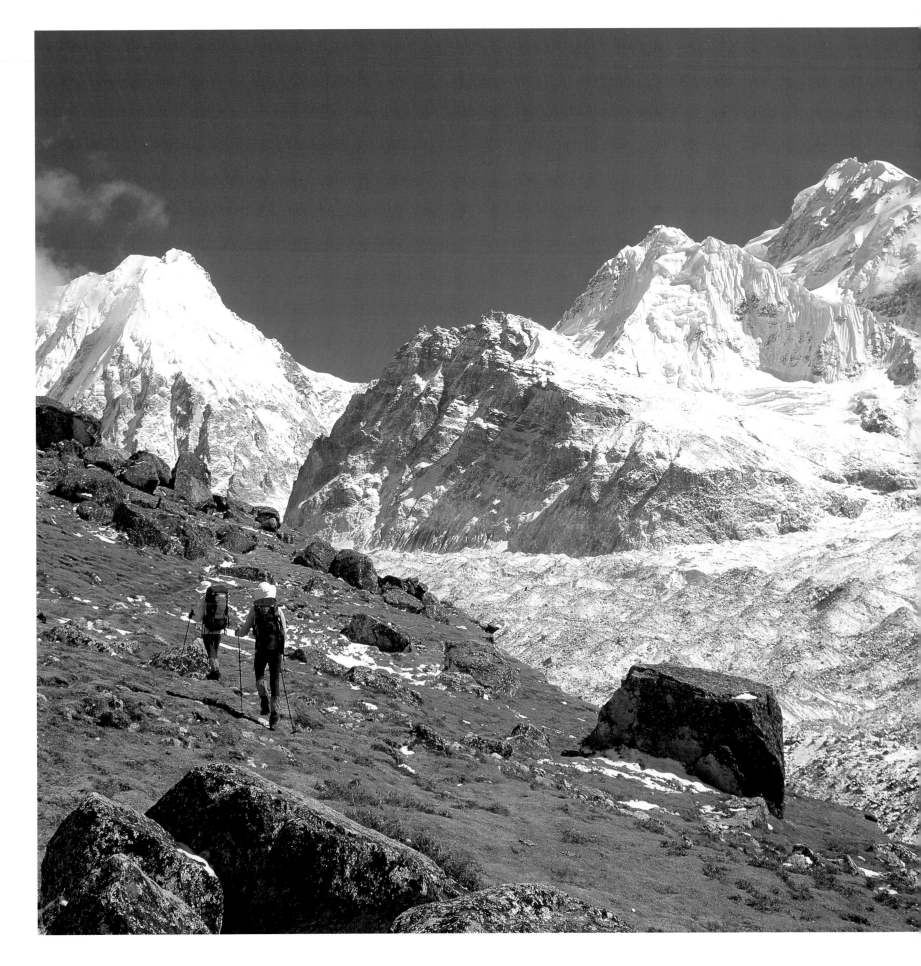

ABOVE *Approaching Pang Pema along the tiny trail above the Kangchendzonga Glacier, with Nepal Peak and The Twins visible in the background.*

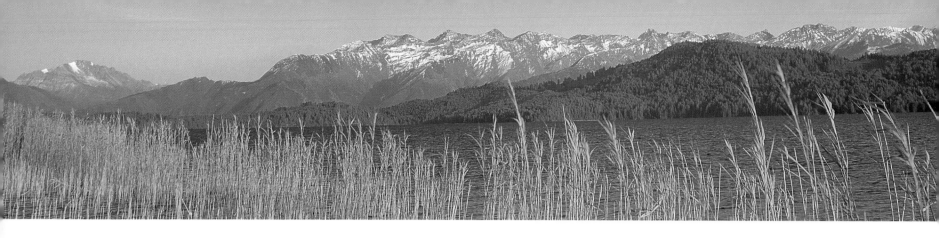

JUMLA TO MOUNT KAILAS

by Steve Razzetti

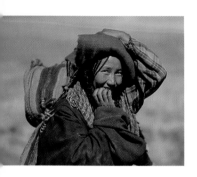

The Himalaya were already the stuff of myth and legend when the first wave of Indo-Aryans crossed the Punjab 2000 years before the birth of Christ. Seeing the Himalaya, they developed a cosmography that recognized these distant snow-clad mountains as divine and the rivers that flowed from them as life-giving.

Hindu, Bon, Buddhist and Jain religions elaborated on these notions, developing mythologies that focus on the idea that a particular mountain in the Himalaya is the 'world pillar' around which all existence revolves. Jains revere this mountain as *Astapada*, where they believe Rishaba, the founder of their creed, attained enlightenment. Hindus, on the other hand, call this mythical peak *Meru*, and believe that upon its lofty summit the great god Shiva sits – meditating, consorting with his goddess Parvati and smoking *ganja* (marihuana). Their sacred river – the Ganga (Ganges) – is believed to fall directly from heaven to its summit, whereon it divides into four streams that flow to the four corners of the earth for its purification.

Time has shown these fantastic legends to have a surprising basis in geographical fact. North of the main Himalayan chain in the remote western Tibetan province of Ngari there does indeed stand a unique mountain, Kailas, near the base of which rise four of the most significant rivers of the Indian subcontinent – the Indus, Sutlej, Karnali and Tsangpo-Bramaputra. The plains around Kailas form the apex of the Tibetan table-land, and the waters that rise there reach the ocean as far apart as the Arabian Sea and the Bay of Bengal.

The ancient pre-Buddhist Bon religion of Tibet saw mountains as power points linking heaven and earth, and Mount Kailas as the Soul Mountain of the kingdom of Zhang Zhung. The struggle for the hearts and minds of Tibetans between traditional Bon and modern Buddhism centred on Kailas, and the story of the contest of magic between the Bon deity Naro Bon Chung and the Buddhist saint Milarepa to decide which cult could claim the sacred mountain is still told today. Legend has it that Milarepa won, but was magnanimous enough in victory to bequeath a nearby peak to the Bon-po and agree that they might still circumambulate Kailas.

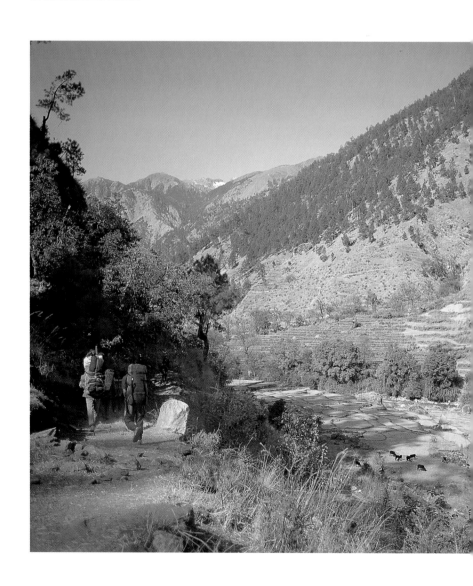

TOP *Looking across into the mountains of the Mugu district from the reed-fringed northern shoreline of Rara Lake.*

INSET *A Tibetan girl on the Kailas* kora. *The energy and spirit of pilgrims, who travel to Kailas from all over the Indian subcontinent, is simply inspiring.*

RIGHT *Idyllic scenery and seldom-travelled trails make the walk up the Humla Karnali to Simikot a memorable experience.*

The Chinese occupation of Tibet in 1951, subsequent internal unrest and the devastation wrought on Tibetan monastic culture during the Cultural Revolution resulted in the hermetic sealing of borders with India and Nepal. Ancient trading links and pilgrimage routes were instantly abolished and many remote frontier communities were pitched into economic oblivion.

In a remarkably conciliatory gesture, the Chinese agreed to reopen the border on the Humla Karnali in northwest Nepal early in 1993, allowing foreigners to approach Mount Kailas on foot legally for the first time in history. Today, it is possible to make your own pilgrimage to Kailas through one of the most enchantingly beautiful and unspoiled corners of Nepal, instead of suffering the week-long ordeal of an overland journey from Lhasa. For travellers interested in the ancient history and culture of the Himalaya, this is a unique opportunity.

Most people heading for Kailas today fly into the airstrip serving the capital of Humla, Simikot. However, by starting further south at Jumla and following the ancient trade routes north into Humla via Rara Lake, a hurried visit to Tibet and Nepal may be turned into an odyssey befitting the approach to a mountain as revered as Kailas.

Rara Lake lies at the heart of the least visited national park in Nepal – its sparkling waters set like a paragon of tranquillity amid a wilderness of primeval woodland and rolling hills – and is three tough days from Jumla. The trail is often faint, always strenuous and the countryside traversed sparsely populated, but Rara is a treasure to behold. Leaving Rara National Park northwards, the way to Humla plunges down to cross the Mugu Karnali Valley before starting the long haul up to the Chankel Lekh (3640m; 11,352ft) and approaching Simikot along the valley of the Humla Karnali. Reaching the crest of the Chankel Lekh, the landscape ahead is instantly transformed, with the blue ridges of Humla fading into the arid distance beneath a wall of lofty snow-capped peaks on the border with Tibet.

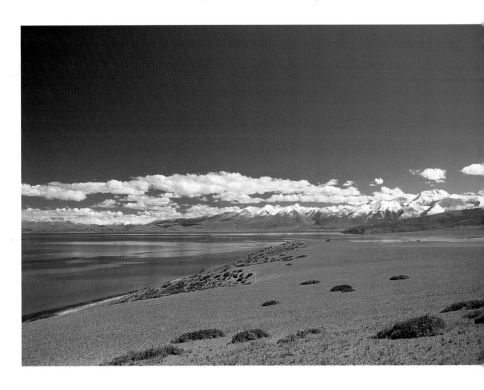

ABOVE *At an altitude of 4510m (14,800ft), Lake Manasarovar is particularly revered by Hindus, many of whom make the difficult 85km (50-mile)* kora *around it.*

Life in Humla continues at a pace unaffected by the schedules and stresses that propel the world beyond. Here the villages are medieval and the lives of their inhabitants intimately entwined with the rhythms of nature. Before you toil up the final 1000m (3200ft) climb to Simikot and head on through highland *bhotia* (people of Tibetan origin) settlements to the Nara Lagna Pass and Tibet, the subtle yet all-pervasive charm of Humla will have you bewitched.

LOCATION Ngari province, southwest Tibet. Approach through Humla, northwest Nepal.

WHEN TO GO May to June; late September to December.

START International flight to Kathmandu, then to Nepalganj by air (50mins) or road (bus 14hrs). Overnight there and early morning flight to Jumla (25mins).

FINISH Simikot; flight to Nepalganj (50mins) and on to Kathmandu by air or road (night bus 12–14hrs).

DURATION 28 to 30 days.

MAX ALTITUDE Dolma La (5600m; 18,400ft).

TECHNICAL CONSIDERATIONS In view of the remoteness of Kailas and the extreme altitude attained on this trek, a close watch should be kept for the onset of altitude sickness. Getting below 4000m (13,000ft) once in this part of Tibet will be difficult and helicopter evacuation impossible.

EQUIPMENT Need to be fully self-sufficient throughout.

TREKKING STYLE Backpacking or expedition.

PERMITS/RESTRICTIONS Standard Nepali trekking permit required for Jumla-Simikot section. Must be obtained through accredited agent. Section from Simikot to border requires a special permit. Arrangements for visas and the Kailas sector must be made in advance through an accredited agency in Nepal or Tibet. Expensive.

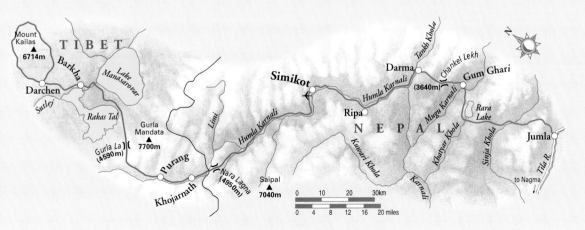

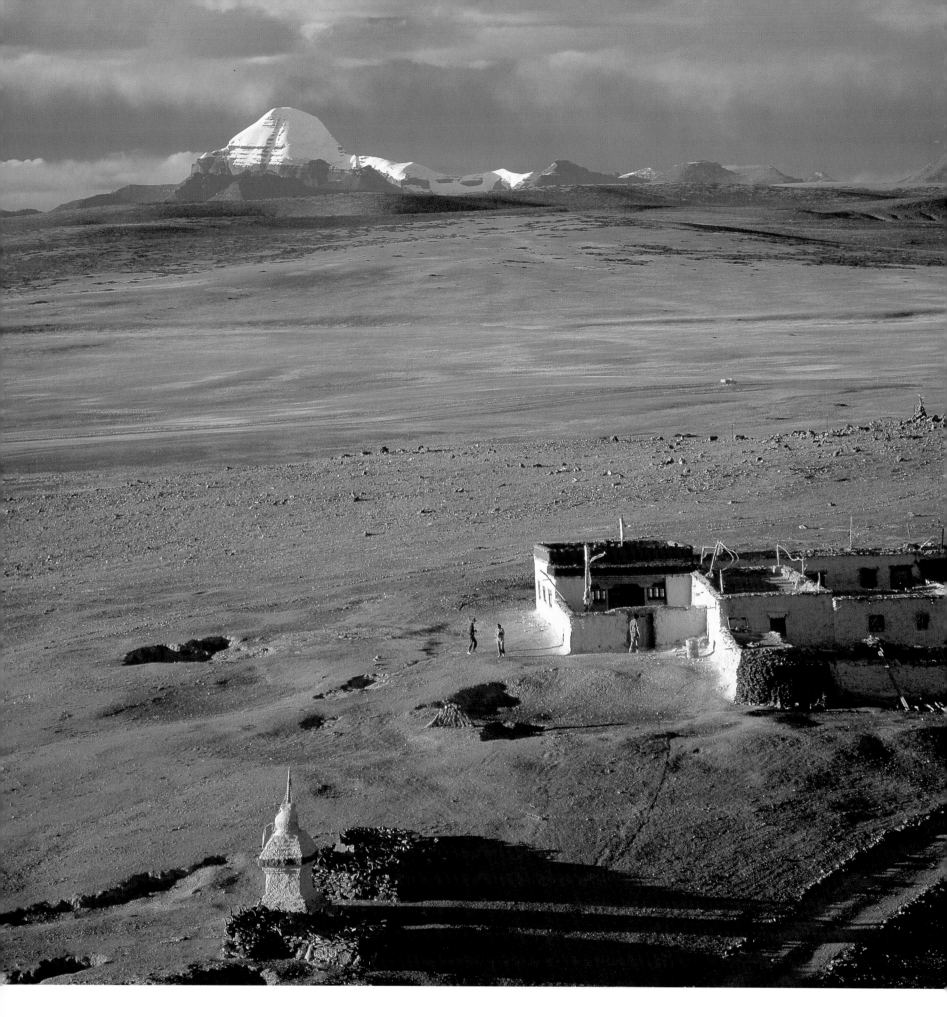

ABOVE *The strange symmetry of Mount Kailas (6714m; 22,029ft), seen here rising above the plains of Barkha from Chiu Gompah on the shores of Lake Manasarovar, has inspired the design of temples as far away as Angkor Wat in Cambodia and Borobadur in Indonesia.*

Formed of the world's highest deposit of tertiary conglomerate, Mount Kailas presents an awesome spectacle as it rises dramatically above the desolate plains of Barkha. Travellers approaching the sacred mountain from the south gain their first view of it upon reaching the crest of the Gurla La (4950m; 16,240ft), from where it appears to float on the horizon above the iridescent turquoise lakes of Manasarovar and Rakas. Setting off from the dusty outpost of Darchen, Tibetans complete the 56km (35 miles) *kora* (circumambulation) of Kailas in a single day. Most foreigners take a more leisurely four days, allowing for the extreme altitude, visits to monasteries and a thorough appreciation of the stunning scenery.

The bitter wind howls while the fierce sun beats down through rarified air. Wayside shrines adorn every turn of the path and prayer flags flutter against the deep azure sky above. Against such an austere landscape, and decades of repression, the joyful countenances of the hundreds of Tibetans who complete the *kora* each day are extremely moving; a most humbling testament to the resilience of the human spirit.

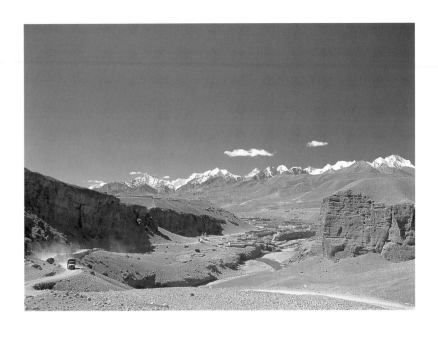

BELOW *Yak horns and mane stones carved with the ubiquitous Tibetan mantra Om Mane Padme Hum (hail the jewel in the lotus) at Chiu Gompah.*

ABOVE *A view south to Purang and the distant Garwal Himalaya in India from the dusty road to the Gurla La (4590m; 15,060ft).*

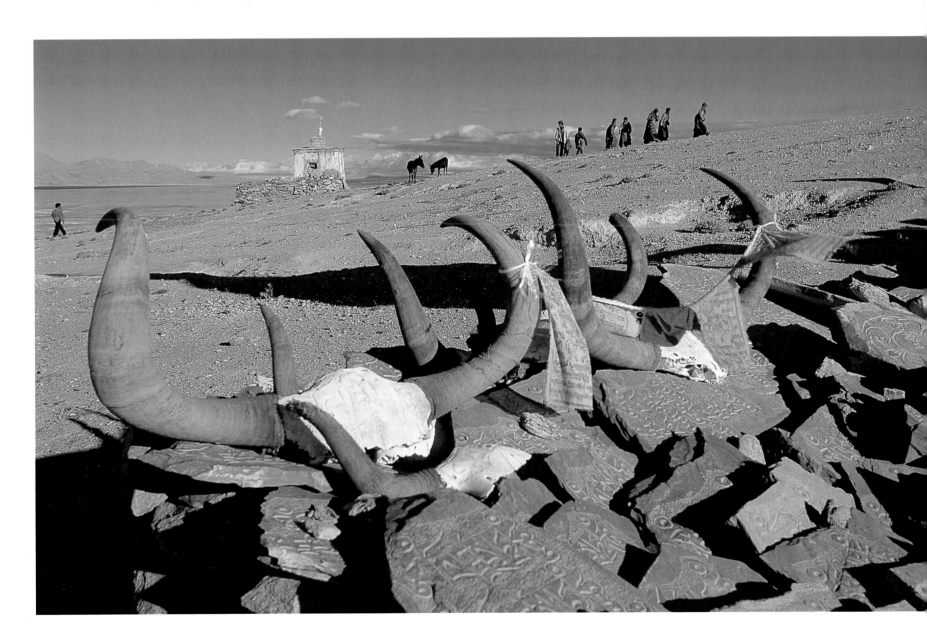

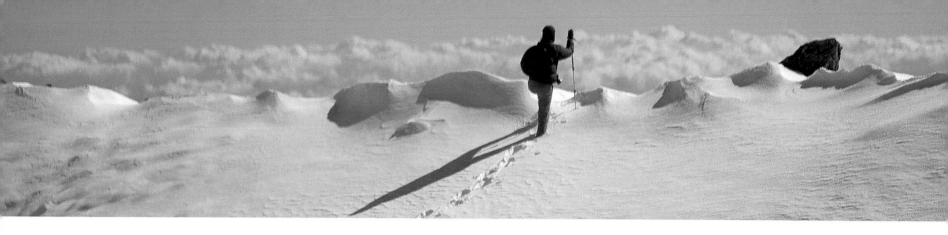

DHAULAGIRI CIRCUIT

by Steve Razzetti

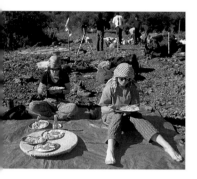

As a rule, the natives of the high Himalaya do not share the Westerner's nomenclaturial tendencies, and on numerous occasions when asked the name of a particular snowy peak the *sherpa* has innocently replied 'Dhaulagiri, sahib' (White Mountain, sir). In the case of the massif we know today as Dhaulagiri, this simple fact led to early confusion as to the topography of Nepal, and resulted in some seriously imaginative mapping.

Dhaulagiri I (8167m; 26,795ft) is the highest peak of a complex massif that is over 55km (35 miles) across, and includes the six summits of Dhaulagiri and their western outliers, Churen Himal and Putha Hiunchuli, all of which are in excess of 7200m (23,600ft). Tukuche Peak is one of the most spectacular in the group, failing to make the 7000m (23,000ft) mark by a mere 80m (260ft).

Swiss geologist Arnold Heim was the first European to actually get close to the peaks of central Nepal, while conducting an aerial survey of the region in 1949. One year later, Bill Tilman's party saw Dhaulagiri from Muktinath after crossing the Thorung La from Manang, but it was the Frenchman Maurice Herzog and his expedition that same year who really got close to this beautiful yet intimidating Himalayan behemoth.

Herzog was the leader of a stellar team, organized under the auspices of the French Alpine Club, which included such seminal alpinists as Gaston Rébuffat, Lionel Terray and Jacques Oudot. Theirs was purely a climbing endeavour, undertaken with the intention of reaching the summit of the first 8000m peak 'for the honour of France'. Dhaulagiri and Annapurna were their selected objectives, and they chose the village

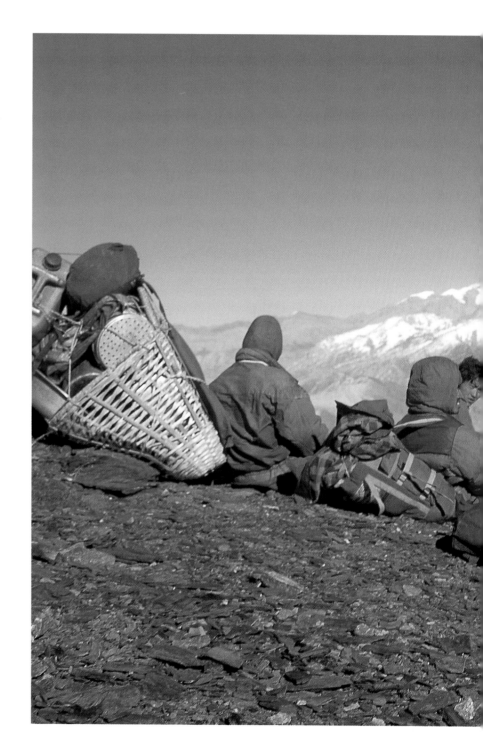

TOP *A walk in the clouds; approaching the knife-edge crest of Budzunge Bara Pass en route to the Kaphe Khola and the base camp of Putha Hiunchuli.*

INSET *A hearty lunch on the trail to Gurja Gaon. Copious amounts of good food are one of the best reasons for organizing your trip through a reputable operator.*

RIGHT *A well-earned rest off the snow on the steep descent from Damphus Pass into the Kali Gandaki above Marpha. Across the valley, the Thorung La can be seen.*

OPPOSITE TOP *Sunset on the Puchhar Wall of Dhaulagiri I from Italian Base Camp – the last place with any vegetation until Marpha, four long days ahead.*

of Tukuche in the Kali Gandaki Valley as their base camp. The approaches to both peaks were unknown, and the team was faced with a daunting task of reconnaissance. Electing to concentrate on Dhaulagiri first, they split into small groups and set about finding a way to the mountain. Formulating their strategy according to an erroneous Survey of India map, several abortive forays were made into the Damphus Khola Valley and up the terrifying East Dhaulagiri Glacier before they reached the watershed west of the Kali Gandaki, at what we now know as Damphus or Thapa Pass.

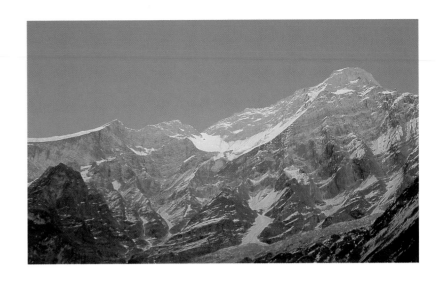

The glaciers on the north side of Dhaulagiri remained a mystery, however. Only when Lionel Terray and Jacques Oudot finally succeeded in crossing Hidden Valley, reaching the col overlooking the Chhonbardan Glacier and the North Face of Dhaulagiri, was the problem finally solved: the glacier drained into the fearsome ravines of the Myagdi Khola. Although French Pass is named after that heroic feat of

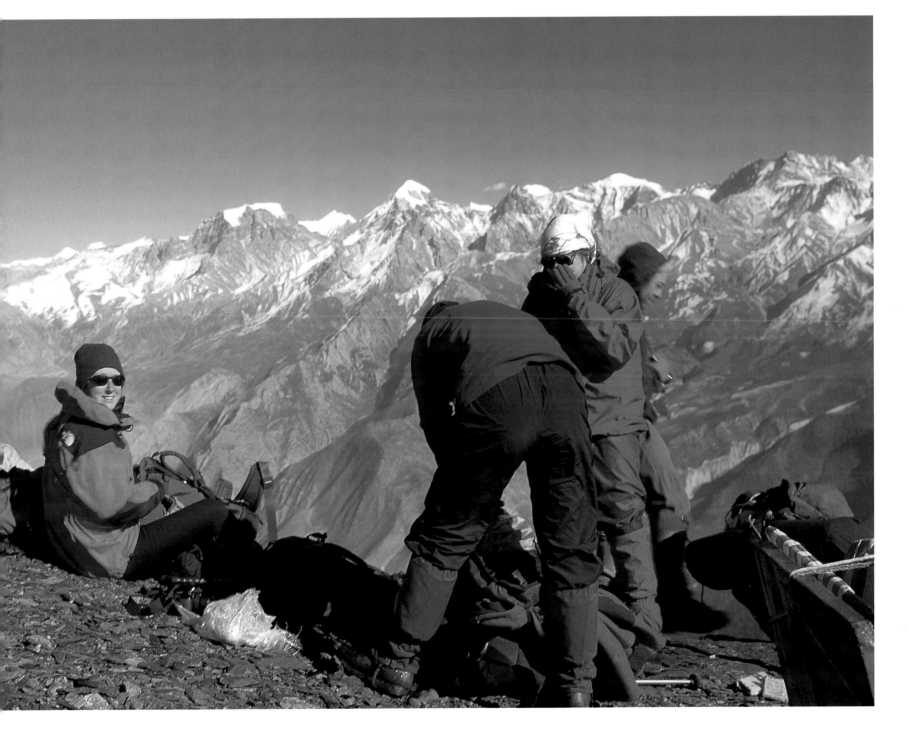

LOCATION Dhaulagiri Himal, Nepal.

WHEN TO GO April to May and September to December.

START Beni; international flight to Kathmandu, then by road or air to Pokhara and on to Beni by bus or jeep (poor road).

FINISH Jomsom; flight to Pokhara (20mins) and on to Kathmandu either by air (25mins) or by road (8hrs).

DURATION 21 to 23 days minimum.

MAX ALTITUDE French Pass (5300m; 17389ft).

TECHNICAL CONSIDERATIONS French Pass in bad weather needs skilful navigation. Though ostensibly close to some of the busiest trails and airstrips in Nepal, much of this route is effectively extremely remote and organizing a retreat/evacuation in an emergency could be time consuming at best. Parties travelling here should prepare, equip and conduct themselves with this in mind.

EQUIPMENT Need to be self-sufficient in accommodation, food and fuel throughout. Security can be a problem around Pokhara, where burglars operate so keep an eye on belongings at all times.

TREKKING STYLE Backpacking or expedition.

PERMITS/RESTRICTIONS Trekking permit required. Must be obtained through accredited agency.

exploration, Herzog and his group eventually retreated, proclaiming the peak 'unclimbable'. The first expedition to approach Dhaulagiri via the Myagdi Khola was led by Swiss mountaineer Bernhard Lauterburg in 1953. Having only one photograph (taken by Terray from French Pass in 1950) to go on, the Swiss set about exploring the Chhonbardan Glacier and tried to find a route onto Dhaulagiri itself. A thorough reconnaissance was carried out and an altitude of 7200m (23,600ft) reached on the peak, but while several of the team left via French Pass and Damphus Pass, the difficulty of climbing the north face remained patently obvious.

In 1960, a second Swiss expedition finally conquered the mountain. They brought with them a single-engined aircraft equipped for glacier landings, complete with veteran pilot and mechanic. After laying on a shuttle service and flying the entire team up to Damphus Pass, pilot Ernst Saxer set a world height record for a glacier landing when he dropped Kurt Diembeurger and Ernst Forrer off at the northeast col, from which point they commenced their ascent.

The basic circuit of Dhaulagiri I remains one of the most challenging and rewarding routes in Nepal. The most popular trail starts at Beni and finishes across Damphus Pass to rejoin the Kali Gandaki at Tukuche or Marpha, committing you to a long and difficult trek, with two remote passes and the highest camp, Dhaulagiri base camp, right at the end of the trail. Contingency plans on this route should be carefully weighed up. Given fine weather and good snow conditions the French and Damphus Pass crossings are unforgettable, with impressive perspectives gained on the north face of Dhaulagiri, but in a blizzard navigation may prove extremely difficult. Similarly, choosing the correct col when crossing into the Kali Gandaki from Hidden Valley is imperative as a mistake could lead to dangerously steep ground.

For a party travelling in expedition mode, the basic circuit can be made even more rewarding by beginning with a side trip to the Kaphe Khola Valley and the base camp of Putha Hiunchuli. This peak was first climbed from the north in 1954 by a small

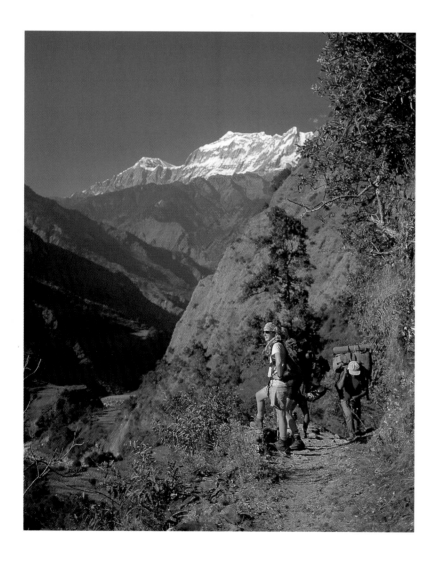

ABOVE *Pausing to admire the view up the Dara Khola valley, towards the Gurja Himal and Budzunge Bara Pass, near the village of Lurang.*

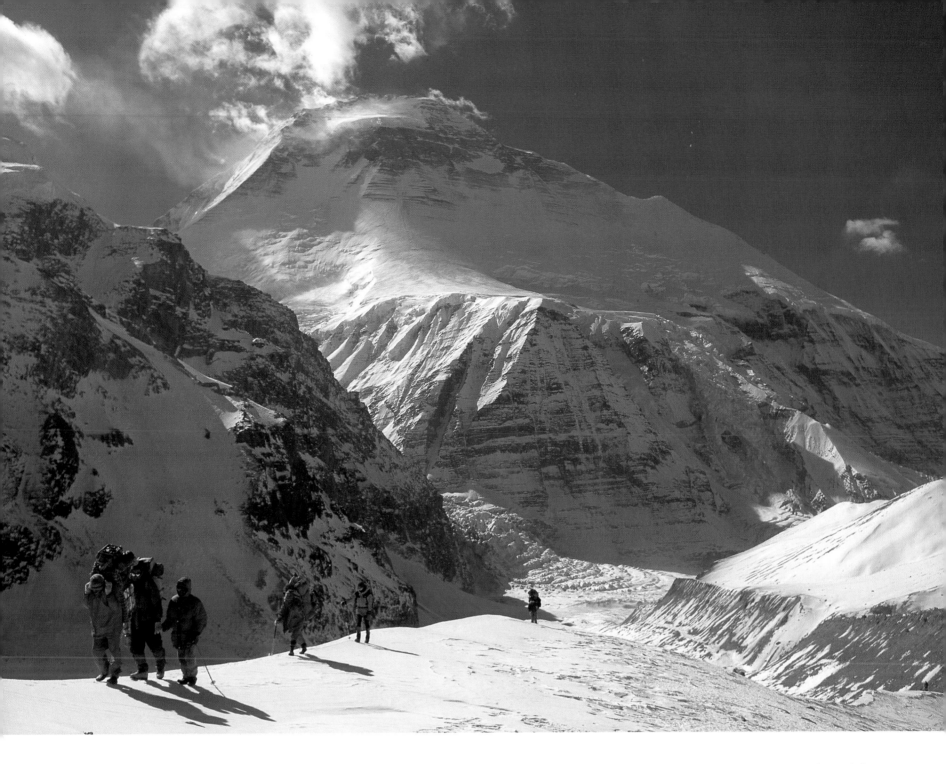

British expedition led by Jimmy Roberts, but it was the second and third ascents, both made in 1972 by Japanese teams, that pioneered the route from Phalai Gaon village in the valley of the Myagdi Khola via Gurja Gaon and the Budzunge Bara Pass.

The roller-coaster trail that constitutes this dramatic ridge walk rises skyward from Gurja Gaon onto the Budzunge Bara. Under snow it would be a most serious proposition, but given fine weather a high camp just east of the col is feasible. Tucked right under the south face of the Gurja Himal, this spot offers spectacular sunset views of Dhaulagiri and Nilgiri; and with no other high ground south, east or west for miles it really does feel like a walk in the clouds.

The thin trail up the Myagdi Khola above the village of Baghar leads through dense primordial jungle. The path zigzags up and down, crossing the tumultuous river on rickety bamboo bridges and surmounting vertical sections of rock by way of bamboo ladders lashed into place with knotted vines, and disappears under enormous, precariously balanced boulders, reappearing over the rotting trunks of gigantic fallen trees.

Only on the fourth day do the deciduous trees give way to conifers and the valley walls retreat to a more respectable distance. Abruptly, the trail emerges into a clearing and straight ahead is Puchhar. The tiny camp, known as Italian Base Camp, is situated in a tiny grassy meadow immediately beneath the west face or Puchhar Wall of Dhaulagiri I. A more awesome and intimidating spot is hard to imagine: with the Rupal Face of Nanga Parbat in Pakistan, this ranks among the highest mountain walls in the world, sweeping skyward over 4600m (15,000ft). The now diminutive waters of the Myagdi Khola issue from between the ice-plastered walls of a dark and forbidding gorge to the north and the savage beauty of the scene is enhanced every evening as the setting sun plays its light-show across the entire face.

ABOVE *The climax of the trip: ascending the final snow slopes high above Chhonbardan Glacier and Dhaulagiri base camp to French Pass, the north face of Dhaulagiri 1 beyond.*

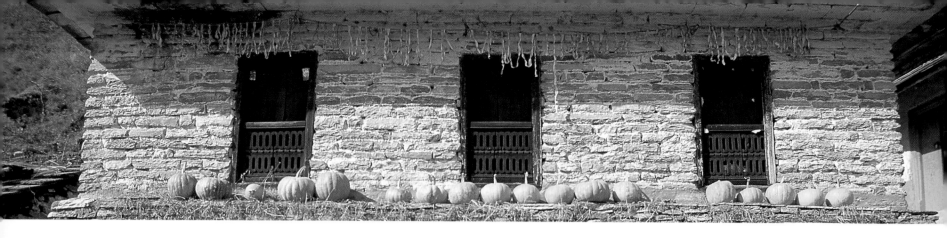

MANASLU & ANNAPURNA CIRCUIT

by Steve Razzetti

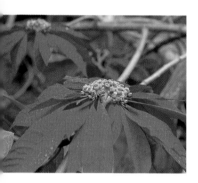

The kingdom of Nepal encompasses 800km (500 miles) of the highest peaks in the Himalayan chain east to west, and 220km (130 miles) north to south at its broadest point. The latest statistics for the number of tourists visiting this mountain realm annually put the figure close to 400,000. Of these, some 80,000 head into the hills on foot, enjoying the magnificent mountain scenery for which the country is renowned worldwide. Nepal first opened to foreigners in 1949 and trekking, as we know it, began in the 1960s. The ensuing 40 years have seen incredible changes in Nepal, unfortunately not all of them benign. Tourism is a mixed blessing. Inconsiderate visitors have tended to erode the ecology of several much-trekked areas and the unsophisticated charm of their inhabitants. Thankfully the Nepalese are strong enough to resist such cultural damage and there are still countless mysteries to enthrall the discerning explorer.

The central part of the Nepal Himalaya is known as the Gandaki Section as it comprises mountain ranges drained by the tributaries of the Gandaki River – the Kali Gandaki, Seti Gandaki, Marsyangdi, Buri Gandaki and Trisuli Gandaki. The highest chain of peaks running east–west throughout Nepal is known as the Great Himalaya, and to the north of this lies a secondary crest zone sometimes referred to as the Ladakh Range or Tibetan Marginal Range. Most of the major rivers both pre-date and actually cut through the Great Himalaya, while a few drain areas in Tibet north of both chains. The practical result of all this physical geography is that the Nepal–Tibet frontier follows the northern crests in some places, and the Great Himalaya in others. Where the former is the case it is often possible to complete circuits of the highest peaks in the Great Himalaya while remaining within Nepal. So it is with Manaslu and Annapurna.

European exploration of the area started modestly in 1864 when Nain Singh Rawat, the 'Chief Pundit' of Montgomerie's Great Trigonometrical Survey (GTS), visited the upper Buri Gandaki on his way to Tibet. 'No. 1', as he also became known, and his cousin Mani were sent to the GTS headquarters at Dehra Dun to be trained as clandestine surveyors. After two years' instruction in the use of sextant and compass, the pair failed to cross surreptitiously into Tibet through their home territory due to their fame in the area. Only after several attempts did Nain Singh finally succeed from Nepal, when he travelled up the Trisuli Gandaki Valley and entered Tibet at Rasua Garhi.

Almost a century passed before the next chapter in the exploration of the area commenced. In 1950, at the start of their second expedition to Nepal, British mountaineers Bill Tilman, Jimmy Roberts and their team spent several weeks around Bimtakhoti, the meadows below the western flanks of the Larkya La. Marked on modern maps as Bimthang, this was still an important trading post at the time. Tilman's real objective during this epic expedition was to scout possible approaches to the Annapurnas and

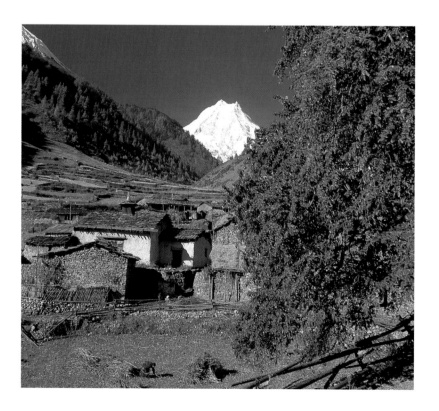

TOP *Pumpkin drying in the autumn sun under the eaves of a Gurung house. Along with rice, dried fruit and vegetables, they form the bulk of the mountain people's diet.*
INSET *Throughout the inhabited regions of upland Nepal, the poinsettia adds a welcome splash of colour to autumnal valleys.*
RIGHT *An early view of the east face of Manaslu, towering over the village of Lo in the upper Buri Gandaki.*

Manaslu for future climbing expeditions, but the team also succeeded in mapping the details of what has today become one of the most celebrated stretches of mountain terrain on earth. Once in Manang, the party split up into pairs and between them explored the upper Marsyangdi Valley, crossed the Thorung La to Muktinath, reached 7200m (23,600ft) during an attempt to climb Annapurna IV, crossed the Larkya La to Nupri and finally left the area down the awesome defile of the Buri Gandaki Valley.

Today, to experience the stupendous revelations that come with crossing remote mountain passes in the heart of the Nepal Himalaya, and appreciate the stark contrast between trekking in real back-country and on the tourist trails, a combination of the Manaslu and Annapurna circuits is unbeatable.

Three of the major tributaries of the Gandaki are featured on this route. In the east, the Buri Gandaki separates the peaks of the Gurkha Himal (Manaslu, Himalchuli and their satellites) from the Ganesh Himal. Next, the Marsyangdi divides the Gurkha Himal from the Annapurnas, and finally the great gorge of the Buri Gandaki cuts between the Annapurnas and Dhaulagiri. North of Manaslu lies Nupri, and north of the Annapurnas lie Manang and Mustang – tracts of barren upland under Nepalese sovereignty still populated by *Bhotias* (people of Tibetan origin).

Those undertaking this journey usually set off from the town of Gorkha, accessible by a paved road from Kathmandu in six hours. From the chaos of Gorkha's dusty main square and bus terminus, the trail climbs a low ridge to the east before plunging down into the sweltering heat of the Buri Gandaki, entering the valley at the sleepy market town of Arughat Bazaar. The journey north along the river from here into Nupri presents a real challenge and takes eight days through one of the longest and most dramatic trans-Himalayan valleys in Nepal.

Though the trail through the gorges has been in use for centuries as a trade route, it is regularly devastated by the monsoon rains and certain sections are always difficult. Expect to have to make high, time-consuming diversions and to sweat profusely as you

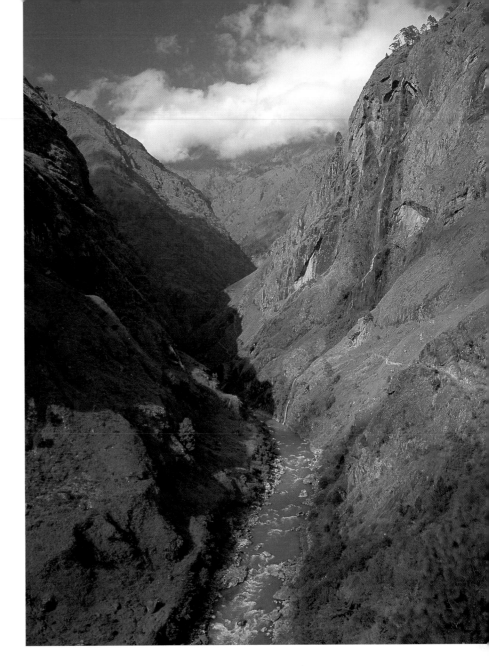

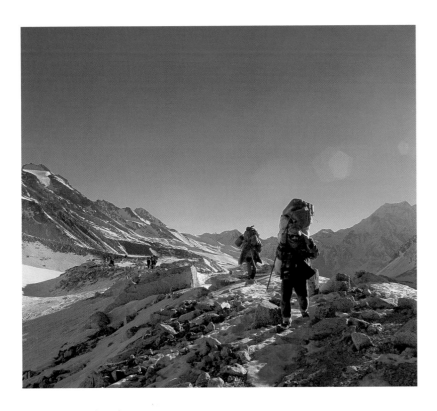

scramble among the twisted debris of avalanche-decimated jungle before reaching the delicious cool air of the upper reaches. Rich rewards await those who venture this way into Nupri. A host of sensational peaks to ogle. Precarious, unspoiled villages nestling amid pristine forest and arable land. Tiny, remote *gompahs* (monasteries) where you may sit sipping *chang* (beer) with *lamas* from as far afield as Lhasa and Sikkim.

Those with sufficient time will find plenty to keep them entertained in and around the biggest village in Nupri, Sama Gaon. Tucked away in the arid upper reaches of the Buri Gandaki, this truly outlandish spot consists of a tight cluster of medieval Tibetan timber dwellings and boasts a picturesque *gompah* and awesome perspectives of the northern and eastern aspects of Manaslu. The ruins of the once prosperous Larkya Bazaar lie a short distance away to the north.

ABOVE *The walls of the Buri Gandaki are incredibly steep. With almost no flat ground in the valley, camp sites are rare and cultivated land virtually nonexistent.*
LEFT *Porters cross the Larkya La. Though not as famous as the Thorung La north of Annapurna, this pass is more enjoyable because of the solitude of its upper reaches.*

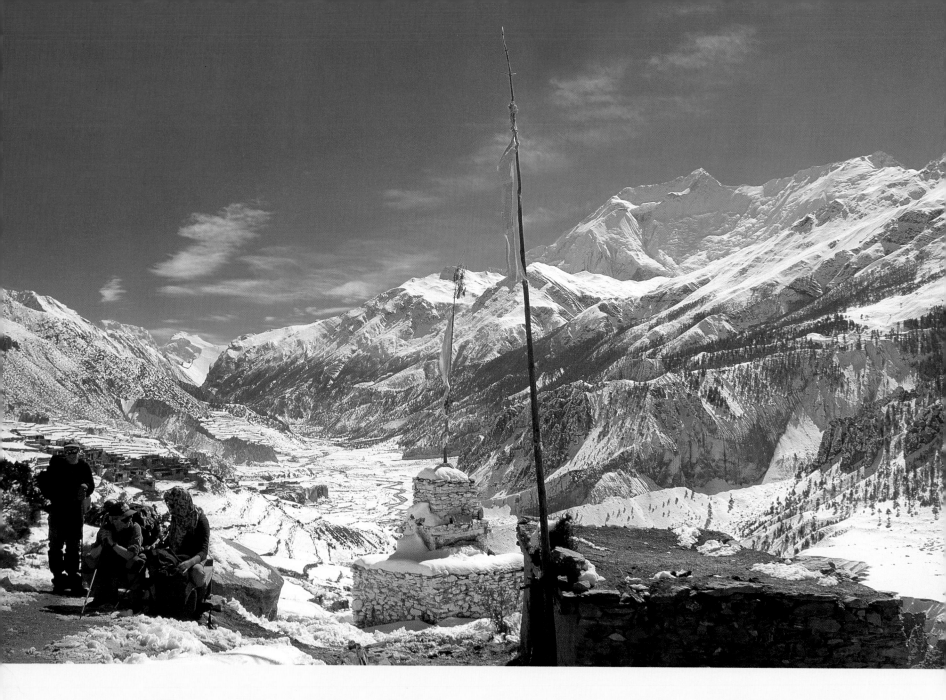

LOCATION Larkya Himal, Nepal.

WHEN TO GO March to May or September to December.

START International flight to Kathmandu, then by road to Gorkha via the Prithvi Highway (7hrs).

FINISH Jomsom; flight to Pokhara (20mins) and on to Kathmandu either by air (25mins) or by road (8hrs).

DURATION 22 days.

MAX ALTITUDE Thorung La (5400m; 17,700ft).

TECHNICAL CONSIDERATIONS None.

EQUIPMENT Must be self-sufficient in accommodation (tents), food and fuel.

TREKKING STYLE Gorkha–Thonje, backpacking. Thonje–Jomsom, tea-houses and lodges available all the way. Most people doing the Manaslu & Annapurna circuit camp all the way.

PERMITS/RESTRICTIONS Gorkha–Thonje stretch is a notified area, and a permit and a liaison officer are required. Thonje–Jomsom is an open area, and no permit is necessary.

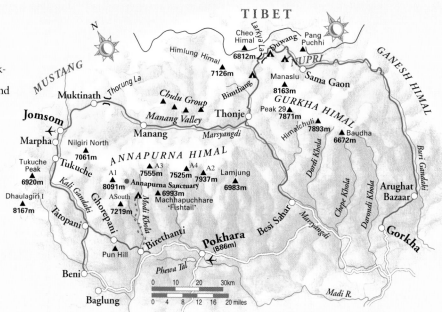

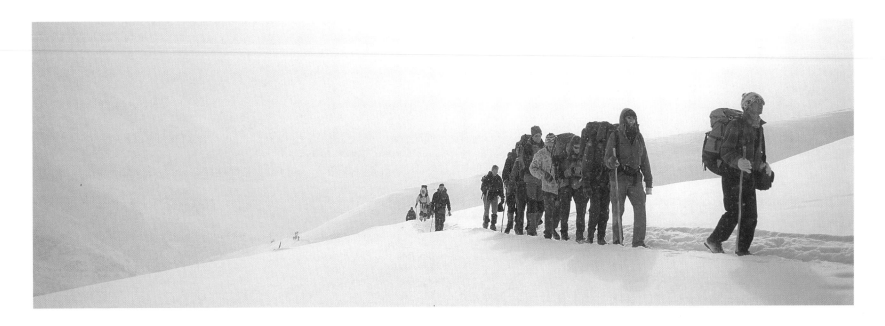

Annapurna III and Gangapurna tower over the Christmas-card scene of the Marsyangdi Valley and Manang after an early-season snowfall.

Trekkers wend their way up over the interminable snowfields on the climb to the Thorung La from Phedi. This busy route can be blocked by unseasonal snowfall at any time.

The Larkya La (5100m; 16,700ft) crossing from Nupri into Manang is straight forward enough in good weather but, like all passes of this height in the Himalaya, it can turn into an epic in the event of a blizzard. The trail sneaks its way over between the Cheo and Manaslu Himalaya, yielding stunning views of the Annapurnas and Himlung Himal ahead and Pang Puchhi and the Ganesh Himal behind. There is a tiny stone shelter at Duwang (4480m; 14,690ft) on the eastern side, and a long, rough descent from the west across loose boulders to the idyllic grassy meadows at Bimthang. This is a truly spectacular spot to camp – a perfectly flat area sheltered beneath ancient glacial moraines and positively dwarfed by a cirque of towering Himalayan giants.

As with many of the places described in this book, there is much to be gained by lingering here and conducting your own 'exploring party'. Those prepared to devote more time to their wanderings will find plenty of scope for adventure in the vicinity of the Larkya La. Thonje village, the Marsyangdi River and the main Annapurna Circuit trail are two long days away from Bimthang down the valley of the Dudh Khola.

This trek could be completed in a couple of days from Thonje by turning south for the roadhead town of Besi Sahar, but it would be a great shame to miss out on the splendours up valley. The Marsyangdi Valley is nowhere as difficult as the Buri Gandaki, and though the villages along the trail have become increasingly devoted to pandering to the whims of tourists, often presenting a garish spectacle of sun terraces bedecked with beer banners, TV satellite dishes, provision stores and trashy trinket bazaars, the surrounding mountain scenery is scintillating.

Crossing the Thorung La (5400m; 17,700ft) from the cramped lodge at Thorung Phedi certainly will not be a peaceful wilderness experience (as many as 500 trekkers set off daily at peak season and there is now a tea-shop on the top), but it is the high point and climax of this route. The Larkya La may be more dramatic and remote,

Looking north into Mustang's kaleidoscope of sand and scree from the trail above Kagbeni as it cuts around the hillside into the Kali Gandaki.

but the contrast between the steep defiles of Manang and the vast, barren vistas of the Kali Gandaki and Mustang that await you on the Thorung La more than justify its popularity. For sheer mountain magnificence, the outlook on Dhaulagiri and Tukuche peak from the descent is unbeatable.

Be sure to visit the exquisite temple complex at Muktinath on your way down from the pass. It is one of the holiest sites in Nepal. Today you can fly out from Jomsom, a day's walk from Muktinath, but that would be to deny yourself the joys of strolling down the Kali Gandaki and savouring the famous hospitality of the Thakali inns in villages such as Marpha and Tukuche. For an unforgettable scenic finale, divert east from Tatopani and head to the road at Birethanti via Ghorepani and Pun Hill. Rise early and get to the top before dawn. Sunrise panoramas don't come any better, even if you do have to share it with hundreds of others.

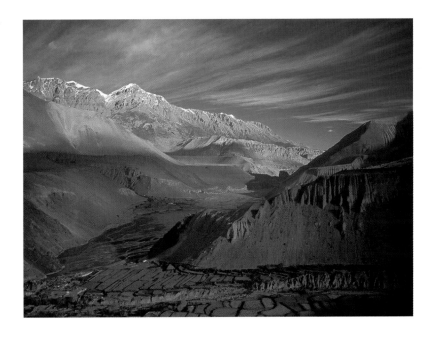

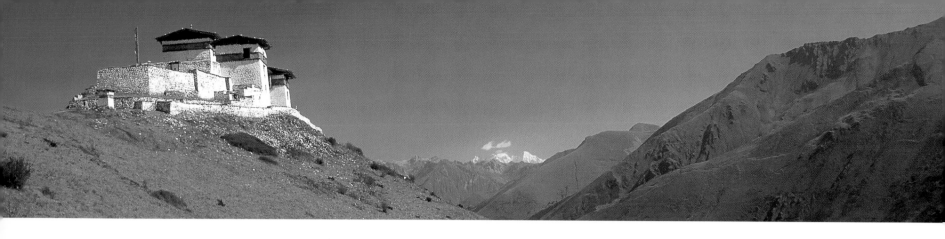

THE SNOWMAN TREK

by Steve Razzetti

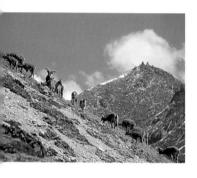

Shangri La may be a tired cliché today, but if there is one place on earth that deserves such an epithet it may well be Bhutan. Like many of the lesser satellite principalities surrounding Tibet, Bhutan has often had to fight for its spiritual and economic independence against powerful, aggressive neighbours. This has inculcated a strong sense of pride and cultural awareness among Bhutan's people, and today it is the only country in the world that embraces Tantric Buddhism as its state religion.

Few countries can claim such a rich traditional heritage, and Bhutan is surely unique in that ancient customs and values continue to inform the daily life of both government and people at almost every level. This is largely due to the enlightened efforts of the king – Jigme Singye Wangchuk – and a few other key figures.

Fleeing persecution in Tibet, Ngawang Namgyal, honoured with the title of Shabdrung (at whose feet one submits), arrived in Bhutan in the 17th century. He succeeded in unifying the 'Land of the Dragon' within 30 years, creating a political and religious establishment that was to last until the 20th century. The most celebrated manifestations of Shabdrung's legacy are the elegant fortress-like *dzongs* that he built, which today serve the dual function of administrative centre and monastery.

The father of modern Bhutan is held to be Jigme Dorje Wangchuk, who reigned from 1952 to 1972. Under his guidance, the long and complete isolation of the country came to an end, and the government adopted a cautious approach to tourism. Independent travel was not permitted but limited numbers of foreigners were allowed in provided they travelled on preplanned, prepaid and guided package tours. This situation prevails, and in the year 1999 the number of tourists reached almost 5400.

Trekking in Bhutan is covered by the same regulations as tourism in general, making exploratory trips almost impossible. Those wishing to travel through Bhutan's pristine and spectacular mountain country on foot must make all their arrangements through an accredited agency and travel on one of the fixed itineraries approved by the Tourist Authority of Bhutan. As the current charge for arranging any tourist activity in Bhutan – trekking or otherwise – is US$200 a day, the longer mountain excursions are very expensive. Whatever one's views on this, the appeal of trekking in such unspoiled mountain country cannot be denied. Neither can the fact that of all Bhutan's currently permitted routes, the 400km (250 miles) Snowman Trek is the roughest, toughest, longest and most rewarding.

From the ruins of Drukyel Dzong in the Paro Valley to Bumthang in central Bhutan, this challenging route crosses no less than 11 passes, three of which exceed 5000m (16,400ft). It also takes in the most dramatic mountain scenery in the country, passing both Chomolhari (7315m; 24,001ft), and Ganker Punzum or Rinchita (7541m; 24,742ft), probably the highest unclimbed peak in the world.

Drukyel Dzong, built to commemorate the Shabdrung's victory over marauding Tibetans in 1644, is situated atop a strategic rocky spur some 20km (12 miles) north of Paro airport. Today there is a paved road as far as this once mighty fortress, and on a fine day the imposing summit of Chomolhari towers above the intervening

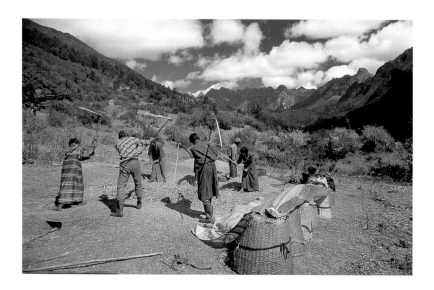

TOP *Lingshi Dzong on the route from Chomolhari to Laya. These imposing fortresses were built as symbols of Drukpa power in the 17th century.*
INSET *Tibetan bharal (blue sheep) on a hillside above the Gombu La. The Bhutan government's cautious development policies have preserved local fauna and flora.*
LEFT *Threshing barley at Woche village in Lunana. Subsistence agriculture is crucial for such remote areas, and villagers may be reluctant to join trekkers during harvest time.*

ridges crowning a scene of quintessential Bhutanese magic. Climbed for the first time in 1937 by Englishman Freddy Spencer-Chapman and Nepali Pasang Dawa Lama, Chomolhari is a sacred peak whose actual summit remains untrodden.

Travellers' baggage and equipment are traditionally carried by yaks in Bhutan. After loading these mighty beasts beneath Drukyel Dzong's crumbling ramparts and setting off up the valley of the Paro Chhu, it is an idyllic three-day hike to the base camp of Chomolhari at Jangothang (3960m; 12,990ft). The trails throughout this route are not really difficult as laden yaks require a broad passage, but the valley walls are precipitous, the forests impenetrable, the population sparse and camp sites few and far between. Trekking days in Bhutan are typically longer than in Nepal, and both facilities and communications in the mountains are far more primitive. The Bhutanese authorities have constructed lodges at the principal camping places on the Chomolhari part of the route, but in practice these are now used by trek crews and are unsanitary and an unattractive alternative.

The valley of the Paro Chhu is a delight to walk up. The turquoise waters of the river flow peacefully through a valley wooded with birch and larch trees that provide a magnificent display of autumn colour in late October. Nearing Jangothang, the woods thin out, and branches of bamboo, juniper and rhododendron are silhouetted against the awesome snow-slopes of Jitchu Drake (6790m; 22,280ft) ahead. Chomolhari

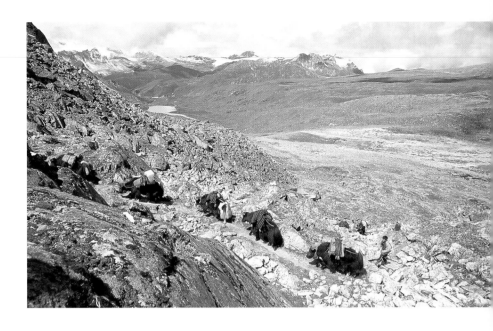

ABOVE *A caravan of yaks carrying gear, winds its way up towards Jazela Pass (5050m; 16,569ft) in the Lunana area on the Snowman Trek.*
BELOW *A trekking group enjoying breakfast at Jangothang beneath the imposing east face of Chomolhari.*

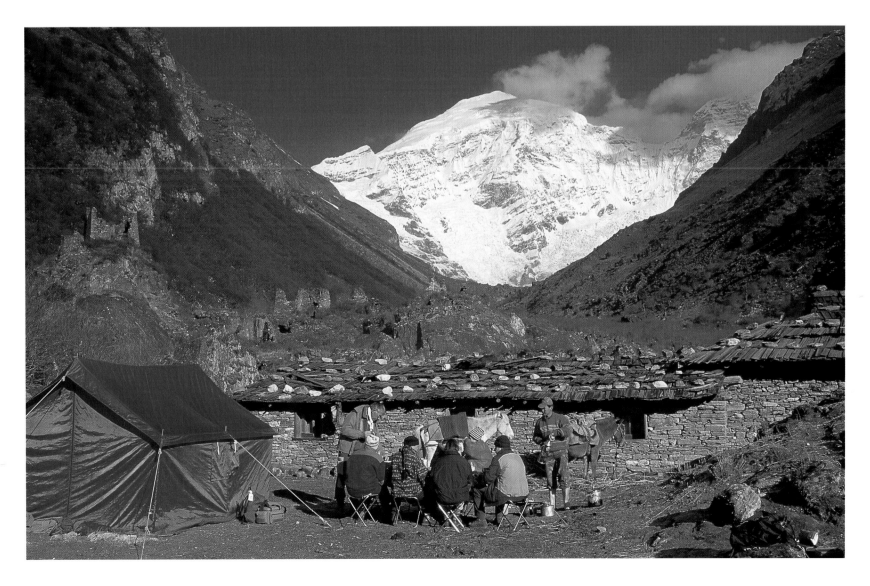

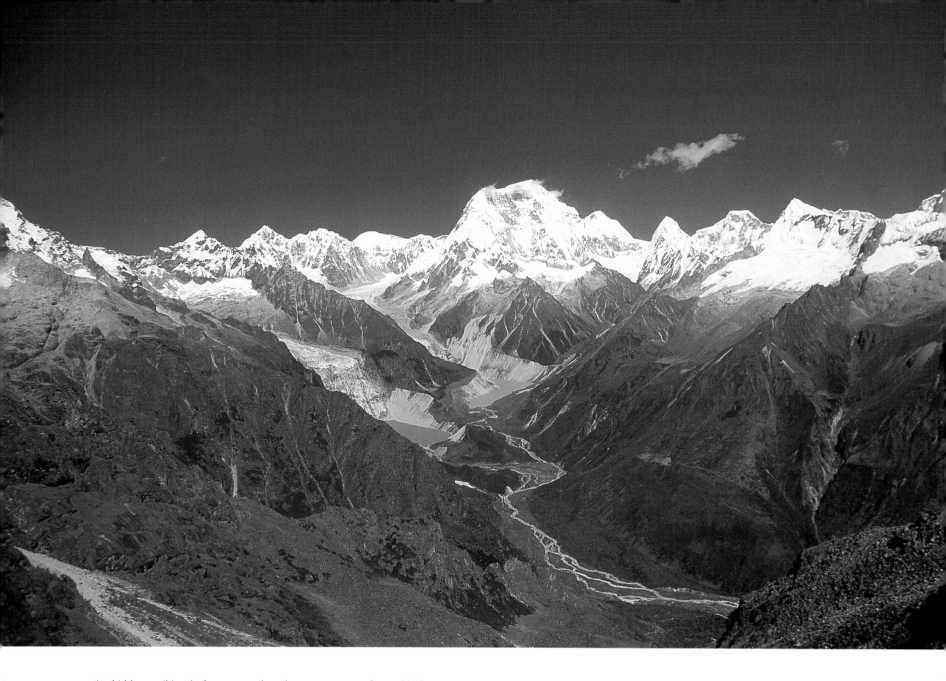

remains hidden until just before camp, when the enormous east face suddenly appears at the head of a glaciated valley, the entrance to which is guarded by an ancient but ruined *dzong*. On a day's hike up grassy slopes immediately north of Jangothang trekkers can easily attain heights in excess of 5000m (16,400ft), achieving excellent acclimatization and revelling in the breathtaking 360-degree panoramas of the surrounding peaks.

Continuing northwestwards and parallel to the Tibetan border, the route to Laya and Lunana then crosses a series of high passes, yielding sensational views of Chomolhari, Jitchu Drake, Kang Bum (approximately 6500m; 21,300ft), Gang Chhen Ta (6794m; 22,291ft)) and Masa Gang (7194m; 23,604ft). The only significant settlement passed on the six-day walk between Jangothang and Laya is Lingshi, where a magnificent whitewashed *dzong* on the crest of a steep ridge above the village presents an unforgettable sight.

Laya (approximately 3800m; 12,500ft) is a large and prosperous village immediately south of Masa Gang, the citizens of which have long traded with their cousins to the north across the passes in Tibet. Agriculture and the breeding of yaks form the mainstay of the local economy, but illicit cross-border commerce is in the men's blood. Many of the houses in the village sport solar panels, and a hunt among them

will produce a surprising variety of Chinese and Tibetan goods for sale. The women dress in striking black yak-hair robes, wear distinctive conical bamboo hats and make the *chang* (beer) with which visitors are plied.

Beyond Laya, the Snowman Trek continues east over the Kanglakachu La (5105m; 16,750ft) into the fabulous district of Lunana. Some cross this major watershed in a single day from the high camp at Rodophu (4350m; 14, 270ft) to Tarina, but an acclimatized party with sufficient time should consider breaking its journey at Narithang (approximately 4800m; 15,700ft). Wending its way between iridescent lakes, over ancient boulder-strewn glacial beds and beneath towering snow-capped peaks, the trail is often thin but always a joy to walk.

Narithang is perched on a moraine shelf immediately opposite the fearsome snow-covered northern ramparts of Gangla Karchung (6395m; 20,982ft). By spending a night here, a 13-hour marathon may be turned into two stunning and enjoyable days' trekking. North of the descent route, a prominent rocky spur can easily be climbed, from which the views of the mountains between Lunana and Tibet are awesome.

ABOVE *Descending from the Kanglakachu La into the Tarina Valley, the full splendour of the peaks in Lunana is revealed. At the centre of this panorama is Jejekangphu Gang.*

LOCATION Bhutan, eastern Himalaya.

WHEN TO GO May to June or October. Bhutan gets a much heavier monsoon than Nepal. The weather is generally less settled, windier and colder.

START/FINISH The only airline serving Bhutan is Druk Air. Fleet of 2 BAe146 aircraft, with services from Bombay, Delhi, Bangkok and Kathmandu. Most people walk Paro–Bumthang and all transport arrangements are made by their Bhutanese hosts.

DURATION Minimum of 25 days, Drukyel Dzong–Dhur. Add 5 days for rests, contingency and/or side trips.

MAXIMUM ALTITUDE Gophu La (5230m; 17,160ft).

TECHNICAL CONSIDERATIONS None.

EQUIPMENT Equipment should be carefully packed in strong duffles, which are carried on yaks. All camping and kitchen equipment will be provided by Bhutanese hosts.

TREKKING STYLE Backpacking or expedition.

PERMITS/ RESTRICTIONS No permits for independent travel are issued for anywhere in the country. All treks must be booked through an accredited agency. Must travel on fixed itineraries approved by the Tourist Authority of Bhutan.

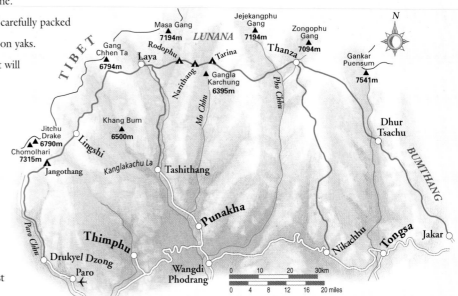

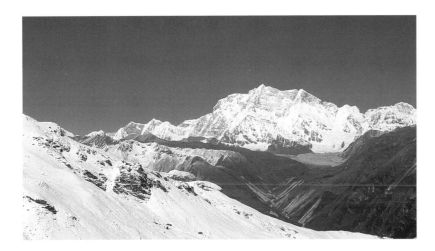

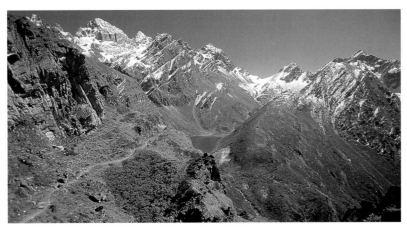

TOP *Gangkar Puensum, or Rinchita, and the headwaters of the Mangdi Chhu, seen from a rocky spur above the Wartang La on the walk from Thanza to Bumthang.*
ABOVE *The sting in the tail! Looking south at the long ascent to the snowy col of the Djule La, the final pass on the route out of Lunana to Bumthang.*

From the beautiful Tarina Valley across a series of steep mountain spurs that descend from Jejekangphu Gang (7194m; 23,604ft) to the head waters of the Pho Chhu and Thanza, Lunana is an arcadian land of intense sunlight, scattered medieval hamlets and hardy pastoral folk. Approaching Thanza along the debris-strewn floor of the valley, the colossal south face of Zongophu Gang (7094m; 23,275ft) rears up above the terminal moraines of invisible glaciers beyond. Held back by these unstable piles of rubble are several enormous glacial lakes, from which cataclysmic floods have periodically burst, wreaking destruction as far away as Punakha Dzong.

Cut off from the outside world by deep snow on the passes between November and April, the people of Thanza (approximately 4100m; 13,500ft) live in one of the most inhospitable yet magical places on earth, and represent a unique and genetically significant community. Tall and strong, they are free of Mong's Disease and the deformities of the heart usually associated with people who live their entire lives at such altitude. Naturally they will be reluctant to take their precious yaks anywhere out of Lunana as the winter snows approach, so careful logistical planning is required if delays are to be avoided here late in the season.

Two possibilities exist for the final part of the Snowman Trek. The westerly route out to Nikachhu from Thanza is high and wild and passes a string of jewel-like lakes, but those anxious to get a closer look at Gankar Puensum will opt for the more rugged eastern route to Bumthang. Both are more strenuous than anything so far encountered and involve camping at over 5000m (16,400ft), but from at least three viewpoints during the seven-day walk out to the road at Dhur in Bumthang, Gankar Puensum presents an absolutely heart-stopping vista. Opportunities abound for side trips and a soak in Guru Rinpoche's hot tub at Dhur Tsachu perfectly rounds off what many veterans believe is the hardest and most wonderful in the world.

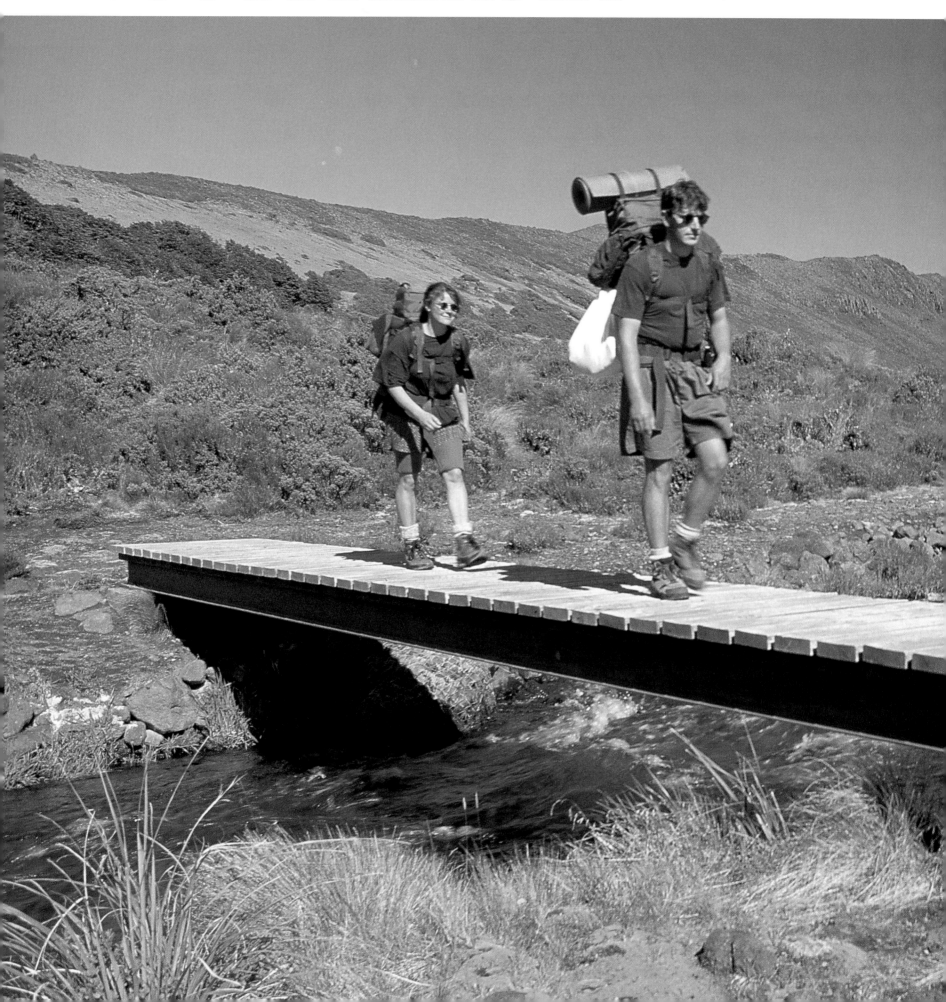

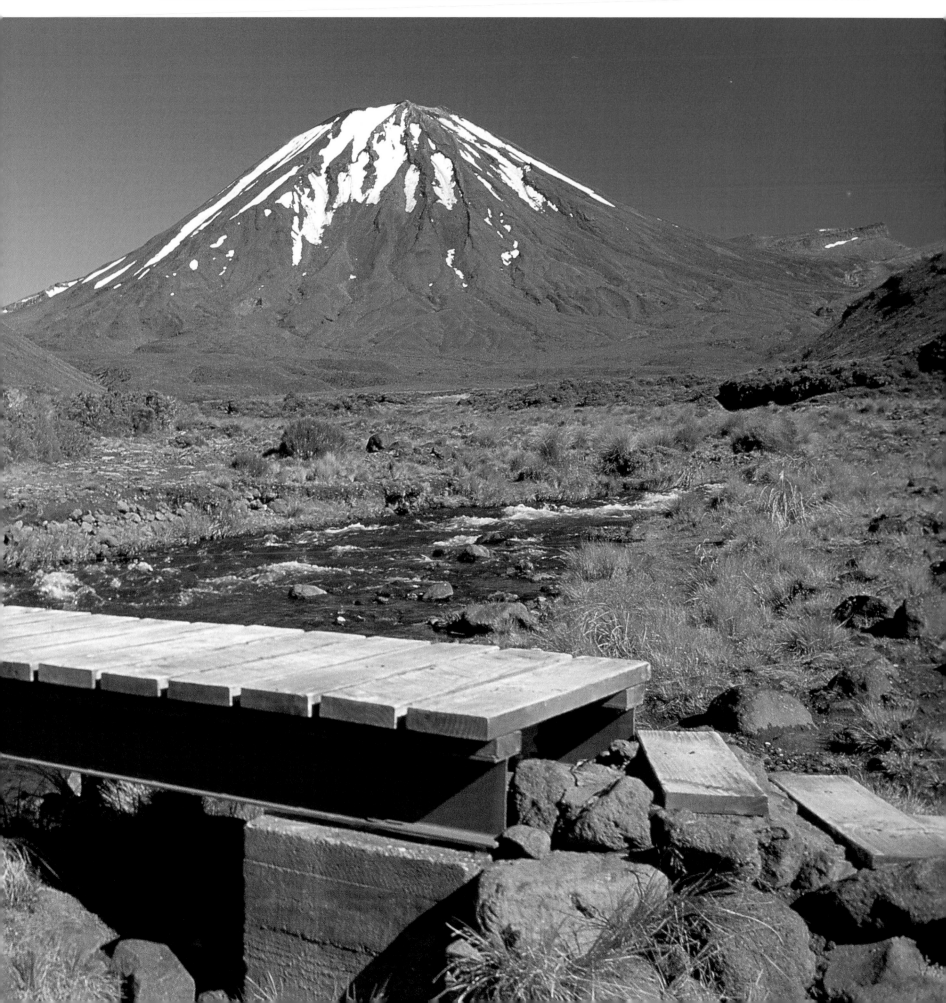

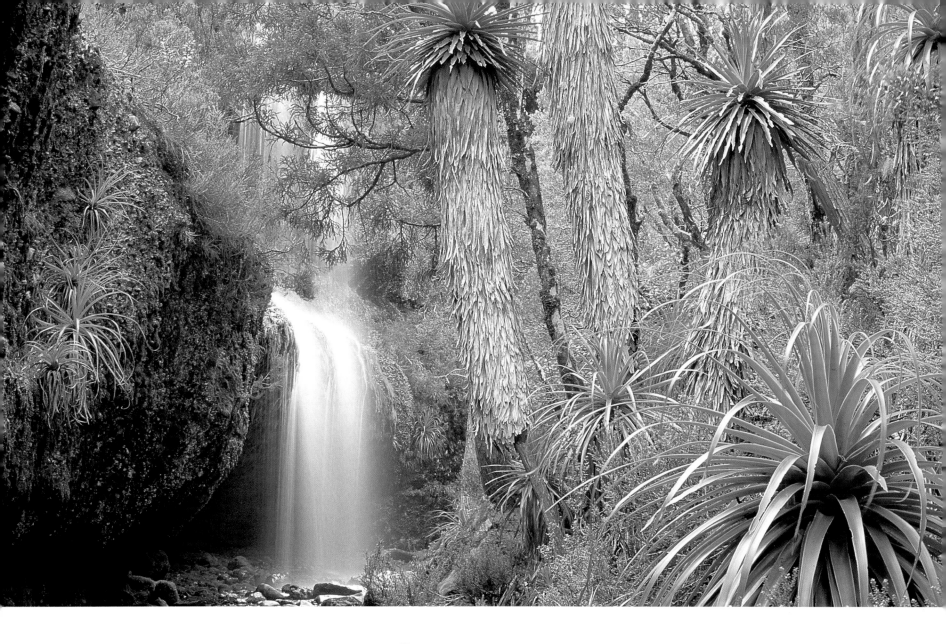

AUSTRALASIA

We simply need that wild country, for it can be a means of reassuring ourselves of our sanity, a part of the geography of hope.

WALLACE STEGNER, 1909–93

ABOVE *The aptly named Waterfall Valley (Overland Track, Tasmania) is a picturesque wonderland of natural water features and lush vegetation.*

OPPOSITE *Standley Chasm, start of the Larapinta Trail, forms an oasis in Australia's arid heartland.*

PREVIOUS PAGES *Park boardwalks and bridges near Mount Ngauruhoe provide easy walking and protect fragile mountain stream and wetland environments.*

Surrounded by the world's greatest oceans, Australia and New Zealand are, despite their physical isolation, popular tourist destinations which offer outdoor enthusiasts a heady cocktail of unique wildlife, vast wilderness areas and modern facilities.

Australia is the sixth largest country in the world, and much of the interior of the island continent is inhospitable desert across which few venture during the sweltering summer months. Nevertheless, it is some of the oldest land surface on earth, and supports a stunning array of flora and fauna that has evolved to survive difficult conditions. The mountains here were formed over 300 million years ago, and those that remain today are but the eroded skeletons of once great ranges. Almost exactly in the middle of Australia lies the town of Alice Springs, and the neighbouring MacDonnell Ranges contain the highest summits west of the Great Dividing Range. Though a sensitivity to the sanctity of Aboriginal lands has prevented the construction of the proposed central sections, the Larapinta Trail takes in some of the Northern Territories' most celebrated tourist attractions and has already been recognized as one of the finest desert walks on earth.

Perhaps the most precious seaboard wilderness in Australia lies on the Sapphire Coast of New South Wales, and this has been acknowledged in the formation of two stunning national parks – Ben Boyd and Nadgee. Walkers making the journey between Eden and Mallacoota may revel in the area's unspoiled sandy beaches, rocky headlands and coastal heathlands.

Van Diemen's Land, known today as Tasmania, was a notorious British penal colony in the 19th century. Today it may be the smallest of Australia's states, but the fact that 20 per cent of its wilderness area has been designated as a World Heritage Site by UNESCO testifies to its ecological significance. Wild

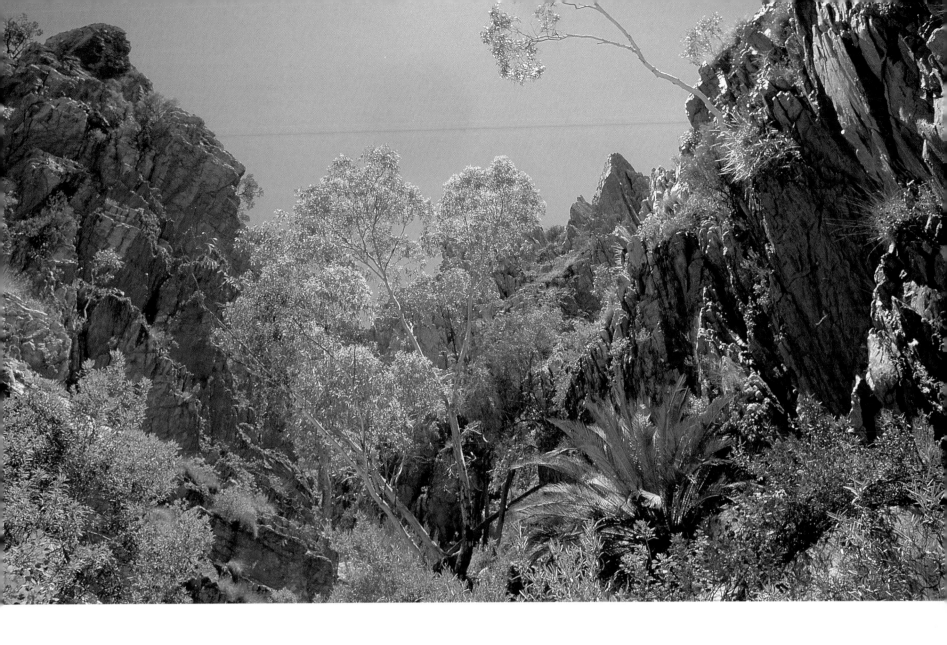

beaches, imposing cliffs, dense rain forests, rugged mountains and rolling moorlands all combine to make Tasmania a trekkers' paradise. In the west of the island, Cradle Mountain and Lake St Clair National Park contains the most spectacular of all the trails here, the world-famous Overland Track.

New Zealanders are fiercely proud and protective of their country's natural heritage and have long been ardent conservationists. Over one-third of the entire land area of New Zealand is legally protected as conservation land. The government's Department of Conservation administers the country's extensive network of trails and huts and entry to national parks is free, although fees are payable for the use of various park facilities.

In 1887 Tongariro National Park, in the central North Island, became New Zealand's first and the world's fourth national park. Taking into account the unique natural splendour of its volcanic landscape and its significant association with the Maori people, UNESCO has declared the park the first ever dual natural and cultural World Heritage Site. The Round the Mountains trek explores the forests and tussocklands, streams, lakes and waterfalls of the three volcanic mountains that form the nucleus of the park.

New Zealand's South Island is dominated by the great mountainous divide known as the Southern Alps/Ka Tiritiri o te Moana. A series of national parks protects the glaciers, snowfields, rivers, lakes, forests and wildlife of these mountains, while valleys and mountain passes have become challenging but popular hiking routes. The Routeburn Track, which traverses the remote wilderness of two of the country's largest national parks, Mount Aspiring and Fiordland, is one of New Zealand's most spectacular and popular walks.

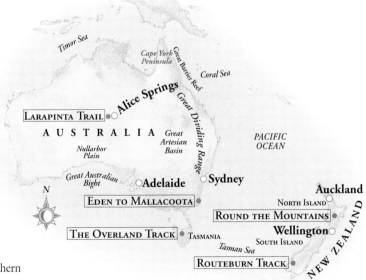

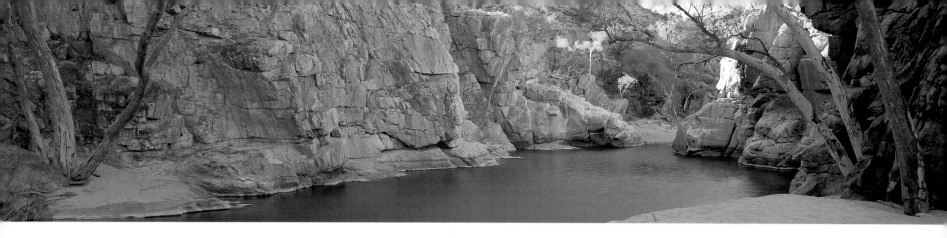

LARAPINTA TRAIL

by John Chapman

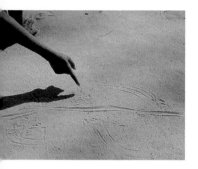

The Larapinta Trail runs along the spine of the West MacDonnell Range, a series of parallel ridges rising above the red inland deserts of central Australia. This is the driest continent on earth and the trail provides the unique opportunity of walking through a desert region. Although the trail is still being constructed, it is already well known to walkers and travellers alike.

In 1989, the government decided to connect the existing reserves (Simpsons Gap, Ormiston Gorge and Redbank Gorge and several smaller parks) together into a single unified national park. Part of this grand plan was the creation of a 220km (140 miles) walking trail along the length of the range. Beginning at Telegraph Station near Alice Springs, the Larapinta Trail is planned to extend west to Mount Razorback at the other end of the range. The first section was opened in 1990 and after 10 years, eight of the 13 sections are open to walkers. The name 'Larapinta' is the local aboriginal name for the Finke River, which drains most of streams in the range. Many aboriginals still live in the area and their agreement is needed to complete the remaining sections; it could be another three years before all sections are open.

The Larapinta Trail has been designed to appeal to trekkers and walkers who wish to experience the desert ranges without the need for extensive planning. An unusual feature of the area is the series of deep gaps where streams cut through the range. As the range was uplifted, the streams kept eroding the rising rock and have remained in essentially the same place instead of being diverted around. The result is a series of gorges where the watertable is exposed in permanent waterholes. These sources of water are of utmost importance to the local aboriginal people and the region's wildlife as well as, these days, walkers. Water is provided either by waterholes or tanks at all camp sites. The track itself is usually well marked with distance posts every kilometre.

Until the central four sections of the Larapinta Trail are completed, the best walk is the 60km (40 miles) traverse from Standley Chasm to Alice Springs. To make transport arrangements easier, take a morning tour bus to Standley Chasm and walk back to Alice Springs. The bus drive provides fine views of the range to the north.

The walk begins with a side trip into Standley Chasm itself. This narrow parallel-sided gorge is a major tourist attraction and is best avoided at midday when large

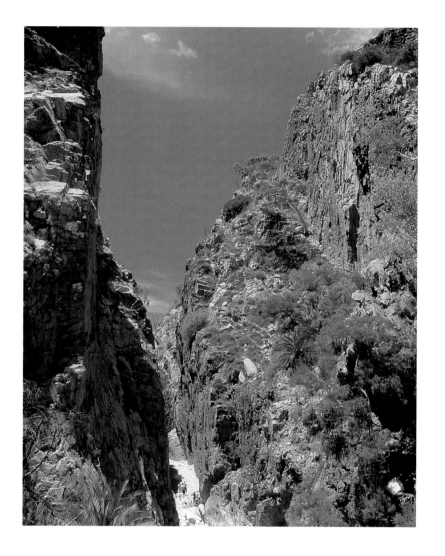

TOP *Fish Hole, a permanent pool on Jay Creek is sacred to the Aborigines and marks the end of the second stage on the Larapinta Trail.*

INSET *A young Aborigine tracks 'bush tucker', following the trail left by a lizard.*

ABOVE *The walls of Standley Chasm are over 150m (500ft) in height and the chasm itself under 10m (30ft) in width.*

OPPOSITE *The Larapinta Trail follows a high ridge of the Chewings Range, west of Fish Hole, between Tangentyere Junction and Millers Flat.*

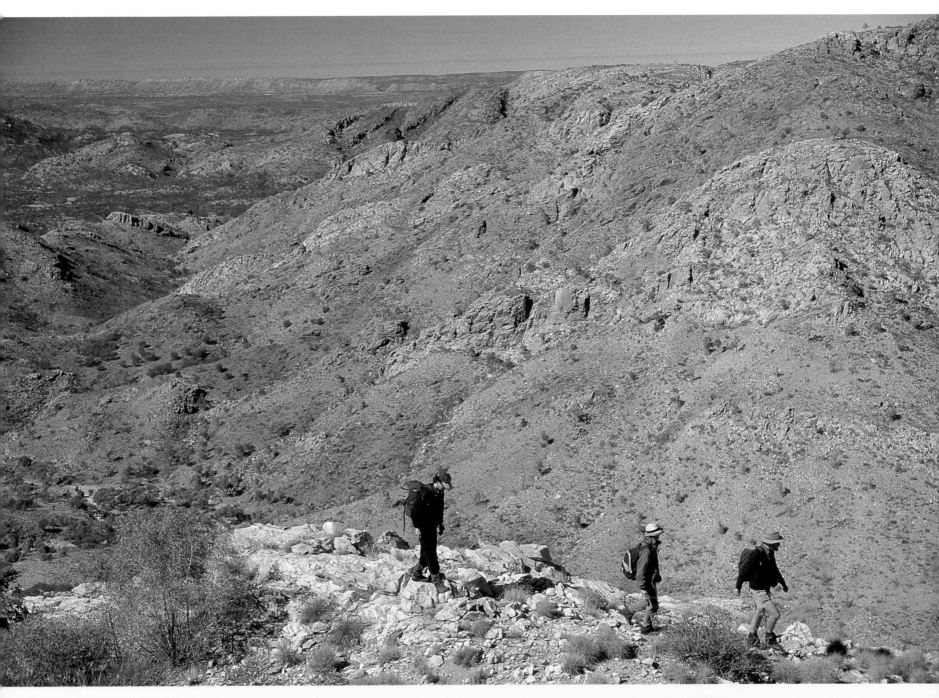

LOCATION Central Australia

WHEN TO GO May to September. Avoid summer months as temperatures can be over 40°C (104°F).

START Standley Chasm. Bus tours run several times a day from Alice Springs; book at the Tourist Bureau.

FINISH Alice Springs.

DURATION 4 to 6 days; 60km (40 miles)

MAX ALTITUDE Lorettas Lookout (1150m; 3770ft).

TECHNICAL CONSIDERATIONS Moderate grade. The Conservation Commission produces a set of strip maps for the trail. Nos. 1 to 3 are required for the described walk.

EQUIPMENT Tent, lightweight camping equipment. This is a desert walk – carry enough water for each day.

TREKKING STYLE Backpacking. Camping at established sites only.

PERMITS/RESTRICTIONS No permits required; no camping allowed near water-holes; use a fuel stove for cooking.

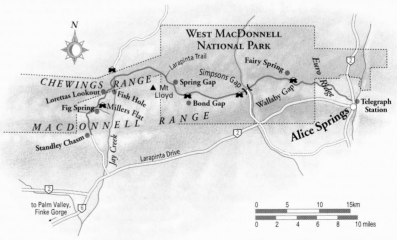

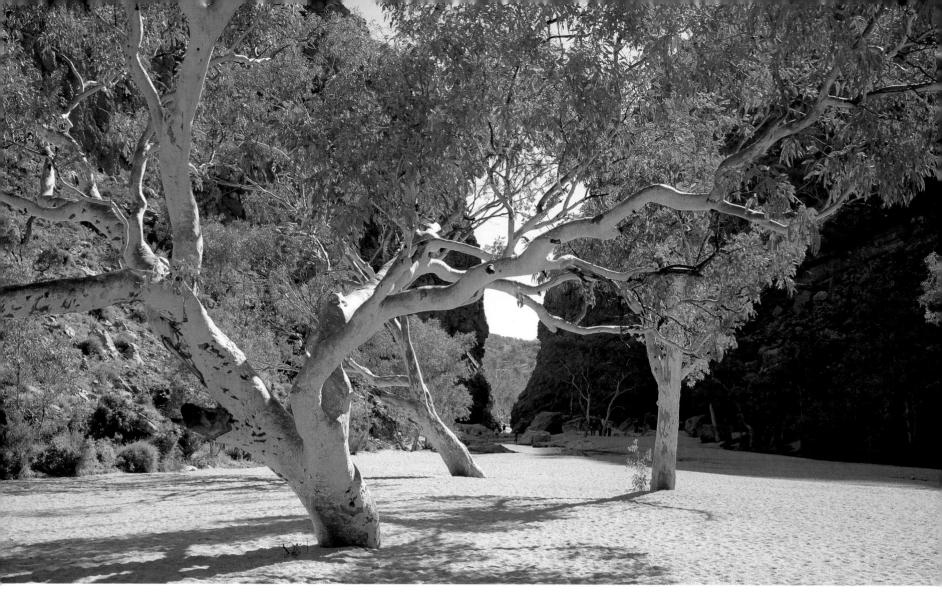

numbers of tourists arrive. At other times of day, however, there are few people around, and there will be ample occasion to wade in the pool at the far end and appreciate the gorge from both sides.

After leaving the chasm, the main trail climbs steadily, providing good views of the surrounding landscape. Only a small amount of bushes and grass grow up here, and barren red rocky slopes tower above. Be careful not to sit on the spinifex grass, as its leaves are as sharp as needles! Entering the heart of the range, the track then leads over a saddle, before heading northeast, following a large, dry creek bed downstream. All around are signs of flood damage, yet no water. Rainfall is rare here but when it does rain, it often takes the form of thunderstorms, which can result in flash floods – for this reason you should avoid camping in a streambed overnight. There are several dry waterfalls to descend along the way, each very different – the first is a straight cliff, then a series of sloping slabs and finally a set of deep bowls separated by vertical steps. The usually well-marked track deteriorates somewhat along the creek as the occasional flash floods wash away signposts, but you do not really need them. Just keep walking downstream.

The only water sites are at Refuge and Fig Springs. Collect water here, as there is none until Fish Hole. Soon after Fig Spring, you cross the open camp site at Millers Flat. The tent sites are nothing special but the surrounding views of red rock slopes and cliffs make it a fine setting for an overnight stop. With nearby springs, the valley also contains a wide variety of plants, including the MacDonnell Range cycad, Peach-leaved poison bush, Central Australian plectranthus and tender brake. Many of these are found only in these small gorges and are plants from wet climates like rain forests. The extremely wide variety of plants and the open landscape they live in is one of the special features of the range.

The trail splits, offering a high route and a low route. The lower trail has been provided for those who hate climbing hills and is not very scenic. Take the high route north. This passes through a small gorge with palm trees, another unexpected sight in this dry landscape. An awkward climb past a large, dry waterfall leads to a saddle. The trail swings northeast and climbs to Lorettas Lookout (1150m; 3770ft) at the top of Chewings Range. This is the finest view on the trail. Looking along the crest of the MacDonnells, it becomes evident that the range is actually a series of disconnected ridges and peaks. The sweeping views of never-ending deserts stretch both north and south.

A steady descent joins the lower track and leads to the spectacular Fish Hole, a deep waterhole surrounded by cliffs. The site is sacred to aboriginals, who allow walkers to visit if they follow simple rules: no camping is allowed and when heading upstream walkers must stay in the creek bed. Follow the bed of Jay Creek upstream through a scenic gorge for 2km (1.3 miles). The track then skirts the northern side of Mount Lloyd (1045m; 3429ft) as the terrain is too rocky and steep for a trail. Several raised granite

ABOVE *The typically dry landscape of Simpsons Gap, the largest gap in the West MacDonnell Range, has only a few waterholes to support the area's flora and fauna.*

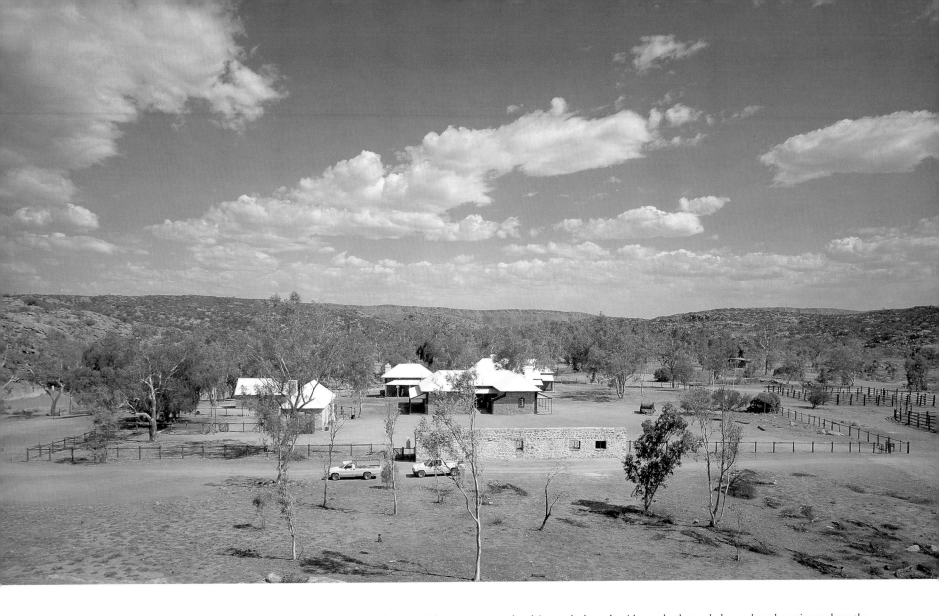

ridges provide good views of this rugged peak. The trail crosses over from the north side of the range to the south by passing through Spring Gap, another permanent spring. A few kilometres further on lies Mulga Camp. The water-tank and unusual tall trees here provide shade from the harsh desert sun, and it is a good place for a rest. Collect water and walk another hour to camp at the foot of Arenge Bluff. This is arguably the best place in the range to view the setting sun, as the crags above turn orange then red.

The next day, Bond Gap is accessed by a marked side trail. This extremely narrow and deep waterhole is one of the best places to sit at and observe bird life. The trail continues east, meandering across a flat, dry desert plain providing fine views of the surrounding ridges. At Simpsons Gap, a walkers' camp site has been provided, with a shaded shelter and hard ground to camp on.

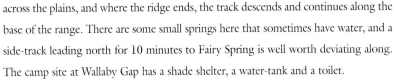

Simpsons Gap is the largest and most spectacular gap in the range and a popular tourist site with a sealed access road. Expect to share it with many other people. The trail continues east and soon leaves the crowds behind, climbing the next ridge. The height provides fine views

across the plains, and where the ridge ends, the track descends and continues along the base of the range. There are some small springs here that sometimes have water, and a side-track leading north for 10 minutes to Fairy Spring is well worth deviating along. The camp site at Wallaby Gap has a shade shelter, a water-tank and a toilet.

Next morning the trail climbs onto Euro Ridge (790m; 2600ft). While not high, this cliff-edged ridge provides fine views of Alice Springs and the surrounding country. Past Euro Ridge, the West MacDonnell Range becomes a series of low-lying hills. The trail meanders across these hills to Telegraph Station, where it officially ends.

The station was the first permanent European settlement in the centre of Australia. Established in 1872, it was used as a telegraphic repeater to enable messages to be transmitted from Adelaide to Darwin. Only 3km (2 miles) away lies Alice Springs, and an easy walk south along good paths by the river leads into the town centre. Free showers are available at the public toilets near the council offices. Wash away the red dust but remember the glowing hills, sharp spinifex and colourful gorges of the Larapinta Trail.

ABOVE *Alice Springs telegraph station, a monument to the tenacious spirit of Australia's first European settlers, is a welcome sight for trekkers completing the Larapinta Trail.*

CENTRE *Euro Ridge (790m; 2600ft) is named after the medium-sized kangaroos, known as 'jurus' by the Aborigines, often spotted here among the spinifex (porcupine grass).*

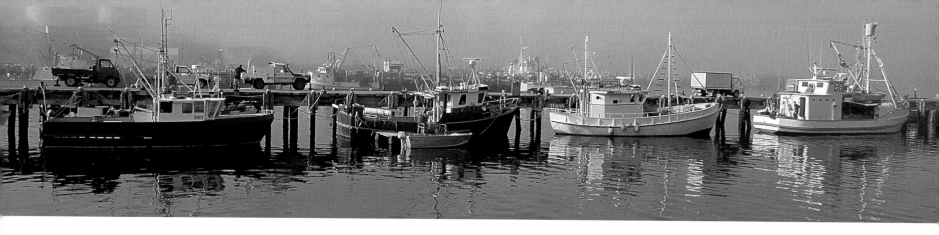

EDEN TO MALLACOOTA

by Peter Cook

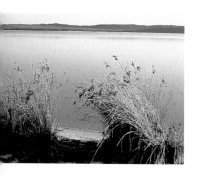

The eight-day trek between the fishing and tourist towns of Eden and Mallacoota will take you through the best coastal wilderness on the east coast of Australia. A major feature of this trek is that special feeling that comes from being part of a pristine, unspoilt and unpolluted environment, untouched by civilization and development.

The area has a fascinating history mainly to do with shipwrecks, the best known of which was the *Sydney Cove*, which ran aground on a small island between Victoria and Tasmania in 1796 when Sydney was the only settlement in Australia. The captain sent 17 men off in the ship's long boat to row to Sydney to get help, but the long boat was wrecked on the Victorian coast. Having survived this, all 17 started off on a trek up the Victorian and New South Wales coast. Only three men survived and made it to Sydney. These men were the first Europeans to trek the Wilderness coast. Walking this area today, it is not difficult to appreciate what an amazing feat of survival theirs was.

The best place to start this trek is the fishing wharf at Eden where you can charter a boat to taxi you across Twofold Bay to Fisheries Beach where the walking begins. The first three days of the trek take you through Ben Boyd National Park, named after colourful Scottish entrepreneur, Benjamin Boyd, who arrived in Australia in 1842. Boyd established two settlements on Twofold Bay, which he named Boydtown and East Boyd. They were to be centrepieces of a trading empire he planned to build based around his expanding farming, whaling and shipping interests. In 1849, Boyd's business empire collapsed and he sailed out of Twofold Bay for the last time, bound for the Californian goldfields. He disappeared in 1851 on a Pacific Island, allegedly killed by natives.

TOP *A misty morning view over the main fishing wharves in Snug Cove, Eden. Boats can be chartered here to transport trekkers to the start of the trail at Fisheries Beach.*
INSET *Another tranquil day comes to an end on the shores of Nadgee Lake. Due to its prolific bird life, the lake is a favourite camping spot for trekkers.*
ABOVE RIGHT *Marred by nothing but footprints, the beaches of Boyd National Park constitute a pristine natural wilderness.*

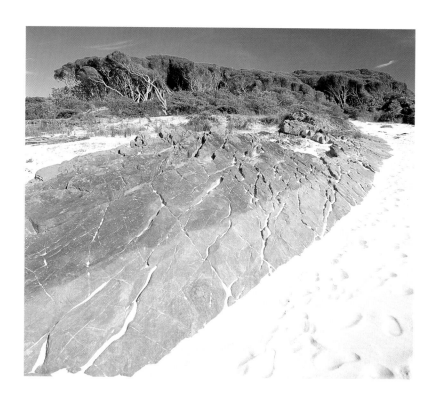

Shortly after beginning the trek, you come across Boyd's Tower at Red Point, one of several impressive structures that Boyd erected in what was then a very isolated area. The tower was intended to give Boyd's whaling crews early warning of approaching whales so that he could have an advantage over his competitors. Named after the vivid red siltstone that is a feature of the headland here, Red Point also offers fascinating insight into the area's geological past. The siltstone, which originated as fine volcanic ash, was laid down in the Devonian Period in horizontal beds that were later compressed and folded by powerful earth movements.

Further along the trail at Bittangabee Bay are the ruins of a whaling station built by the Imlay Brothers, Boyd's main competitors. The buildings here were never completed because the Imlay Brothers, like Boyd, suffered a financial crisis that forced them to scale back their operations.

Ben Boyd National Park has impressive sea cliffs along which the trail often traverses, affording great views up and down the coast. The best-known landmark on this section of the trek is Greencape and its lighthouse. The lighthouse was built in 1886, just three years before the ship the *Ly-ee-moon* was wrecked there with the loss of 71 lives. Several of the graves can still be seen near the lighthouse.

When you walk from Ben Boyd National Park into Nadgee Nature Reserve you are entering a wilderness. Nadgee was never settled or developed and until the 1980s it was closed to the public and only accessible to scientists doing wildlife research. All these factors have kept Nadgee relatively pristine.

Nadgee has many special places, including the mouth of the Merrica River, a beautiful, hidden cove in a rocky coastline that makes a fabulous lunch spot, and Newton's Beach, with caves that can be explored at low tide and a dawn chorus of resident lyrebirds. Lyrebirds are expert mimics of a host of other bird calls and their melodic repertoire makes waking up at Newton's a memorable experience.

Osprey Lookout is another highlight, and its views of the surrounding sea cliffs and the rock pools below are magnificent. Not far from Osprey Lookout is Nadgee Beach, where the Nadgee River flows across the sand and into the sea. Nadgee Lake, home to a large number of black swans and pelicans, is a favourite camp site among trekkers. Here, magical sunsets over the lake can be appreciated, with Howe Hill silhouetted against the skyline. Birds are a major feature of trekking in Nadgee. When walking

across the heathlands of Nadgee Moor and Endeavour Moor, you will often catch fleeting glimpses of the endangered ground parrot. During the night at Nadgee Lake you often hear dingoes howling. Dingoes are now very rare in southeastern Australia, and wildlife scientists have been researching this species at Nadgee for the last 20 years.

After three days of trekking through Nadgee, you enter Croajingolong National Park, and the landscape changes completely as the wilderness takes on a new form – the estuaries, sea cliffs and heathlands are replaced by sand dunes and long beaches. The name Croajingolong is derived from the name of a local aboriginal clan called Krowathunkoolung, which means 'the country belonging to the men of the east'.

The sand dunes you walk across on day seven, between Cape Howe and Lake Wau Wauka, are the biggest coastal sand dunes in Australia and an utterly amazing landscape. The best time to cross the dunes is early morning or late in the day when the sun is low in the sky and the lack of glare makes it easy to see the array of patterns the wind has left in the bright, white sand. The supply of sand comes from the sea near

BELOW *Dingoes give chase to a Lace monitor in the shallows of Nadgee Lake. Due to their depleting numbers, the dingo population at Nadgee is under close observation.*

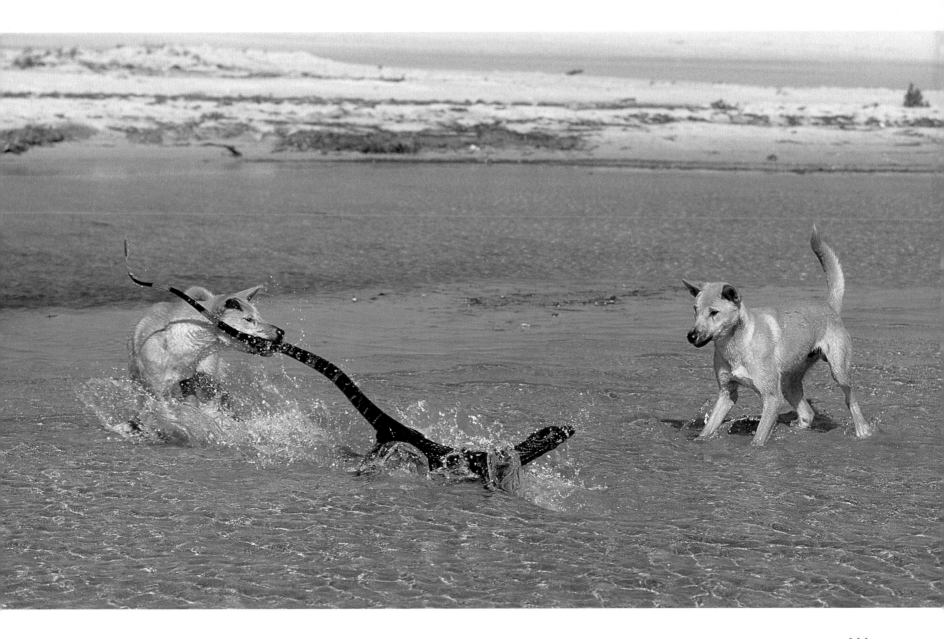

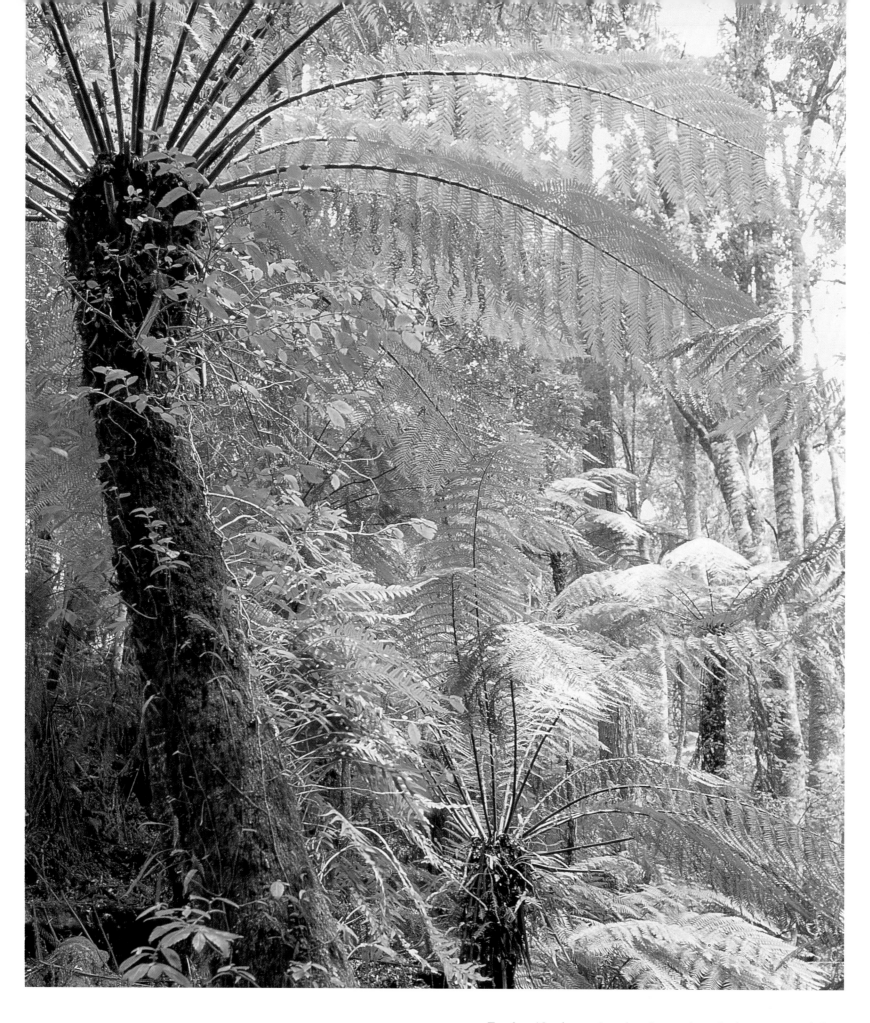

ABOVE *Tree ferns* (Cyatheaceae), *such as these specimens in the temperate rainforest near Eden, have tall, trunk-like stems with foliage at the top.*

Gabo Island, courtesy of the prevailing southwesterly wind that blows the sand back into the sea at the northeastern end of the dunes, not far from Bunyip Hole. Making your way across the dunes is straightforward as the desired route is parallel to the beach, which is visible most of the way. The walking is easy despite the ups and downs, and interesting sights along the way include small waterholes that form between the dunes and thickets of small trees, in the process of being swallowed up by the shifting sands. Rolling down the dunes becomes a popular pastime at every rest stop.

Beyond Lake Wau Wauka lie Gabo Island, Tullaberga Island, Lake Barracoota and Big Beach. Lake Barracoota is a beautiful camp site for the last night with great views offering a different perspective across to Howe Hill. This area has its own fair share of shipwreck sagas, such as the story of the *Monumental City*, which ran onto Tullaberga Island in 1853, resulting in 37 deaths. This disaster was the reason why the Gabo Island lighthouse was built nine years later.

The trek ends on Big Beach on the eastern side of Mallacoota Inlet. At Mallacoota trekkers can celebrate their arrival with a sumptuous meal of local seafood at a restaurant with spectacular views of the wilderness that has been explored.

The walk from Eden to Mallacoota is just one section of a much longer trek along the wilderness coast, which stretches from Lakes Entrance in Victoria to Pambula in New South Wales. Eden to Mallacoota is surely the most varied part of this coastline, but once in the area there are many other beautiful places well worth visiting. Its pristine scenery, history and geomorphology, together with its abundant bird, animal and plant life are the reasons why trekkers keep coming back to walk the wilderness coast.

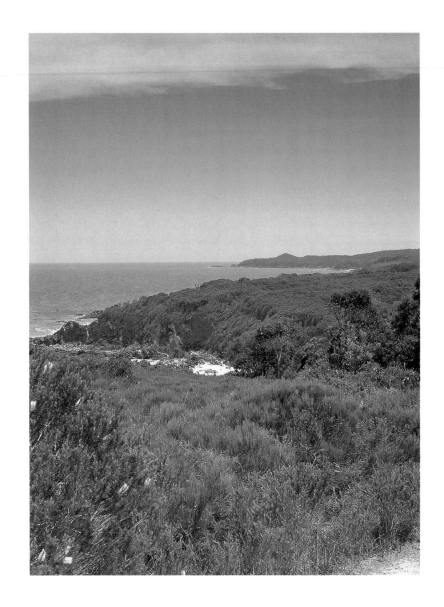

RIGHT *As trekkers enter Croajingolong National Park, heathlands and sea cliffs give way to spectacular sand dunes and long stretches of white sand beaches.*

LOCATION Roughly halfway down the coast between Sydney and Melbourne.

WHEN TO GO March to September.

START Fishing wharf at Eden. Take a boat across Twofold Bay to Fisheries Beach where the trek begins.

FINISH Big Beach on the eastern side of Mallacoota Inlet. Water-taxi arrangements can be made through the Eden Tourist Information Centre.

DURATION 8 days; 95km (60 miles)

MAX ALTITUDE 260m (850ft)

TECHNICAL CONSIDERATIONS None.

EQUIPMENT Standard backpacking equipment. Must be self-sufficent in food. Waterproof clothing and sun protection. Relevant maps available from bushwalking shops in Melbourne, Sydney and Canberra.

TREKKING STYLE Backpacking. Most of the walking at the start of the trek is done on 4x4 tracks or narrow foot tracks. After Bunyip Hole on Day 6, it is mainly beach walking.

PERMITS/RESTRICTIONS Number of people allowed to visit Nadgee and Croajingolong at any one time is limited. Permits are required and can be obtained from the New South Wales National Parks and Wildlife Service or Parks Victoria.

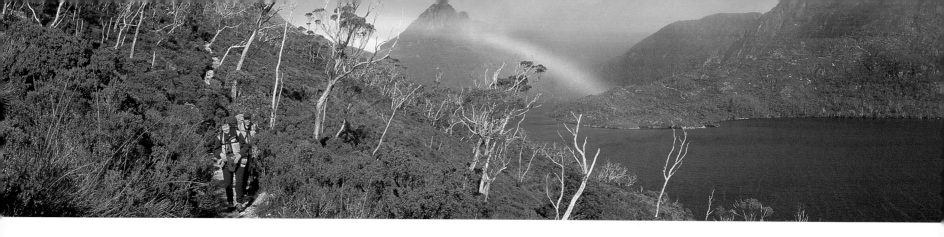

THE OVERLAND TRACK

by Shaun Barnett

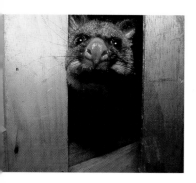

Tasmania's Overland Track has in recent years developed a reputation as Australia's finest trek. The 73km (45-mile) trek certainly has it all, with the spectacular Cradle Mountain, numerous alpine lakes, distinctive Australian wildlife and forests, and interesting Aboriginal and European history. The mountains are some of the most rugged in Australia, and the trek passes close to Tasmania's highest peak, Mount Ossa (1617m; 5305ft). Although no glaciers exist today, the landscape bears the marks of heavy glaciation from the last ice age, which ended some 10–14,000 years ago.

The trek crosses an impressive chunk of central Tasmania, part of one of the largest wilderness areas remaining in Australia. In 1982, along with several areas in south-west Tasmania, Cradle Mountain–Lake St Clair National Park was granted World Heritage status, rightly identifying its importance on a global scale.

Aboriginal people have lived in Tasmania for over 30,000 years, and survived even the last ice age by retreating to coastal refuges. Although you always feel you are passing through pristine wilderness, many of the buttongrass plains that characterize the central part of the trek are actually the result of past Aboriginal fires. By lighting fires, Aboriginal hunters encouraged buttongrass to grow on the damp peaty soils, displacing eucalypt (gum) forest. The resultant plains made superb places for them to hunt wombats, wallabies and kangaroos.

Europeans arriving in the late 1700s and early 1800s also quickly recognized the hunting possibilities of the high plateau, with trappers hunting possums, wallabies, wombats and Tasmanian devils for their skins. It was an Austrian man who proved instrumental in getting protection for Cradle Mountain. Gustav Weindorfer emigrated to Australia in 1900, and with his wife Kate made many visits to the mountain. Enraptured by the beauty of the peak, he developed a firm conviction that the area deserved national park status. To encourage people to visit, Gustav built a chalet, Waldheim, a short distance from the mountain. He served as guide and host there, continuing to campaign for the area's protection until his death in 1932.

Cradle Mountain was declared a scenic reserve in 1922, but only gained national park status in 1971. Trapper Bert Nicholls first blazed the Overland Track itself in 1930, and the first walk along the entire route was completed in January 1931.

Although it can be walked in either direction, most people begin the Overland Track from Cradle Mountain, an impressive turreted peak that bears the chiselled imprint of the last ice age. Officially, the Overland Track begins at Waldheim, but from here it is not possible to get good views of the mountain. A much more impressive vista is found at the shores of nearby Lake Dove, and trekkers can opt to begin the trail here, by joining tracks that link the main trail at Crater Lake.

On either route, trails pass through a mixture of eucalypt and beech forest, crossing bubbling streams, and climbing steadily to Marion's Lookout (1200m; 4000ft). Here, on a good day, are uninterrupted views of Cradle Mountain (1545m; 5070ft), now much more imposing, and the more distant monolith of Barn Bluff (1559m;

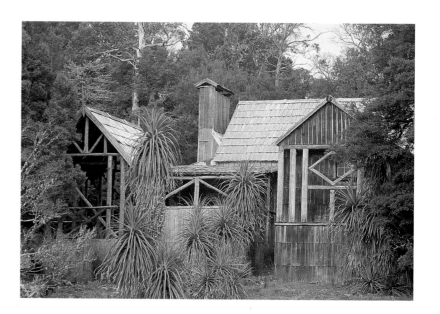

TOP *During the last ice age, a thick glacier formed on the flanks of Cradle Mountain and carved out the bed of Dove Lake, today one of the best viewpoints in the park.*

INSET *Possums are the least shy of Tasmanian marsupials, their inquisitive nature often leads them to investigate huts or tents at night.*

ABOVE *Waldheim, Gustav Weindorfer's chalet, near the start of the track was opened in 1912. The original chalet was demolished in 1976 and this replica built in its place.*

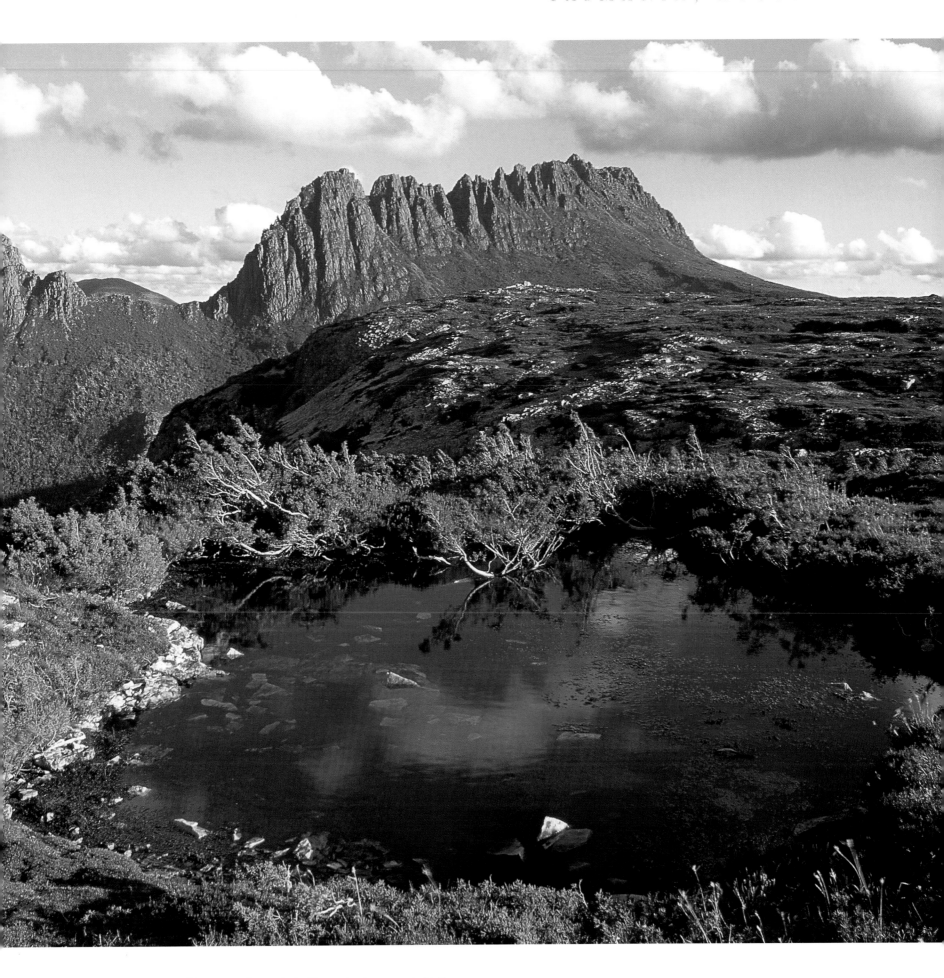

ABOVE *Cradle Mountain, like many other peaks in Tasmania, is composed chiefly of dolerite, a highly weather-resistant volcanic rock.*

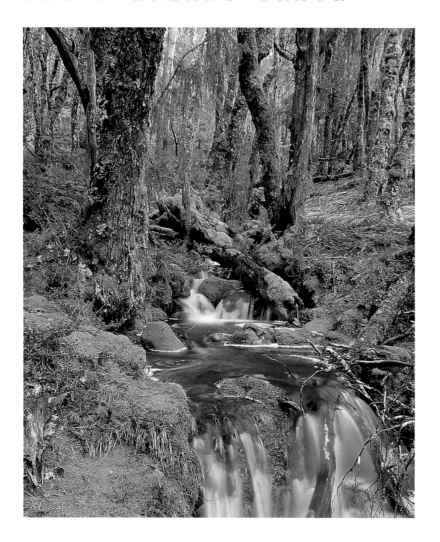

ABOVE *While myrtle grows into a large attractive evergreen (seen here), other species of* Nothafagus *beech adopt a more bushy form and lose their leaves during autumn.*

5115ft). On many days, however, there are no views. Unimpeded by any landmass for over 14,000km (8700 miles), westerly winds can bring snow, hail and rain at any time of year to Tasmania, making the island deserving of its reputation for stormy weather. This climate may sound bleak and uninviting, but rainforests as distinctive as Tasmania's inevitably require a lot of rain.

From Marion's Lookout, the trail begins a long sidle around the western flanks of Cradle Mountain, passing the rustic shelter of Kitchen Hut before entering patches of endemic subalpine shrubs known as *pandanni*.

Tasmania's plants share a common ancestry with those of New Zealand and South America when all were part of the super-continent Gondwana. Since the fragmentation of the continent some 80 million years ago, many Gondwanan plants have survived in comparatively cooler Tasmania while their counterparts were replaced by more modern plants on the sun-baked Australian mainland.

Past a turn-off indicating the route to Barn Bluff, the Overland Track begins a descent to the two huts at Waterfall Valley. The next day sees a considerable stretch of travel across buttongrass plains, with the bulky Mount Pelion (1554m; 5098ft) visible for much of the day. Much of the route is now boardwalked, a necessary track development in the notoriously peaty soils. Past use had turned much of the track into a quagmire, and the boardwalks, while jarring to walk on, are necessary both to prevent environmental damage, and to allow trekkers to make a reasonable pace.

Lake Windermere Hut appears set in a welcoming forest enclave, nestled near the attractive Lake Windermere. Trekkers attempting the trail in five days will need to continue on to Pelion Hut, while those with more time may wish to spend a night here.

Across the Pine Forest Moor, the trail begins to reach the edge of Mount Pelion, and here winding through eucalypt forest it leads eventually to the swampy Frog Flats, and beyond to Pelion Hut. From Pelion Plains, the track climbs into the heart

LOCATION Cradle Mountain, Lake St Clair National Park in central Tasmania.

WHEN TO GO Any time of year. December to March is most popular, but the trail can get crowded. During winter, snow may cover large sections of the track.

START Cradle Mountain, near Devonport in northern Tasmania.

FINISH Lake St Clair, some 100km (62 miles) northwest of Hobart, the state capital. Daily buses service both ends during the summer season.

DURATION 5 to 7 days; 73km (45 miles).

MAX ALTITUDE Marion's Lookout (1200m; 4000ft).

TECHNICAL CONSIDERATIONS Moderate grade, suitable for people of moderate fitness. No climbing or scrambling necessary. Tasmap produces a 1:100,000-scale park map.

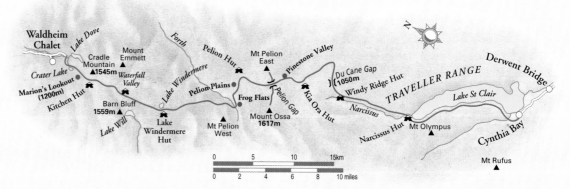

EQUIPMENT Sturdy boots, pack, sleeping bag and mat, food, warm clothes and wet-weather gear.

TREKKING STYLE Backpacking. Well-formed and marked track with several huts en route. Camping is possible near most huts, and in a few other locations. Guided walks using private huts, with meals supplied, are also available.

PERMITS/RESTRICTIONS Currently no booking system exists for independent trekkers although this may change in the near future. There are modest entry fees for all Tasmania's national parks. Trekkers intending on visiting more than one park should consider the good-value two-month Backpacker Pass.

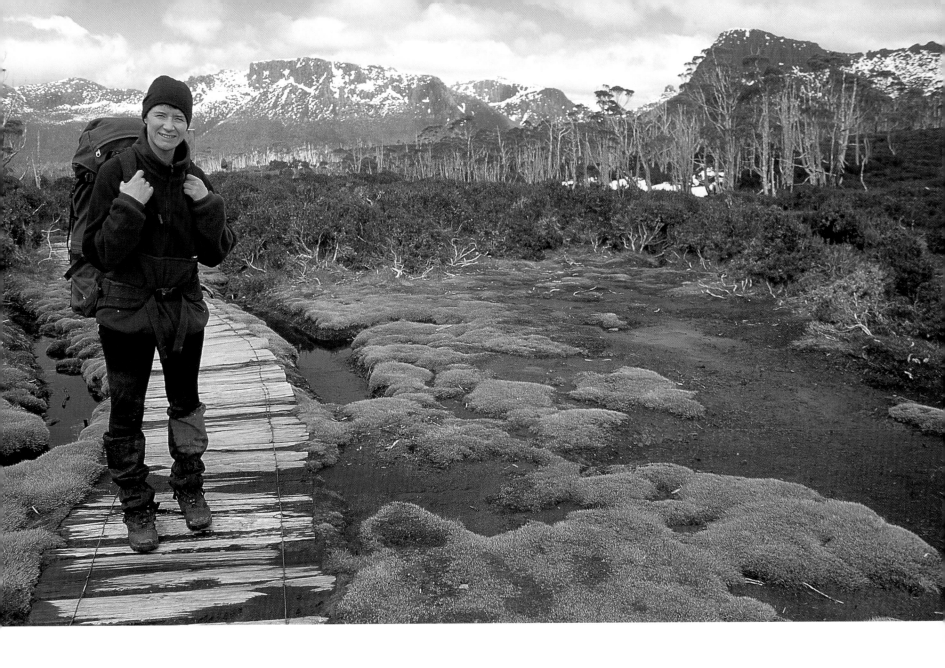

of Tasmania's highest peaks, rising in long fluted columns at geometric angles. A steady climb with numerous steps leads to the open expanse of Pelion Gap (1126m; 3694ft), a pass with commanding views.

Taking fittingly ancient names from Greek mythology, Mounts Thetis, Achilles, and Ossa crowd the horizon. Mount Ossa is hardly a giant at 1617m (5303ft), but its buttresses and steep approaches demand respect from would-be climbers. In summer the summit can be reached via a track from Pelion Gap, but snow may deter an attempt.

From Pelion Gap, the track descends into the Pinestone Valley and eventually to Kia Ora Hut. Here's a good place to observe Bennetts wallabies, one of Tasmania's 31 marsupial species. Wombats are more shy creatures with short stout bodies; you're more likely to see evidence of them in the form of their distinctive square droppings.

Passing through soaring eucalypt forests, the trail from Kia Ora Hut at first crosses a low pass known as Du Cane Gap (1050m; 3450ft), then descends the Narcissus Valley, flanked by steep escarpments of the Traveller Range. As the tallest flowering plants on earth, eucalypts can reach heights of 90m (300ft), with their trunks peeling bark in great sagging strips. Loud birds such as the sulphur-crested cockatoo are likely to interrupt quiet contemplation in these forests. Other birds likely to make their presence felt are black currawongs – crow-like birds with beady yellow eyes and quick reflexes.

ABOVE *Year-round, spectacular Pelion Gap is covered in cushion plants which have adapted a low, wind- and snow-resistant form.*

At the end of the valley, the darkly stained waters of the Narcissus River ebb into the head of Lake St Clair. Many of Tasmania's streams become coloured by tannins leached from buttongrass plains, giving them the appearance of strong tea. Narcissus Hut is nearby.

Lake St Clair is a more traditional blue, despite having several tannin-stained streams feeding it. After the last ice age gouged out its bed between Mount Olympus and the Traveller Range, Lake St Clair became Australia's deepest lake (167m; 548ft). Here, platypus – primitive egg-laying mammals – are quite common, and are best seen in the early morning or evening, quietly moving across the surface of the lake.

On the lake edge, Narcissus Hut is the last one on the Overland Track if you're heading north to south. A trail skirts Lake St Clair past Echo Point to the track end at Cynthia Bay. Alternatively, take a leisurely cruise across the lakes on the launch that operates on demand during summer. It's an enjoyable way to round off one of Tasmania's most spectacular outdoor experiences.

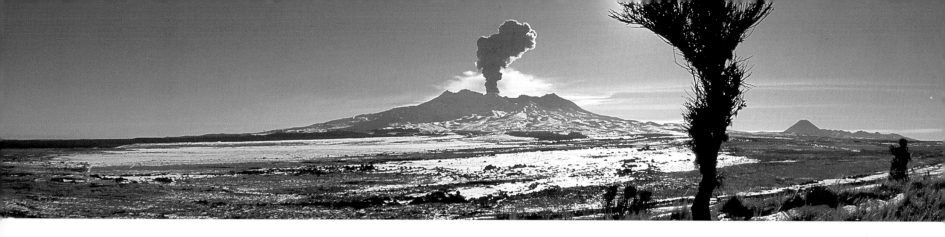

ROUND THE MOUNTAINS

by Kathy Ombler

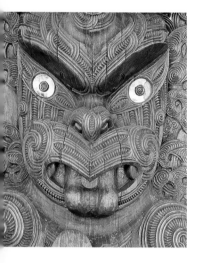

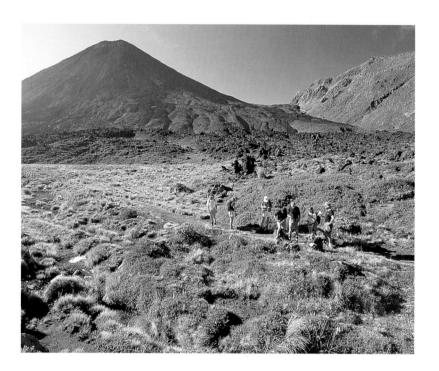

The volcanic landscape of New Zealand's Tongariro National Park holds a special place on the stage of world conservation. The park, dominated by three magnificent volcanic mountains, is the fourth national park ever created and the first site to be granted dual World Heritage status for its outstanding natural and cultural values.

Ruapehu, Tongariro and Ngauruhoe stand at the southern end of the Pacific Rim of Fire, a vast zone of volcanic and earthquake activity that results from tectonic movement of the great Pacific crustal plate. Mount Ruapehu, the highest of the three at 2797m (9177ft), dominates the surrounding countryside and is the only North Island mountain with real glaciers. Indeed glacier ice completely surrounds its volatile steaming Crater Lake, one of the few such phenomena anywhere in the world. Ruapehu is an extremely active volcano, erupting every few years. As recently as 1996, massive showers of ash, rock and steam were blasted hundreds of metres from the Crater Lake and lahars (rivers of mud and water) streamed down the mountain slopes.

Mount Tongariro (1968m; 6459ft) may be lower than Ruapehu but its huge massif extends over 18km (11 miles) in length and encompasses numerous craters, steaming fumaroles, geothermal springs and volcanic vents, one of which is in fact the higher, classical cone-shaped Ngauruhoe (2291m; 7519ft). The Round the Mountains trek travels over and around these mountains, passing through stunning, stark and variable volcanic landscapes, barren desertlands, beech forests, alpine herbfields, lakes and glacier-carved river valleys. The entire trek takes about seven to nine days, but there are several access points that allow options for shorter trips.

TOP *Mount Ruapehu is the highest and most recently active of the three volcanoes that form the nucleus of Tongariro National Park.*
INSET *Ancestors of Ngati Tuwharetoa, the local Maori people, are remembered in carvings at the park's visitor centre.*
ABOVE RIGHT *Trekkers take a well-earned break among open rock and tussock fields between Mount Ngauruhoe and Whakapapa Village.*

Within the northern circuit is the Tongariro Crossing, arguably one of the most popular and spectacular one-day walks in New Zealand. This six- to eight-hour walk climbs high between Mounts Ngauruhoe and Tongariro, past volcanic features such as steaming vents, old lava flows and variably coloured, water-filled explosion craters. The southern sector of this trek traverses the mid slopes of Mount Ruapehu, where the stark volcanic landscape softens. The slopes are covered with a mix of beech forest, tussock fields and alpine herbfields and punctuated by mountain streams and waterfalls.

The Tongariro volcanoes are of deep spiritual significance to Ngati Tuwharetoa, the Maori people who have lived in the region for nearly 1000 years. The mountains represent the home of their ancestors and are sacred areas to be treated with respect. Traditional stories describe the origins of volcanism in the park.

When the ancestors of Ngati Tuwharetoa migrated to New Zealand, the navigator of their canoe, Te Arawa, was the high priest Ngatoroirangi. After landfall, he led his people inland, looking for land they could claim as their own. They settled by the great lake of Taupo, and Ngatoroirangi continued south to 'claim' the summit of Tongariro. As he crossed the barren desert, he spied a second priest travelling towards the mountain so he called for help from his gods, who sent a savage storm to vanquish his rival. Later, as Ngatoroirangi neared the icy summit, he became frozen in a snowstorm and prayed to his priestess sisters in Hawaiiki, his traditional Polynesian homeland, for warmth. The name Tongariro, referring to the cold south wind being carried away, comes from this prayer. Ngatoroirangi's sisters blasted a fiery response, sending fire via an underground passage – known today as the Pacific Rim of Fire – which erupted from a new crater we know today as Mount Ngauruhoe.

Thus the fires of occupation for Ngatoroirangi's people were lit. As the years passed, the spiritual stature of the volcanoes grew. To climb them was forbidden; travellers crossing the desert flanking Tongariro's eastern slopes used leaves as blinkers to prevent them even looking at the sacred summit. Early European explorers' attempts to climb the sacred mountains were either thwarted by local Maori, or they disregarded protocol and made their journeys in secret. In the 1800s, European immigration increased and the European system of land law was introduced throughout New Zealand, changing the very basis of traditional Maori tribal land ownership.

In 1887, to prevent the sale of the sacred mountain summits, Ngatoroirangi's descendent, Ngati Tuwharetoa chief Te Heuheu Tukino IV (Horonuku), made a historic decision and gave the three summits to the Crown to preserve them for ever as sacred places. They became the core, the very essence, of Tongariro National Park.

From Whakapapa Village, the Tongariro Northern Circuit heads north, through a mix of open tussock fields and small stands of beech forest, across the lower slopes

BELOW *The Round the Mountains trek explores Tongariro National Park, home to the Tongariro (front), Ngauruhoe (middle) and Ruapehu (distant) volcanoes.*

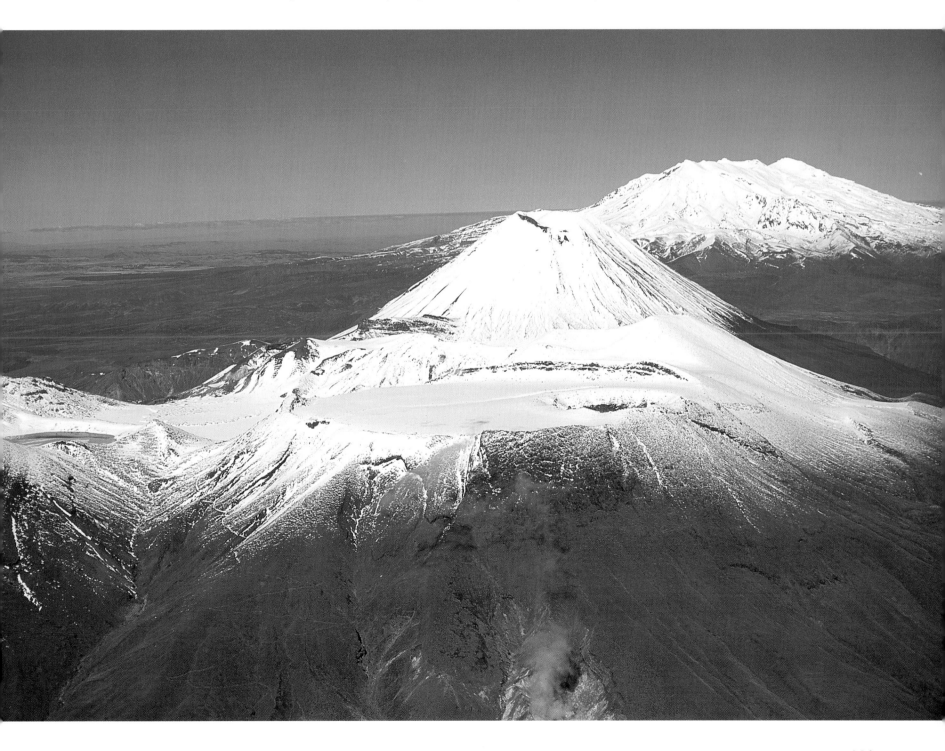

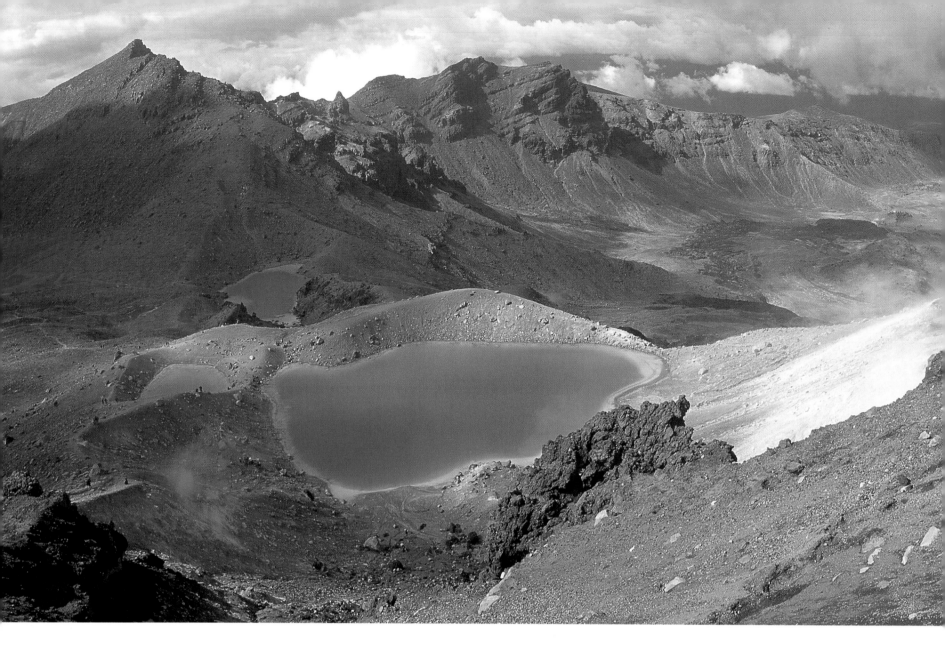

ABOVE *High on Mount Tongariro, the Emerald and Blue lakes, old craters filled with mineral waters, bring colourful contrast to the stark volcanic landscape.*

of Mount Ruapehu. The giant, classic cone of Ngauruhoe looms ahead, alongside the lower yet greater mass of Tongariro. The trail skirts around Pukekaikiore, one of the older vents of the Tongariro volcanic complex, and enters Mangatepopo Valley, close to Mangatepopo Hut.

From here the trek turns into the valley, now following the route of the one-day Tongariro Crossing, climbing a succession of lava flows that poured from Ngauruhoe during eruptions in 1949 and 1954. A five-minute detour at the head of the valley leads to Soda Springs, which emerge from beneath an old lava flow and provide a fertile little oasis that fills with summer flowers in this otherwise bleak volcanic landscape.

The hardest climbing of the trek starts here, as the rocky track wends its way high onto a saddle between Mounts Tongariro and Ngauruhoe, then crosses the flat, dusty moon-like South Crater before climbing again to the trek's highest point, Red Crater (1800m; 5900ft). The going is steep, but the view more than compensates. Here is volcanic landscape at its finest; the stark blacks, reds and browns of lava rock contrasting strongly with the brilliant green and blue mineral waters of Emerald and Blue lakes, old explosion craters, and beside them the massive wrench in the earth that is Red Crater. If the weather is clear – and it needs to be to tackle this high, exposed section

of the trek – the view extends eastwards, beyond volcanic landscape to the forest-covered Kaimanawa Ranges, part of the mountainous divide of the North Island.

Side trips from Red Crater include a walk to the summit of Tongariro (about two hours there and back) or a walk down the northern side of Tongariro to Ketetahi Hut (two hours one way). From the hut can be seen steam from Ketetahi Springs a couple of ridges away. These springs are in a private enclave of land, belonging to the Ngati Tuwharetoa people.

Back on the main stretch, the trail to Oturere Hut branches southeast from beside Emerald Lakes, and descends through fields of jagged lava into Oturere Valley. Some respite from open, rocky terrain comes while passing through the beech forest of Waihohonu Valley, where there is a restored historic hut and a track that heads west, over the low saddle between Mounts Nguaruhoe and Ruapehu.

The Round the Mountains trek continues across the Rangipo Desert, vast plains of wind-sculpted sands and volcanic rock flanking the eastern foothills of Ruapehu. Here, in the only true desert landscape of New Zealand, the altitude and harsh climate have

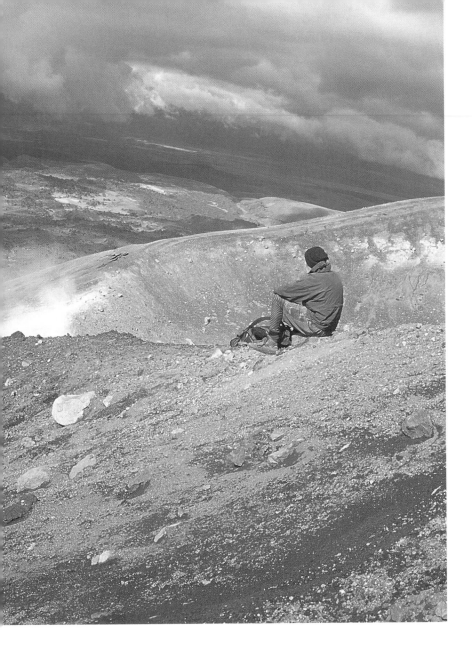

combined to prevent the regrowth of forests devastated hundreds of years ago by volcanic eruption. Rangipo Hut sits near the southern end of the desert, and from here the trek continues, traversing the slopes of Mount Ruapehu, undulating through beech forest, tussock and steep river gorges to reach Mangaehuehu Hut, from whence a gradual downhill traverse weaves through more open alpine tussock country and beech forest. About three hours from Mangaehuehu, the track passes the highest falls in the park, Waitonga Falls, tumbling over the edge of an old lava flow, then crosses a boggy clearing where a boardwalk protects fragile wetland plants from hikers' boots. On a clear day, views of Ruapehu's snowy peaks can be appreciated from here.

The trail briefly joins the sealed Ohakune Mountain Road, a road that provides access to one of Tongariro's commercial skifields. It then descends into a steep valley, crosses a lava ridge that is covered with alpine herbs and drops into the Mangaturuturu Valley, where Mangaturuturu Hut nestles on the bush edge.

The final day's walk passes by a delightful mix of mountain lakes, steep river gorges and waterfalls, beech forest, subalpine tussock and shrubs and wetlands, filled with summer flowering herbs. In good weather the views are expansive; Ruapehu's peaks loom above, while in the distant west the classic volcanic cone of Mount Egmont stands above and beyond the forest-covered wilderness of Whanganui National Park.

From Whakapapaiti Hut there are two options to end the trek: a higher level track that climbs above bushline to reach the Bruce Road (which provides access to the park's northern skifield) 4km (2.5 miles) above Whakapapa Village, or the lower forest track that heads directly to the village. At Whakapapa Village there is a park visitor centre, camping ground, motel, cafés and the historic hotel, The Grand Chateau. There are also several walks, with information signs that tell about the natural and historic features of the park.

LOCATION Central North Island

WHEN TO GO December to March is the safest and most popular time. In winter snow, ice and avalanche danger are likely.

START/FINISH Whakapapa Village, 40 minutes' drive from Turangi. Regular public transport and tramper shuttle services available.

DURATION 7 to 9 days; 85km (55 miles)

MAX ALTITUDE Red Crater, Mount Tongariro (1800m; 5900ft).

TECHNICAL CONSIDERATIONS Route is marked by poles and in places is a well-formed, benched track or boardwalk. Much of it is exposed to changeable mountain weather at any time of the year. During winter snow and ice may cover much of the route, thus climbing equip-ment and experience is necessary. Some river crossings may not be feasible during or after heavy rain.

EQUIPMENT Strong hiking boots, warm, waterproof clothing as well as standard hiking clothing.

TREKKING STYLE Backpacking. Nine park huts with facilities including toilets, mattresses, water supply and benches for cooking. During summer, the three huts on Mount Tongariro also have gas cookers and heaters. Camping is permitted.

PERMITS/RESTRICTIONS Hut space is available on a first come, first-served basis; maximum stay is two nights. Hut tickets should be purchased in advance. During the summer season, 'Great Walks' passes are required for huts on the Tongariro Northern Circuit and camping on this section is not permitted within 500m (1600ft) of the track.

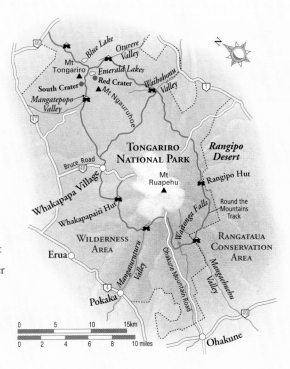

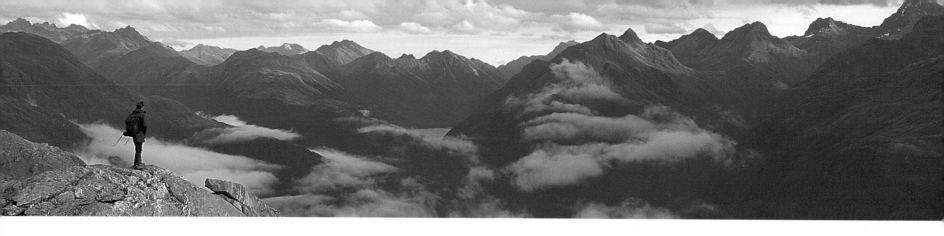

THE ROUTEBURN TRACK

by Kathy Ombler

The Routeburn Track is one of New Zealand's most spectacular and popular walks. At the heart of the Te Wahipounamu/South Westland World Heritage Area, the historic, high-quality trail traverses the remote mountains of southwestern New Zealand, through two of the country's largest national parks, Fiordland and Mount Aspiring.

Routeburn walkers pass through a veritable kaleidoscope of natural landscapes. Each day – even hour – on the trail reveals a changing outlook: dense rainforests, tussock grasslands and summer-flowering alpine herbfields, mountain streams, waterfalls and lakes, valley flats, glacier-gouged valleys, alpine passes, remnant glaciers and towering mountain peaks. Bird life is as diverse as the landscape, with more than 30 species of native birds living in the forest, open river flats and alpine habitats along the track.

The unpredictable mountain weather, too, has a huge impact on the Routeburn experience. Hot sun, moody mist, torrential rain, wind and snow; even in summer it is not unusual to meet all of these elements in the duration of one Routeburn trip.

Because of its beauty and popularity, the Routeburn walk is well served by park management and tour operators. The track itself, bridges, huts and camp sites are high quality, designed with careful environmental considerations, and well maintained.

No high-class track or hi-tech boots graced the rock and tussock slopes when humans first crossed these mountains. New Zealand's first settlers, the Maori, were tenacious travellers, particularly when in pursuit of pounamu – a greenstone or nephrite jade that was highly valued by them for use as jewellery, tools and weaponry – which was found in West Coast rivers. In their pursuit of the valuable jade, these early people forged a number of 'pounamu trails' over the great mountainous divide of the South Island.

Traces of the much-valued pounamu were also found in the Routeburn River and the Routeburn became one such trail. For centuries, flax-sandal-wearing Maori travellers negotiated the beech forests of the Routeburn Valley, then climbed over

LOCATION Southwest of the South Island.

WHEN TO GO November to April. During winter the track can be blocked by snow and should be tackled only by those with climbing experience.

START/FINISH The track can be walked in either direction, from Routeburn Shelter (72km or 45 miles from Queenstown) or 'The Divide' (on the Milford Road, 85km or 53 miles from Te Anau). Several bus companies and tour operators offer transport services from Queenstown and Te Anau to both ends of the track.

DURATION 4 days; 33km (20 miles). Bad weather may cause delays over open, exposed track sections.

MAX ALTITUDE Harris Saddle (1280m; 4200ft).

TECHNICAL CONSIDERATIONS On this alpine trail storms can occur at any time of the year. Walkers should

be cautious and carry suitable clothing for cold, wet and windy conditions.

EQUIPMENT Pack, sleeping bag, hiking boots, wet-weather gear, food, warm, quick-drying clothing, insect repellent.

TREKKING STYLE Backpacking. There are four park huts on the track, each supplied with gas cookers, cold running water, lighting, heating, communal bunkrooms and flush toilets. Two camp sites on the track.

PERMITS/RESTRICTIONS Advance bookings essential. Accommodation bookings required between October and April. Camping is not permitted within 500m (1600ft) of the track, except at the two designated camp sites.

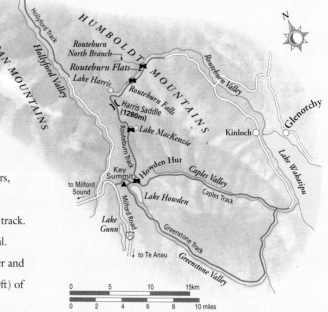

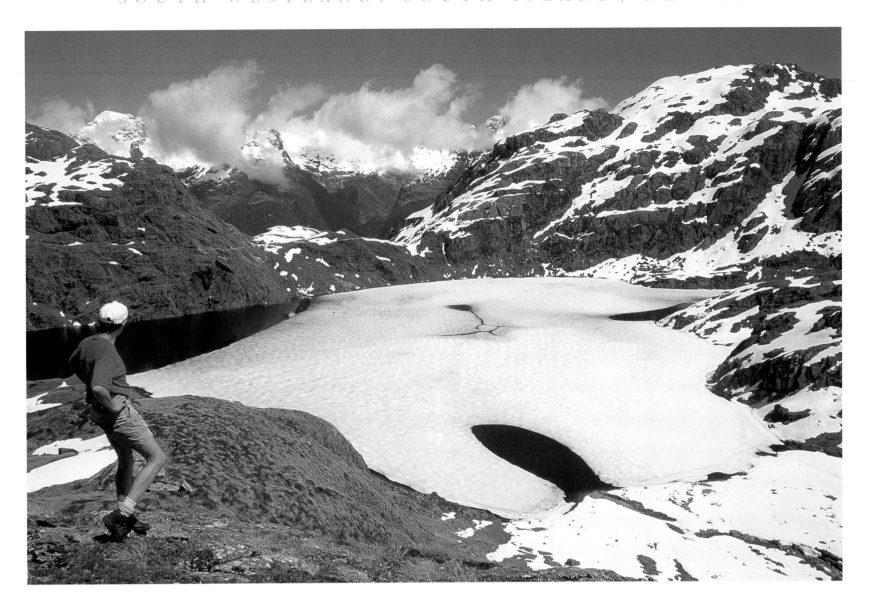

the steep mountains via the Harris Saddle (1280m; 4200ft), which they knew as Tarahaka Whakatipu and which marks the highest point of today's Routeburn Track.

Later, British surveyors sought advice from Maori about routes through the mountains. In 1870, in a thoroughly optimistic manner, a new settlement was established at Martins Bay, on the remote, southwestern coast. The provincial government plan was to build a bridle road to the settlement through the mountains via the Routeburn Valley and Harris Saddle, but construction was painfully slow.

In the meantime, with sea approaches thwarted by atrocious conditions, the new settlement was cut off and ran short of provisions. One settler, William Homer, decreed to be the settlement's most experienced bushman, set off overland to Queenstown. Travelling in September, in the New Zealand spring when snow and

avalanche danger is prevalent in the mountains, Homer climbed for days to reach Harris Saddle. He struggled through deep snowdrifts, often sinking to his waist, until finally the ground gave way beneath him and he fell into a 3m-deep (10-ft) ice cave. He managed to climb out, but retreated downhill and eventually found a way into the neighbouring Greenstone Valley, and thence to Queenstown, where he was described upon his arrival as a 'moving bundle of rags, scratches and bruises'. All attempts to establish roads and settlements were abandoned, and thus the old Routeburn pounamu trail still traverses a remote mountain wilderness, one that is appreciated today by thousands of walkers from more modified environments. Names of landscape features reflect the historic associations of both early Maori travellers and British explorers.

There is a gentle start to the Routeburn Track. A well-formed, easily graded trail wends its way along the Routeburn Valley floor, through beech forest where dappled light filters through the trees and friendly native birds, fantails and bush robins, will likely follow walkers' footsteps in search of insects. Footbridges cross side creeks, and for a time the track sidles above the Routeburn Gorge, a spectacular jumble of giant boulders and deep, hidden chasms. About one and a half hours from the start, the track emerges from the bush onto the wide, open expanse of the Routeburn Flats. Towering mountain walls enclose the grassy flats, providing a hint of the alpine grandeur that lies ahead.

OPPOSITE *The Routeburn Track traverses the remote, mountain wilderness of two of New Zealand's largest national parks. From Conical Hill, above Harris Saddle, views encompass Fiordland National Park's Darran Mountains.*

ABOVE *Lake Harris, nestled between the mountains near the track's highest point, slowly starts to shed its cover of snow. Even in summer, snow can occur on the Routeburn Track, although falls are generally shortlived.*

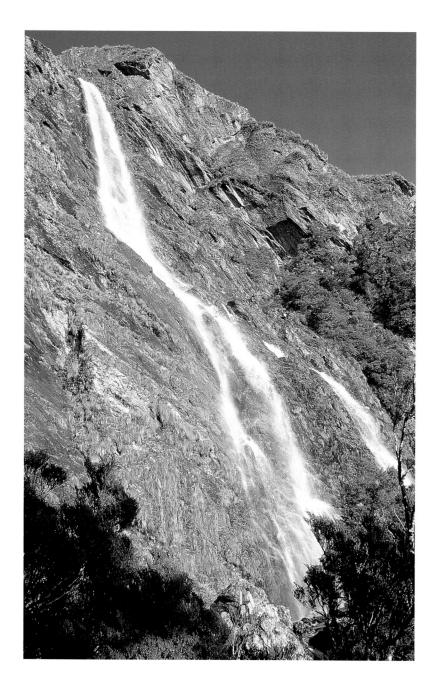

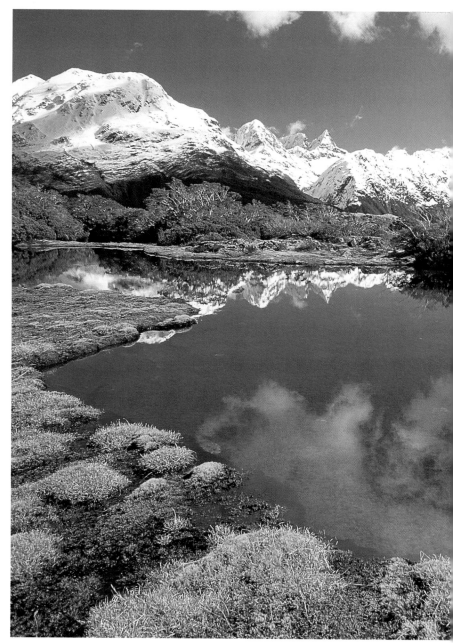

ABOVE *Earland Falls, which cascade down a sheer, mountainside bluff just above the trail, are particularly stunning after heavy rain.*

ABOVE *Key Summit, where alpine lakes are surrounded by fragile, flowering bog-lands and stunning mountain views, is a must-do scenic side trip.*

The Routeburn Flats Hut and camp site nestle by the bush edge, where the peculiar 'honking' sound of paradise shelducks is likely to be heard echoing across the flats. From the flats, the Routeburn Track starts climbing into true alpine terrain. The first hour is a steep pitch through beech forest, crossing a renovated section of track that was obliterated by a massive slip in 1994. The higher portion of track here is also within reach of avalanches, a reminder of why this route should be avoided in winter and early spring.

Routeburn Falls Hut (1000m; 3300ft) sits above the bushline, on an imposing site overlooking Routeburn Flats, 500m (1600ft) below. Behind the hut, the Routeburn River itself cascades over a series of rock ledges before plunging steeply to the valley floor below. Above the forest line now, the trail climbs over rocky terrain, among low-growing subalpine herbs and shrubs, snow tussocks and speargrass. Speargrass, with its stunning summertime flower, is yet the bane of hikers who absentmindedly

touch its vicious, spear-like leaves. Above the bush line a different collection of birds proliferate; tiny rockwrens shelter among the rocks and tussocks, New Zealand falcon may soar above and kea, New Zealand's mountain parrot, are bound to make their cheeky presence known.

On a clear day, the climb to the highest point of the trail, Harris Saddle (1280m; 4200ft), can be straightforward and stunning, with mountain views expanding as altitude is gained. However, rain, cloud and wind can quickly combine to make this exposed section of the trail a more dangerous adventure, one requiring appropriate clothing and careful navigation of track markers to find the way.

At Harris Saddle, weather permitting, magnificent views of the sheer diorite faces of the Darran Mountains, the highest of Fiordland National Park, reveal themselves across the forest-filled expanse of the Hollyford Valley. Lofty Mount Tutoko (2746m;

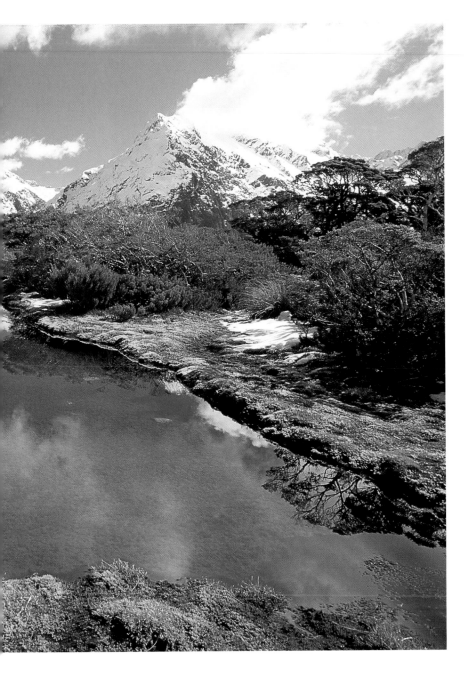

great weather is synonymous with great views in this subalpine terrain. However, if mist and cloud conspire to hide the mountains there are other visual delights to enjoy beside the track itself, such as the summer-flowering ourisias, gentians, daisies and the showy *Ranunculus lyalli*, commonly misnamed as the Mount Cook lily.

The track descends a series of zigzags into the forested shelter of MacKenzie Basin, where in calm conditions the dark blue waters of Lake MacKenzie shimmer magnificent reflections of surrounding mountain peaks. About three to four hours' walk from Harris Saddle lies Lake MacKenzie Hut and camp site, nestled at the forest edge beside the lake. The private Lake MacKenzie Lodge sits just beyond the lake in a forest clearing.

From the stark and wild beauty of the exposed uplands, the track continues now in a more sheltered environment, sidling along the bush margin through a mix of mountain beech trees, snow tussock and passing small mountain tarns (lakes). Soon after passing a small clearing dotted with distinctive-looking ribbonwood trees, the track cuts hard against near-vertical bluffs beneath the Earland Falls. These 80m-high (260ft) falls are a highlight of the track, particularly after heavy rain.

As the track continues to descend, it enters denser forest, where silver beech trees dominate with a profusion of smaller trees and shrubs, ferns, lichens and mosses flourishing beneath. The mountain views are now all but hidden, until the track emerges in a clearing near Howden Hut, nestled beside the lake of the same name.

A must-do side trip, just 15 minutes from Howden Hut, is the 30-minute climb to Key Summit. Once more, the surrounding mountains are revealed in all their splendour, and on the ground boardwalks lead walkers around delightful small tarns and over fragile, swampy areas matted with alpine herbs, mosses and bog plants.

The Routeburn Track ends beside the Te Anau to Milford Road at The Divide, the lowest east–west crossing of the South Island's Southern Alps. From here, transport connections can be made to Te Anau, the Hollyford Valley (another major trekking route that starts just a few kilometres along the road) or to the scenic wonders of Milford Sound, one of New Zealand's most sought-after tourist destinations.

RIGHT *One of the four trekkers' huts on the Routeburn Track nestles beside Lake MacKenzie, where mountain reflections often shimmer.*

9069ft) is the highest mountain in all of Fiordland's 1.2 million hectares (3 million acres), and the glacial-gouged Hollyford one of the longest rivers. Closer at hand, in the swampy basin by the Saddle, is a delightful profusion of plants, such as sundews, orchids, daisies, bog pines and bladderworts, which flourish in the boggy conditions.

After the steady climb to the summit, a small daytime shelter provides welcome respite for walkers, particularly in the event of inclement weather. On the other hand, if the weather is clear and the body willing, a magnificent, albeit steep option for a side trip is the 250m (800ft) climb from the Saddle to Conical Hill. The views, even greater from this higher vantage point, extend all the way to the South Island's West Coast.

From here on, the Routeburn Track is virtually all downhill. From the Saddle, the trail descends steeply at first, then winds on a gradual grade, still above bush line, along the exposed Hollyford Face at the very head of the Hollyford Valley. Again,

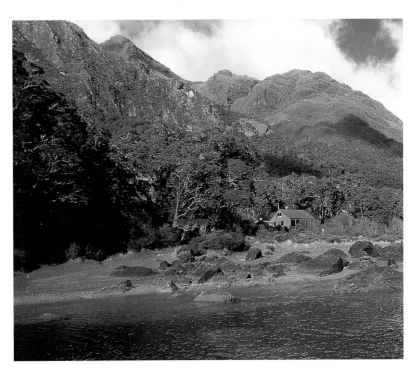

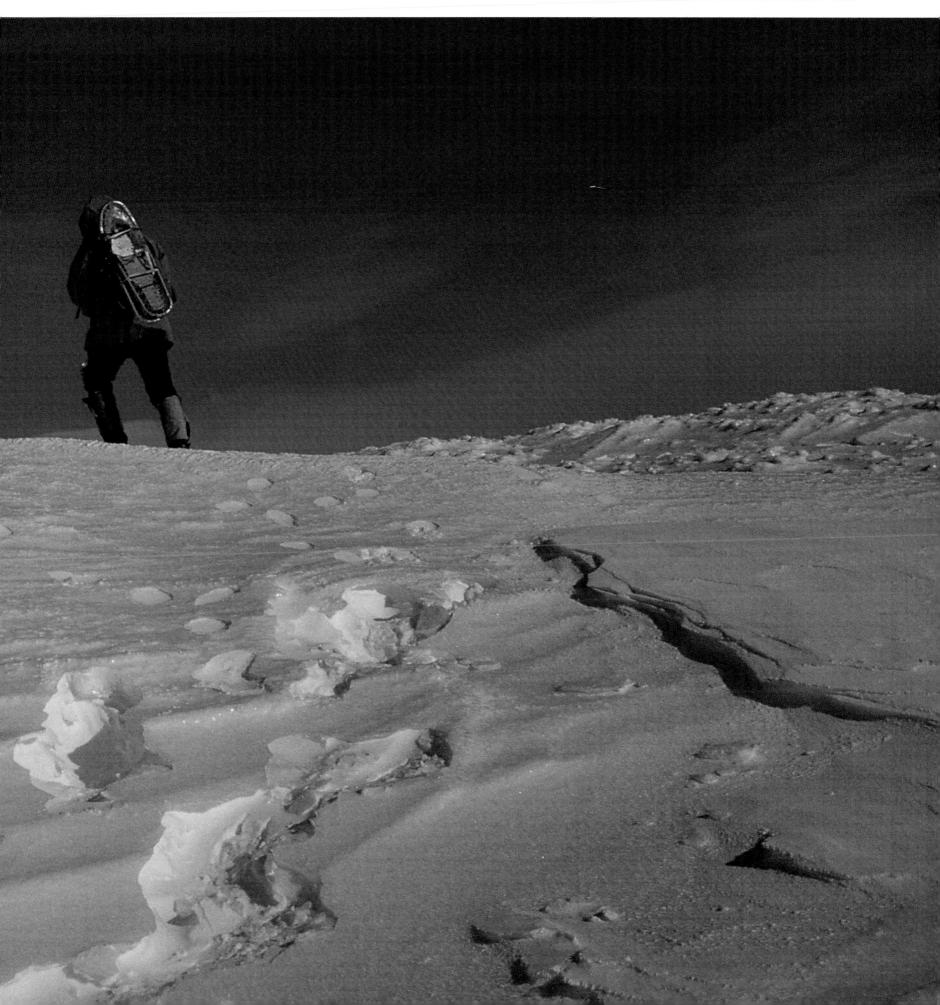

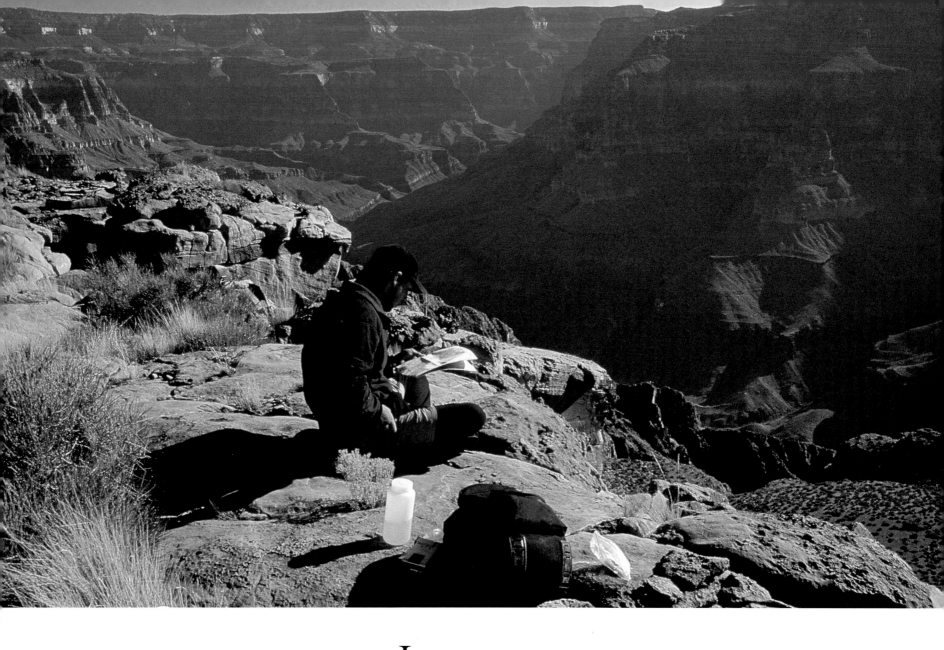

NORTH AMERICA

What would a man do, if he were compelled to live always in the sultry heat of society, and could never bathe himself in the cool solitude?

NATHANIEL HAWTHORNE

AMERICAN NOTEBOOKS

ABOVE *A Grand Canyon hiker pauses at Cogswell's Butte (North Rim) to contemplate his route into the void.*

OPPOSITE *Descending Blood Mountain (1360m; 4461ft) in Georgia, a hiker walks through the Appalachian Trail's green tunnel. Visible is the familiar white blaze painted on trees and rocks in 11 states.*

PREVIOUS PAGES *Partnering along the Appalachian Trail is recommended, especially in wilderness areas such as here in the Green Mountains.*

In 1689, British philosopher John Locke wrote, 'In the beginning, all the world was *America*, and more so than that is now'. Today, the United States consumes more food, electricity and oil per capita than any other nation on earth. Technology may play a larger role in the lives of Americans, but, as US historian Peter Carroll put it, central to the identity of this most powerful nation is the idea that its rural areas remain in a 'mythical state of nature, virtually uncorrupted by civilization and practically devoid of government and laws.'

This can best be summed up in the notion of the 'frontier'; that on the edge of civilization there exists a wild and natural place where animals roam and man must live by his wits alone. This has been an obsession of Hollywood film makers for decades, perfectly encapsulated in the Western genre and expressed at the beginning of every episode of *Star Trek:* 'Space – The Final Frontier'. To preserve what is indisputably an absolutely stunning natural heritage, the USA has protected its wild and beautiful places by establishing the most diverse, efficiently run and popular network of national parks in the world.

America is big. Everything in America is big. Cars, steaks, office blocks and billboards. The exploration of this vast country by the 19th-century pioneers produced journeys as epic as any in the annals of Asian travel. Meriwether Lewis, William Clark and their specially selected team of 'good hunters, stout, healthy, unmarried men, accustomed to the woods' set off up the Missouri in the spring of 1804 to cross the Rockies. In November 1805, having followed the river to its head waters, crossed the Bitterroot Range and then followed the Clearwater, Snake and Columbia rivers west, they reached the Pacific coast and dug in for the winter. By the time they made it back to St Louis in September 1806,

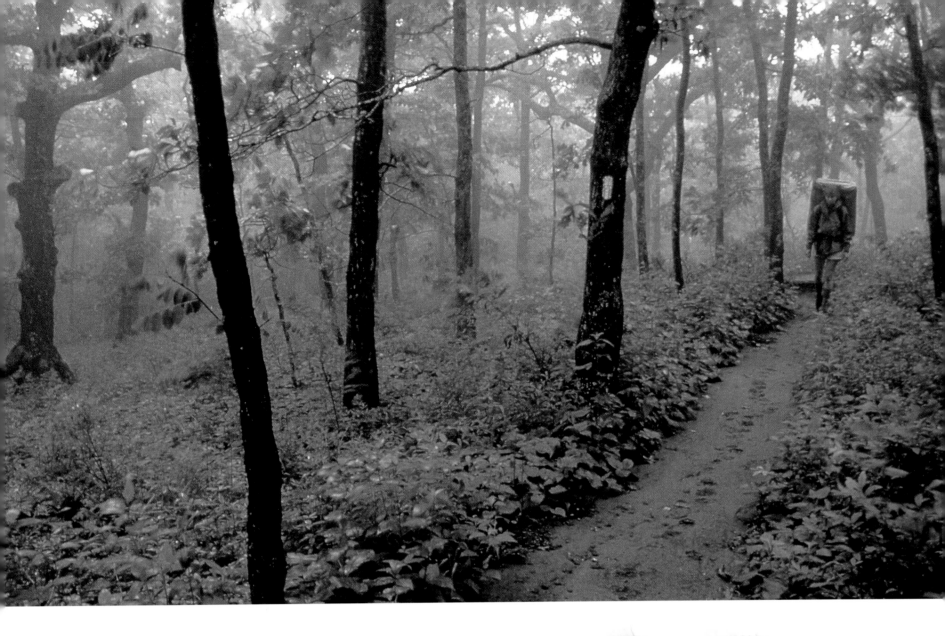

they had been gone two and a half years, travelled 13,000km (8000 miles) and made contact with over 50 Native American nations. Every American child learns about the Lewis-Clark expedition at school, and doubtless their story sowed the seeds of roaming that have led so many of their heirs out into the backcountry.

The USA today has the longest way-marked backpacking trails in the world and those that travel them form a unique and colourful counter culture, rich in literature and anecdote. Of all these routes, the 3460km (2150-mile) Appalachian Trail from Georgia to Maine inspires the fiercest loyalty and closest camaraderie among its veterans. A trip to most US outdoor bookstores will reveal a shelf full of guide books, histories, personal memoirs, anthologies and pictorials. Each hiker adopts a trail nickname, and you can find out how *Jumpstart, The Philosopher, Lo-Tec, Singing Horseman* and many others earned their stripes. Whether you set out to through-hike or complete just a portion of this marathon route, the minute you start the trail you step onto something much larger than a mere footpath.

Almost 3200km (2000 miles) west of the Appalachians, the Colorado River reaches the state of Arizona and almost immediately enters what is unquestionably one of the greatest natural wonders on this planet. For a distance of 450km (280 miles), the waters of the mighty Colorado snake through the Grand Canyon hemmed in by towering walls of multicoloured and fantastically eroded bedrock. Grand Canyon National Park may be one of the biggest tourist attractions in America, but drop below the rim on one of the many rugged trails that descend to the river and the world of RVs and clamouring visitors is soon forgotten.

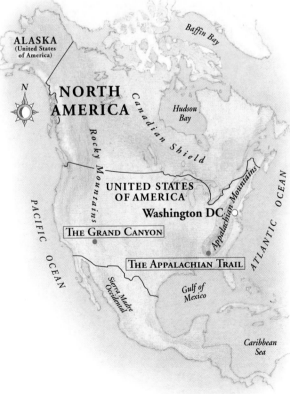

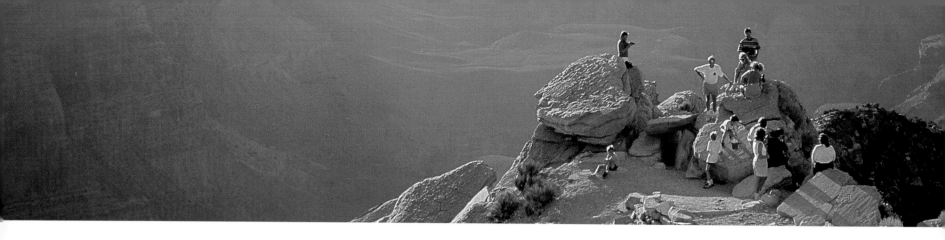

THE GRAND CANYON

by David Emblidge

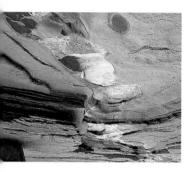

Almost all treks take us up to new heights. Paradoxically, a walk into the Grand Canyon takes us down, to new discoveries in a world so gloriously beautiful that the superlatives of everyday language do not suffice. Indeed, 'Grand' is a modest name for one of the world's natural wonders. Proclaimed a World Heritage Site in 1979, a trek here leaves an indelible impression. It also often leaves sore feet and knees, parched throats and sun-burned skin. The canyon's climate is harsh, with intense heat, dry air, and steep, relentless descents and ascents. The rewards are commensurate, however, especially for those who come prepared to cope well with the elements and who can appreci-ate the silent, haunting beauty of ancient wind- and water-carved rocks, of feisty plant life in the desert environment, and of ever-changing light shows as sunshine and shadows inch through the canyon. While brief walks into the canyon's upper levels on the South Rim are the most popular, the big ticket is a rim-to-rim traverse, over several days, with a stopover at Phantom Ranch by the banks of the rushing Colorado River on the canyon's distant floor.

The geological history of the Grand Canyon stretches back over two billion years. Human habitation here began long before the first European explorers arrived. At first glance, the dry canyon may seem frozen in time, but imperceptibly it grows wider and deeper. In the beginning, volcanic eruptions pushed up mountains that eroded and reformed again over long periods. Sediments from the erosion were compressed and under heat they metamorphosed into the base rocks we see today, deep in the canyon.

TOP *Hikers pause at Ooh Aah Point on the South Rim, where hiking trails connect the scrub dryness of the South Rim with the forest-shaded North Rim.*

INSET *Precious, infrequent rain water and snow melt are captured in sandstone pools on the Grand Canyon's countless ledges.*

ABOVE RIGHT *Most Grand Canyon hiking trails are wide enough for donkey trains and hikers to pass safely.*

OPPOSITE *Dusk view from Angel Point. Precipitous walls, revealing layer upon layer of compressed sedimentary rock, display the Grand Canyon's geological record.*

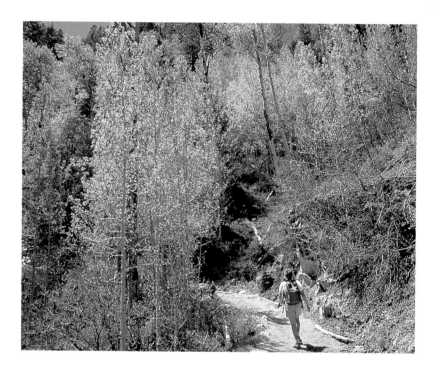

In a mere six million years the river now called the Colorado eroded the canyon as it sliced through the area. Over the millennia, wind and rainwater erosion carved and reshaped the canyon's towering walls. A mile deep and 30km (18 miles) wide at some points, the sheer scope of the Grand Canyon is hard to take in visually or emotionally.

The Anasazi (Native Americans) settled here about 11,000 years ago. Until the mid-13th century they shared the canyon with the Coconino Indians. Villages, trading and some agriculture developed. A drought in the 13th century forced a move away from the canyon and other native Americans, such as the Cerbats, replaced the Anasazi.

Spanish explorer Garcia Lopez de Cardenas was the first European to see the Grand Canyon, in 1540, but the earliest documentation of exploration here stems from the intrepid John Wesley Powell, a one-armed Civil War veteran who led an expedition by boat down the raging Colorado in 1869. Powell's colourful account of his two trips through the canyon set the tourism and prospecting ball rolling. When the Santa Fe Railroad finished laying track around 1900, public access to the canyon was vastly improved and tourism became big business. Grand Canyon Village, on the South Rim, took shape shortly after the railroad's arrival and is still the trailhead for most trekking.

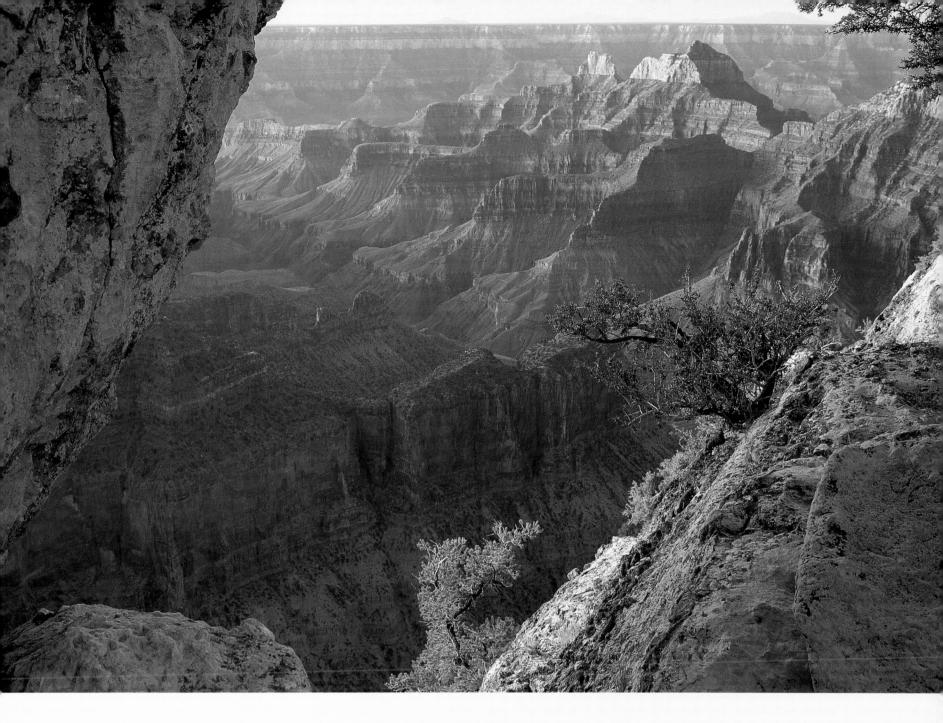

LOCATION Northwest Arizona, 126km (78 miles) north of Flagstaff.

WHEN TO GO May to June and October to November. South Rim trailheads and Grand Canyon Village open all year; North Rim trailheads from mid-May to mid-October.

START/FINISH The route can be walked in either direction. Start at South Rim, Grand Canyon Village, with shuttle bus to South Kaibab trailhead. Finish at trailhead for North Kaibab Trail, North Rim, then shuttle to Grand Canyon Lodge or exit transportation.

DURATION 5 days; 35km (22 miles).

MAXIMUM ALTITUDE 2400m (8000ft) at North Rim.

TECHNICAL CONSIDERATIONS Both winter and summer weather can make trekking in the Grand Canyon impossible or dangerous. Snow and ice at the highest points on the 'rims' is common well into spring. Blistering heat from late spring onwards in the canyon makes sunburn and dehydration likely. Drink plenty of water even if you are not thirsty. Footpaths are generally wide and flat, but often with precipitous drop-offs. All refuse must be carried out.

EQUIPMENT Comfortable boots, emergency shelter (lightweight tarp), water filter, flashlight, sunscreen and a hat.

TREKKING STYLE Backpacking.

PERMITS/RESTRICTIONS The Park Service limits access to the canyon's deeper sections to prevent crowding, but this makes reservations difficult. Backcountry permits (free) are required for all overnight treks into the canyon.

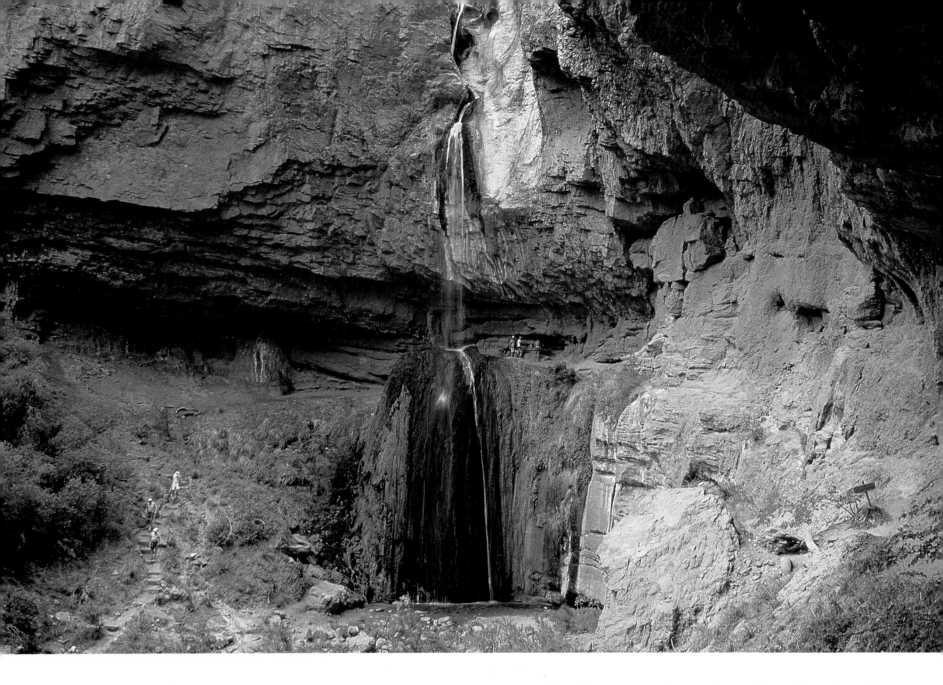

No matter when you arrive at the Grand Canyon, your first glimpse down into and across the void will no doubt take your breath away. Early mornings and sunsets in particular reveal the canyon in its richest light. The South Rim, at Grand Canyon Village, is intensely busy, clogged with auto and RV traffic as well as tourist buses throughout the summer. Do not despair. The North Rim gets only 10 per cent as many visitors.

A traverse of the canyon can go either way, South to North or North to South rims. In either case, transportation arrangements to or from the North Rim are the big problem. Highway access to the canyon itself is far easier from the south; the northern access road closes in winter and is a long haul through vacant territory in summer. However, from Grand Canyon Village, it can take a full day to reach the North Rim trailheads on Park Service roads in your own car or by chartered vehicle (350km; 215 miles). Trekkers who have the time and resources to position cars on both rims before hiking can do as they please, but most will arrive at the South Rim, stay a night in lodgings there, then head down with the crowd into the canyon on Bright Angel Trail (the most popular) or on South Kaibab Trail for a more isolated walk. A couple of hours down into the canyon, after fatigue and heat persuade most day hikers to return to the top, trekkers will have the place mostly to themselves, depending on the season.

ABOVE *Ribbon Falls, a spring cascading from the Grand Canyon's North Rim along the Kaibab Trail, leaves deposits of travertine, which is composed of calcium carbonate.*

Starting at the South Rim lets you walk away from civilization rather than back into it. The trek described here uses the South Kaibab Trail, whose Yaki Point Trailhead is accessible by shuttle bus from Grand Canyon Village. The panorama from Yaki is superb and the drop-off a challenge. Pray that your hiking boots fit well – you are about to descend 1460m (4800ft) to the Colorado River, almost continuously steeply, over the next 10km (6 miles). There is almost no shade and water is scarce at best. Carry a map and use it. Although the path is easy to follow, keeping track of where you are by distance and time requires concentration, especially in the heat and glaring sunshine, which may make even the most in-shape hikers light-headed. Hiking alone is not recommended.

Cedar Ridge appears just 2.4km (1.5 miles) down the path, one of several ridges this zigzagging path follows (most trails use side canyons). Ominously named Skeleton Point is reached at 4.6km (2.9 miles). Vast Redwall Formation (largely wind-sculpted sandstone) hosts numerous miles of South Kaibab Trail as it meanders downward on huge switchbacks.

Though steep-sided, the Grand Canyon is actually desert, lying on the borders of two deserts, the hot Mojave and the cold Great Basin. The most striking fact is dryness, of soil and air. Desert plant life is a marvel of adaptation. Blackbrush, the dominant shrub, sprouts hairy, small leaves suited to water catching and holding. In drought times, the plant turns deciduous and essentially shuts down its metabolism. About once every decade a blooming spring of desert plants appears, with abundant phlox and lupines.

Tonto Trail Junction, at 7km (4.4 miles), is followed shortly by The Tipoff, the final plunge into the Colorado River Gorge. By this time, you will hear the river if not see it. Upon reaching the Colorado, you will have walked over 9km (6 miles) and may well feel like taking a swim. Don't. The current is vicious. Cross the suspension bridge and carry on to either Bright Angel Campground or Phantom Ranch, where a soak for tired feet in a quiet brook will be safer. The ranch is reachable only by foot, horse, or river raft. Set amid cottonwood trees beside singing Bright Angel Creek, this is a canyon oasis that feels, and is, far from the outside world. While water supplies can be replenished here, there is no food for sale. The ranch is not a spa, conditions are Spartan, but the privilege of staying here leaves a luxury of good memories.

The Colorado River is a matter of endless political debate. Built in 1963, Glen Canyon Dam, some 140km (90 miles) upstream, changed the ecology of the river

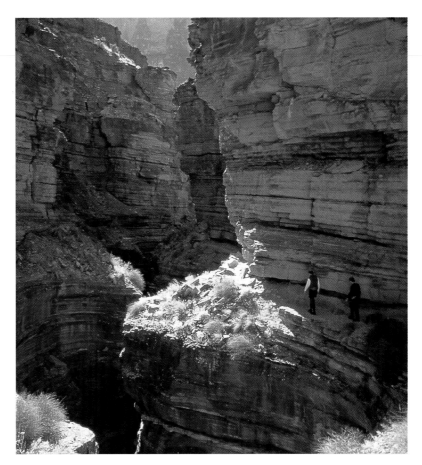

basin in unanticipated ways. Sediment flow that formerly carved the canyon has been stalled. Plant and animal life were adversely affected, and some people now argue that the dam should be breached. Whitewater rafters relish the wild ride on the Colorado, and many call for letting mother nature take its course. Far downstream, the states of Arizona, Nevada and California siphon off almost every last drop of the Colorado's water so that it ends nearly dry at the sea.

Hiking out to the North Rim on North Kaibab Trail through Bright Angel Canyon is a long climb that is best broken into two parts. At 10.2km (6.3 miles) up from the Colorado River, there is a respite at Ribbon Falls. A night at Cottonwood Campground (12.2km; 7.6 miles) requires packing in all equipment and food and packing out garbage. The effort is worth it, however, both to extend your stay in the Grand Canyon and because climbing the north side of the canyon in one fell swoop is more than most hikers can manage.

Roaring Springs/Bright Angel Creek Junction at 15.3km (9.5 miles) is the next major landmark, but there are still 7.6km (4.7 miles) to go before the trailhead. Grand Canyon Lodge lies about 3km (2 miles) beyond the trailhead, and by the time you have hiked that far you will be ready for an overnight rest in a bed before driving out. Chances are – blisters, parched throat, and sore muscles notwithstanding – you will have trouble tearing yourself away from views back down into and across the Grand Canyon from the North Rim. By then, you will know you have walked through a true natural wonder.

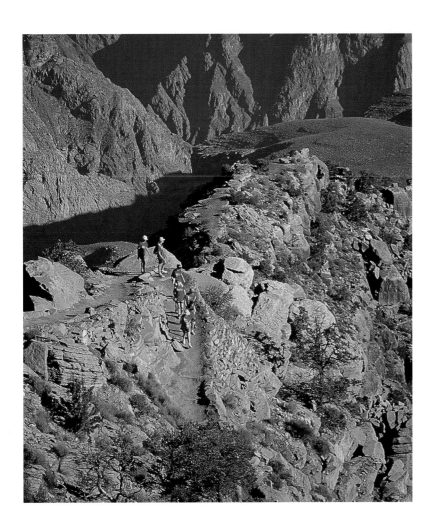

ABOVE *Hikers walk into the Grand Canyon on the South Kaibab Trail, which begins near Yaki Point on the South Rim and descends 10.2km (6.3 miles) to the Colorado River.*

ABOVE *In the inner Grand Canyon, intense light and dark shadows make for sharp contrasts in a labyrinth of twisting footpaths, here above Deer Creek.*

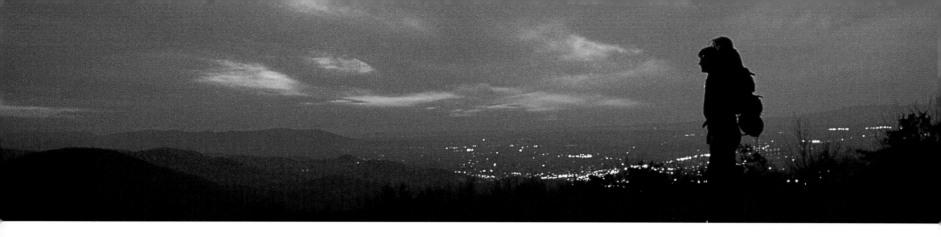

THE APPALACHIAN TRAIL

by David Emblidge

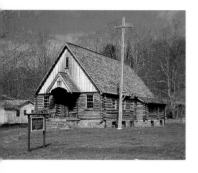

Grandfather of North America's long footpaths, the Appalachian Trail (AT) is also its most well-trodden trek. At 3460km (2150 miles), traversing 11 states through a variety of landscapes and climates near the United States' Atlantic coast, the trail serves an estimated 4,000,000 walkers each year. A hardy few attempt to through-hike. Each year about 2500 start out; barely 10 per cent make it to the other end, four to six months later.

Most AT trekkers are day hikers, weekend backpackers, and those on expeditions of a week or two. Despite heavy use in some favoured sections within easy reach of seaboard cities, vast stretches of the track pass through protected wilderness areas offering extreme solitude and backpacking challenges between re-supply stations.

Forested by a colourful mix of deciduous trees and conifers, the Appalachian region is home to hundreds of bird species and scores of mammals, including black bear and moose. Many AT miles in southern and northern states offer superb vistas, alpine flora, wild weather and exciting above tree line hiking. Winter closes the trail in all but the most southern states, and even there at higher elevations, major storms can dump several feet of snow.

The trek generally follows the crest line of the Appalachian Mountains, arcing from the southern state of Georgia toward the mid-Atlantic states, into New England, culminating in the rugged wilderness areas of New Hampshire and Maine. Great Smoky Mountains and Shenandoah national parks, as well as a number of state parks, play host to the meandering track. A northern extension is under construction – the International Appalachian Trail – reaching into Canada and the Gaspé Peninsula.

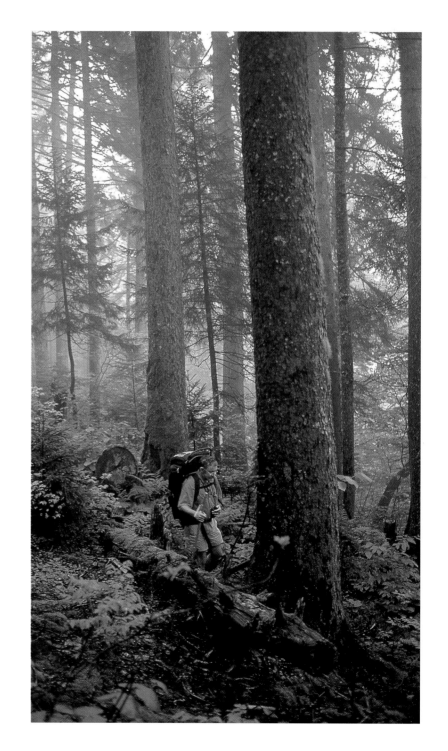

TOP *A lone through-hiker gazes down at the lights of Waynesboro, Virginia before bedding down for the night.*

INSET *Breaking away from wilderness areas, AT hikers will on occasion come across small mountain communities such as this one, in Laurel Valley, Virginia.*

RIGHT *A through-hiker picks his way through old growth forest of red spruce in the Great Smoky Mountains National Park, Tennessee.*

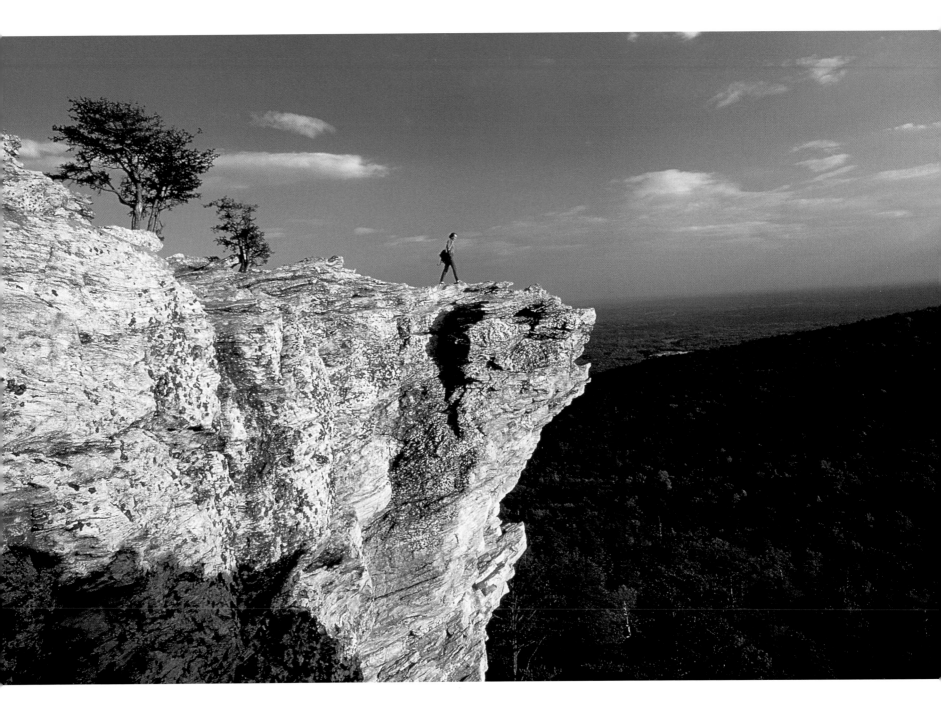

ABOVE *A solitary hiker looks over the Blue Ridge Mountains from Hanging Rock, a 60m (200ft) overhang in Virginia that gives Hanging Rock State Park its name.*

The AT is not, as many believe, a Native American footpath. A modern creation, the trail was the brainchild of hiking enthusiasts in the late 19th and early 20th centuries. Boston's venerable Appalachian Mountain Club and Vermont's Green Mountain Club began trail building in New England during the Gilded Age (1880s) when the expansion of railroads into mountain areas first brought tourists to the wilderness.

In 1921, Harvard-educated forester Benton MacKaye published 'An Appalachian Trail, A Project in Regional Planning' in the *Journal of the American Institute of Architects*. MacKaye envisioned a linear park from Georgia to Maine, including the trekking path, campgrounds, and mountain lodges with recreation programmes for weary urban workers. His plan challenged capitalist work-ethic values, drawing on a philosophical attitude toward nature rooted in 19th-century Romanticism and American Transcendentalism. MacKaye, an avid reader of Thoreau, Emerson, and John Muir, celebrated the moral and aesthetic virtues of American wilderness.

Thousands of volunteers and many legislators collaborated over a 25-year period to make the AT a reality. During the Depression, a government work-relief programme for unemployed urban young men – the Civilian Conservation Corps (CCC) – built numerous trail sections and many camps and lodges. Not until 1948 did anyone attempt to through-hike; credit goes to Earl Shaffer, now a celebrated AT hero.

The National Trails System Act of 1968 put the trail under the authority of the National Park Service which, by 2000, had nearly completed real-estate purchases to create a minimum 300m wide (1000ft) trail corridor. In many places the corridor is several miles wide. Environmentalists and legislators are now engaged in heated debates over environmental impact concerns (wear and tear, sustainability) and hiker management issues (overuse, low-impact camping and safety).

135

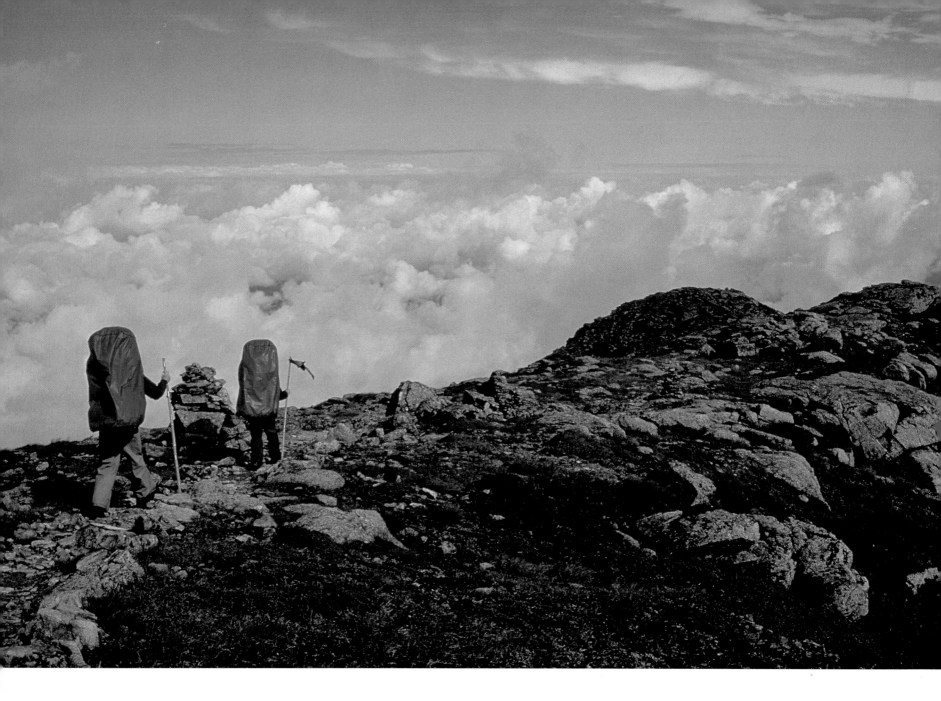

The typical AT through-hiker starts out, between March and April, at Springer Mountain, Georgia, after a robust climb to the peak through Amicalola Falls State Park. The trail is a narrow, often rugged and rocky footpath, usually traversing the highest peaks and most delightful valleys it can find en route northwards. Rivers are bridged but many streams require fording.

In the southern states of Georgia, North Carolina and Tennessee, the trail runs through several national forests and spends 110km (70 miles) in Great Smoky Mountains (GSM) National Park where it crosses Clingman's Dome, 2024m (6642ft), the trail's highest point but a disappointment due to nearby road development and resulting crowds. Except in the first wave of the through-hiking season, this southernmost territory on the trail is largely empty. Expect certain ironies, however – GSM National Park is the busiest in the country and near its major crossing highways, the trail is heavily used. A mile or so away, crowds mercifully disappear.

Heat, humidity and abundant rain, plus the latitude, favour a varied forest of soft and hardwoods, with wildflowers galore, abundant birdsong and frequent sightings of black bear. Evidence of the unfortunate impact of acid rain (from coal-fired industrial plants to the west) appears in numerous dead stands of trees. Blights wiped out the American chestnut and elm, and the woody adelgid attacks the balsam firs. The southern Appalachians are steep though less rugged than New England and the area remains a botanist's paradise. Rhododendron, dogwood, trillium and countless other flowering plants grace the footpath – drawing crowds of day hikers during peak bloom season.

Atop several of the highest southern peaks, mostly rounded (these are very old mountains), are large open areas – the 'balds' – offering spectacular vistas across endless ridges and valleys. No one knows why the balds exist. Despite their 1500m (5000ft) elevation, they are not above the tree line thanks to the warm climate. Native American myths say the gods burned off the mountaintops to keep a clear view of human activity in the valleys. Botanists know that some native people and early white settlers grazed cattle on the balds, but the explanation is incomplete.

At over 640km (400 miles), the AT covers more distance in Virginia than any other state. Damascus, Virginia, hosts Trail Days in May to celebrate the passing tide of annual through-hikers. The southern Virginia Highlands rise above 1500m (5000ft) while passing through Jefferson and Washington national forests en route to the second national park on the trail – Shenandoah – near the northern state border. Proximity to Washington DC, Baltimore, Maryland and an easy, level trail make northern trail sections in Virginia busy. Summer in Virginia can be beastly hot, but fall hiking here is long and glorious. The trail's arguably most photogenic spot is McAfee Knob, a promontory in central Virginia affording views westwards off a giant overhanging rock.

A few miles of trail pass through neighbouring West Virginia into a National Historical Park at the village of Harpers Ferry where the Appalachian Trail Conference headquarters welcomes all hikers and provides abundant trail information. Across the wide Potomac River, the path takes a 60km (40 miles) hop through Maryland before crossing the Pennsylvania border and the culturally significant Mason Dixon Line separating southern Confederate (pro-slavery) states from northern Union (anti-slavery) states. The political line is a relic of the mid-19th-century Civil War.

The AT's mid-point comes just north of Pennsylvania's southern border. Accents, cuisine, climate and architecture change noticeably in the Mid-Atlantic states. Pennsylvania's Appalachians curve gently northeastwards, but the walking is tough in 'Rocksylvania'. Long ridges, often treeless (from logging and harsh soils), are littered with sharp-edged rocks thrust upwards by colliding tectonic plates and stirred into disarray by glaciers. Compensating factors on the Pennsylvania section of trail are Civil War historical sites and sweeping pastoral views. Pennsylvania's northern edge is a mighty river set in a handsome gorge, the Delaware Water Gap National Recreation Area.

New Jersey, one of the densely populated states, offers segments of the AT in the Pocono Mountains and along Kittatinny Ridge which – if hiked midweek – are quiet and beautiful. Elevations top out at 520m (1700ft) with no distinct peaks, but occa-

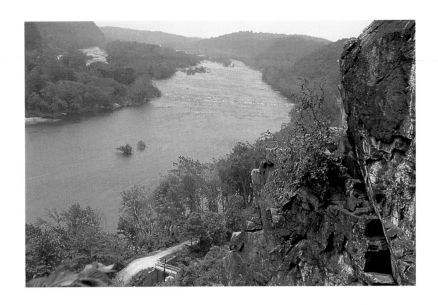

ABOVE *At Harper's Ferry the village can provide lonely hikers with some welcome social contact and amenities, as well as offering abundant trail information.*

sional gems such as Sunfish Pond are rewarding. The trail skirts a corner of New York State about 80km (50 miles) north of the Big Apple, managing to find stunning views in Bear Mountain and Harrison and Hudson Highlands state parks on opposite sides of the Hudson River. Isolation is harder to come by here, but trekkers enjoy the vistas painted by famed Hudson River School artists in the 19th century who defined the American Romantic view of nature as sublime and fearsome.

Entering Connecticut in rolling hill country, the trail is finally in New England, its last distinct region en route north, but there are still five states and hundreds of miles to go – plus the bulk of the climbing. New England villages make the AT's most

LOCATION USA; eleven east coast states (Georgia, North Carolina, Tennessee, Virginia, West Virginia, Maryland, Pennsylvania, New Jersey, New York, Connecticut, Massachusetts, Vermont, New Hampshire, Maine).

WHEN TO GO Spring through autumn: southern states March through November; northern states April through mid-October. Nearly year-round trekking is common in southern lowlands. Best hiking is August through colourful autumn, especially in New York and New England.

START/FINISH AT through-hikers generally start in Georgia and walk north to Maine. Many people make the trek in sections over a number of years.

DURATION 4 to 6 months for a continuous through-hike. Discrete sections (one of the national parks, for example) make a fine two- to three-week expedition.

MAXIMUM ALTITUDE Clingman's Dome, North Carolina (2024m; 6642ft).

TECHNICAL CONSIDERATIONS Winter conditions can close the trail in early spring or mid-autumn. The entire AT is blazed white, with a simple vertical bar painted on trees and rocks. Side trails are blazed blue, orange, red, etc. Lean-tos generally provide outhouses and spring water, but backcountry AT hikers should come prepared to camp well off the trail and without amenities.

EQUIPMENT Backpack, sleeping bag, hiking boots, wet-weather gear, food (light weight, high energy), warm, quick-drying clothing, insect repellent.

TREKKING STYLE Backpacking.

PERMITS/RESTRICTIONS No permits are required for the Appalachian Trail. Within Great Smoky Mountains National Park, lean-tos are reserved for through-hikers. Trekkers on shorter trips should carry a tent.

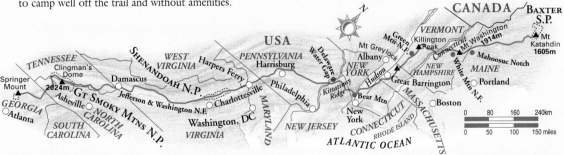

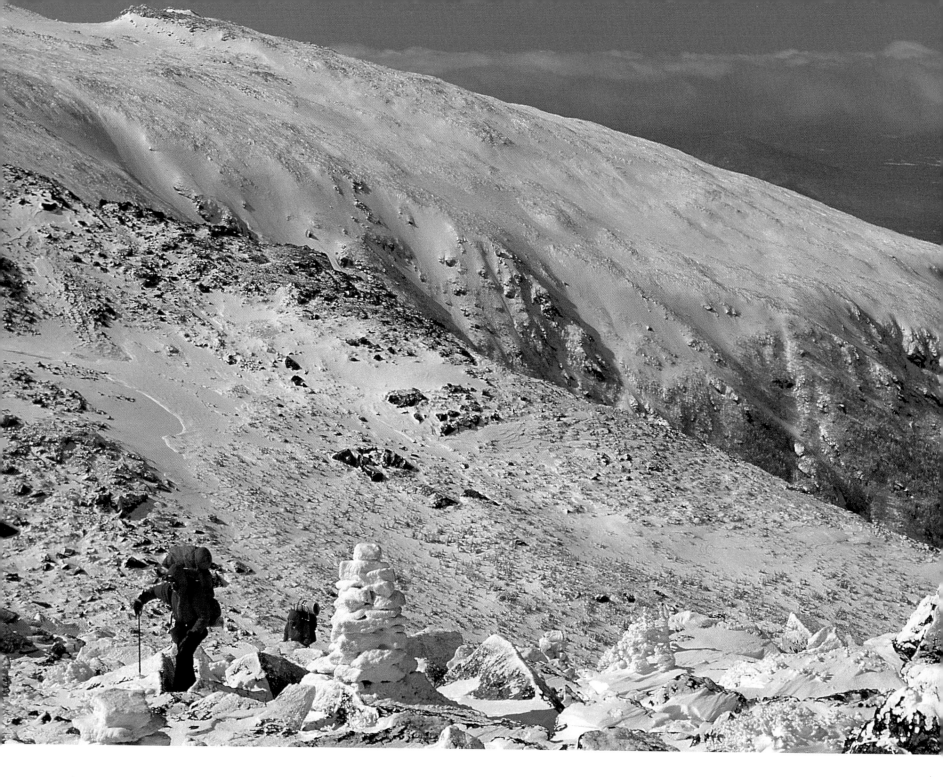

charming stopovers as the footpath wends its way through remarkably lovely countryside. Increasingly as it marches north, the trail climbs the first real 'mountains' since Virginia. Connecticut's northwest uplands are the Litchfield Hills, where the trail rollercoasters from ridge tops to valleys, keeping close to the Housatonic River. Between gentrified Salisbury and southern Berkshire County in neighbouring Massachusetts, the track navigates a superb forest and ridgeline path on the Taconic Range in contiguous state parks, passing through Sage's Ravine – a naturalist's paradise, with waterfalls – and peaking at Mount Everett, 793m (2602ft).

Crossing the Housatonic River, the trail passes near Great Barrington, Massachusetts, a bustling, upscale market town, then rises onto the Berkshire Massif for most of this state's 130km (80 miles) of trail. Trekkers with a yen for cultural entertainment off-trail love the Berkshires where numerous towns boast everything from the Boston Symphony Orchestra, to the Jacob's Pillow Dance Festival,

various theatres and several superb museums. Mount Greylock in Massachusetts' northwest corner, at 1064m (3491ft) southern New England's tallest peak, is the first where wild weather may pose a threat. Bascom Lodge, atop Greylock, offers pricey but welcome bunks.

Green Mountain National Forest hosts most of the trail's miles in Vermont, here heading almost due north. Vermont's Long Trail is contiguous with the AT from Massachusetts to Killington Peak, mid-state. The Long Trail predates the AT and has its own legendary through-hikers who walk to Quebec, Canada. Federal wilderness areas in Vermont, within the national forest, remain untouched by mechanized equipment, have few if any roads, and offer a chance to escape even the amenities of estab-

ABOVE *Reaching the alpine zone above the tree line on Mount Madison in the White Mountains, hikers have little access to shelter from the cold and characteristic fierce winds.*

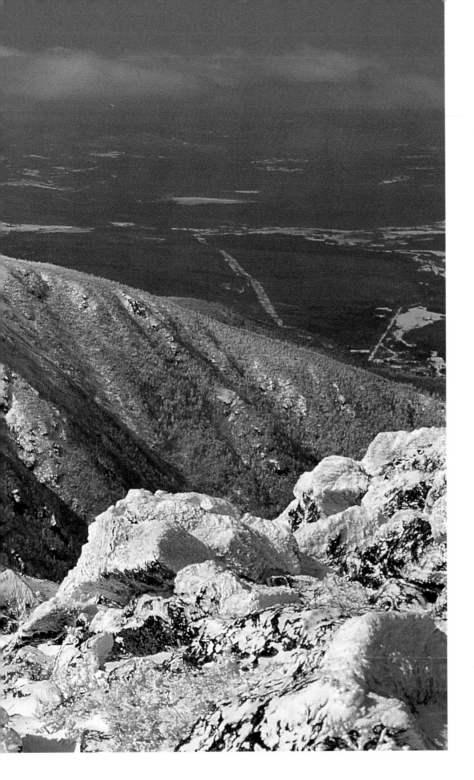

above the tree line into the alpine zone for the first time. After a harrowing descent from Franconia Ridge into Crawford Notch the trail rises even higher onto the Presidential Range for the longest alpine walk in eastern America, certainly the finest views and undoubtedly the most dangerous weather. At Mount Washington (1914m; 6280ft) the trail achieves its second highest elevation but greatest exposure to the elements. A bizarre state park concession building mars the treeless peak (19th-century tourism developers carved a road to the top). A superb series of alpine lodges, managed by the Appalachian Mountain Club (AMC), provides respite from the powerful winds common in the White Mountains above the tree line. No camping is permitted in the extremely fragile alpine zone where diapensia, Lapland rosebay, alpine azalea and lichens cling to the rocks, surviving by means of astonishing adaptive chemistry.

Trekkers not using the AMC huts, which are expensive and booked months in advance, generally must descend significantly to reach permissible tenting sites. A trek across the Presidential Range requires careful expedition planning and attention to safety. Several people die every year from accident or foolhardiness in the Presidentials where lightning, fierce winds, rock slides, avalanches and falls lead to tragedy. A well-planned safe trip here, however, is unquestionably *la crème de la crème* of the AT. Hiker's Mecca is Pinkham Notch, on the AT in the valley below the Presidentials, where a lodge, restaurant, bookstore, natural history programmes, and shuttle service to dozens of trailheads attract exuberant crowds of mountaineering aficionados.

The trail rises sharply again, crosses into Maine and encounters infamous Mahoosuc Notch, the 'toughest mile on the AT', a torturous jumble of colossal boulders and twisted, dark passages too tight for full backpacks. A few more peaks in western Maine rise briefly into the alpine zone and the trail passes a busy ski resort, Sugarloaf, but soon elevations drop off and a week-long trek through the most isolated wilderness in eastern America begins. Hours from any city in the USA or Canada, the Maine woods are home to logging companies and hunting and fishing camps and not much else. Pristine glacial lakes dot the rolling landscape, with moose grazing in the wetlands and black bear roaming freely. The 100-Mile Wilderness requires full provisioning. Stream and river crossings in Maine are potentially treacherous. At the Kennebec River, where fording hikers have drowned, the Maine Appalachian Trail Club provides canoe-ferry service.

Baxter State Park, a vast territory in north central Maine, brings the story to a fitting close with Mount Katahdin, which in Abenaki means 'greatest mountain'. At 1605m (5267ft), Katahdin is the most isolated alpine peak on the trail, with no roads, no mountainside shelters, and no protection from the elements. Snow and ice linger well into May, returning in early or mid-October. The AT spends its last northbound hours well above the tree line, with a rousing finish at Baxter Peak (1605m; 5267ft) where many a champagne bottle cork has been popped by through-hikers and day hikers, though often in a chilly fog and bone-rattling winds. On a clear day a descent on the mountain's northern side, after crossing the Knife Edge with its precipitous drop-offs, provides the trekker with a big bonus – if the knees will tolerate it. Most hikers return to 'base camp', south on the AT. However, the Katahdin climb finishes, trekkers here go home with a sense of satisfaction and closure. If you have walked all the way from Georgia to Maine, you have now passed through the gates of the AT's hall of fame.

lished camp sites. A stark surprise awaits trekkers at Vermont's popular mountains – Stratton (1200m; 4000ft) and Killington (1293m; 4241ft) – where adjacent ski area chairlifts hoist crowds to the peaks. Magically isolated Stratton Pond, with shelters and tent sites scattered around pristine waters, is a piece of protected heaven.

North of Killington, the AT turns east, leaves the Long Trail, and heads down towards the Connecticut River Valley. It takes 80km (50 miles) to get there, in undistinguished rolling forest, on rarely used trail, passing near only one interesting town, Woodstock, a moneyed place brimming with boutiques and elegant Federalist period mansions. Dartmouth College, Hanover, New Hampshire, a venerable Ivy League university, lies on the AT. Resupply and rest are easy to arrange here for through-hikers, though purists may find the town too busy and pricey. After lowland rambling northeast of Hanover, the AT begins its toughest ascents and descents, through White Mountain National Forest. Mount Moosilauke (1464m; 4802ft) takes the trail

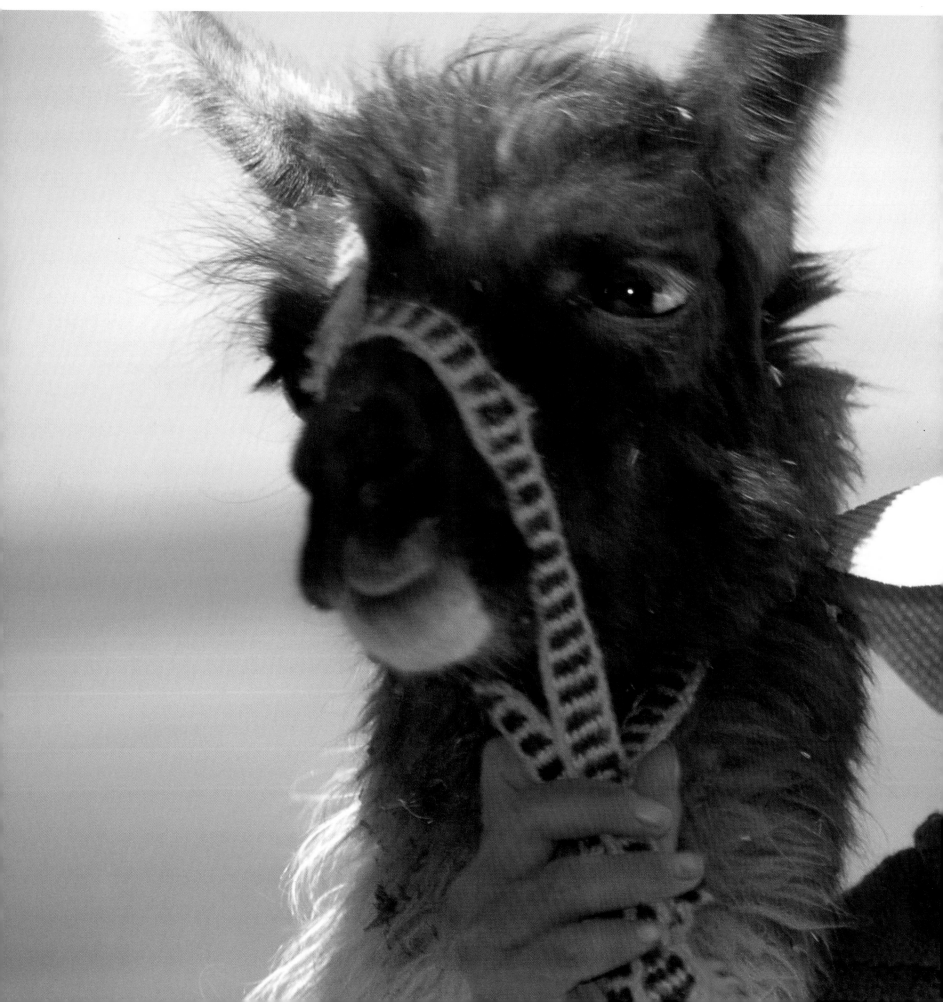

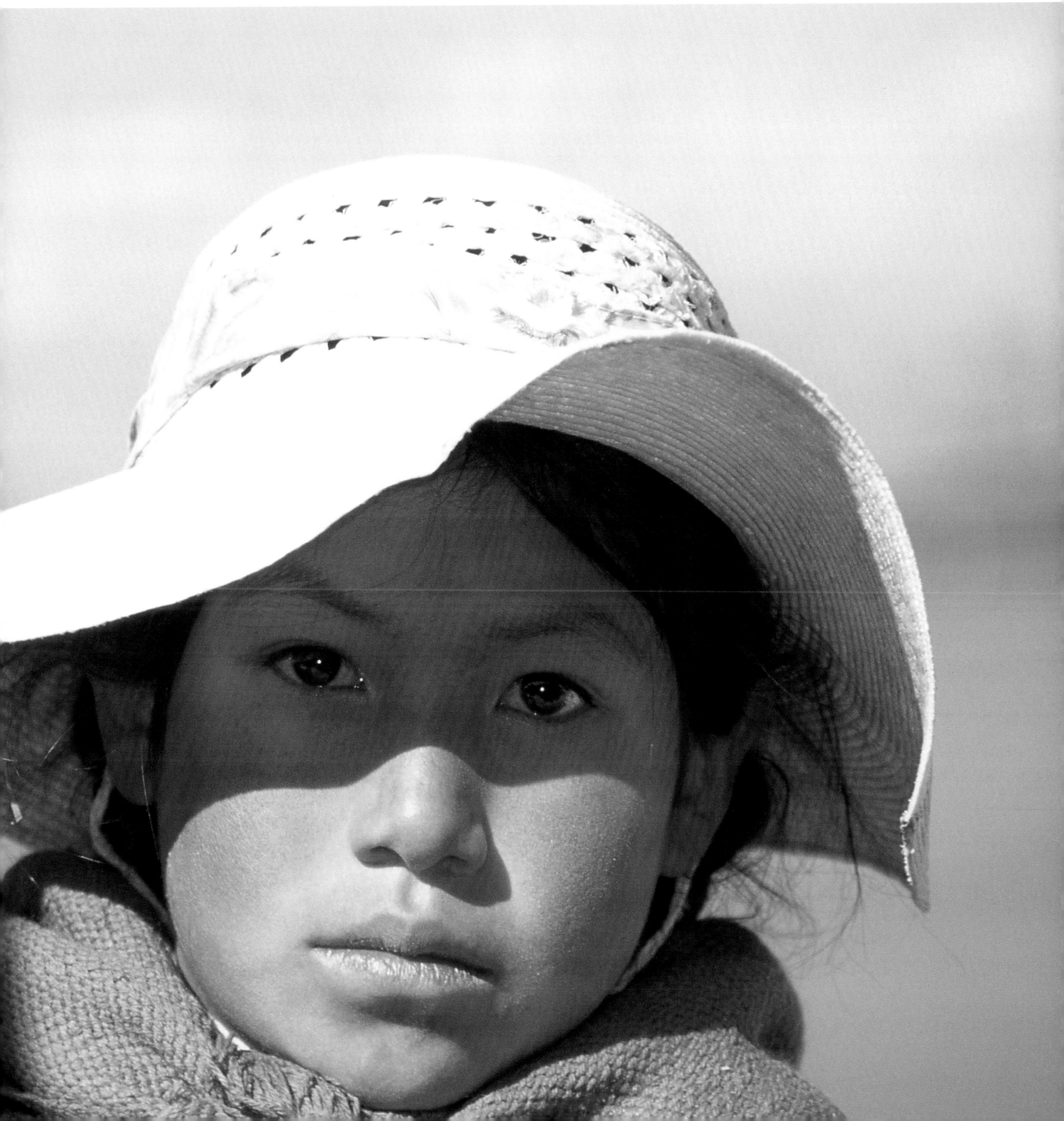

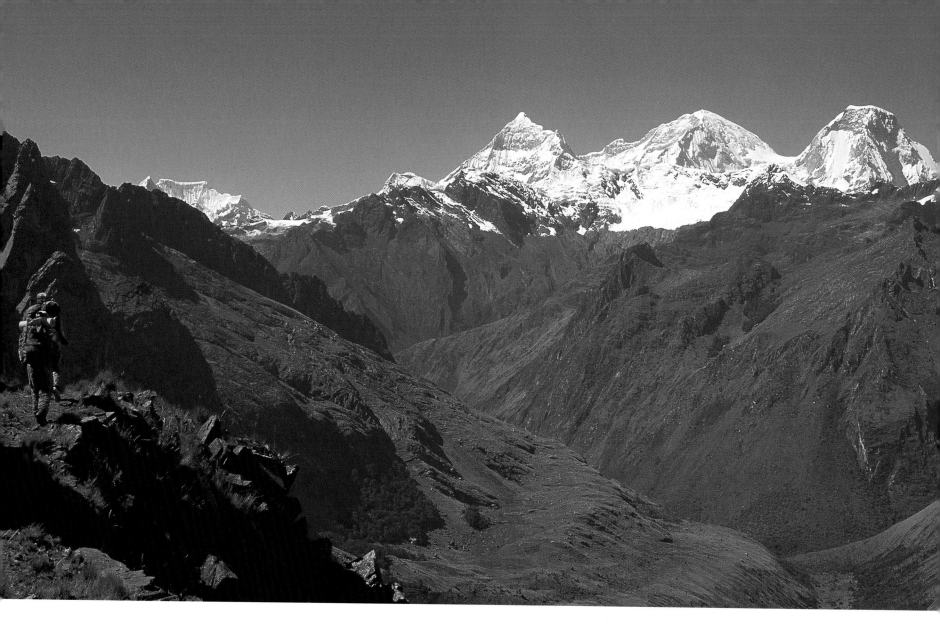

SOUTH AMERICA

For my part, I travel not to go anywhere,
but to go. I travel for travel's sake.
The great affair is to move.

ROBERT LOUIS STEVENSON, 1850–94
TRAVELS WITH A DONKEY

ABOVE *Huascarán (6768m; 22,205ft), the highest peak in Peru,*
seen here from the Alto de Pucaraju Pass, Cordillera Blanca.

OPPOSITE *Donkeys drinking from Guanacpatay River.*
Although the donkey's load-carrying capacity is greater than
that of the llama, the latter retains a niche due to its unpara-
lelled resistance to cold and altitude.

PREVIOUS PAGES *A young Aymara girl with a baby llama*
grants a rare photo opportunity on the shores of Lake Titicaca.

From balmy palm-fringed beaches lapped by the languid waters of the Caribbean, to the monstrous granite pillars of Patagonia, ravaged by the perpetual gales of the Roaring Forties, South America is the fourth largest of the earth's continents. By far the most dominating physical feature of this vast tract of land is the Andes, a stunningly beautiful range of mountains that lines the entire western edge of the continent. Fringed by the deserts of the Pacific coastal strip in the west and the boundless rainforests of the Amazon Basin in the east, the Andes includes many volcanoes and some of the world's most celebrated mountain scenery.

Though they do not stretch as far back into the mists of time as those in Asia, the ancient civilizations spawned in South America produced a wealth of architectural wonders and material treasures that certainly rival those of the East. The Incas represented the climax of an urbanized culture that developed over 3000 years, only to be abruptly terminated with the arrival of the Spanish *conquistadores* in the 16th century. The destruction wrought by the *conquistadores* and the ferocity of their cruelty towards the indigenous Indians of South America are unparalleled in the history of European colonization.

Trekking in South America has attracted a growing band of enthusiastic devotees. Unlike the Indian subcontinent, most of the countries in South America are relatively sophisticated and modern. Communications work and facilities are akin to those available in Europe and North America. This is certainly true of Chile and Argentina, less so of Peru and Bolivia, where highland Indians still speak their native tongues. Set all this against a backdrop of Spanish colonial architecture and you start to get an inkling of the South American scene.

Peru, boasting the most impressive Inca ruins, rainforest reserves teaming with wildlife and – in the Cordillera Blanca – the highest mountain anywhere in the tropics (Huascarán, 6768m; 22,205ft), offers

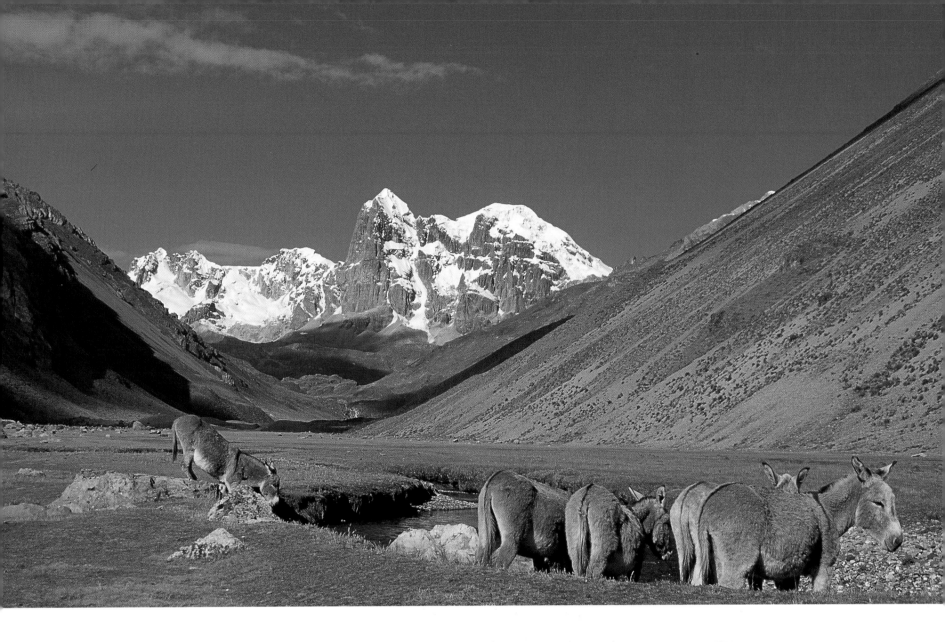

treks to rival any in the Himalaya. Alpamayo (5947m; 19,512ft) may not be one of the giants of the Cordillera Blanca but it is often described as the most beautiful mountain in the world, and a hike around it yields peerless views of the entire range. Equally challenging and scenically wonderful is the circuit of the Cordillera Huayhuash, the next group of mountains to the south of the Cordillera Blanca. Access is slightly more difficult here, and the route less frequented, but with Yerupajá (6634m; 21,766ft) and a host of others this compact range appears like the upturned teeth of a giant saw. An unforgettable sight.

South of Peru, the Andean chain enters Bolivia, where the frontier divides the shimmering waters of Lake Titicaca between the two nations. Bolivia has the highest percentage of indigenous Indians of any South American country. Sparse population and slow economic development have rendered Bolivia one of the poorest nations on the continent, but on the other side of this coin there remains the fact that much of the natural beauty to be found here is unblemished by human activity. The Cordillera Real is the jewel in Bolivia's mountain crown and the circuit of Illampu from the sun-drenched, palm-shaded Spanish colonial courtyards of Sorata unbeatable.

There can be few places in the world to which Patagonia does not offer a complete contrast. Lashed by some of the most ferocious weather imaginable, this wonderland of glaciers and lakes, of stunted temperate rainforest and boundless *pampas* defines the word elemental. Under enormous, constantly changing skies featuring surreal cirrus and lenticular cloud formations, it is often referred to as the uttermost part of the earth. Though trekking here is no casual affair, those suitably equipped and prepared will find it utterly captivating. No route better displays the multiple facets of Patagonia than the circuit of the Torres del Paine.

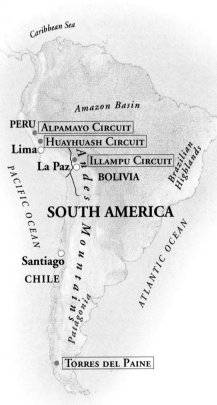

143

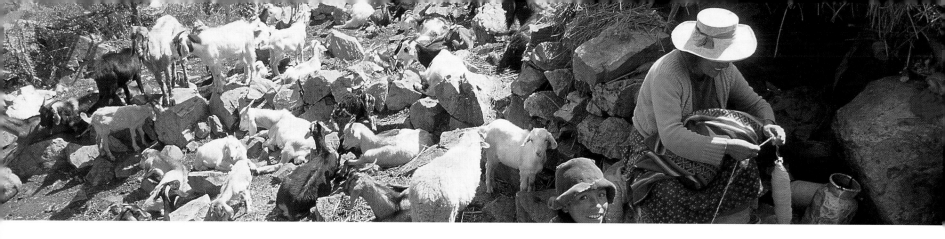

HUAYHUASH CIRCUIT

by Chris Hooker

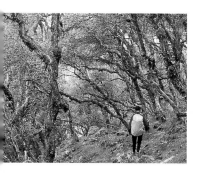

The Cordillera Huayhuash looks insignificant on most maps of Peru, running as it does just 30km (19 miles) from north to south. Yet this compact range is one of the most magnificent in all the Andes. One of 20 glaciated ranges within Peru, the Huayhuash rises abruptly from rolling grassland 50km (30 miles) south of the Cordillera Blanca and, like it, forms the Amazon watershed. From a distance, its profile resembles that of a giant saw – a dozen serrated summits line a single ice-clad ridge, with Yerupajá (6634m; 21,766ft), the second highest peak in Peru, standing out above the rest.

At the heart of the *cordillera* (mountain range), a pristine wilderness is revealed. Below the fissured glaciers, cirques and valleys lie adorned with sparkling lakes and abundant bird life. Wild *puna* (high-altitude grassland) predominates, punctuated by the occasional patch of *quenual* (rosewood) forest. The elusive wild *vicuña* (similar to the llama) is occasionally sighted, but more common on this bleak terrain are scattered herds of cattle brought for grazing by seasonal croft-dwellers. This is the setting for a spectacular and hugely rewarding trek, the 170km (110-mile) Huayhuash Circuit, one of very few to loop an entire mountain range. Though strenuous, requiring some 12 days and crossing several passes above 4500m (14,700ft), it takes trekkers into a world of unsurpassed natural beauty.

Ancient Andean people revered certain snow peaks, imbuing them with great powers. If an *apu* (mountain spirit) needed appeasing, the priest might climb its flanks to perform a sacrifice. A number of high-altitude archaeological discoveries even suggest that, in so doing, such priests may have become the first humans to reach an altitude of 6000m (19,700ft). There is, however, no evidence to date of

TOP *A campesino woman and her daughter tend their goats on a summer pasture at an altitude of some 4200m (13,700ft) near the pass of Punta Llamac.*
INSET *Trekker in* quenual *forest. This tough red-barked species is endemic to the high Andes, with pockets of* quenual *forest found at altitudes in excess of 4000m (13,000ft).*
CENTRE *Trekkers above Lake Carhuacocha. Behind centre is the east face of Yerupajá Grande (6634m; 21,766ft), the highest point on the Amazon watershed.*

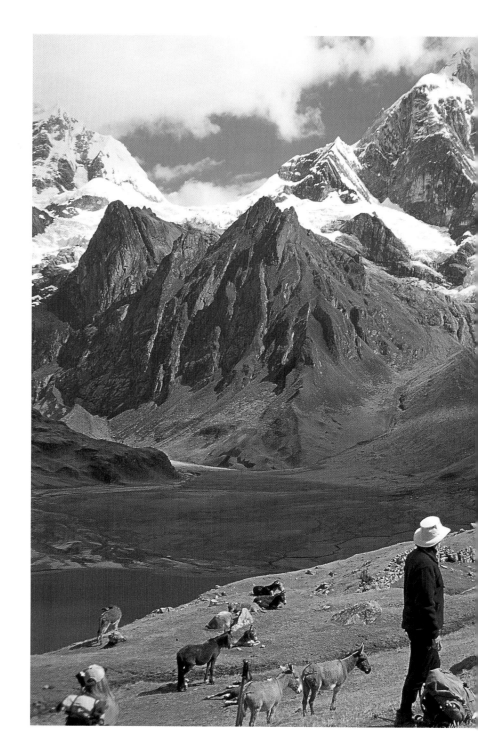

ancient mountaineering exploits in the Huayhuash; and there probably never will be, given the no-nonsense verticality of its snow peaks and the technical skills they demand.

The Austrian geographic team of Erwin Schneider and A Awerzger made the first important ascent in the Huayhuash, reaching the summit of Siula Grande (6344m; 20,815ft) in 1936. Schneider went on to solo Rasac (6017m; 19,742ft) and Yerupajá was first climbed in 1950 by Americans David Harrah and Jim Maxwell, but one particularly chilling story has become an epic associated with climbing in the Huayhuash. In 1986, the unclimbed west face of Siula Grande was the scene of a singular feat of survival, recounted in British climber Joe Simpson's acclaimed book *Touching the Void*. Badly injured after a fall near the summit, Simpson was being lowered through a blizzard by his partner, Simon Yates. With light failing, and Simpson hanging over a precipice, Yates started to slip. He was obliged to cut the rope. Simpson plummeted into a crevasse and was left for dead. Despite several broken bones, he managed miraculously, over the next two days, to crawl out and across the glacier to safety. The Huayhuash Circuit trek may not require quite such extraordinary endurance, but a degree of perseverance will certainly come in handy!

Chiquián, the gateway to the Huayhuash, is easily reached by public transport. Approached by road, the massif is first glimpsed from a high plateau, but only later does the entire glacier-encrusted wall reveal itself. The town lies two full days' walk from the north flank of the range. A well-used track descends steeply from Chiquián's plateau (3400m; 11,100ft) into the hot, dry Pativilca Valley 500m (1600ft) below. Once there, the trail turns east and traverses a dusty cactus-and-scrub environment. Over the next two weeks, the trekker will encounter quintessential examples of Andean ecosystems, the range of altitudes and the tropical latitude combining to produce a fascinating variety of environments.

Two hours from Chiquián, riverside camping spots abound, although there is precious little shade as the trail follows the Pativilca downstream through arid scrubland for two hours before turning north. So begins a two-day ascent via the Pacllón and Llamac valleys into the heart of the *cordillera*. Turning into the Llamac Valley, the landscape changes as the trail passes stands of eucalyptus, the odd walnut and a variety of blooms. Hummingbirds flit among brilliant red, trumpet-shaped *cantuta*, national emblem of Peru and sacred flower of the Inca.

Llamac (3200m; 10,500ft), one of only three villages encountered on the circuit, is surrounded by corn fields and lies some seven hours from Chiquián. One hour upstream, the trail passes Pocpa – its two small shops the last for a week – and very soon trekkers pick up a vehicle track and follow it steadily up for five hours. On this stretch the first effects of altitude might be felt. It's important to avoid over-exertion. Pace must be adapted to the scarcity of oxygen: at the higher passes on the circuit, the body absorbs only 60 per cent of the oxygen absorbed at sea level.

Three hours east of Pocpa, the terrain changes once again. At around 3800m (12,400ft), *puna* of pale, coarse *ichu* grass predominates. Patches of dark *quenual* forest mark the landscape, too. This red-barked species, endemic to the Andes, thrives at up to 4800m (15,700ft) and is prolific hereabouts. Many mammal species, including the elusive puma and Andean mountain cat, shelter here.

Trekkers lose the road at Cuartel Huain (4150m; 13,610ft), a tiny scattering of *chozas* (grazier crofts) at the foot of the circuit's first major ascent, up over the high ridge to the east. Cuartel Huain also affords the first close-ups of the massif. To the southeast, Rondoy (5870m; 19,260ft) and Ninashanka (5607m; 18,397ft) loom large. Camping here is adequate, if somewhat exposed. With clear skies, early morning temperatures can drop to minus 4°C (24°F), providing a taste of what's to come as from here on the circuit descends only once below 4000m (13,000ft).

Giant condors may be spotted circling on the ascent to the Cacanampunta pass (4700m; 15,400ft), the first of seven passes above 4500m (14,700ft). Flora is varied and features several medicinal plants, notably *wamanripa* (for pneumonia) and *anqush* (an expectorant). The pass marks the Amazon watershed and transition from 'dry' to 'rainy' *puna*. An hour and a half after the pass there are breathtaking views over Lake Mitucocha to several towering snow peaks from which the twin summits of Jirishanka (6094m; 19,994ft) stand out. The light here is intense, lending a crisp

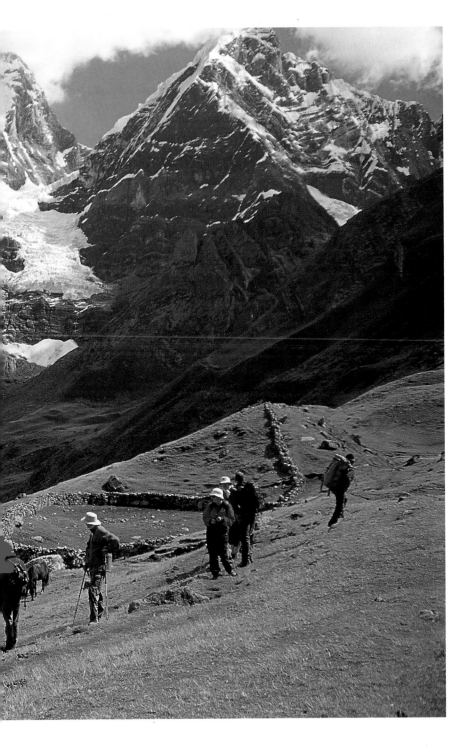

LOCATION The Andes of northern Peru. Nearest towns are Chiquián and Cajatambo.

WHEN TO GO May to September, dry season.

START/FINISH Chiquián; several daily buses from Lima (8hrs) and Huaraz (3hrs). When the Chiquián to Llamac road is completed, Llamac will become the ideal start/finish point, reducing duration of all treks by 2 days.

DURATION 11 to 14 days; 160km (100 miles). Longer if side valleys are explored. Alternative half-circuit (7 to 9 days) from Chiquián to Cajatambo or vice versa.

MAX ALTITUDE Punta Cuyoc (4950m; 16,240ft). Average altitude is well above 4000m (13,000ft).

TECHNICAL CONSIDERATIONS Steady acclimatization before starting trek is essential. For security and health reasons, the trek should not be attempted alone.

EQUIPMENT Take in all food. Backpack, tent, sleeping bag and mat, hiking boots, wet-weather windproof outer shell, thermals, layers and warm jacket, high SPF sunblock, insect repellent. Huaraz has several agencies that rent camping and trekking equipment.

TREKKING STYLE Backpacking or expedition. Recommend hiring donkeys to transport gear. No designated camp sites but good wild camping spots abound. No huts on circuit.

PERMITS The Huayhuash has no protected status and no permit is required.

sharpness to the scenery. There is great camping at Mitucocha, and a possible three-hour side trip to the lateral moraine above Laguna Ninacocha. To resume the circuit, the southern edge of the boggy Janca Plain is skirted until 45 minutes from Mitucocha, the trail cuts south up a narrow valley and ascends gently to Punta Carhuac (4650m; 15,260ft). From here the towering form of Yerupajá stands out among a rank of gigantic peaks. Descending to the stunning Laguna Carhuacocha (4200m; 13,700ft), the choice of camp sites is wide with Carnicero (5960m; 19,560ft), Siula Grande (6344m; 20,815ft) and Yerupajá providing a majestic backdrop.

Resuming the loop, the most interesting route is via Laguna Siula, cutting up steeply to the Carnicero ridge (4850m; 15,910ft). With patience, distant *vicuña* may

be sighted on the far side. In the shadow of Carnicero, Jurao (5600m; 18,400ft) and Trapecio (5644m; 18,528ft) a vast expanse of cushion grass covers the flooded valley floor, and it is surprisingly easy to hop, cushion by cushion, right across the valley! Two-house Huayhuash (4350m; 14,270ft) provides good camping.

The 400m (1300ft) ascent to the Portachuelo pass is gentle. From the pass, the spectacular Raura range comes into view. Large herds of alpaca (related to the llama) can often be seen between here and Laguna Viconga (4450m; 14,600ft), situated at the end of the descent. A soak in the nearby al fresco thermal bath provides welcome muscular relief before tackling Punta Cuyoc (4950m; 16,240ft). The three-hour ascent to the trek's highest point forks half way: go left for amazing views of both

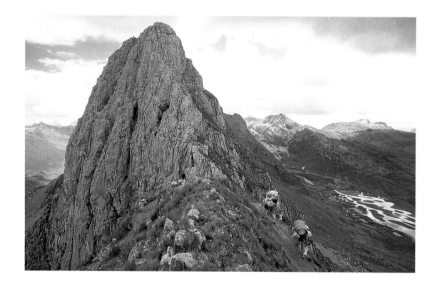

ABOVE *Pack donkeys cross Cacanampunta, one of only two passes across the main Huayhuash range. The narrow limestone crest lies on the Continental Divide.*

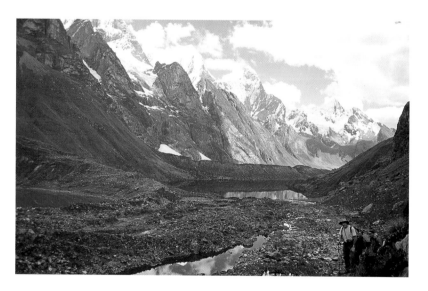

ABOVE *Lake Siula and the serrated eastern flank of the Cordillera Huayhuash. Trekkers make their way slowly to the Carnicero Ridge (4850m; 15,910ft).*

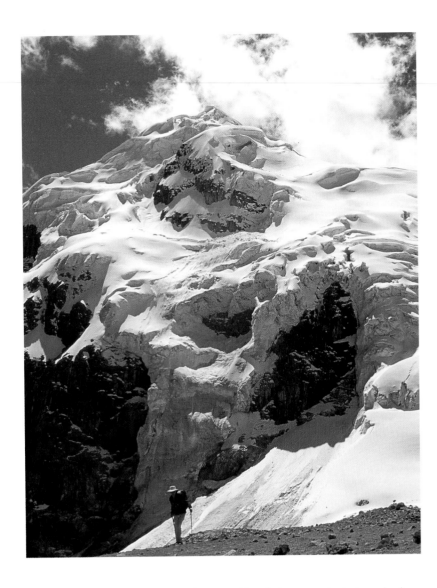

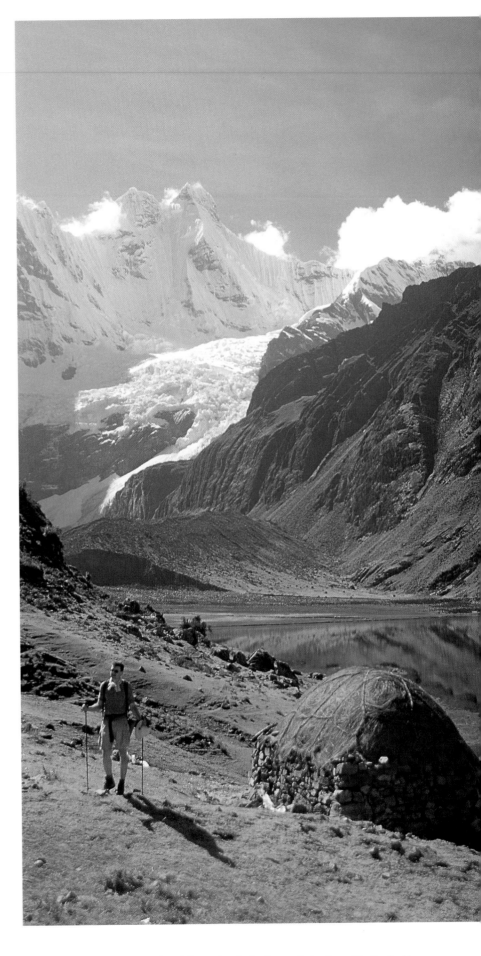

cordilleras. The descent back to the west side of the range leads into the long Huanacpatay Valley and three hours later it is a steep, dusty descent to the Huayllapa Valley. The air warms up as the trail, turning west below an impressive waterfall, approaches the village of Huayllapa (3550m; 11,648ft), the lowest point since Pocpa. Some supplies are available here and camping is permitted on the football pitch.

The 1250m (4100ft) ascent to the Tapush Pass is long and steep. It eases off after the Huatia plateau (4300m; 14,000ft), where there is good camping, and ends after five hours. It's then an hour down to the Cashpapampa plateau and another half-hour to the junction with the Yaucha Valley. Heading east, a two-hour ascent culminates in a scree traverse to the Yaucha Pass (4800m; 15,700ft). On a clear day, the razorback ridge of Rasac (6017m; 19,742ft) dominates the skyline. A two-hour descent via the Huacrish Valley ends on the shores of Lake Jahuacocha (4050m; 13,288ft), where a line of magnificent snow peaks forms the perfect backdrop for an overnight stop. The final pass, Pampa Llamac (4300m; 14,000ft), is reached on an undulating path through *quenual* forest. It's a dusty, three-hour descent to Llamac and a further hour downstream to the camp site at Huarangallo. The final five-hour leg to Chiquián culminates in a sweaty, 500m (1600ft) ascent.

ABOVE *Punta Cuyoc Pass (4950m; 16,240ft), the highest point of the trek, marks the return from the eastern (right) to the western (left) slopes of the Andes.*

ABOVE *A* choza *(grazier croft) at Jahuacocha, the background dominated by the double summits of Jirishanka and the glacier that feeds Lago Solterococha.*

147

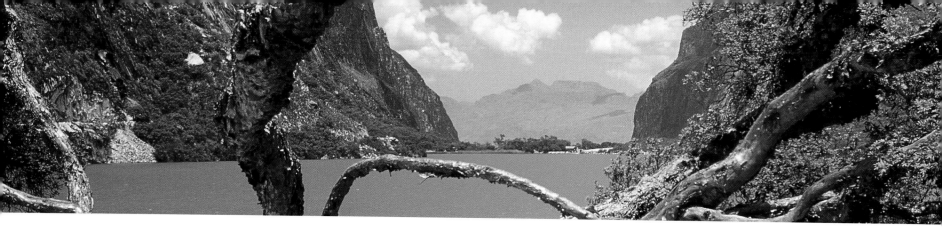

ALPAMAYO CIRCUIT

by Kathy Jarvis

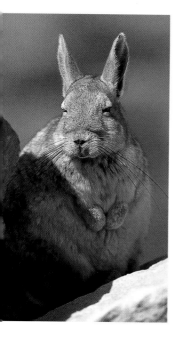

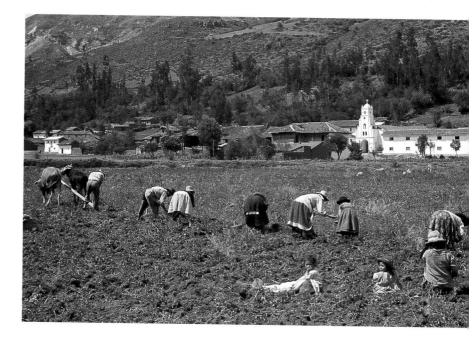

The Alpamayo trek is one of the most scenically spectacular walking routes of the Andes, no small claim given the infinite choice in this dramatic mountain range. The Andes rise steeply from the Pacific Ocean on the western edge of the continent of South America. They run from the Santa Marta range in Colombia to the very tip of Cape Horn in the south, a total distance of more than 7000km (4300 miles). The Cordillera Blanca, just a short part of the entire range, has 33 immense peaks towering over 6000m (19,600ft). It is home to Huascarán, at 6768m (22,205ft) Peru's highest mountain.

Exploration of the area came relatively recently – Alpamayo was first climbed in 1957 by a German expedition – but the Cordillera Blanca has become world renowned for serious mountaineering and breathtaking high-altitude trekking. Long before adventurous foreigners arrived to discover the beauties of the Andes, generations of highland Indians had lived, worked and fought beneath the towering peaks. Visiting some of the Indian communities that still inhabit the area is one of the highlights of this trekking route.

The Alpamayo Circuit can be walked in either direction. Scenically, it is preferable to start at the northern end and trek south, but trekkers must be fully acclimatized because of the rapid altitude gain during the first two days. There is no escape route between the first and second pass, so it is not possible to evacuate anyone suffering from altitude sickness. All food should be purchased in Huaraz as there is no possibility of restocking along the way. The local market has a large variety of good-quality local produce.

TOP *The peeling copper-coloured bark of the quenual (*Polylepis sericea*) frames the sapphire waters of Laguna Chinacocha, deep in the heart of the Cordillera Blanca.*
INSET *Rabbit-like* viscacha *are commonly spotted sunning themselves among the boulder fields throughout the high Andes.*
ABOVE RIGHT *Quechua Indians living in the fertile Callejón de Huaylas make a living from grazing livestock and growing a surprising variety of Andean crops.*

To get to the trail head an early start from Huaraz is recommended. Hired transport is needed for the four-hour journey to Hualcayán. The drive along the agricultural valley of Callejón de Huaylas provides tantalizing views of some of the Cordillera Blanca's highest, most impressive peaks. Copa (6188m; 20,303ft), Hualcán (6122m; 20,086ft), the towering form of Huascarán (6768m; 22,206ft), the three jagged peaks of Huandoy (the highest is 6359m; 20,864ft) and soaring Santa Cruz (6259m; 20,536ft). At Hualcayán (3000m; 10,000ft) locally hired donkeys are loaded up with kit and food for the next eight days. The path leads upwards, zigzagging steeply and offering superb views back over the Callejón and the Rio Santa Valley. The gorge of Quebrada de Los Cedros plunges away to the west, peeling red-barked *quenual* forests lining the valley sides, deep blue lagoons below. The first taste of the beauty of this trek is experienced as camp is set up high on the mountainside at Huishca (4000m; 13,000ft).

On the second day, passing Laguna Cullicocha (dammed for hydroelectric power) the trail cuts close beneath the three sharp and spectacular peaks of Santa Cruz. Rabbit-like *viscacha* scurry about among the boulders. The first pass, Paso de Los Cedros, is a challenging 4850m (15,910ft), the highest on the trek. Following this there is a welcome descent to the camp at Osoruri (4600m; 15,000ft).

A short climb the next morning takes trekkers over Osoruri Pass (4750m; 15,580ft) and onto a long descent into the Quebrada de Los Cedros below. There is a farming community here with scattered adobe houses nestled on the valley floor, terraced potato fields perched precariously high up on the valley sides and goats tended by remarkably young children. Strolling up the valley, with the hard walking done for the day, there is time to appreciate the surroundings. The trail follows the banks of the bubbling Los Cedros River, waterfalls tumbling off the glaciers of Milluacocha to the west, a superb panorama of snow-capped peaks appearing ahead. This gentle walk culminates at Jancarurish Camp (4200m; 13,700ft) just beneath the famous peak of Alpamayo (5947m; 19,512ft), voted the most beautiful mountain in the world in an international competition held in Germany in 1966. Alpamayo rises spectacularly, a steep, perfectly shaped pyramid of ice, smaller than its neighbours but unique and unmistakable in form: two sharp summits separated by a corniced razor ridge.

Day four begins with a tough climb to the pass of Jancarurish (4830m; 15,850ft), affording excellent views back over rocky moraines and jewel-like lakes to the immense glaciers and peaks of Alpamayo, Jancarurish (5578m; 18,301ft), Quitaraju (6036m; 19,804ft), Pumapampa (5785m; 18,980ft) and Santa Cruz. From the pass, the trail diverts northeast and Pucajirca (6050m; 19,850ft) can be seen in the distance. A gentle descent takes trekkers through rolling landscapes reminiscent of the Scottish highlands, with views towards the Callejón de Conchucos, a productive farming area lying between the high peaks of the Andes and the lowlands of the Amazon Basin. A short, 400m (1300ft) ascent leads over into Quebrada Tayapampa and the hamlet of Huillca (4000m; 13,000ft), where camp is set up for the night.

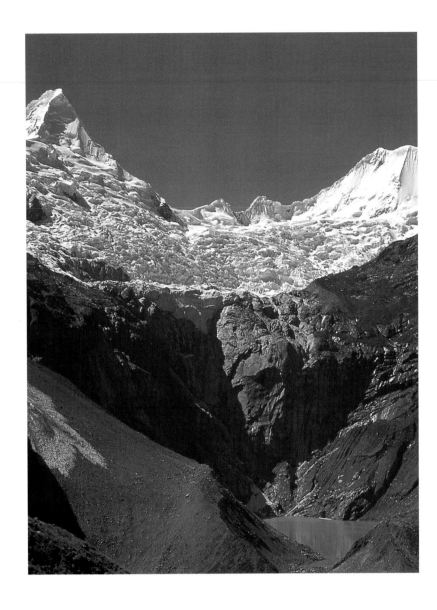

RIGHT *The steep climb out of the Quebrada de los Cedros towards Jancarurish Pass gives trekkers excellent views of the unmistakable pyramid form of Alpamayo.*

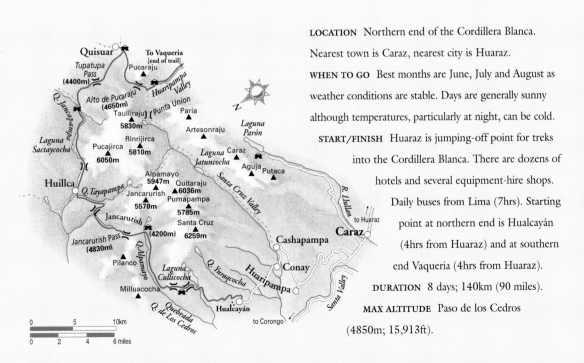

LOCATION Northern end of the Cordillera Blanca. Nearest town is Caraz, nearest city is Huaraz.

WHEN TO GO Best months are June, July and August as weather conditions are stable. Days are generally sunny although temperatures, particularly at night, can be cold.

START/FINISH Huaraz is jumping-off point for treks into the Cordillera Blanca. There are dozens of hotels and several equipment-hire shops. Daily buses from Lima (7hrs). Starting point at northern end is Hualcayán (4hrs from Huaraz) and at southern end Vaqueria (4hrs from Huaraz).

DURATION 8 days; 140km (90 miles).

MAX ALTITUDE Paso de los Cedros (4850m; 15,913ft).

TECHNICAL CONSIDERATIONS Adequate acclimatization before setting off is essential. Weather conditions in the mountains can change rapidly so carry suitable clothing to cover all eventualities. There is plenty of stream water, which should be purified before drinking.

EQUIPMENT Backpack, light-weight waterproof tent, sleeping bag and mat, waterproof boots and clothing, thermals, hat, gloves, light-weight high-energy food, snacks, sun protection, map, compass, first-aid kit.

TREKKING STYLE Backpacking or expedition. There are no huts and no designated camp sites on this route; wild camping in remote and beautiful valleys.

PERMITS/RESTRICTIONS The trek falls within the Huascarán National Park and a trekking permit is required. Available from the National Park office in Huaraz, US$25.

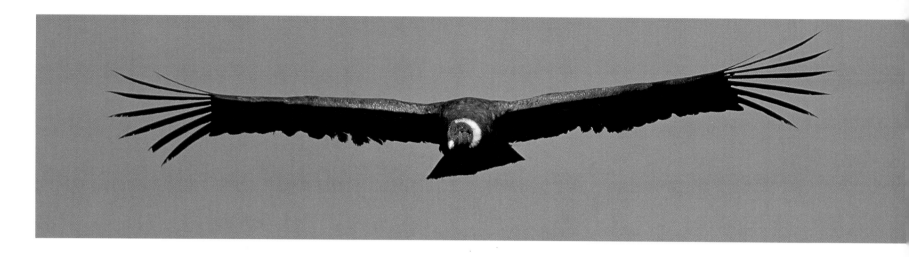

From Huillca the trail climbs steadily through high-altitude *puna* grassland to the next pass at 4600m (15,000ft). A surprising vista opens up below of the enchanting Laguna Sactaycocha, its wooded slopes of quenual forests home to the *oso de anteojos* (Andean bear) and timid mountain deer. Pucajirca towers above the pass. The trail descends through this wonderland to the vast flat valley of Jancapampa (3500m; 11,400) at the foot of Taulliraju (5830m; 19,128ft) and Rinrijirca (5810m; 19,060ft). The fifth night is spent camping in this dramatic spot; glaciers overhead, waterfalls cascading to the valley and farming communities dotted around the slopes below.

The climb out of the valley leads through a highland village of thatched adobe houses. Using traditional farming methods, local Quechua Indians grow nutritious native crops such as beans, potatoes and lupins, aided only by oxen and wooden ploughs. One of the highlights of the trek is the pass of Tupatupa (4400m; 14,400ft)

from where the entire panorama of the northern massif of the Cordillera Blanca spreads out ahead. The views provide a dramatic backdrop during the descent to the village of Quisuar (3800m; 12,400ft). The next day the gentle start towards the Alto de Pucaraju Pass (4650m; 15,260ft) steepens as it zigzags up. From the top another breathtaking panorama of snow-capped peaks unfolds, ample reward for the stresses of the climb – the jagged top of the peak of Taulliraju is impressive to the northwest. Majestic Andean condors may be spotted soaring in the Quebrada Huaripampa just below.

A steep rocky track winds down to join the Huaripampa Valley and the final day is a gentle wander down the valley to the road head. Leaving the trek at Vaqueria, catch a bus in the village for a memorable return journey to Huaraz. The narrow mountain road crosses back into the Santa Valley over the Portachuelo Pass (4767m; 15,640ft), with postcard views over the Llanganuco Lakes and close-ups of Huascarán.

ABOVE *The majestic Andean condor, often over 1m (3ft) tall, soars over steep mountainsides searching for carrion on which to feed.*

BELOW *Pack horses are used by local communities in the Andes. Many families supplement their income by working as* arrieros *(donkey drivers) during the trekking season.*

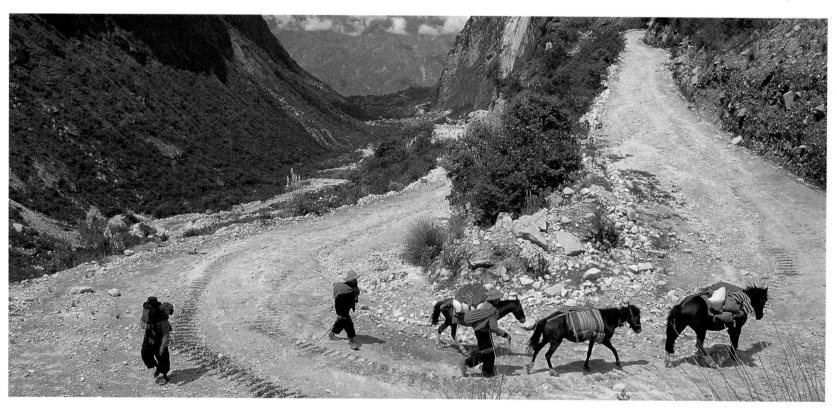

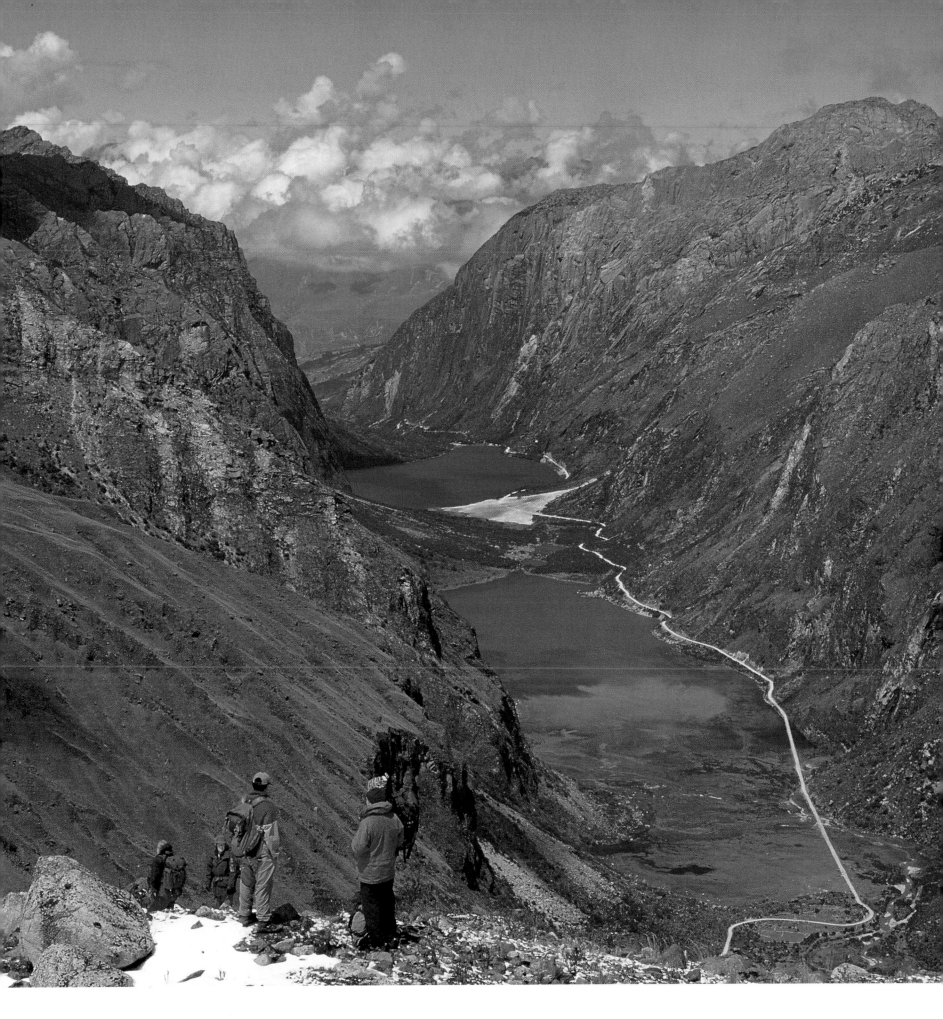

ABOVE *Trekkers gaze at the deeply cut Llanganuco Valley below. Day trippers often make the journey from Huaraz to the scenic Orcancocha and Chinacocha lakes.*

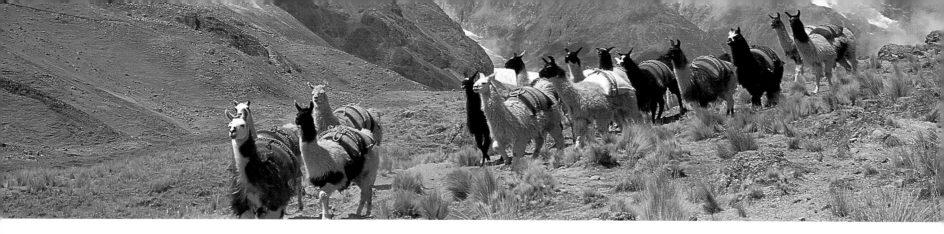

ILLAMPU CIRCUIT

by Kathy Jarvis

The Cordillera Real rises from the eastern shores of Lake Titicaca on the Bolivian high plains known as the *altiplano*. This awe-inspiring range of jagged icy peaks is a part of the immense Andes chain, which runs over 7000km (4300 miles), the full length of the South American continent. The Cordillera Real stretches 150km (93 miles) from southeast of Bolivia's largest city, La Paz, to the massif of Illampu (6368m; 20,893ft) and Ancohuma (6427m; 21,087ft) to the northwest. Several ancient paved paths cross the range, evidence of pre-Colombian civilizations. These laboriously constructed roads run from the high *altiplano* to the fertile tropical lowlands of the eastern Andean slopes and are usually attributed to the Incas, who ruled most of Bolivia and Peru in the 15th and 16th centuries. It is thought that much of the Inca gold in the ancient capital of Cusco came from the Tipuani area on the eastern side of the Andes. Gold is still mined in this area. Solid stone roads were also needed for the movement of Inca armies as they expanded their empire. Since then a whole network of routes has developed, for trade and to transport valuable minerals such as gold and silver. This labyrinth of paths provides remote Indian villages with their only line of communication to the outside world.

The Illampu Circuit follows these well-trodden trails over seven days as it takes trekkers high around the flanks of the Illampu-Ancohuma massif. The regular circuit may be lengthened by taking time to trek high above Sorata to Laguna Chillata (4204m; 13,793ft) and Laguna Glaciar. At a breathtaking 5038m (16,530ft) Laguna Glaciar is fed directly from the glaciers of Illampu. This area is sacred to the local Aymara Indians and it is recommended to take a local guide on this three– to

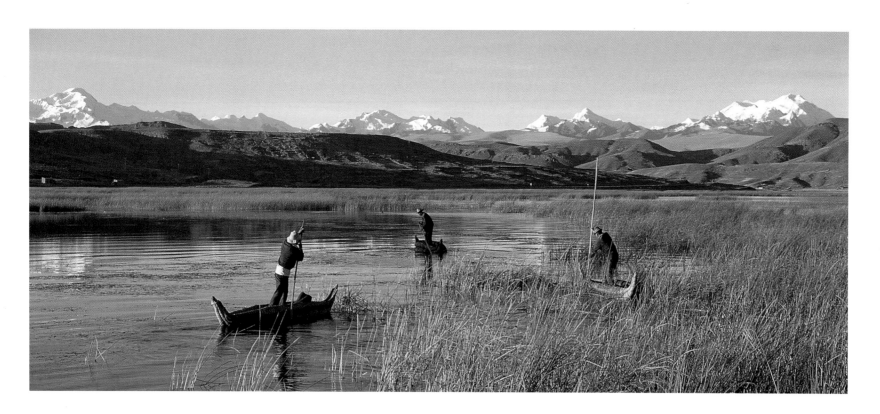

TOP *In the Cordillera Real, llamas are still used as pack animals, as they were in Inca times. From more remote villages, locals may take several days to transport their produce.*

ABOVE *Aymara Indians living on the altiplano around the shores of Lake Titicaca use handmade* totora *(reed) boats for fishing.*

four-day diversion. The main Illampu trail passes through isolated settlements, travers-ing various vegetation zones, from lush subtropical palm trees through semiarid val-leys, terraced and cultivated for thousands of years, to elfin forest of stunted gnarled *polylepis* trees. The trail finally emerges in stark alpine-type *puna* (a high, cold dry plateau), where only a few well-adapted plants cling to barren permanently frozen ground. At lower levels on the trail, where plant life is prolific, there is also a variety of animal life: the shy members of the camelid family *vicuña*, graze warily, once hunted almost to extinction for their fine coats; *viscachas* (rabbit-like rodents) scuttle to and fro among the boulders; Andean geese and other water birds populate the many lakes. Most majestic of all, the Andean condor soars overhead in search of carrion for its next meal.

Leaving behind the waving palms of balmy Sorata (2678m; 8787ft), the track heads steeply up out of town winding along above the Lakathiya River valley towards the small village of Quilambaya. Route finding at this early stage can be tricky so tak-ing a guide and donkeys, at least on this first day, is recommended. At Quilambaya go left at the fork through an avenue of tall cacti and continue climbing steeply. The path levels out and contours left, then sharply right to cross a bridge over the Lakathiya River. Climb the winding track ahead to reach the village of Lakathiya. Walking through the village, keep an eye out to the left for the point where two branches of the river meet. Follow the left bank of the left branch, crossing the river on a small stone bridge and heading on up the track until the valley widens out and there are good grassy camping areas (4000m; 13,100ft).

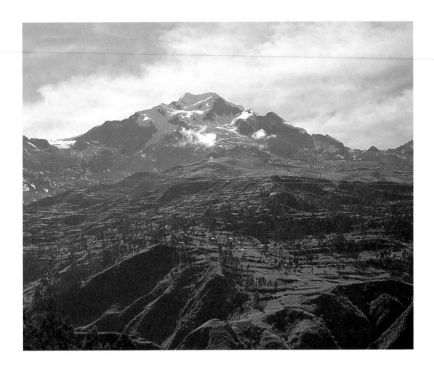

ABOVE *The west face of Ancohuma. Having circumnavigated its icy slopes, trekkers spend the last day on the trail in the subtropical gardens of the green terraces below.*

BELOW *A steep climb brings trekkers high up on the slopes of Illampu to Laguna Glaciar (5038m; 16,530ft), which is often littered with icebergs from the glacier above.*

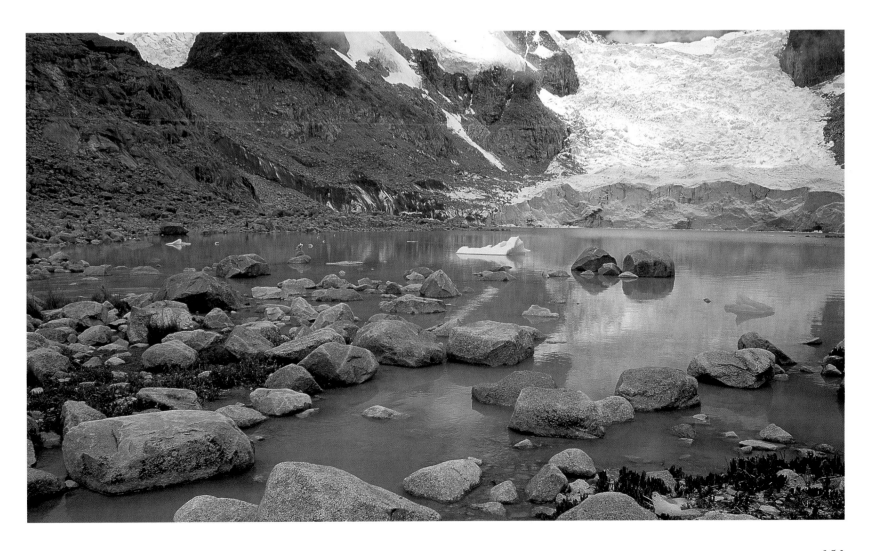

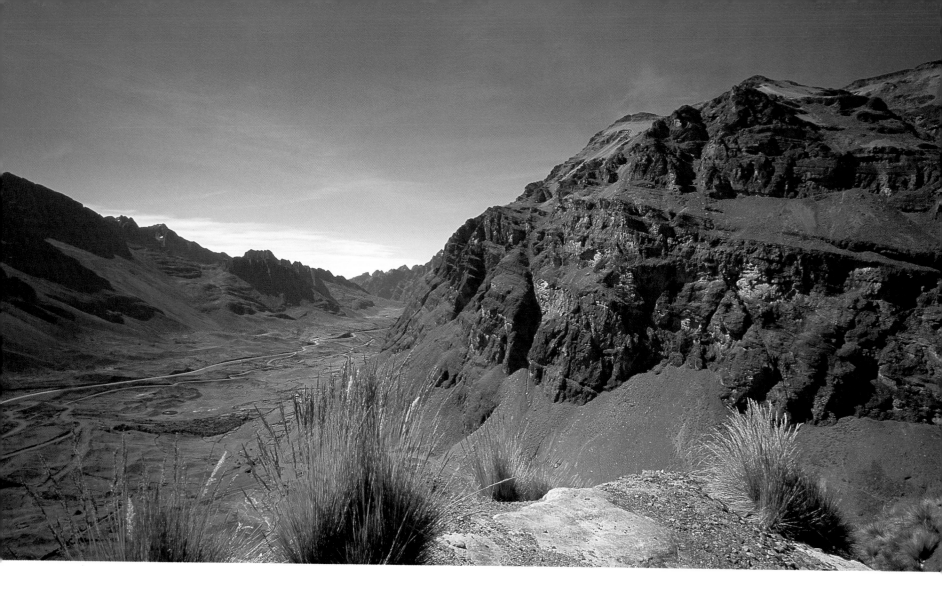

The next day the climb to the pass continues. As the valley widens, the route swings to the north alongside a stream. The track steepens, zigzagging almost vertically to the first pass on the trek, Abra Illampu (4741m; 15,555ft). Herds of llamas lift their heads from grazing the tough *ichu* grass, seemingly to admire the magnificent view, oblivious to tired trekkers. Ahead, the sight of the glacier-covered Illampu peak is inspiring. Deep-green valleys plunge away behind, and the vast inland sea of Lake Titicaca shimmers in the far distance.

From the pass, the track descends the grassy valley of Quebrada Illampu to the river Chuchu Jahuira and the dirt road from Sorata to Ancohuma and Cocoyo. Follow the road gently downwards before heading southeast at the small hamlet of Estancia Utaña Pampa. Ancient-looking stone houses with thatched roofs have wall-encircled plots, ploughed and planted with native crops. *Quinoa*, a high-protein cereal crop with distinctive red fronds, is widely grown. It makes the most delicious soup. Look out for potatoes spread out on the ground being freeze-dried into *chuño*, to be stored and later reconstituted in stews. Highland life has changed little over the centuries in these far-flung valleys of the Andes. Cross the Anco Huma Jahuira River on a stone bridge and continue up the valley for good overnight camping spots.

Next day continue walking steeply southeast, up into the hanging valley below Abra Korahuasi (4479m; 14,696ft), the second pass. Once over the pass, follow the path down through luxuriant vegetation, dropping 1000m (3200ft) to the flat-bottomed, green valley with the village of Cocoyo ahead. It may be possible to buy fresh trout from local children tending llama herds and fishing in the stream that

meanders through the valley. Cocoyo is a village of llama herders and miners; unaccustomed to seeing trekkers, giggling, inquisitive children often peek nervously from behind corners. Follow the bank of the thundering waters of the Sarani River, keeping the river on the left. There are many excellent camping spots within an hour of the village. Four hours of gentle climbing from Cocoyo bring trekkers to Paso Sarani (4600m; 15,090ft). Climbing steeply out of the Sarani Valley a few hours later, look ahead: water cascades dramatically into the boggy pampa at the top end of the valley. Watch for condors overhead and *viscachas* on the boulders on the way up the pass.

Over the pass, the trail descends steeply towards the remote village of Chajolpaya where there are several houses, but little sign of life other than llamas and sheep. Aymara is the only language spoken here and the nearest shops are two days' walk away in the town of Achacachi far beyond Abra Calzada. Spectacular views of the deep blue-green lakes of Carrizal and Khota reward trekkers for the long, steady climb from the village to the final and highest pass on the trek, Abra Calzada (5045m; 16,553ft). There are abundant camping spots on the way up and even a few at the top, rubbing shoulders with the glaciers, rugged icy peaks towering above. The pass itself is broad and almost barren, with the ubiquitous *ichu* and just a few other hardy plants clinging to the earth, struggling for survival amid ice-scraped boulders and meltwater lakes.

The initial descent from the pass is steep and tricky for donkeys. The track soon levels out and passes close to lakes Carrizal and Khota, crossing a scree slope of deep red-coloured rock. From Laguna Khota, head towards Laguna San Francisco across the grassy pampa of the Quebrada de Kote, and on to the grassy ridge up to the right. From the top of the ridge, an impressive 360-degree panorama unfolds; the vast inland ocean of Lake Titicaca to the west, the high peaks of the Cordillera behind. The colour of the landscape, accentuated in the unique light over the altiplano, is unsurpassably beautiful. There are several places to camp before reaching Laguna San Francisco, although it is best not to camp within sight of any houses, as local farmers are not always friendly.

Crossing Laguna San Francisco at the north end, look out for the large black-and-white Andean geese often feeding along the lakeshore. The trail heads towards the top of the ridge on the far side where there is a rocky cairn (4867m; 15,969ft). From here the route is cross-country, with little evidence of a track of any sort. Traverse the next small valley before turning west, down across the pampa and past the head of the valley of Quebrada Tiquitini. Eventually, a path is reached. Follow this to join a dirt road, which goes to the village of Alto Lojena. It may be possible to catch a truck down to Sorata from here. Alternatively, it is a further day's walk down the road, through the small village of Millipaya to Sorata. There are good camping spots on the way; try just beyond the old mine, one hour from Millipaya before the village of Cochipata.

The landscape changes dramatically as trekkers descend from the stark grassy *puna* of high mountain passes to cultivated fields adjoining small colourful villages. There are still fabulous views of the towering glaciated massif of Ancohuma and Illampu above, meltwater cascading down deep gullies towards the valley bottom. Vegetation becomes prolific, the temperature rises and birdsong is abundant as Sorata and a welcome rest are approached.

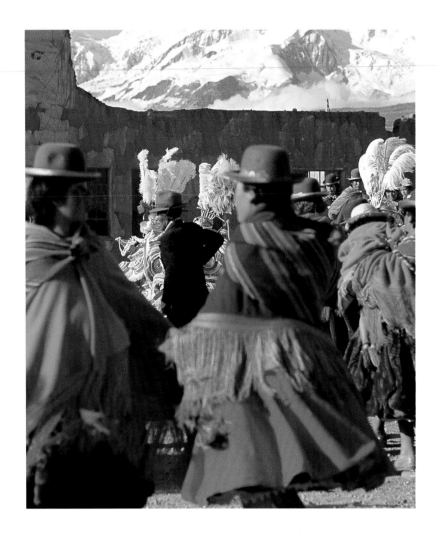

ABOVE *Festivals, often rooted in pre-Hispanic tradition, are lively, colourful events. Aymara Indians come from far and wide to celebrate in the streets of Sorata.*

LOCATION Cordillera Real, western Bolivia. Approximately 150km (90 miles) from La Paz.

WHEN TO GO May to September (dry season) are best months for trekking. Sunny days and cold nights.

START/FINISH Trek starts and finishes at subtropical Sorata (2695m; 8842ft) at the foot of the Illampu and Ancohuma mountains. Bus service from La Paz (4hrs).

DURATION 6 to 7 days; 90km (60 miles).

MAX ALTITUDE Abra Calzada (5045m; 16,553ft)

TECHNICAL CONSIDERATIONS Trek goes into remote highland areas. Spend several days at altitude before setting off to ensure adequate acclimatization. Strong sun and high altitude combine to make the risk of dehydration high; drink plenty of water. Stream water is readily available but should be sterilized before drinking. Rubbish should be carried out, and human waste disposed of responsibly.

EQUIPMENT Take in all food. Backpack, waterproof tent, sleeping bag and mat, waterproofs, good walking boots, sun protection, warm clothes, thermals, hat, gloves, compass, map, first-aid kit, light-weight nutritious food and high-energy snacks. Maps can be bought and equipment is available for hire in La Paz. Guides and donkeys are available in Sorata.

TREKKING STYLE Backpacking and expedition. Wild camping; no designated sites. Don't camp near villages.

PERMITS/RESTRICTIONS There are no restrictions on trekking or climbing in the area and no permits are required for the trek.

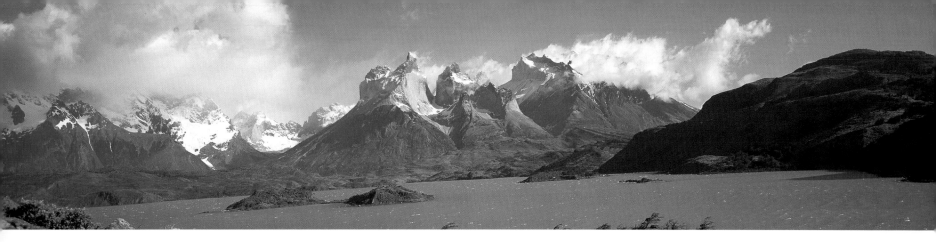

TORRES DEL PAINE

by Chris Hooker

The Parque Nacional Torres del Paine lies in the wilds of deepest southern Chile, sandwiched between the windswept Patagonian steppe to the east and the vast Continental Icecap to the north and west. To the southwest are the fjords and islands of the Chilean Archipelago. The Paine is one of South America's most spectacular national parks. A wonder of natural sculpture, its 2422 square kilometres (935 square miles) display many of southern Patagonia's most spectacular and idiosyncratic landscape features: soaring granite spires, glaciers, jewel-like lakes and dense Magellanic forest. As for wildlife, Paine's contrasting vegetation zones harbour many bird and mammal species, some endemic. UNESCO recognized this uniqueness in 1978 when it granted the park World Heritage Status.

There is something otherworldly about the improbably contoured Paine massif (3000m; 10,000ft). It rises abruptly from a low-lying plateau and forms the centrepiece of the park. It is also the hub of the great Paine trekking circuit, a demanding 10-day loop that takes trekkers to the pristine heart of one of the world's most breathtaking glaciated wildernesses. The ferocious westerly winds that buffet this region throughout the trekking season are an integral part of the Paine experience. These are due largely to the presence nearby of the vast South Patagonian Icefield, a huge anomaly given the moderate latitude – some 50 degrees south. Relatively recently (in geological terms), this entire area was choked with ice; the colossal glaciers that snake their way into the park today are a legacy of this era.

The breathtaking granite wall of the Paine range is first viewed from afar on the approach from Puerto Natales and its various distinct features come into sharp focus on rounding the eastern shore of Lago Sarmiento. The monolithic Cerro Paine Grande

TOP *The Paine massif seen from the south across the glacial meltwaters of Laguna Pehoe. In the background are the Cuernos (right) and Cerro Paine Grande hidden by cloud.*

LOCATION Southern Chile, 12th Region. 110km (68 miles) north of Puerto Natales, 400km (250 miles) north of Punta Arenas.

WHEN TO GO October to April; long daylight hours.

START/FINISH Several daily bus trips to the park from Puerto Natales. Stops include Laguna Amarga gate, Pudeto (3 daily lake crossings) and park headquarters. Exit from same points.

DURATION 10 days; 135km (80 miles) including side trips and rest day(s). Alternative 5-day 'W' trek: Grey–Pehoe–Valle Francés–Torres, exiting via Laguna Amarga.

MAXIMUM ALTITUDE Paso Paine (1250m, 4100ft).

TREKKING STYLE Backpacking.

TECHNICAL CONSIDERATIONS Trails, marked with orange paint, are not immaculate. Occasional bogs to cross, streams to ford and gullies to negotiate. Anti-clockwise recommended as avoids toughest ascent early on. Winds around 160kph (100mph), can hinder progress and require caution on exposed ground. Snow often lies deep near the pass and can obscure the trail, especially early in the season.

EQUIPMENT Take in all food (light-weight, high-energy). Topographical map, backpack, tent, sleeping bag and mat, hiking boots, wet-weather wind-proof gear, thermals, quick-drying clothes, sun block, insect repellent. Most camping equipment can be hired at Puerto Natales.

PERMITS/RESTRICTIONS Park fee (US$13) payable in Chilean pesos. Register with passport on arrival, sign out on leaving. Park is well managed by CONAF. Wardens are helpful.

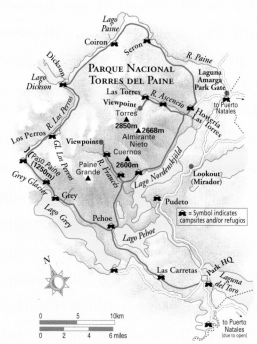

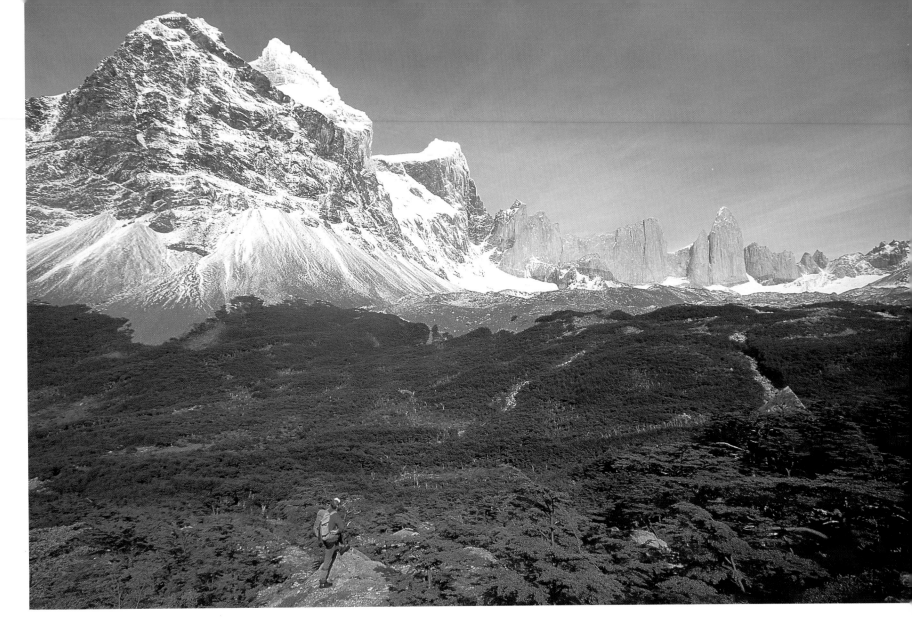

(3000m; 10,000ft) dominates its western flank while, to its right, the aptly named Cuernos (horns) thrust skyward. Cerro Almirante Nieto forms the eastern shoulder of the massif, obscuring from view the eponymous Torres. These three frost-polished columns of pink granite first appear in the distance on approaching the Laguna Amarga park gate from the east. Entering the park, grey *coiron* (bunchgrass) gives way to lush, rolling pre-Andean heath, one of Paine's four floral communities. This is *guanaco* country, and close encounters with groups of the wild camelid (once on the brink of extinction) are commonplace.

Inside the park now and heading towards the Pudeto refuge and ranger post, the dirt road winds through a zone characterized in spring by bright yellow *calafate* (burberry) flowers, and blazing red *notro* (firebush). The route veers westward and passes high above turquoise Lago Nordenskjöld, sparkling at the base of the massif. Awestruck onlookers are confronted here, for the first time, by the sheer scale of the landscape; the lake lies a mere 60m (200ft) above sea level while the sheer granite peaks to its north soar 3000m (10,000ft) above. Pudeto is just over

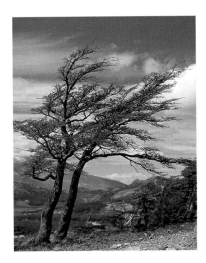

three hours from Natales by bus. Strong westerlies can turn Lago Pehoe into a seething cauldron of whitecaps, but with benign conditions and clear skies, the catamaran crossing from Pudeto to Refugio Pehoe is a pleasure. To the north, the Cuernos thrust skywards to 2600m (8500ft). Their unusual stratification and tapering – teat-shaped crowns – are the result of a dark, crumbly shale overlying their granite base. The Cuernos, indeed the whole massif, have their geological origins a mere 12 million years ago in a tectonic convulsion that thrust a large body of intruded igneous rock violently upward. (This compact range does not, strictly, belong to the much older Andean range, whose median lies to the west.) Since then, frost action and glacial erosion have cracked and polished the batholith to its current wonderful profile. Heading west, the boat is soon in the shadow of the frequently cloud-bound Cerro Paine Grande.

Refugio Pehoe's setting is spectacular, but exposed. The camp site has windbreaks, but gales can shred a badly pitched tent in minutes. The circuit begins with an undulating walk towards the Cuernos through mixed grassland and sparse forest, passing

ABOVE *View across the Valle Francés. In the distance (right) are the granite forms of Cerro Castillo, Cota, Catedral, Aguja de los Quirquinchos and Gemelos.*

CENTRE *A* lenga *(southern beech) tree permanently bent by decades of 160kph (100mph) winds. The deciduous* lenga *dominates the Paine's dense Magellanic forest.*

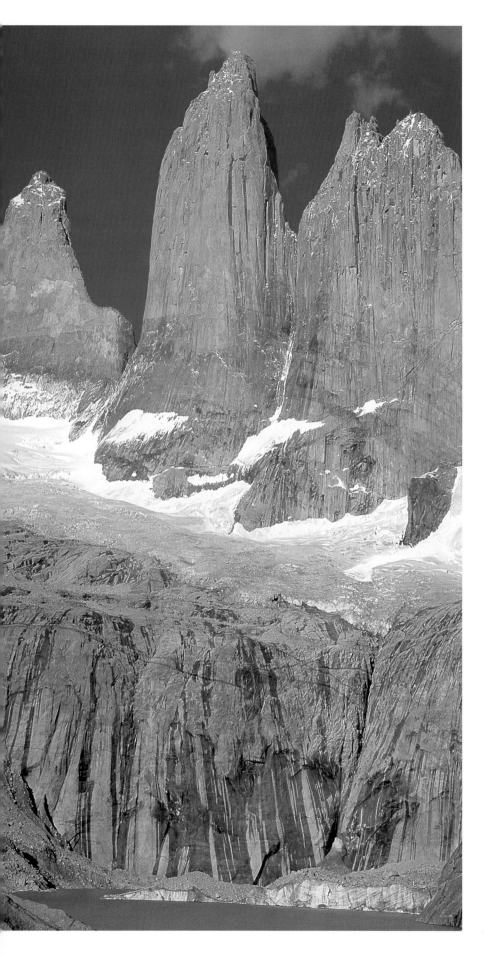

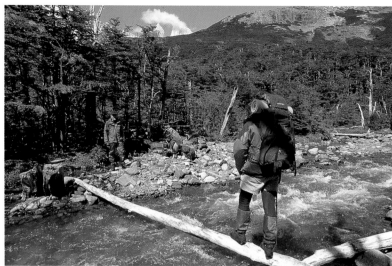

two large tarns occupied by ducks, coots and the occasional grebe. After two hours, the trail descends to the Rio Francés and crosses a suspension bridge. To the left is the free Campamento Italiano consisting of several clearings within deciduous Magellanic forest. The first side trip, steep in places, goes up the dramatic Valle Francés.

Much of the main ascent is through *lenga* (southern beech) forest, which becomes steadily more skeletal and stunted. Early on, the trail emerges from forest onto moraine boulders, requiring a few short, steep clambers. Periodic, ear-splitting cracks announce the calving of ice from hanging glaciers on the sheer east face of Paine Grande to the left. The disintegrating glaciers are usually clear of cloud since the valley lies in the lee of the mountain. When conditions are totally clear, ice mushrooms, a feature unique to Patagonian peaks, are seen perched atop Paine Grande's summits way above. The ascent continues via a cascade and on to a wind-buffeted moraine ridge. Some bogland has to be negotiated before the Campamento Britanico is reached after two hours. A rickety climbing hut used by pioneering British climbing expeditions stands in a clearing. A viewpoint just beyond affords stunning panoramas of the Cuernos to the east. To the north, a sheer wall of shale-capped granite has been sculpted by ice and wind into several weird shapes, among these, the Aleta de Tiburon (shark's fin). The return to Campamento Italiano takes one and a half hours.

A long exposed slog around the north shore of Lago Nordenskjöld, the next stretch traverses mixed terrain before reaching the Los Cuernos *refugio* and campsite. It is a further four hours northeast across open, undulating terrain before the trail emerges onto grazing plains near the Hostería Las Torres hotel. Energy permitting, the recommended route is left and up, into the Ascencio Valley via a steep, zigzagging path that turns into the ravine high above the foaming river. The trail soon drops to river level and the Refugio Chileno. It is a further hour and a half uphill to the Las Torres camp site, involving two stream crossings. With patience you may spot (or hear) one of Patagonia's extrovert forest-dwelling bird species, such as the screeching Austral parakeet (southernmost parrot species in the world), flame-crested Magellanic woodpecker or mottled Chilean flicker.

ABOVE *The magnificent Torres del Paine. These technically challenging walls are subject to extreme climatic conditions and provide some of the most extreme climbing on earth.*

ABOVE *The precarious crossing over Rio Los Perros close to Laguna Los Perros before the long ascent to John Gardiner Pass. Such crossings are typical of the Paine backcountry.*

The path emerges onto a sandy slope above the concealed woodland camp site. Trail markers lead left to a broad, steep boulder slope and up to the Laguna Torre *mirador* (lookout). Aim to be there in the morning for ideal light conditions. A final clamber over boulders ends at the moraine lip (1000m; 3300ft), with dramatic views of the three pillars soaring above the glacier-encrusted cirque. The descent to Hostería Las Torres hotel, *refugio* and private camp site takes three hours, and the circuit trail continues anti-clockwise to Campamento Seron. Hooting buff-necked ibis and the dive-bombing southern lapwing abound in the eastern sector of the park. Pairs of upland goose are also commonplace. The track follows the Rio Paine, crossing flower-filled meadows. Stands of skeletal *lenga* are the legacy of ranchers' slash and burn. This, the most sheltered sector of the park, only obtained protected status in 1975.

An hour on from Seron, the trail climbs left to a shoulder and descends westward, revealing new panoramas to the north. Two hours on is Campamento Coiron, then a level, three-hour trail across boggy floodplain ends at Refugio Dickson. House-sized icebergs cross Lago Dickson, the source of the park's hydrological system.

The 1000m (3300ft) ascent beginning at the Refugio Dickson is the circuit's toughest. The path follows the Los Perros torrent through dense forest. Five hours on, the trail reaches iceberg-filled Laguna Los Perros, and the dramatically located Los Perros camp site. Above the tree line, the final few hundred metres are on bare rock. Careful route finding is required in poor visibility or deep snow. Also beware severe winds at the Paso Paine (1250m; 4100ft). With clear conditions, the view amply rewards effort: the broad, blue Grey Glacier tumbling 1000m (3300ft) below.

The marked track drops to the tree line, where it continues through grotesquely-knotted, branch-strewn forest. The going is very slippery when wet. The first camp, Campamento Paso, is two hours from the pass and Campamento Los Guardas a further three hours. The trail improves for the final forest section down to the popular Refugio Grey, sited near the fast-receding glacial snout.

The final four hours to Refugio Pehoe are fabulous. After an hour of steady then steep ascent, trekkers have a stunning view back to the forest-fringed Grey Glacier. In autumn, when the *lenga*'s leaves turn a dramatic red, the spectacle is amazing. A little further on the iceberg-cluttered southern end of Lago Grey comes briefly into view. The quantity of ice has been such that for two years the lake's small passenger boat could not get through – one of many alarming signs that glacial retreat is accelerating. Finally, the path crosses a low ridge, veers southeast and descends for an hour to Refugio Pehoe. Exit is either via park HQ or back across Lago Pehoe by boat.

BELOW *Giant icebergs calve off the snout of Grey Glacier, before drifting the length of Lago Grey and beaching on the lake's southern shore some 7km (4 miles) away.*

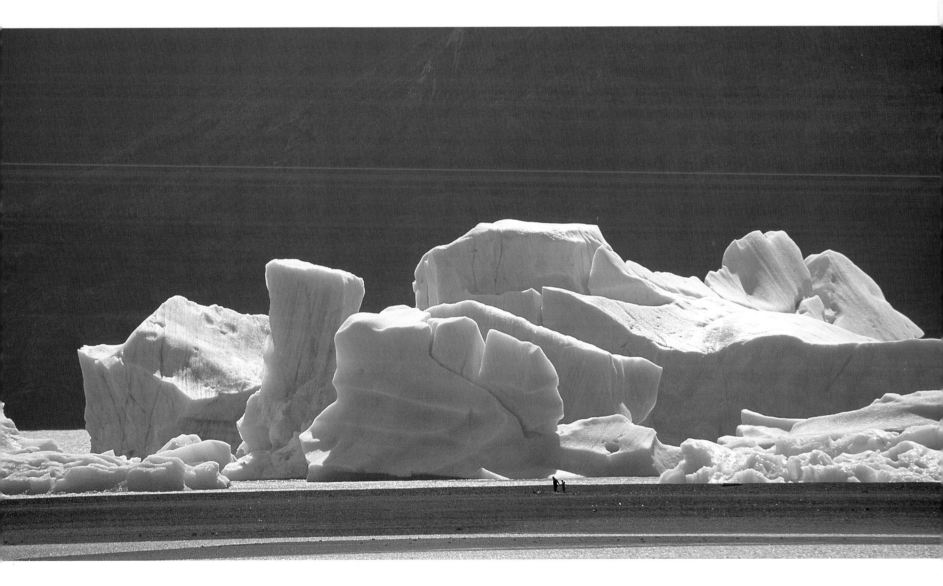

AUTHOR BIOGRAPHIES

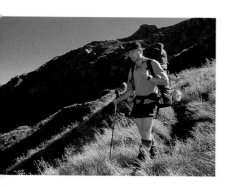

SHAUN BARNETT

Shaun Barnett's passion for mountains and tramping developed during his teenage years in New Zealand. Since then he has tramped throughout New Zealand and also in Australia, South America, Canada, Nepal and Alaska. Shaun trained as an ecologist, and worked for the New Zealand Department of Conservation for several years. Since 1996 he has been a full-time writer and photographer, and his first book *Classic Tramping in New Zealand*, co-authored with Rob Brown, won the 2000 Montana Book Award in the Environment category. He lives in Wellington with his wife Tania.

Hamish Brown is a professional author, mountaineer, photographer, educationist and lecturer who has become the English-speaking authority on the Atlas Mountains of Morocco. Born in Colombo to Scottish parents, he discovered the great outdoors early in life and has wandered the world ever since. His climbs and expeditions have ranged from the Arctic to the Andes, from the Alps to the Himalaya – but it is the Atlas Mountains which have 'stolen his heart away'. Having spent winters there in 1965 and 1966, he now leads small exploratory treks into the Atlas for up to five

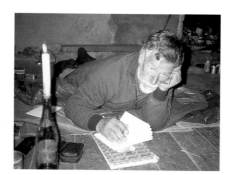

HAMISH BROWN

months each year. Along with local guide Ali, from Taroudant, Hamish was the first to realize the potential of the Western Atlas and, again with Ali, has made complete traverses afoot of the Anti- and the High Atlas, the latter a 96-day, 900-mile (560km), 30-peak venture.

Hamish starred in a television feature on the Western Atlas and, in 2000, was made an honorary Fellow of the Royal Geographic Society. He is currently working on a book about the early exploration of the Atlas Mountains.

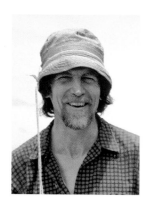

JOHN CHAPMAN

John Chapman is one of the most experienced bush walking writers and photographers in Australia. He has explored every Australian state extensively, in over 1600 days of walking. Over the last 22 years he has written five books, 16 editions in total, shared a bush walking column for five years in a major metropolitan newspaper, *The Age*, and written over 100 articles for walking magazines. John has also led many commercial treks in Tasmania, Nepal and India. His photography, in both black and white

and colour, features in a variety of publications. In addition, John has won many international photographic exhibitions and now judges exhibitions himself. He has also been awarded various photographic honours including that of Fellow of the Australian Photographic Society.

Kate Clow was born and educated in the UK, and pursued a career in the computer business while indulging a hobby of off-road motor-cycling. On annual motorcycle journeys through France and Spain she followed the Roman road network, and visited many historic sites in the mountains.

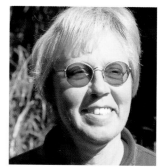

KATE CLOW

Taking a job in Istanbul, Kate learned Turkish while selling computers to the Turkish government and studying at Istanbul University. Eight years ago she moved to Antalya at the foot of the fabulous Taurus range. Immediately, she started collecting maps and researching the ancient road system on foot and motorbike. Turkey's first long distance walk, the Lycian Way, is a result of this research. Today, Kate earns a living from writing and photography, and leading groups of trekkers on the old paths.

Peter Cook developed a love of the outdoors and a strong interest in Australia's unique fauna and flora early on in life. He has spent over 25 years trekking in all of Australia's states and territories as Outdoor Education Instructor and Outdoor Recreation Club leader, as well as part of his own recreation and leisure. He has completed a number of formal qualifications in outdoor leadership and outdoor safety and has been an active volunteer member of search and rescue organizations. In 1993, Peter published a book entitled *Walking in the Wilderness Coast*, in conjunction with close friend and colleague, Mr Chris Dowd.

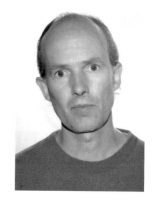

PETER COOK

David Emblidge has spent much of his adult life in a pair of hiking boots. Born in Buffalo, New York, he grew up sailing on Lake Erie from his family's Canadian summer home. Emblidge frequently blends his literature and journalism background with adventuring in the mountains or at sea. On the Appalachian Trail, he has hiked sections in seven of 11 states, completing Connecticut, Massachusetts and Vermont while writing *Hikes in Southern New England*, in a series he edited called *Exploring the Appalachian Trail* (Stackpole). Emblidge also created *The Appalachian Trail Reader* (Oxford). His trek into the depths of the Grand Canyon and his sailing voyage from Bermuda to Connecticut were done 'because the opportunities were too delicious to resist'. Urban life attracts Emblidge as well. He worked in New York as an editor for Cambridge University Press. Emblidge now lives in Seattle, Washington where he is Editor in Chief at The Mountaineers Books.

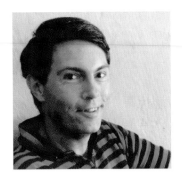

DAVID EMBLIDGE

Chris Hooker's love of the great outdoors and his work as a guide have taken him to many remote corners of the globe. But Chris's great love remains Latin America, where he was born, grew up and has spent much of his adult life.

Years of guiding, trekking, climbing and cycling, from the Amazon to the Andes and from Peru to Patagonia, have given him an intimate knowledge of the continent. He is usually to be found (or not) somewhere remote, either leading treks or planning new routes.

Chris is co-owner of Andean Trails, a travel company based in the UK, specializing in wilderness expeditions to South America.

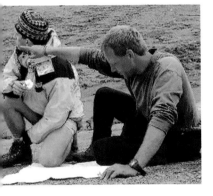

CHRIS HOOKER

Kathy Jarvis grew up in Scotland, where she was introduced to the joys of hill walking at an early age. Her career in South America began when she went to work as a tour guide in Chile and Peru in the early 90s, and she has been going back regularly ever since. For a few years all of her free time between tours was spent exploring the Andes, but now she spends more time in her office as a partner in the trekking and mountain biking company, Andean Trails, organizing tours to Peru, Bolivia and Patagonia. This provides a great excuse for leading groups on her favourite treks and spending a few months each year exploring new routes throughout the Andes. Kathy has no particular favourite among the Andean countries, anywhere with dramatic scenery, empty spaces, local people or wildlife and the freedom to walk, is just fine.

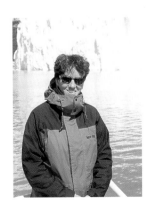

KATHY JARVIS

Mike Lundy has spent a lifetime trekking through many parts of Southern Africa. He has written five books and numerous magazine features on the subject. He has been a columnist for two South African newspapers, producing over 200 hiking features, as well as a weekly hiking report on radio.

In 1996, Mike received the Merit Award from the Hiking Federation of Southern Africa for what they described as his 'exceptional service to the hiking community of Southern Africa'. Mike lives in Cape Town, which he describes as the 'scenic hiking capital of the world'. Having travelled extensively to over 50 countries worldwide, he feels both qualified and, hopefully, forgiven for such home-town chauvinism. He and his wife Barbara work from home as trader and travel agent respectively.

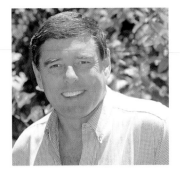

MIKE LUNDY

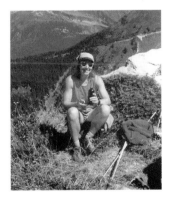

KATHY OMBLER

Kathy Ombler is a freelance writer whose interests include ecotourism, travel and conservation. In the past 20 years, Kathy has either lived in, or visited all of New Zealand's national parks. She has also enjoyed many years of tramping and camping with friends and family in her country's diverse and beautiful natural wilderness. Kathy has written several books and magazine articles on conservation and has been involved in writing and research for park management and other conservation organizations. Her most recent book is *National Parks and other Wild Places of New Zealand* (New Holland).

Hilary Sharp has enjoyed walking in the mountains since childhood. A qualified teacher of Outdoor Education, Hilary spent several years working in outdoor centres in Britain before settling in the French Alps, near Chamonix. Based here, she leads treks throughout the European Alps, the Pyrenees, Corsica and the Mediterranean islands.

Also a keen skier and runner, Hilary spends much of her time, winter and summer, exploring the mountains around her home and

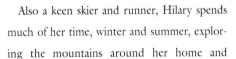

HILARY SHARP

further afield. She has walked and climbed extensively in Europe, Africa, North America, Australia and Thailand, and is particularly interested in the flora and fauna of the mountain areas she visits.

Hilary is the author of the New Holland Globetrotter Adventure Guide *Trekking and Climbing in the Western Alps* and is currently working on a guide to snow shoeing in the Alps. She writes regularly for the British magazine *High*.

FOLLOWING PAGES *Balti porters on Snow Lake in the Karakoram. Taking local men into glaciated, high mountain environments is a grave responsibility – they should be properly equipped and looked after at all times.*

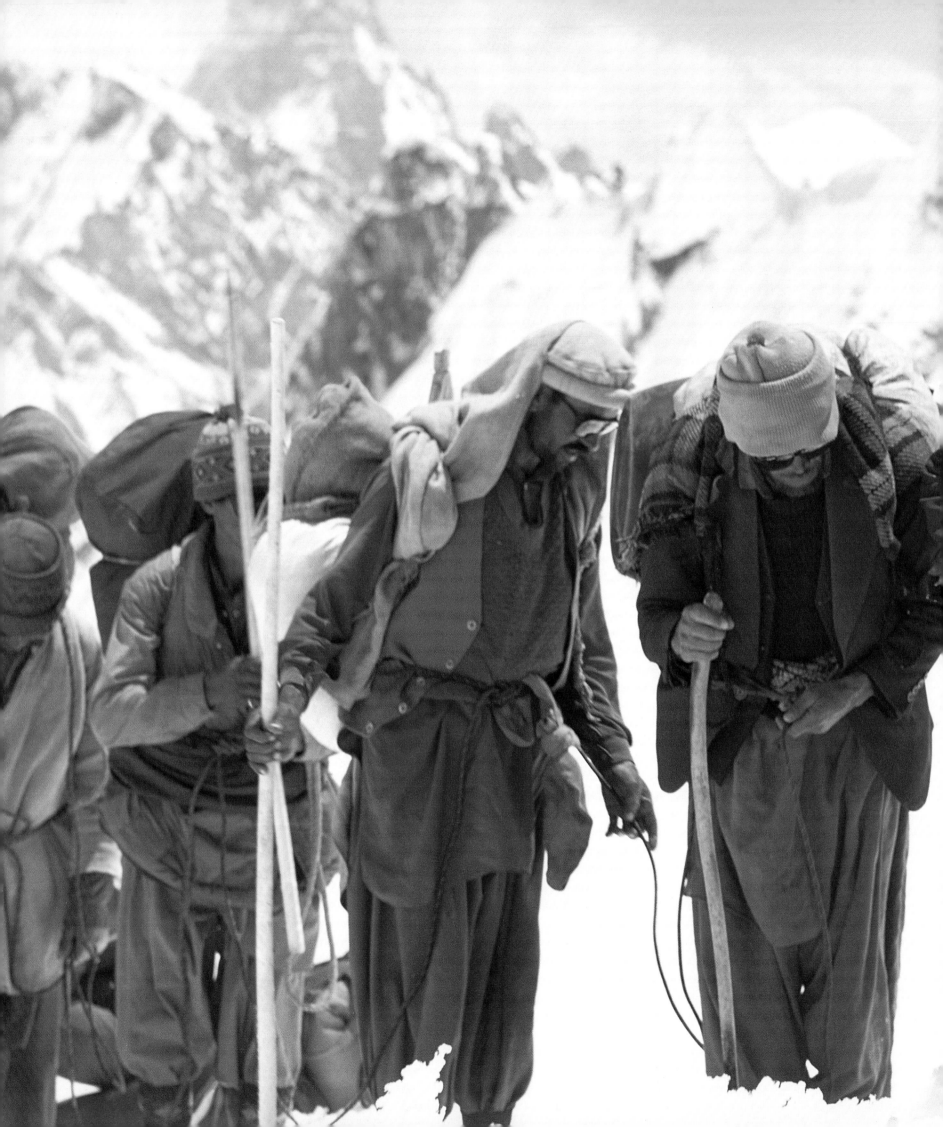

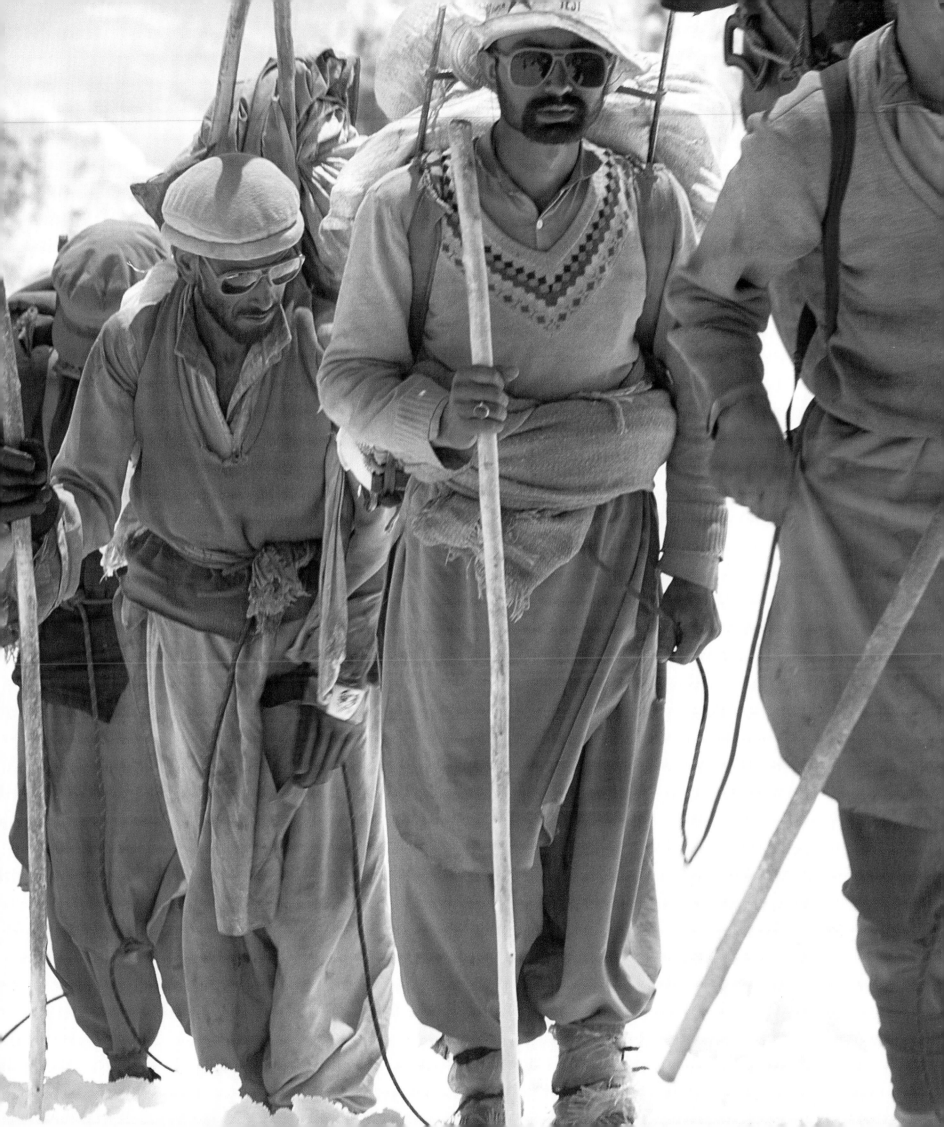

BIBLIOGRAPHY

SOUTH AMERICA

BRADT, HILARY. *Peru and Bolivia Backpacking and Trekking*, Bradt Publications, Bucks, UK (1999)

JARVIS, KATHY. *Ecuador, Peru and Bolivia The Backpacker's Manual*, Bradt Publications, Bucks, UK (2000)

AFRICA

ALLAN, IAIN. *Guide to Mount Kenya & Kilimanjaro*, Mountain Club of Kenya, Nairobi (1998)

BRISTOW, DAVID. *Best Hikes in South Africa*, Struik Publishers, Cape Town (1992)

BURMAN, JOSE. *Cape Trails and Wilderness Areas*, Human & Rousseau, Cape Town (1992)

ELSE, DAVID. *Walking in Africa 1 – Kenya*, Robertson McCarta, London (1991)

FINLAY, HUGH & CROWTHER, GEOFF. *Kenya – A Travel Survival Kit*, Lonely Planet, Australia (1997)

GRAHAM, ROBERT CUNNINGHAME. *Mogreb-el-Acksa*, Heinemann, London (1898)

MAXWELL, GAVIN. *Lord of the Atlas*, Cassel, London (2001)

OLIVIER, WILLIE & SANDRA. *The Guide to Backpacking & Wilderness Trails*, Southern Book Publishers, Johannesburg (1989)

OLIVIER, WILLIE & SANDRA. *The Guide to Hiking Trails*, Southern Book Publishers, Johannesburg (1988)

THOMSON, JOSEPH. *Travels in the Atlas & Southern Morocco*, George Philip & Son, London (1889)

The Rough Guide to Morocco. Rough Guides, London (2001)

WAGNER, PATRICK. *The Otter Trail*, Struik Publishers, Cape Town (1993)

EUROPE

CASTLE, ALAN. *The Corsica High Level Route*, Cicerone Press, Cumbria, UK (1992)

REYNOLDS, K. *Walks and Climbs in the Pyrenees*, Cicerone Press, Cumbria, UK (1993)

TOWNSEND, CHRIS. *Long Distance Walks in the Pyrenees*, The Crowood Press, Swindon, UK (1991)

Translated by PRETTY, HARRY & MCPHAIL, HELEN. *Walks in Corsica GR20*, Robertson McCarta, London (1990)

ASIA

ARMINGTON, STAN. *Trekking in the Nepal Himalaya*, Lonely Planet, Australia (1997)

ARMINGTON, STAN. *Trekking in Bhutan*, Lonely Planet, Australia (1999)

BEAN, GEORGE. *Lycian Turkey*, Ernest Benn, London (1971)

BEZRUCHKA, STEPHEN. Trekking in Nepal, Cordee, Leicester (1997)

BOOZ, ELIZABETH. *A Guide to Tibet*, Collins, London (1986)

CLOW, KATE. *The Lycian Way*, Upcountry (Turkey) Ltd, Buxton, UK (2000)

DUBUN, MARK & LUCAS, ENVER. *Trekking in Turkey*, Lonely Planet, Australia (1989)

JACCARD, PIERRE & FOLLMI, OLIVIER et al. *Ladakh-Zanskar*, Artou, Geneve (1984)

KAPADIA, HARISH. *Across Peaks & Passes in Ladakh, Zanskar & East Karakoram*, Indus, New Delhi (1999)

MACDONALD, DAVID. *Touring in Sikkim and Tibet*, OBS, Siliguri (1943)

NAKANO, TORU. *Trekking in Nepal*, Yama Kei, Tokyo (1984)

POMMARET, FRANCOISE. *An Illustrated Guide to Bhutan*, The Guidebook Company, Hong Kong (1990)

RAZZETTI, STEVE. *Trekking and Climbing in Nepal*, New Holland, London (2000)

SHAW, ISOBEL. *Pakistan Handbook*, John Murray, London (1989)

SHAW, ISOBEL & BEN. *Pakistan Trekking Guide*, Odyssey, Hong Kong (1993)

SNELLING, JOHN. *The Sacred Mountain*, East/West, London (1990)

STARK, FREYA. *Alexander's Path*, John Murray, London (1958)

SWIFT, HUGH. *Trekking in Nepal, West Tibet & Bhutan*, Hodder & Stoughton, London (1990)

SWIFT, HUGH. *Trekking in Pakistan and India*, Hodder & Stoughton, London (1990)

VERMA, RAJESH. *Sikkim, Darjeeling, Bhutan – A Guide and Handbook*, Verma, Gangtok (1996)

AUSTRALASIA

BELL, CHRIS. *Beyond the Reach, Cradle Mountain-Lake St Clair National Park*, Laurel Press, Tasmania (1990)

CHAPMAN, JOHN & SISEMAN, JOHN. *Cradle Mountain-Lake St Clair and Walls of Jerusalem National Parks*, John Chapman, Melbourne (1998)

COOK, PETER & DOWD, CHRIS. *Walking the Wilderness Coast: Lakes Entrance to Pambula. A Bushwalking, Canoeing and Holiday Guide*, Wildcoast Publications, Victoria, Australia (1995)

GIORDANO, MARGARET. *A Man and a Mountain, The Story of Gustav Weindorfer*, Regal Publications, Launceston, Tasmania (1987)

GREENAWAY, ROB. *The Restless Land – Stories of Tongariro National Park*, Department of Conservation/Tongariro National History Society, Turangi (1998)

OMBLER, KATHY. *National Parks and Other Wild Places of New Zealand*, New Holland, Cape Town (2001)

PEAT, NEVILLE. *Land Aspiring – The Story of Mount Aspiring National Park*, Craig Potton Publishing, Nelson (1994)

The Overland Track, A Walkers Notebook. Parks and Wildlife Service, Tasmania (1996)

NORTH AMERICA

BRUCE, DAN 'WINGFOOT'. *The Thru-Hiker's Handbook*, Center for Appalachian Trail Studies, Hot Springs, North Carolina (annual)

CHAZIN, DANIEL. *Appalachian Trail Data Book*, Appalachian Trail Conference, Harpers Ferry, West Virginia (annual)

EMBLIDGE, DAVID (Series Editor). *Exploring the Appalachian Trail*, Stackpole Books, Mechanicsburg, Pennsylvania (1998)

EMBLIDGE, DAVID (Editor). *The Appalachian Trail Reader*, Oxford University Press, New York (1996)

HOUK, ROSE. *Grand Canyon Trail Guide: South Kaibab*, Grand Canyon Natural History Association, Arizona (1981)

O'BRIEN, BILL (Editor). *Appalachian Trail Thru-Hiker's Companion*, Appalachian Trail Long Distance Hikers Association, Harpers Ferry, West Virginia (annual)

WHITNEY, STEPHEN. *A Field Guide to the Grand Canyon*, The Mountaineers Books, Seattle, Washington (1996)

Grand Canyon Magazine, Pali Arts Communications, San Francisco, California (1989)

CREDITS & ACKNOWLEDGEMENTS

The Publishers would like to thank everyone involved with the title for their continued enthusiam and dedicated effort.

Steve Razzetti would like to thank Jon Tinker, Val Pitkethly, Kate Harper, John Cleare and Pete Royall for their creative and moral support, all at KE for keeping me off the streets over the years, all at New Holland for entrusting me with this project and Natalie Hawkrigg for putting up with my interminable late nights at the computer. Humble thanks also go to all my friends and accomplices in Asia; To Shukor Ali for six fantastic trips across the Hispar, to Anwar Ali and Abdullah Javed of Hushe, to Bikrum Pandey and all his staff in Kathmandu and Dago Beda and all her staff in Thimpu. I am not worthy.

KEY TO PHOTOGRAPHERS

Copyright rests with the following photographers and/or their agents.
Key to Locations: t= top; tl = top left; tc = top centre; tr = top right; b = bottom; bl = bottom left; bc = bottom centre; br = bottom right; l = left; r = right; c = centre; i = inset. (*No abbreviation is given for pages with a single image, or pages on which all photographs are by same photographer.*)
Photographers: AB = Andy Belcher
ABQ = Anders Blomquist
AC = Auscape (JPF = Jean-Paul Ferrero)
AW = Art Wolfe
BB = Bill Bachman
BBC = British Broadcasting Corporation (JF = Jeff Foott; PO = Peter Oxford; JBR = Jose B Ruiz; SW = Staffan Widstrand)
BCC = Bruce Coleman Collection (JF = Jeff Foott; JC = Jules Cowan)
BO = Bill O'Connor
BP = Bigpie Pictures (NS = Nicholas Sumner)
CH = Chris Hooker
BR = Black Robin (SB = Shaun Barnett; DP = Darryn Pegram)
COP = Christine Osborne Pictures
DR = David Rogers
DW = David Wall
ES = Edward AM Snijders
FF = ffotograff (MG = Mike Greenslade)
GG = Gary Gentile
HB = Hamish Brown
HG = Henry Gold
HH = Hedgehog House (BA = Bill Atkinson; SB = Shaun Barnett; RB = Rob Brown; JM = Jim Harding; LH = Lynda Harper; CM = Colin Monteath; AR = Andy Reisinger)
HL = Holger Leue Photography
HS = Hilary Sharp
JDP = Jeff Drewitz Photography
KJ = Kathy Jarvis
LE = Leopard Enterprises (JK = Johann Kloppers)
LT = Lochman Transparencies (JL = Jiri Lochman; ML = Mari Lochman)
MC = Mountain Camera (CC = Chris Craggs; JC = John Cleare)
NG = National Geographic (SA = Sam Abell; SLA = Steven L Alvarez; RG = Raymond Gehman; LG = Lowell Georgia; DH = David Hiser; CJ = Chris Johns; TL = Timothy Laman; JR = Johan Reinhard)
NHIL = New Holland Image Library
(SA = Shaen Adey; AJ = Anthony Johnson)
NV = Neil Vincent
PAPL/G = Photo Access Picture Library/Getaway (DB = David Bristow; DP = D Pinnock)
PM = Peter Mertz
RDH = Roger de le Harpe
RS = Robin Smith
SAP = South American Pictures (KJ = Kathy Jarvis; KM = Kimball Morrison; TM = Tony Morrison; KR = Kim Richardson)
SC = Sylvia Cordaiy Photo Library (AB = Anthony Bloomfield)
SR = Steve Razzetti
TI = Travel Ink (MD = Mark Dubin; AW = Andrew Watson)
TR = Terry Richardson
WK = W Koch

Page		Credit	Page		Credit	Page		Credit	Page		Credit	Page		Credit
Endpapers		NV	35–36		HS	89	tr	SR		br	HH/SB	142		KJ
1		BR/SB	37		PM		b	HH/CM	115		HH/SB	143		CH
2–3		SR	38–39		PAPL/G/DP	90–93		SR	116–117		BR/SB	144	t	MC/JC
4–5		BBC/JF	40		SR	94	t	FF/MG	118	t/l	AB		i	KJ
6–7		DW	41		LE/JK		i	BR/SB		i	BR/SB		r	CH
8		BBC/JBR	42	t/i	HB		br	SR	119		DW	146	bl	MC/JC
9		LE/JK		r	BR/DP	95–97		SR	120–121		HL		br	CH
10–13		SR	44–45		HB	98	t	SR	122		HH/AR	147		CH
14		ABQ	46	t/i/br	SR		i	HH/CM	123		HH/CM	148	t	SAP/KJ
15	l	WK		bl	PAPL/G/DB		bl	SR	124	l	HH/CM		i	BBC/PO
	r	SR	47–48		SR	99	tr	HH/JH		r	HH/LH		tr	SAP/TM
16		SR	49		WK		b	HH/CM	125	br	HH/CM	149		SAP/KJ
17	l	SAP/TM	50–52		LE/JK	100–101		SR	126–127		GG	150	t	BBC/SW
	r	SR	53	tl/tc	PAPL/G/DP	102–103		HH/RB	128		NG/JR		b	SAP/KR
18–21		BO		tr	LE/JK	104		LT/JL	129		NG/SA	151		KJ
22–24		HS	54	t/bl	LE/JK	105		AC/JPF	130	t	NG/DH	152	t	SAP/KM
25	tl	HS		i	RDH	106	t	BB		i	BCC/JF		b	SAP/TM
	br	TI/MD	55		LE/JK		i	COP		r	NG/TL	153	t	KJ
26	t	MC/CC	56		DR		l	AC/JPF	131		BCC/JC		b	BR/SB
	i	BO	57		LE/JK	107		BB	132		NG/DH	154–155		SAP/TM
	r	AW	58–61		SR	108		NHIL	133	bl	NG/DH	156		HH/CM
27–29		BO	62–63		KC	109	t	NHIL/AJ		tr	NG/JR	157	t	HH/CM
30	t	WK	64	tl	SC/AB		b	BB	134	t	NG/CJ		b	KJ
	i	HS		br	KC	110	t	NHIL/SA		i	TI/AW	158	l	BR/SB
	r	AW	65		KC		i	HG		r	NG/SA		r	MC/JC
31	tl	HS	66–74		SR		l	JDP	135		NG/RG	159		RS
	br	BO	74	c	COP	111		AC/JPF	136		NG/SA		b	HH/CM
32–33		HS	75	t	SR	112		LT/ML	137		GG	162–163		SR
34	t/i	PM		bl/c/br	BP/NS	113		JDP	138–139		GG	168		SR
	r	HS	76–88		SR	114	t/i	HL	140–141		ES			

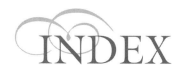

INDEX

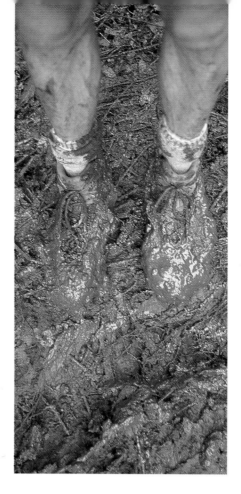

They say travel broadens the mind;
but you must have the mind.

GK CHESTERTON